Boulainvilliers and

the French Monarchy

Boulainvilliers and the French Monarchy

Aristocratic Politics in Early Eighteenth-Century France

HAROLD A. ELLIS

Cornell University Press

Ithaca and London

First published 1988 by Cornell University Press.

International Standard Book Number 0-8014-2130-6
Library of Congress Catalog Card Number 87-47971
Printed in the United States of America
Librarians: Library of Congress cataloging information appears on the last page of the book.

The paper in this book is acid-free and meets the guidelines for permanence and durability of the Committee on Production Guidelines for Book Longevity of the Council on Library Resources.

FOR LINDA

Contents

Contents

Preface

Henri de Boulainvilliers is a familiar figure, if not an endearing one. Historians probably know him best as one of the Old Regime's leading aristocratic reactionaries. And specialists are well acquainted with the controversies about the Frankish Conquest, French feudalism, and the nobility's origins which erupted after his death, when his writings on French history got into print. But virtually no one has asked when and why he wrote those works in the first place, despite some intriguing leads in the work of Franklin Ford, Jean-Dominique Lassaigne, the late Jean-Pierre Labatut, and André Devyver. One aim of this book is to answer those questions by restoring Boulainvilliers and his works to the circumstances in which he wrote them. The result is a book about Boulainvilliers' career—a paradoxical career, perhaps, since he published next to nothing—as a political writer and controversialist at the end of Louis XIV's reign and at the beginning of the duc d'Orléans' regency.

This book has several goals, but a rehabilitation of Boulainvilliers' reputation will not be among them. It may seem that a full-length work on such a figure should justify itself by justifying him: thus the only modern monograph on him, Renée Simon's *Henry de Boulainviller* (1941), portrays him as a learned and moderately forward-looking man who might have ranked among the "patriotic" nobles of 1789. In the following pages Boulainvilliers will remain an aristocratic reactionary. True, the monstrous ideological throwback whom some historians write about will not reappear here. But his invidious and scandalously *nobiliaire* convictions can be understood only as the convictions of an aristocratic reactionary, and so they shall be understood here.

Boulainvilliers will not be relegated to the backwaters of French history, however. Aristocratic reactionaries were not peripheral to the evolving but still monarchical political culture of the Old Regime—a fact

ix

appreciated by those historians who seek to discover "constitutionalist" or even "liberal" implications in their thought—and as much may be said of Boulainvilliers. In the following pages the reader will watch him work for princes as he picks his way through thickets of historical and constitutional controversy occasioned by the French monarchy's problems: dynastic problems that led aristocratic elites to fashion competing visions of a French constitution, to engage in public debate about them, and to mobilize historical learning and writing to sustain them. This book, therefore, is not just a study of Boulainvilliers' career. It is also a chapter in the history of Old Regime political culture, designed to examine the by no means unambiguous role played in it by aristocratic ideologies and the historical arguments mobilized on their behalf.

In writing this book I have contracted many debts of gratitude. Some are to scholars I do not know or I barely know. Although I dissent from much that André Devyver has had to say about Boulainvilliers and the social and ideological contexts to which he may be assigned, I could not have written my book had Devyver not written his own massive and learned study of noble "race consciousness" in the Old Regime. Nor could I have so confidently proceeded with my work on an often rebarbative character such as Boulainvilliers had not François Furet already urged historians to discard their "Manichaean" assumptions about the forces of Progress and Reaction in the Old Regime. Even aristocratic reactionaries may be found among the artisans of change in the history of France's political culture.

I am pleased to acknowledge personal debts, too. The competent and courteous staffs of French libraries and archives provided invaluable assistance. Here at Washington University, Olin Library's Interlibrary Loan Office filled countless requests for recent publications and fragile volumes printed hundreds of years ago. As my work took shape, personnel in Computing Facilities helped me impose my will on recalcitrant word processors. And from the beginning my teachers and colleagues in the Department of History offered intellectual, moral, and material support, the last in the form of graduate fellowships, a 1983 Summer Faculty Research Grant, and a semester's leave of absence in 1986.

My first debt and one of my greatest is to J. G. A. Pocock. He first suggested that I examine Boulainvilliers' historical work, and he continues to guide my efforts by his example. Orest Ranum, too, has taught me much in the occasional conversations we have had over the years, far more, in fact, than he may suspect. Keith Michael Baker and Natalie Zemon Davis have encouraged me by their continued interest in my work. Steven Englund, Thomas Kaiser, and Marina Valensise kindly read all or part of this book's penultimate draft. Like Terry Maher, who read a still earlier draft, they did much to help an author clarify his own arguments. So too did my anonymous readers at Cornell University Press, where John Ackerman's interest in this project is warmly appreciated by its author. Finally, I thank the University of Chicago Press for permission to use material from my article "Genealogy, History and Aristocratic Reaction in Early Eighteenth-Century France: The Case of Henri de Boulainvilliers," which appeared in *Journal of Modern History*, 1986, copyright © 1986 by The University of Chicago Press.

It is pleasing to know that this book has friends. It is equally pleasing to know that I do too: my wife lived with me while I lived with this book, listening to me rehearse it far more often than mere conjugal duty required. In some ways it is as much hers as mine. I gladly dedicate it to her.

HAROLD A. ELLIS

St. Louis, Missouri

Abbreviations

NOTE ON TRANSLATIONS

Unless otherwise stated all translations are mine. Context determined my renderings of the term *françois (français),* which historians of the Old Regime used to denote both Franks and Frenchmen.

Boulainvilliers and

the French Monarchy

1

---◆◆◆►---

Introduction

On January 23, 1722, Henri comte de Boulainvilliers died in his apartment at Paris. The *Mercure de France* duly recorded the event, but Parisian society and those who liked to read about it in the *Mercure*'s pages were not alone in taking note of the count's demise.[1] "This death caused a lot of talk," Mathieu Marais wrote in his journal for January 23. The Parisian lawyer explained that "the vulgar," aware that Boulainvilliers had been working on a life of Mohammed when he died, "said that he died a Mohammedan."[2] By "the vulgar" Marais may have meant the literary hangers-on and coffee-house habitués of regency Paris, always pleased to gossip about unorthodoxies of all kinds. But respectable citizens of the Republic of Letters were equally concerned to take stock of the late Boulainvilliers' work: within weeks of his death his friend Nicolas Fréret, young member and future secretary of the Académie des Inscriptions et Belles-Lettres, sent a provincial correspondent a long letter describing the man, his major works on French history and genealogy, and his writings on astrology.[3] Finally, no less a personage

---

[1]*Mercure de France* (January 1722): 193–94.

[2]Mathieu Marais, *Journal et mémoires*, ed. M. Lescure, 4 vols. (Paris: Firmin Didot, 1863–68), 2:227.

[3]Nicolas Fréret, "Lettre de M. Fréret de l'Académie des Belles-Lettres, écrite à M.***, au sujet de la personne et des ouvrages de M. le comte de Boulainviller," in M.-H. Guervin, "Deux Amis. Nicolas Fréret (1688–1749). Henry de Boulainviller (1658–1722)," *Dix-septième Siècle*, nos. 7–8 (1950): 201–4. Guervin prints Fréret's letter from Bibliothèque Mazarine, Paris, MS. 1577. But see B.M., Troyes, MS. 1288, for an "extract" of the same letter dating it to February 1722. On Fréret see Renée Simon, *Nicolas Fréret, académicien*, in *Studies on Voltaire and the Eighteenth Century*, ed. Theodore Besterman, vol. 17 (Geneva: Institut et Musée Voltaire, 1961). Marais' journal too was a vehicle for news in the Republic of Letters, for Marais habitually showed it to visitors and correspondents, chief among them President Jean Bouhier of Dijon who was at the center of a well-organized network of literary correspondence. See Marais, *Journal*, 4:143 (letter to President Bouhier, Paris, July 3, 1730), and Françoise Weil, *Jean Bouhier et sa correspondance*, 3 vols. (Paris: Université Paris-Sorbonne, 1972–76), 1:iii and xiii–xlii, and passim.

than the regent of France, Philippe duc d'Orléans, sought to acquaint himself with the count's writings. On January 25—only two days after Boulainvilliers' death—Orléans had Secretary of State Claude Le Blanc order the dead man's heirs to go to his Norman château at Saint-Saire, pack up his manuscripts on "history and other sciences," and send them to Paris for examination. By January 29, they had complied.[4]

Why this interest in an author who had published next to nothing? That question probably has as many answers as there are subjects on which Boulainvilliers wrote. Even before he died, cognoscenti were paying booksellers for manuscript copies of his essay on Spinoza's metaphysics.[5] Boulainvilliers' astrological interests also intrigued contemporaries. Indeed, they long remembered his efforts to vindicate that strange and suspect science in the salons of regency Paris.[6] But Boulainvilliers probably owed the lion's share of his notoriety to his historical writings about France. These alone among his works inspired printed comment and efforts at publication while he lived. In 1716, for example, a literary gazette published at The Hague reported on the "great eagerness" with which "people of condition" at Paris awaited the (vainly) projected publication of his history of Merovingian and Carolingian France.[7]

Whatever the reasons for contemporary interest in Boulainvilliers' philosophical and astrological work, it is likely that his writings on French history attracted readers because of their political and even polemical character. Historians have long since appreciated that in the last years of Louis XIV's reign Boulainvilliers wrote for the Burgundy Circle, the reformist coterie of the Sun King's grandson and heir the duc de Bourgogne.[8] Less well known is the likelihood that Boulainvilliers

[4]A.N., Y. 10976 [fols. 3–5ᵛ] (procès verbal de mise sous scellés).

[5]Guervin, "Deux Amis," 203.

[6]Ibid.; Chansonnier historique du XVIIIe siècle, ed. E. Raunié, 6 vols. (Paris: 1879–84), 2:25 and 289 (1716 and 1717 squibs); Jean Buvat, Journal de la Régence (1715–1723), ed. E. Campardon, 2 vols. (Paris: Plon, 1865), 2:171. For later recollections see [Louis de Rouvroy, duc de] Saint-Simon, Mémoires, ed. A. de Boislisle et al., 43 vols. (Paris: Hachette, 1879–1930), 16:246–47, 40:240, and works cited in Gustavo Costa, "Un Collaboratore italiano del conte di Boulainviller: Francesco Maria Pompeo Colonna (1644–1726)," Atti e memorie dell'Accademia Toscana di Scienze e Lettere: La Colombaria, 29, n.s., no. 15 (1965): 219–20.

[7]Nouvelles littéraires, contenant ce qui se passe de plus considérable dans la republique des lettres, 4 (The Hague: Henri de Sauzet, 1716): 156–57 (August 22). See also Jacques Lelong, Bibliothèque historique de la France (Paris: Gabriel Martin, 1719), 21, 339, 607, 845, 931, listing French historical works by Boulainvilliers, among them the minor pamphlet of 1717 which was his only piece to be printed while he lived.

[8]G. Tréca, Les Doctrines et les réformes de droit public en réaction contre l'absolutisme de Louis XIV dans l'entourage du duc de Bourgogne (Paris: Librairie de la Société Générale des Loix & des Arrêts & du Journal du Palais, 1909), 47 and passim; Nannerl O. Keohane, Philosophy

wrote for the regent, the duc d'Orléans, in the first years of Louis XV's minority. According to Nicolas Fréret, Orléans commissioned Boulainvilliers to write his history of the "parlements or estates general" of Capetian France. Fréret added that Boulainvilliers left that work unfinished when "circumstances" changed.[9] "Circumstances," it is inviting to suppose, led Boulainvilliers to write (and sometimes to abandon) his other pieces on French history, too.

In fact, one of this book's aims will be to establish that politics did indeed occasion Boulainvilliers' major writings on French history. Working in the shadow of princes, it will be argued, Boulainvilliers wrote to them and for them as a client, counselor, and controversialist. In so doing he elaborated a distinct vision of the French past. His was not a consistent vision: ambiguities and equivocations abound in his works and they need to be explained. By restoring Boulainvilliers' historical writings to the largely political and polemical contexts in which he wrote them, one may identify the conflicting ideological aims he sought to serve. Those aims, it will soon be apparent, have been a matter of debate and merit attention. So do the political and polemical contexts in which Boulainvilliers worked. It has been said that studies of an individual's thought may let historians identify the possibilities and constraints inherent in that individual's culture.[10] That remark is particularly applicable to works such as this one, in which contexts are objects of study no less important than the principal texts under examination.[11] Here, paying attention to the contexts in which Boulainvilliers worked entails paying attention to France's political culture at a critical moment in its history. At the end of Louis XIV's reign and at the beginning of the regency, cracks and fissures opened up in the political consensus binding the elites of the Old Regime, particularly the aristocratic elites, to the crown and assigning all political authority to it. Why that happened remains to be seen, but because that happened Boulainvilliers composed the bulk of his French historical writings. This book, therefore, is

and the State in France: The Renaissance to the Enlightenment (Princeton, N.J.: Princeton University Press, 1980), 332–57, esp. 346–50.

[9]Fréret, "Lettre de M. Fréret," 202.

[10]Carlo Ginzburg, The Cheese and the Worms: The Cosmos of a Sixteenth-Century Miller, tr. John Tedeschi and Anne Tedeschi (Harmondsworth: Penguin, 1982), xx–xxi. Ginzburg had members of the "subordinate classes" in mind, but his remark may be applied to studies on members of the educated elites as well.

[11]It will be apparent that I am much indebted to the methodological precepts and examples set by J. G. A. Pocock and Quentin Skinner, particularly Skinner, "Meaning and Understanding in the History of Ideas," History and Theory, 8 (1969): 3–53; Pocock, Politics, Language, and Time: Essays on Political Thought and History (New York: Atheneum, 1971), 3–41, and Pocock, Virtue, Commerce, and History: Essays on Political Thought and History, Chiefly in the Eighteenth Century (Cambridge: Cambridge University Press, 1985), 1–34.

not about Boulainvilliers alone. It is also about the French monarchy and the aristocratic debates over its history and character which prompted him to take up his pen.

French history was not the only subject to capture Boulainvilliers' attention. Readers of Renée Simon's massive *Henry de Boulainviller* (1941) will be acquainted with his writing on philosophy, astrology, ancient history and the history of religion. He was in fact one of the first Frenchmen to read and write about Spinoza with something like sympathy.[12] This diverse intellectual activity suggests a man with a mind of his own and with aims of his own—even when writing French history for French princes.

What were Boulainvilliers' aims when he wrote French history? According to an old and vigorous historiographical tradition, his were the aims of a paradigmatic aristocratic reactionary.[13] That unattractive rep-

---

[12]Renée Simon, *Henry de Boulainviller: Historien, Politique, Philosophe, Astrologue: 1658–1722* (Paris: Boivin, 1941). See also Simon's *thèse supplémentaire* on MSS and editions of Boulainvilliers' works, and her editions of some of his less-well-known astrological, philosophical, and historical texts: *A la recherche d'un homme et d'un auteur: Essai de bibliographie des ouvrages du comte de Boulainviller* (Paris: Boivin, 1941); *Traité d'astrologie par le comte Henry de Boulainviller (1717)*, ed. Renée Simon et al. (Garches: Editions du Nouvel Humanisme, 1947); *Un Révolté du grand siècle: Henry de Boulainviller*, ed. Renée Simon et al. (Garches: Editions du Nouvel Humanisme, 1948); *Astrologie mondiale: Histoire du mouvement de l'apogée du soleil; ou, Pratique des règles d'astrologie pour juger des événements généraux, 1711*, ed. Renée Simon et al. (Garches: Editions du Nouvel Humanisme, 1949); *Oeuvres philosophiques*, ed. Renée Simon, 2 vols. (The Hague: Martinus Nijhoff, 1973). Simon spells Boulainvilliers' name as he spelled it himself. On his Spinozist writings see also Paul Vernière, *Spinoza et la pensée française avant la Révolution*, 2 vols. (Paris: Presses Universitaires de France, 1954), 1:306–22.

[13]For this traditional interpretation see Augustin Thierry, *Récits des temps mérovingiens, précédés de Considérations sur l'histoire de France*, 2 vols. (Paris: Garnier, [1867]), 1:53–136, esp. 60, 66; Gabriel Monod, "Du progrès des études historiques en France depuis le XVIe siècle," *Revue historique*, 1 (1876): 25; A. Lombard, *L'Abbé Du Bos: Un initiateur de la pensée moderne (1670–1742)* (Paris: Hachette, 1913), 412–64; Erwin Hölzle, *Die Idee einer altgermanischen Freiheit vor Montesquieu: Fragmente aus der Geschichte politischer Freiheitsbestrebungen in Deutschland, England und Frankreich von 16.–18. Jahrhundert*, Beihefte 5 der Historischen Zeitschrift (Munich: R. Oldenbourg, 1925), 47–58; Albert Mathiez, "La Place de Montesquieu dans l'histoire des doctrines politiques au XVIIIe siècle," *Annales historiques de la Révolution française*, 7 (1930): 97–98; Jacques Barzun, *The French Race: Theories of Its Origin and Their Social and Political Implications prior to the Revolution* (New York: Columbia University Press, 1932), 138–47; Friedrich Meinecke, *Historism: The Rise of New Historical Outlook*, tr. J. E. Anderson (New York: Herder and Herder, 1972), 132–35; Dorit Drews, *Das fränkisch-germanische Bewusstsein des französischen Adels im 18. Jahrhundert*, Historische Studien 368 (Berlin: Emil Ebering, 1940), 25–35; Martin Göhring, *Weg und Sieg der modernen Staatsidee in Frankreich (vom Mittelalter zu 1789)* (Tübingen: J. C. B. Mohr, 1947), 126–28; Franklin L. Ford, *Robe and Sword: The Regrouping of the French Aristocracy after Louis XIV* (Cambridge: Harvard University Press, 1953), 222–45; René Herval, "Un Historien normand oublié: Henri de Boulainvilliers (1658–1722)," *Etudes normandes*, 34 (1960): 51–53; Franz Neumann, "Introduction" to Montesquieu, *The Spirit of the Laws*, tr. Thomas

utation seems well deserved. Born in 1658 into an ancient noble family
and educated at the exclusive Oratorian academy at Juilly, Boulainvilliers pursued a military career until forced by disordered family finances to abandon it in the 1680s. Thereafter he devoted himself to
raising and educating his children and to writing the corpus of texts
studied by the admiring Renée Simon, among them the works on
French history whose putative erudition she warmly applauded.[14]
Boulainvilliers was not a dispassionate historian, however. He exalted
"feudal government" as "the masterpiece of the human mind" and
condemned modern social circulation and royal absolutism as "confusion" and "despotism."[15] He celebrated the "blood," "birth," and putative Frankish extraction of France's "true and old nobility," and—here is
probably his most celebrated and controversial claim—he insisted that
when they conquered Roman Gaul, his noble Franks reduced the Gallo-
Romans living there to serfdom and founded "a sort of aristocracy" well
before anything like a monarchy established itself.[16] Such views have
long since convinced historians that Boulainvilliers was an aristocratic
reactionary. In our own century, for reasons that need no explanation,
his rhetoric about noble "blood" and "birth" has persuaded historians
that he was also a racist. The most vigorous exponent of this view is
André Devyver. Drawing attention to Boulainvilliers' failed army career
and to his later complaints about his "little fortune,"[17] Devyver argued
that Boulainvilliers' ideas were racist symptoms of his poverty and that
his history was nothing but "myth" fabricated to console or to animate a
hopelessly "proletarianized" and reactionary nobility.[18]

Nugent (New York: Hafner, 1966), xix–xxix. Even scholars who acknowledge substantive
or conceptual merit in Boulainvilliers' historical writing agree. See Gioacchino Gargallo di
Castel Lentini, *Boulainvilliers e la storiografia dell'Illuminismo francese* (Naples: Giannini,
1954), 33–39, 48–67; Vincent Buranelli, "The Historical and Political Thought of
Boulainvilliers," *Journal of the History of Ideas*, 18 (1957): 475–94; Gian Carlo Corada, "La
Concezione della storia nel pensiero di Henri de Boulainviller," *A.C.M.E.: Annali della
Facoltà di Lettere e Filosofia dell'Università degli Studi de Milano*, 28, fasc. 3 (1975): 311–33.

[14]Simon, *Henry de Boulainviller*, 46–255 (esp. 86–88) and 682–83. For biographical
details see ibid., 9–43, and Harold A. Ellis, "Genealogy, History, and Aristocratic Reaction
in Early Eighteenth-Century France: The Case of Henri de Boulainvilliers," *Journal of
Modern History*, 58 (1986): 420–22, 435–37, 449–51.

[15]*Etat . . . Tome III*, 37, 164–88.

[16]*Essais*, 10 and passim; *Etat*, 1, "Mémoires historiques" (separately paginated): 8, and
(on the "Etat de la Nation Françoise" after its establishment in Gaul) 15–49.

[17]Boulainvilliers, *Oeuvres philosophiques*, 2:141.

[18]André Devyver, *Le Sang épuré: Les préjugés de race chez les gentilshommes français de
l'Ancien Régime (1560–1720)* (Brussels: Editions de l'Université de Bruxelles, 1973), 11, 14,
243, 250, 260, 285–95, 353–90. For Boulainvilliers as racist see also Hannah Arendt, *The
Origins of Totalitarianism* (2d ed., Cleveland: Meridien, 1958), 162–63, 171–72; Barzun,
French Race, 138–47; François Bluche, *La Vie quotidienne de la noblesse française au dix-
huitième siècle* (Paris: Hachette, 1973), 230–31; G. Gerhardi, "L'Idéologie du sang chez

Though plausible, these accounts of Boulainvilliers' aims cannot be accepted without reservations. His poverty and racism have probably been exaggerated.[19] And the very existence of aristocratic reaction in eighteenth-century France now seems doubtful. Little evidence of it or of the protracted noble-bourgeois conflict associated with it is forthcoming from the growing body of monographs on social mobility in the Old Regime, on the monarchy's recruitment of its servants, or on the nobility's economic condition and conduct.[20] In fact, a new social history of the Old Regime now insists on the vitality of its nobility and on the vigor of its social "fusion," which, it is argued, drew richer nobles and bourgeois alike into a new "elite" of wealth, title, and power.[21] It has even been possible to neglect programs or proponents of aristocratic reaction and to insist instead on the nobility's (or at least the richer nobility's) "liberalism."[22]

Of course, aristocratic reactionaries will not go away—even the historian who denies that an aristocratic reaction happened can call Boulain-

Boulainvilliers et sa réception au 18e siècle," in *Etudes sur le XVIIIe siècle*, vol. 11, *Idéologies de la noblesse*, ed. Roland Mortier, Hervé Hasquin (Brussels: Editions de l'Université de Bruxelles, 1984), 11–20; Pierre Goubert, *The Ancien Régime: French Society, 1600–1750*, tr. Steve Cox (New York: Harper and Row, 1974), 160; Leon Poliakov, *The Aryan Myth: A History of Racist and Nationalist Ideas in Europe*, tr. Edmund Howard (London: Chatto-Heinemann/Sussex University Press, 1974), 24–28; Ernest Seillière, *Le Comte de Gobineau et l'aryanisme historique* (Paris: Plon, 1903), x, and *L'Impérialisme démocratique* (Paris: Plon, 1907), 42–51.

[19]For a critique of that case see Ellis, "Genealogy, History, and Aristocratic Reaction," 419–23.

[20]See the following publications and works cited in them: William Doyle, "Was There an Aristocratic Reaction in Pre-Revolutionary France?" *Past and Present*, 57 (November 1972): 97–122; Doyle, *Origins of the French Revolution* (Oxford: Oxford University Press, 1980), pt. I; François Furet, *Interpreting the French Revolution*, tr. Elborg Forster (Cambridge: Cambridge University Press; Paris: Editions de la Maison des Sciences de l'Homme), 81–131; Colin Lucas, "Nobles, Bourgeois and the Origins of the French Revolution," *Past and Present*, 60 (August 1973): 84–126. On the vigorous social mobility in France on the eve of the Revolution see David D. Bien, "La Réaction aristocratique avant 1789: L'exemple de l'armée," *Annales. E.S.C.*, 29 (1974): 43–48 and 505–15.

[21]Bluche, *La Vie quotidienne de la noblesse;* Guy Chaussinand-Nogaret, *La Noblesse au XVIIIe siècle: De la féodalité aux lumières*, intro. Emmanuel Le Roy Ladurie, 2d ed. (Brussels: Editions Complexe, 1984); Chaussinand-Nogaret, *Une Histoire des élites 1700–1848: Recueil de textes présentés et commentés* (Paris: Mouton, 1975); Lucas, "Nobles, Bourgeois and the Origins"; Robert Forster, "The French Revolution and the 'New' Elite, 1800–50," in *The American and European Revolutions, 1776–1848: Socio-political and Ideological Aspects*, ed. Jaroslav Pelenski (Iowa City: University of Iowa Press, 1980), 182–207; Goubert, *Ancien Régime*, 70–1, 82, 101–7, 122–38, 244, 247, 252; Denis Richet, "Autour des origines idéologiques lointaines de la Révolution française: Elites et despotisme," *Annales. E.S.C.*, 24 (1969): 1–24.

[22]Chaussinand-Nogaret, *La Noblesse*, 23–38, 181–226; Richet, "Autour des origines," 14–24; Richet, *La France moderne: L'esprit des institutions* (Paris: Flammarion, 1973), 144–46, 148–63. See also Bluche, *La Vie quotidienne de la noblesse*, 230–57, on "Réacteurs et libéraux" among the nobility.

villiers an aristocratic reactionary—but explaining them and their aims is harder than it used to be.[23] Since it is now doubtful that the nobility of early-modern France suffered a cumulative "decline," André Devyver's attempt to explain aristocratic reaction and race thinking as symptoms of it is unconvincing.[24] François Bluche also sees aristocratic reaction as the ideological property of the poor—not Devyver's "proletarianized" nobility, however, but a marginalized country gentry left behind by social change and excluded from the new "elite" of wealth, title, and power emerging at court and in the capital.[25] Yet even Bluche's account of aristocratic reaction, though more plausible than Devyver's, is inadequate because ideologies and programs of aristocratic reaction were not monopolies of the marginalized. According to David D. Bien, the men responsible for the Ségur regulation of 1781—a celebrated measure of aristocratic reaction restricting the army officer corps to men boasting at least four degrees of noble extraction—were hardly poor country gentry or *hobereaux* seeking safe sinecures for their comrades. Rather they were reform-minded lieutenant generals in the War Ministry seeking able officers for an army badly beaten by Prussia in the Seven Years' War and badly in need of a renewed military professionalism. To encourage that professionalism the reformers sought to close the officers' corps not to bourgeois (they were largely absent anyway) but to unprofessional new nobles from court and magistracy, who used army commissions as vehicles of social advancement. Old nobles alone were to be preferred because their family traditions (it was supposed) formed them for military careers. Bien concludes that the Ségur regulation was not an "aristocratic reaction" mounted by a united nobility against nonnobles, but rather a "professional reaction" mounted by one socioprofessional group against others, all of them *within* a divided nobility.[26]

At this point it may seem that ideologies of aristocratic reaction have not been explained but explained away. A fairer and more useful sug-

[23]Doyle, "Was There an Aristocratic Reaction?" 105.

[24]Devyver, *Le Sang épuré*, 39–43, 46–55, 59–63, 70–80, 243–78. Cf. J. H. M. Salmon, "Storm over the *Noblesse*," *Journal of Modern History*, 53 (1981): 242–57, and works cited there. On the character of rural noble poverty—not cumulative but endemic and therefore not the product of progressive impoverishment—see James B. Wood, *The Nobility of the* Election *of Bayeux, 1463–1666: Continuity through Change* (Princeton, N.J.: Princeton University Press, 1980), 122–26. On possible noneconomic causes of noble poverty see Jean Meyer, "Un Problème mal posé: La noblesse pauvre, l'exemple breton au XVIIe siècle," *Revue d'histoire moderne et contemporaine*, 18 (1971): 175–88.

[25]Bluche, *La Vie quotidienne de la noblesse*, 230–31; Bluche, *La Vie quotidienne au temps de Louis XIV* (Paris: Hachette, 1984), 313–14.

[26]David D. Bien, "The Army in the French Enlightenment: Reform, Reaction and Revolution," *Past and Present*, 85 (November 1979): 68–98, esp. 95–97; and Bien, "La Réaction aristocratique," esp. 529, 530.

gestion is that they have been redefined. Socioprofessional rather than socioeconomic in character, they no longer appear to have been weapons of a decaying nobility united against a rising and aggressive bourgeoisie. Instead, they seem to have been instruments of endemic conflict among diverse socioprofessional elites within an open but differentiated noble order. As such, ideologies of aristocratic reaction are integral neither to that traditional social history of the Old Regime which puts noble-bourgeois conflict at its center, nor to that newer social history which takes the "fusion" or integration of "elites" as its organizing principle. On the contrary, the very existence of these divisive ideologies of aristocratic reaction amidst the Old Regime's noble elites suggests that their "fusion" or integration into a single "liberal" "elite" must have been limited indeed.[27]

This is not a plea to abandon efforts at identifying an "aristocratic constitutionalism" or "liberalism" in the Old Regime and associating Boulainvilliers with it. Such efforts—Denis Richet's and Nannerl O. Keohane's are only the latest and subtlest—must be welcomed.[28] Historians no longer need to accept the "Manichaean" premise that the French nobility was thoroughly archaic and addicted to atavisms that only the Revolution could destroy. It is now possible to admit that even the nobility's "reactionary" challenges to French royal absolutism could contribute to France's evolving political culture. Thus Richet can call Archbishop Fénelon's politics "liberal": "liberal because it was aristocratic" at a time when "the hierarchy of orders was the only rampart to raise against absolutism." Thus Keohane can credit the aristocratic critics of Ludovican absolutism—notably Fénelon, Boulainvilliers, and

---

[27] As Bien has already observed ("The Army," 95–97). See also Michel Vovelle, "L'Élite ou le mensonge des mots," *Annales. E.S.C.*, 29 (1974): 49–72; and (on divisions in the nobility) Doyle, *Origins of the French Revolution*, 116–27; Furet, *Interpreting the French Revolution*, 100–16; and Bailey Stone, *The Parlement of Paris, 1774–1789* (Chapel Hill: University of North Carolina Press, 1981), 92–120.

[28] Richet, "Autour des origines," 9–11, 18–23; Richet, *La France moderne*, 141–50, 160–61, 174; Keohane, *Philosophy and the State*, 332–57, esp. 346–50. For earlier exponents of these views see Jacques Denis, "Politiques: Fleuri, Saint-Simon, Boulainvilliers et Duguet," *Mémoires de l'Académie des Sciences, Arts et Belles-Lettres de Caen* (1871): 251–68; Henri Duméril, "La Légende politique de Charlemagne au XVIIIe siècle et son influence à l'époque de la Révolution française," *Mémoires de l'Académie des Sciences, Inscriptions et Belles-Lettres de Toulouse*, ser. 7, vol. 10 (1878): 149–54; Tréca, *Les Doctrines*, 47 and passim; Henri Sée, *L'Évolution de la pensée politique en France au XVIIIe siècle* (Paris: Marcel Giard, 1925), 21–32; Elie Carcassonne, *Montesquieu et le problème de la constitution française au XVIIIe siècle* (Paris: Presses Universitaires de France, 1927), 18–25 and passim; Jean-Jacques Chevallier, "Montesquieu ou le libéralisme aristocratique," *Revue internationale de philosophie*, 9, nos. 33–34 (1955): 333–34. Cf. André Jardin, *Histoire du libéralisme politique de la crise de l'absolutisme à la constitution de 1875* (Paris: Hachette, 1985), 14, where Boulainvilliers belongs to a "reaction against absolutism" but is not linked explicitly to a tradition of "liberalism."

Introduction

the men in the Burgundy Circle—with reviving "constitutionalist" thinking in France. Similarly, Franco Venturi can restore Boulainvilliers to the history of the Enlightenment and applaud "the acrid savor of discovery" exuded by his work. And in a persuasive article, Mona Ozouf and François Furet can argue that Boulainvilliers cracked the monarchical mold in which Old Regime historians customarily cast French history, in order to write a history of the "nation," not of the crown and the princes who wore it.[29] In effect, *nobiliaire* ideologues such as Boulainvilliers have been retrieved from the backwaters of French history and returned to its mainstream. Now they number among the artisans of France's modern political culture, and their aspirations and ideals may be given due attention by historians seeking to find the "distant ideological origins of the French Revolution."[30]

But as work on the French Revolution's ideological origins progresses—and it is progressing rapidly—historians must take care in assessing the role played in that story by aristocratic political ideologies.[31] To begin, the aristocratic liberalism of the Old Regime could be

[29]Furet, *Interpreting the French Revolution*, 81 (against the "Manichaean" assumptions of traditional historiography); Richet, *La France moderne*, 145; Keohane, *Philosophy and the State*, 345, 350; Franco Venturi, *Europe des lumières: Recherches sur le 18e siècle* (Paris: Mouton, 1971), 12; Mona Ozouf and François Furet, "Two Historical Legitimations of Eighteenth-Century French Society: Mably and Boulainvilliers," in Furet, *In the Workshop of History*, tr. Jonathan Mandelbaum (Chicago and London: University of Chicago Press, 1984), 140–49. On the crown-centered character of narrative histories of France in the early modern period see Philippe Ariès, *Le Temps de l'histoire* (Monaco: Editions du Rocher, 1954), 141–256; Goubert, *Ancien Régime*, 3–4; Orest Ranum, *Artisans of Glory: Writers and Historical Thought in Seventeenth-Century France* (Chapel Hill: University of North Carolina Press, 1980); Michel Tyvaert, "L'Image du roi: Légitimité et moralité royales dans les histoires de France au XVIIe siècle," *Revue d'histoire moderne et contemporaine*, 21 (1974): 521–47; Jürgen Voss, *Das Mittelalter im historischen Denken Frankreichs: Untersuchungen zur Geschichte des Mittelalterbegriffs und der Mittelalterbewertung von der zweiten Hälfte des 16. bis zur Mitte des 19. Jahrhunderts* (Munich: Wilhelm Fink, 1972), 321–24, 370.

[30]Richet, "Autour des origines." For the Revolution as (initially) a revolution of enlightened Old Regime elites—noble and nonnoble—see also François Furet and Denis Richet, *The French Revolution*, tr. Stephen Hardman (New York: Macmillan, 1970).

[31]Keith Michael Baker, "On the Problem of the Ideological Origins of the French Revolution," in *Modern European Intellectual History: Reappraisals and New Perspectives*, ed. Dominick LaCapra and Steven L. Kaplan (Ithaca, N.Y.: Cornell University Press, 1982), 197–219; Furet, *Interpreting the French Revolution*, 11–109; Lynn Hunt, *Politics, Culture, and Class in the French Revolution* (Berkeley and Los Angeles: University of California Press, 1984); Mona Ozouf, "War and Terror in French Revolutionary Discourse," *Journal of Modern History*, 56 (1984): 579–97; William H. Sewell, Jr., "Ideologies and Social Revolutions: Reflections on the French Case," and Theda Skocpol, "Cultural Idioms and Political Ideologies in the Revolutionary Reconstruction of State Power: A Rejoinder to Sewell," in *Journal of Modern History*, 57 (1985): 57–96; Dale Van Kley, "Church, State, and the Ideological Origins of the French Revolution: The Debate over the General Assembly of the Gallican Clergy in 1765," *Journal of Modern History*, 51 (1979):629–66; Van Kley, *The Damiens Affair and the Unraveling of the Ancien Régime* (Princeton, N.J.: Princeton University Press, 1984); and Van Kley, "The Jansenist Constitutional Legacy in the French Prerevolution 1750–1789," *Historical Reflections/Réflexions historiques*, 13 (1986): 393–453.

"timid" indeed and its aristocratic constitutionalism "reactionary in substance."[32] Second, if aristocratic political ideologies could be reactionary (despite their liberal or constitutionalist implications) then they could be divisive too, functioning not as platforms for an antiabsolutist consensus but as apologies for competing aristocratic constitutionalisms ("liberalisms" seems inappropriate here) no less invidious than the competing socioprofessional ideals and ideologies of Old Regime noble elites. Finally, to introduce yet one more complication into this analysis, such aristocratic reactionaries as Fénelon and the duc de Saint-Simon could wed nobiliaire social concerns with monarchical political convictions. They could maintain not only that France was (or should have been) a society of orders but also that France was (and should remain) a monarchy in which kings alone take decisions and make laws.[33] Compromised by reactionary impulses, the aristocratic constitutionalisms and liberalisms of the Old Regime could also be constrained by its still powerfully monarchical political culture.

Since the Old Regime's nobiliaire ideologues appear to have pursued conflicting aims with diverse implications in a fundamentally monarchical political culture, the historian may legitimately ask how and why. A study of Boulainvilliers' efforts to write history for princes and put it to political use furnishes an obvious occasion for answering those questions. For although his liberalism may have been exaggerated, his place in the ranks of aristocratic reactionaries and constitutionalists need not be contested, and he may even be included in the ranks of extreme royalists.[34] Like other nobiliaire ideologues of the Old Regime, therefore, he appears to have been ideologically polyvalent, and reducing his ideological character to any of its conflicting implications or possibilities may risk reducing it to a caricature of itself. Yet, although Boulainvilliers pursued conflicting aims, neither he nor (it is arguable) any other nobiliaire ideologue pursued them arbitrarily. His political culture constrained and enabled him to produce his writings on French history. And his political circumstances impelled him to elaborate, by turns, the reactionary or constitutionalist or royalist arguments that may be encountered in his work.

[32]For these admissions see Tréca, *Les Doctrines*, 6, 77, 90; and Keohane, *Philosophy and the State*, 345, cf. 350 on Boulainvilliers' "rankest obscurantism."

[33]Françoise Gallouédec-Genuys, *Le Prince selon Fénelon* (Paris: Presses Universitaires de France, 1963); Jean-Pierre Brancourt, *Le Duc de Saint-Simon et la monarchie* (Paris: Cujas, 1971). See also Brancourt, "Un Théoricien de la société au XVIIIe siècle: Le chevalier d'Arcq," *Revue historique*, 250 (1973): 337–62; Jean-Marie Constant, *La Vie quotidienne de la noblesse française au XVIe–XVIIe siècles* (Paris: Hachette, 1985), 267–73, 296–97.

[34]See Henri Morel, "Les 'Droits de la nation' sous la Régence," in *La Régence* (Paris: Armand Colin, 1970), 254–55. See also chapter 6.

This book, consequently, may be called a *political* biography of a nobiliaire ideologue and historian. Based on fresh bibliographical foundations, it traces the itinerary that Boulainvilliers followed as he wrote history for French princes as a client, counselor, and controversialist.[35] That itinerary begins around 1700 when, in his Norman château, Boulainvilliers busied himself with writing for his sons' education and his own enlightenment. The texts he wrote and the aims he pursued in those years were familial and private, but politics and the possibilities of writing for princes occasioned the composition of virtually everything else he wrote on France and French history. To observe him at work, therefore, will require following him from his château to the circle of the duc de Bourgogne (Louis XIV's grandson and heir) and then, after Bourgogne's death in 1712, into the entourage of the duc d'Orléans, where Boulainvilliers remained until he died. His most strenuous efforts at writing the history of France date to Orléans' regency. During the by no means trivial *affaire du bonnet* (1715–16) and *affaire des princes* (1716–17), when France's contending aristocratic elites made Orléans' tenuous political and dynastic position an object of public debate, Boulainvilliers leaped to the prince's defense. Boulainvilliers sought also to counsel Orléans, whose regency he regarded as a rare occasion for restoring the old nobility's preeminence and the Estates General's powers. It cannot be said that Boulainvilliers' efforts to put French history to polemical and political use were successful. He never finished and published what would have been his major contribution to early-eighteenth-century public political debate: his history of representative institutions in Capetian France. And the duc d'Orléans never performed the historical roles that Boulainvilliers invited him to play. Not surprisingly, Boulainvilliers' last works are bitter reflections on France's "despotic" destiny and his own failed career. Writing the history of Boulainvilliers' career can illuminate his conflicting ideological aims and the circumstances in which he pursued them.

Before we turn to the larger lessons of this study, it will be useful to identify its limits. Some may be apparent already. Boulainvilliers' writings on philosophy, astrology, ancient history, and the history of religion will claim no attention here, although their possibly radical philosophical and religious character—a matter of debate since his death—may be germane to the subject of this study.[36] Margaret C. Jacob has discovered

---

[35]See Bibliographical Appendix.
[36]For eighteenth-century comments see Marais, *Journal*, 2:227; Louis Moréri et al., *Le Grand Dictionnaire historique*, ed. M. Drouet, 10 vols. (Paris: 1759), 2:133. Early-twentieth-

links between the religious and political radicalisms of the Enlightenment; historians of Old Regime political culture will want to examine them.[37] Pursuing that line of inquiry here, however, would have swelled the proportions of this book or required writing an entirely different one on the scientific, philosophical, and religious culture of early-eighteenth-century France and on Boulainvilliers' place in it. An account of his philosophy of history, it is true, cannot ignore his astrological treatises.[38] An account of his efforts to make polemical and political use of French history can do so, however, since Boulainvilliers addressed those efforts to audiences that need not have been privy to his speculations about the astral determination of historical events.

Doubtless those audiences were sensitive to questions about French

century scholars unequivocally claimed Boulainvilliers for deism or even atheism: F. Colonna d'Istria, "Introduction," in Baruch Spinoza, *Ethique*, tr. Boulainvilliers [?], ed. F. Colonna d'Istria (Paris: Armand Colin, 1907), xvi–xxiii, xxviii–xliii, esp. xxviii on Boulainvilliers as an "athée de tempérament"; Gustave Lanson, "Questions diverses sur l'histoire de l'esprit philosophique en France avant 1750," *Revue d'histoire littéraire de la France*, 10 (1912): 17–20; Ira O. Wade, *The Clandestine Organization and Diffusion of Philosophic Ideas in France from 1700 to 1750* (Princeton, N.J.: Princeton University Press; London: Oxford University Press, 1938), 97–123. Norman Torrey and Renée Simon have sought to describe Boulainvilliers as a *bien pensant* Catholic. See Torrey's reviews of Wade's *Clandestine Organization* in *Revue d'histoire littéraire de la France*, 45 (1938): 529–31, and in *Romanic Review*, 30 (1939): 205–9; Torrey, "Boulainvilliers: The Man and the Mask," in *Travaux sur Voltaire et le dix-huitième siècle*, ed. Theodore Besterman, vol. 1 (Geneva: Institut et Musée Voltaire, 1955), 159–73; and Simon's commentaries in Boulainvilliers, *Oeuvres philosophiques*. Recent scholars have restored Boulainvilliers to the ranks of early-eighteenth-century deists, Spinozists, and free-thinkers: Massimo Petrocchi, "Il Mito di Maometto in Boulainvilliers," *Rivista storica italiana*, 9 (1948): 367–77; Vernière, *Spinoza et la pensée française*, 1:306–22; John Stephenson Spink, *French Free-Thought from Gassendi to Voltaire* (London: University of London Press/Athlone, 1960), 267–72; Antoine Adam, *Le Mouvement philosophique dans la première moitié du XVIIIe siècle* (Paris: Société d'Edition et d'Enseignement Supérieur, 1967), 15, 128, 249–50; A. Robinet, "Boulainviller auteur du 'Militaire philosophe'?" *Revue d'histoire littéraire de la France*, 73 (1973): 22–31; Ann Thomson's review of Simon's edition of Boulainvilliers' *Oeuvres philosophiques* in *XVIIIe siècle*, 7 (1975): 364–65; Maria G. Zaccone Sina, "L'Interpretazione della *Genesi* in Henry de Boulainvilliers. Fonti: Jean Le Clerc e Thomas Burnet," *Rivista di filosofia neo-scolastica*, 72 (1980): 494–532, 705–33, and 73 (1981): 157–78; C. J. Betts, *Early Deism in France: From the So-Called 'Deistes' of Lyon (1564) to Voltaire's 'Lettres philosophiques' (1734)* (The Hague: Martinus Nijhoff, 1984), 171–78. Despite this growing consensus, one must not ignore the problems of attribution which surround the "philosophic" literature of the early eighteenth century, problems underlined by Simon and Torrey; see also Pierre Clair, *Libertinage et incrédules (1665–1715?)*, in *Recherches sur le XVIIe siècle*, vol. 6 (Paris: Editions du Centre National de la Recherche Scientifique, 1983), 8, 233, 239, 255; and Betts, *Early Deism*, 173–75. These problems bedevil the inconclusive account of Boulainvilliers' religious thought in James O'Higgin, *Yves de Vallone: The Making of an Esprit-Fort* (The Hague: Martinus Nijhoff, 1982), 209–13.

[37]Margaret C. Jacob, *The Radical Enlightenment: Pantheists, Freemasons and Republicans* (London: Allen & Unwin, 1981).

[38]See Diego Venturino, "Metodologia della ricerca e determinismo astrologico nella concezione storica di Henry de Boulainvilliers," *Rivista storica italiana*, 95 (1983): 389–418.

church history, theology, and the "Constitution," that is, the notorious papal bull *Unigenitus* (1713) that declared Jansenism heretical. Such questions interested Boulainvilliers too.[39] One may find traces of them in his passing remarks on how Gaulish bishops helped Merovingian kings subvert Frankish liberty, or in his contempt for the "pontifical operations" of Pope Steven who reconsecrated Pepin, the first Carolingian, king of the Franks in 754, or in his diatribe against the "superstition" of Capetian kings, which by redoubling their "ignorance" helped them destroy France's "feudal government."[40] The ambition of clerics and the credulity of laymen are recurring themes in Boulainvilliers' historical writing. But he developed no sustained account of French church history. And he contributed nothing at all to the regency's noisy disputes about *Unigenitus* beyond a sour remark that Frenchmen neglect historical study unless impelled by "party" to pursue it.[41] For these reasons religious history and controversy will claim only passing attention here.

Boulainvilliers' remark about "party" may suggest that he was a scholar serenely detached from controversy and that he intervened in it solely to correct the mistakes of mere pamphleteers. Indeed, his one published piece (itself a slim pamphlet) has been taken to be such a gesture.[42] Boulainvilliers did do original research, but he did not write the learned little dissertations sometimes adduced as evidence that he was an *érudit* writing for others; most of his works were narratives and he was not above cribbing them from earlier writers.[43] He did know Nicolas Fréret and enjoy the young academician's esteem. And like Fréret he may have frequented a private "academy" that met in about 1707 in the shadow of the Académie des Inscriptions et Belles-Lettres.[44] Nonetheless, he had undisguised contempt for that body's members, no doubt having them in mind when he condemned scholars "who make the capital of history consist in certain minutiae which they anxiously seek to

[39]See his notes on Catholic and recent Protestant writers in B.N., MSS. n.a.f. 11071–76 (the "Extraits des lectures de M. le comte de Boulainviller, avec des réflexions").

[40]*Essais*, 16–17. *Etat*, 1, "Mémoires historiques": 11, 47–48, 74, 75, 82, 83, and 105 (see also 93, 102–3, and 108 on the cooperation between clergy and Carolingians in securing the latter's authority). *Etat . . . Tome III*, 165–69.

[41]Boulainvilliers, "Préface critique au Journal de Saint Louis," in *Un Révolté du grand siècle*, 87–8: "Today men must be animated by party to apply themselves to study, and perhaps that is why the dispute about the Constitution seems to have lifted spirits."

[42]Simon, *Henry de Boulainviller*, 109; R. E. A. Waller, "Men of Letters and the *Affaire des Princes* under the Regency of the Duc d'Orléans," *European Studies Review*, 8 (1978): 131, 140.

[43]See Bibliographical Appendix, pp. 228–30, 233–36, 239–40.

[44]For this possibility—it is conjectural—see Simon, *Henry de Boulainviller*, 86–88, 682; and Lionel Gossman, *Medievalism and Ideologies of the Enlightenment: The World and Work of La Curne de Sainte-Palaye* (Baltimore: Johns Hopkins Press, 1968), 48–52.

discover in medals and old marbles." He continued: "These men, ambitious to make discoveries, neglect the true utility of history and spend their time deciphering inscriptions, proposing only conjectures, and failing to take care that were they to succeed, which happens very rarely, they would adorn only the academies for which they work, academies worthy of their fruitless remarks about facts that are already known or neglected for their little importance."[45] The worlds of historical writing and historical research were by no means impervious to each other in Boulainvilliers' generation, but he cannot be located firmly and comfortably in the learned and academic milieus of his age.

The final limitations on this book may be the most important, as they directly concern Boulainvilliers' political and polemical applications of French history. There will be nothing here on the Polysynody—the regency experiment in expanding the Royal Council, dividing it into subcouncils, and staffing them with great nobles—because Boulainvilliers had nothing to say about it. Nor will contemporary disputes about royal finances and the royal debt claim more than passing attention, because Boulainvilliers probably did not write the remarkable memoranda on fiscal equity and social welfare that admiring historians have ascribed to him. Equally conspicuous by its absence will be any account of his leadership in the illicit noble assemblies that gathered in regency Paris during the *affaire du bonnet* and the *affaire des princes*. Historians have lately sought to insist that Boulainvilliers was the "ideological expert" for the assembling nobles, but that is a myth based on the erroneous ascription to him of their petitions and memoranda.[46]

[45]Boulainvilliers, "Lettre à Mademoiselle Cousinot sur l'histoire et sa méthode (1707)," in *Un Révolté du grand siècle*, 74. Cf. the similar remarks of Louis Ellies Du Pin, who wrote to glorify the achievements of contemporary ecclesiastical erudition and yet condemned what we would call antiquarianism in almost identical terms: "I pity some savants who have applied their lives to minutiae of [historical] criticism, who have made it the capital of their studies and who have composed fat volumes on useless and frivolous subjects" (*Bibliothèque des auteurs ecclésiastiques du XVIIe siècle* [1708], "Avertissement," as quoted in Bruno Neveu, "La Vie érudite à Paris à la fin du XVIIe siécle d'après les papiers du P. Léonard de Sainte-Catherine (1695–1706)," *Bibliothèque de l'Ecole des Chartes*, 124 (1966): 432–36. This sententious rhetoric was clearly the common property of contemporaries, whatever their aims. Boulainvilliers' aims, it is obvious, were to vilify the academicians. For his doubts about the collective organization of historical research and writing see also *Etat . . . Tome III*, 5.

[46]See chap. 6, n. 64. Cf. Jean-Dominique Lassaigne, *Les Assemblées de la noblesse en France aux dix-septième et dix-huitième siècles* (Paris: Cujas, 1965), 131–52, esp. 144, 146, 162; Jean-Pierre Labatut, *Les Ducs et pairs de France au XVIIe siècle: Etude sociale* (Paris: Presses Universitaires de France, 1972), 393–427, esp. 394; and above all Devyver, *Le Sang épuré*, 250, 260, 393–94, 397. Recent studies are reinforcing the unfounded tendency to impute the assembling nobles' petitions and memoranda to Boulainvilliers (see notably Robin Price's intelligent "Boulainviller and the Myth of the Frankish Conquest of Gaul," in *Studies on Voltaire and the Eighteenth Century*, vol. 197 [Oxford: Voltaire Foundation at the Taylor Institution; Paris: Jean Touzot, 1981]: 155–85).

Boulainvilliers was a nobiliaire ideologue, of course, and the nobility's difficulties—refracted through the prism of his own experience—never ceased to concern him. Though a proud yet anxious "genealogical consciousness" of the burdensome glory of birth informed his work as historian and nobiliaire ideologue, princely service did so too, for he composed most of his work on French history as a princely client, counselor, and would-be controversialist: hence his equivocal thought, here neofeudal, there intensely royalist; here reactionary, there at home in a purely monarchical modernity. Hence too his oscillation between cautious optimism and a numbing historical fatalism inimical to that reactionary "ideology of combat" that one historian has imputed to him.[47] For this nobiliaire ideologue invariably vested his hopes and fears in the good or bad will of princes and sought to discover nobiliaire possibilities in the monarchy's problems.

Hence the broader lessons of this narrow study. The monarchy's problems—dynastic difficulties that entailed diplomatic, political, and constitutional questions—elicited other nobiliaire responses besides Boulainvilliers'. Parisian parlementaires, court nobles, and dukes and peers all produced competing aristocratic constitutionalisms of their own. It follows that these constitutionalisms, even those that may be called reactionary, cannot be dismissed as myths for the marginalized since their authors lived and worked at the center of power and preeminence in the Old Regime. A fortiori they participated in its monarchical political culture. They addressed respectful counsel to the prince. They relayed his real or putative will to each other. And as a rule they refrained from addressing a "public" rather than a prince or from courting that public's good "opinion" rather than a prince's goodwill. In the first years of the regency, however, the monarchy's problems led them to defend their competing constitutionalisms in that "public sphere" which eventually dominated French political culture in the eighteenth century.[48] They still depended on manuscript communication, that discreet and selective medium of counsel and aristocratic controversy in the reign of Louis XIV, but they also used print to reach the "public" whose "opinion" they sought to sway. This is not to claim for the early eighteenth century a distinction usually reserved to the 1750s, when "public

---

[47]Devyver, *Le Sang épuré*, 394–95, 397. Cf. Peter Stadler, *Geschichtschreibung und historisches Denken in Frankreich, 1789–1871* (Zurich: Berichthaus, 1958), 27, on Boulainvilliers' "romantic yearning for an innocent age lost through the fatality of modern state development."

[48]See chapters 5 and 6; Jürgen Habermas, *Strukturwandel der Öffentlichkeit: Untersuchungen zu einer Kategorie der bürgerlichen Gesellschaft* (Neuweid: Hermann Luchterhand Verlag, 1962); and Habermas, "The Public Sphere: An Encyclopedia Article (1964)," *New German Critique*, 3 (1974): 49–55.

opinion" began to challenge the crown's authority and when the Old Regime began to "unravel."[49] Nothing of the sort happened in Boulain-villiers' lifetime. French monarchical political culture was still too strong, the noble elites were still too divided, and their aspirations were still too self-serving in the eyes of contemporary observers for a consensus to emerge which might have challenged the monarchy or at least the bureaucratic absolutism created by the Bourbons in the seventeenth century. By asserting and defending their competing constitutionalisms in the early eighteenth century, however, the noble elites did develop historical arguments and polemical strategies that cannot be ignored by students of Old Regime political culture.

[49]See Van Kley, *The Damiens Affair,* and discussion in chapter 7.

2

Early Works: Genealogy and the Problem of French Feudalism

Although Boulainvilliers wrote his major works on French history for princes, he did not owe them his interest in it. On the contrary, he acquired his passion for the past while a student at Juilly, the prestigious and aristocratic *collège* in the diocese of Meaux run by the Oratorian fathers.[1] He developed some of his central concerns as political writer and controversialist while writing his first and still private works for his sons' education and for his own illumination. Well before he embarked on his journey as a political writer and controversialist, he had acquired his own ideological baggage. Examining its contents is the task of this chapter.

Genealogical Consciousness: Family, Noble, and French History

Boulainvilliers attended Juilly in the 1670s. His first known efforts at writing French history date to about 1700, when his thoughts turned to the educations and future careers of his sons, now ten and nine years old. Soon they would enter Juilly themselves, and then begin careers in the army and the church. Boulainvilliers, actively engaged in their educations, was already preparing for them a series of remarkable texts: a Helmontian treatise on natural philosophy (actually an earlier work which an older and more skeptical Boulainvilliers had recopied in 1700 as an example of youthful intellectual presumption); a sometimes recondite ancient history that he never finished; and finally a history of his own family prefaced by a "Dissertation" on the "true and old nobility" to

---

[1]Moréri et al., *Le Grand Dictionnaire historique*, 2:132.

which it belonged. For present purposes, and arguably for Boulainvilliers' too, the last two works are the most important.[2] Read in their
contexts—the personal and familial circumstances in which he wrote
them and the genealogical and historiographical traditions in which he
worked—those works reveal Boulainvilliers' proud but troubled "genealogical consciousness"[3] and announce one of his abiding historiographical and ideological tasks: the rehabilitation of French feudalism.

The genealogical consciousness here ascribed to Boulainvilliers may
be understood as the consciousness of belonging to a noble lineage and
of inheriting its "glory," a duty to uphold it with one's own, and a
treasury of ancestral examples of "virtue" to imitate in one's pursuit of
"glory."[4] This constellation of aristocratic assumptions and ideals may
be encountered in the Old Regime genealogical histories of noble
houses, and in Boulainvilliers' own family history too. To begin, however, this genealogical consciousness must be distinguished from the
"race consciousness" that André Devyver sought to discover among the
Old Regime nobility and impute to Boulainvilliers.

According to Devyver, Boulainvilliers was the leading proponent of
the French nobility's race consciousness and that race consciousness was
the leading symptom of the French nobility's "decline." By the end of
Louis XIV's reign, Devyver argued, a century and a half of noble "decline" had produced in rural France a desperately poor "noble proletariat" ready to mount an "aristocratic reaction" under the ideological

---

[2]The family history survives only in scattered MS notes and extracts, but the "Dissertation" may be consulted in *Essais* (see p. 10 on the "true and old nobility"; usually Boulainvilliers wrote only of the "nobility" or "old nobility"); on MSS, editions, and dating see
Bibliographical Appendix, Part 2.

[3]I borrow that term from Georges Duby, *Hommes et structures au Moyen âge: Recueil
d'articles* (Paris: Mouton, 1973).

[4]See Ellis, "Genealogy, History, and Aristocratic Reaction." Note that Boulainvilliers'
pedagogical works do not include the remarks on the education of young "persons of
condition" ascribed to him there (ibid., 423): that lost work has been found and turns out
to be by Anne-Thérèse marquise de Lambert (Geneviève Menant-Artigas, "Boulainvilliers
et Madame de Lambert," in *Studies on Voltaire and the Eighteenth Century*, vol. 219 [Oxford:
Voltaire Foundation at the Taylor Institution; Paris: Jean Touzot, 1983], 147–51). On
Boulainvilliers' efforts as a paternal pedagogue see Renée Simon, *A la recherche d'un homme
et d'un auteur: Essai de bibliographie des ouvrages du comte de Boulainviller* (Paris: Boivin, 1941),
9–12; and (for the non–French historical works mentioned earlier) Simon, *Henry de
Boulainviller*, 256–320 (on the ancient history), 358–417 (on the Helmontian treatise),
582–89 (on the misascribed notes on education). The last two are printed in Boulainvilliers, *Oeuvres philosophiques*, 2:145–276, and 134–41. The role of paternal or familial
education among the traditional nobility deserves further study; it was very important
among the robe nobility, which transmitted professional traditions and charges from
generation to generation (Roger Chartier, Marie-Madeleine Compère, and Dominique
Julia, *L'Education en France du XVIe au XVIIIe siècle* [Paris: Société d'Edition et d'Enseignement Supérieur, 1976], 171–73).

leadership of its representative and spokesman Henri de Boulain-villiers.[5] Given Boulainvilliers' rhetoric about noble "blood" and "birth" and the case that can be made for his poverty, that interpretation is attractive.[6] Upon examination, however, Boulainvilliers' poverty and racism disappear.

The case for Boulainvilliers' poverty collapses under the weight of new evidence from Parisian notarial archives and genealogical collections which suggests that his income from land and *rentes* (annuities) may have amounted to 9,000 or 10,000 *livres* a year.[7] Such revenues hardly lift Boulainvilliers into the ranks of court nobility, whose members could indeed call incomes like his (or nobles like him) "poor."[8] Nevertheless, Boulainvilliers's 9,000 *livres* a year certainly removed him from the ranks of "proletarianized" *hobereaux* such as the average petty noble in the Beauvaisis, for example, who in the 1690s was scraping by on only 1,150 *livres* a year.[9] Besides, contemporaries admitted that 10,000 *livres* a year might suffice handsomely for a provincial noble, even for one who took the title of count or baron.[10] Finally, the assistance that Boulainvilliers received from friends and patrons (among them Adrien-Maurice duc de Noailles, Louis-François d'Aumont duc d'Humières, and probably the duc d'Orléans, too) let him live respectably in Paris for much of his life. There he contracted both of his marriages, and there he died in 1722.[11] Boulainvilliers was no plutocrat, but he was no "proletarianized" noble either.

Nor was he a racist. Despite his rhetoric about noble "blood" and "birth," he developed no explicitly biological theory of noble excellence or "virtue." He never employed the argument (an undying commonplace in early-modern France) that noble "virtue" was a biological trait transmitted from generation to generation by a family's "blood" or

[5]Devyver, *Le Sang épuré*, 243, 342, 353–90.

[6]Simon, *Henry de Boulainviller*, 28–31, on Boulainvilliers' poverty.

[7]See Ellis, "Genealogy, History, and Aristocratic Reaction," 449–51. Taking 9,000 *livres* in income as 5 percent on capital—an overestimated rate of return for land and annuities in the period—one safely underestimates Boulainvilliers' fortune as about 180,000 *livres*.

[8]For example, see Louis-F. Du Bouchet, marquis de Sourches, *Mémoires*, ed. Gabriel-Jules de Cosnac et al., 13 vols. (Paris: Hachette, 1882–93), 9:246; cf. Henri Carré, *La Noblesse de France et l'opinion publique au XVIIIe siècle* (Paris: Honoré Champion, 1920), 109–10 (quoting the comte de Preux, a country gentleman). See also Labatut, *Les Ducs et pairs de France*, 324–26, for estimates (based on Parisian notarial archives for 1713–14) of average fortunes of ducal, sword, and robe nobles in the capital. The average for all nobles was 207,900 *livres;* averages for parlementaires, for sword nobles with titled fiefs or officers' commissions, and for dukes and peers were higher still.

[9]Pierre Goubert, *Beauvais et le Beauvaisis: Contribution à l'histoire sociale du XVIIe siècle*, 2 vols. (Paris: S.E.V.P.E.N., 1960), 1:212–13.

[10]Carré, *La Noblesse*, 109–10 (quoting the comte de Preux).

[11]See Ellis, "Genealogy, History, and Aristocratic Reaction," 422.

"seed."[12] In his family history Boulainvilliers did boast that such "virtues" as "piety" were "hereditary" in his house.[13] But like Anne-Thérèse marquise de Lambert, whose private reflections on the education of young nobles may have reached him in manuscript, Boulainvilliers probably imagined that good upbringing in a noble family could "render certain virtues hereditary."[14] By construing heredity as habit, and hereditary virtue as a product of noble education, one could easily claim—as Boulainvilliers did indeed claim—that "virtue . . . is more common in good lines than in others."[15]

If Boulainvilliers was not a "proletarianized" noble wallowing in "race consciousness," what was he doing in 1700, when he wrote his family's history for his sons? To answer that question one may turn to the Old Regime tradition of genealogical history, to which Boulainvilliers clearly adhered.[16] Genealogical histories of noble families first appeared in print in the middle of the sixteenth century, but they acquired their paradigmatic form and their vogue among the high nobility of early-modern France in the early seventeenth century, thanks to the efforts of the great scholar André Duchesne. Combining eloquence and erudition, Duchesne and later genealogical historians produced branch-by-branch and generation-by-generation narratives followed by appendixes or even separate volumes of "proofs."[17] Boulainvilliers owned copies of Duchesne's "Maisons" and borrowed their format when he wrote his own family history in 1700.[18] He also borrowed from Duch-

[12]For these commonplaces see Devyver, *Le Sang épuré*, 33–36; and Arlette Jouanna, *L'Idée de race en France au XVIe et au début du XVIIe siècle (1498–1614)*, 3 vols. (Lille: Atelier de Reproduction de Thèses; Paris: Honoré Champion, 1976), 1:1–3.

[13]B.M., Toulouse, MS. 598 (II 31), fols. 83r–v (see Bibliographical Appendix).

[14]Boulainvilliers, *Oeuvres philosophiques*, 2:135; cf. Menant-Artigas, "Boulainvilliers et Madame de Lambert," 151; and see n. 4 above.

[15]*Essais*, 98.

[16]The Old Regime literature on genealogy and genealogical history still awaits its historian, but for a fuller account than can be given here see Ellis, "Genealogy, History, and Aristocratic Reaction," 424–35, and works cited there.

[17]On Duchesne and French genealogical historiography in the seventeenth century see Martine Deschamps-Juif, "L'Historiographe André Du Chesne (1584–1640)," *Ecole nationale des chartes: Positions des thèses soutenues par les élèves de la promotion de 1963* (Paris: Ecole des Chartes, 1963), 47; and Henri-Jean Martin, *Livre, pouvoirs et société à Paris au XVIIe siècle (1598–1701)*, 2 vols. continuously paginated (Geneva: droz, 1969), 201, 531, 653–54, 845, 941, 942, 944. Most of the printed genealogical literature of early-modern and modern France is catalogued in B.N., *Catalogue de l'histoire de France*, 16 vols. (Paris: B.N., 1968), 9:129–75 and 16:15–75 (for family genealogies and histories), and 9:117–29 (for national or provincial collections of genealogies). Family histories, not collective genealogies, are of principal concern here.

[18]For Boulainvilliers' format see *Essais*, iv, and B.M., Toulouse, MS. 598 (II 31), passim, esp. fols. 36v, 89, 90r–v, 112v–113. For Boulainvilliers' copies of Duchesne's genealogies see A.N., M.C., XIV, 255 (Feb. 13, 1722) (postmortem inventory), under July 18.

esne and his epigones their conviction that genealogical history was a literature of noble pedagogy and panegyric, a literature designed to encourage noble "virtue" and advertise noble "glory." Such claims were plausible, given contemporary assumptions about the uses of history. History was still a didactic literature teaching virtue by example rather than by the sterner precepts of philosophy.[19] Genealogists repeated that commonplace tirelessly, adding only that the examples of virtue that family history afforded were the most powerful of all because they were "domestic."[20]

Not surprisingly, genealogy served pedagogical purposes in early-modern France; there are even printed genealogical histories expressly described by their authors as texts for the wellborn young.[21] Of course, pedagogical family history was not a noble monopoly in early-modern France. French history—that is, the history of French kings—was itself a form of familial history replete with ancestral examples for young princes and reigning monarchs.[22] So too were the memoirs of magistrates of the robe nobility.[23] In fact, at all levels of propertied society in early-modern France, one encounters lineages engaged in consolidating themselves, their patrimonies, and their family traditions, to which end their members composed *livres de raison:* manuscript books of accounts, autobiography, advice, local antiquities, and, finally, family history that served the aims of familial pedagogy.[24]

Noble genealogical history (unlike some other forms of familial history in early-modern France) was also panegyrical history. To the end of

---

[19]George H. Nadel, "Philosophy of History before Historicism," *History and Theory,* 3 (1963): 291–315.

[20]See, for example, Louis and Scévole de Sainte-Marthe, *Histoire généalogique de la maison de France,* 2 vols. (Paris: Abraham Picard, 1619), 1: dedication to the king (unpaginated); André Duchesne, *Histoire de la maison de Chastillon sur Marne* (Paris: Sebastien Cramoisy, 1621), dedication (unpaginated); Nicolas Chorier, *Histoire généalogique de la maison de Sassenage* (Grenoble: Jean Nicolas, 1669), 2; [B. de Maynier], *Histoire de la principale noblesse de Provence* (Aix: Joseph David, 1719), 1.

[21]See, for two examples widely separated in time, François de L'Aloüete, *Traité des nobles et des vertus dont ils sont formés . . . : Avec une histoire & description généalogique de la très-illustre & très-ancienne maison de Couci, & de ses alliances* (Paris: Robert Le Manier, 1577); and François-Augustin de Vipart, *Généalogie de la maison de Vipart, en Normandie* (n.p.: 1751).

[22]Ranum, *Artisans of Glory.*

[23]Orest Ranum, "Fathers and Sons: Social Values in Seventeenth-Century Robe Society," in *Proceedings of the Annual Meeting of the Western Society for French History, 1982,* 10 (1984): 215–26.

[24]See Natalie Zemon Davis, "Ghosts, Kin, and Progeny: Some Features of Family Life in Early Modern France," *Daedalus,* 106, no. 2 (Spring 1977): 96–100, and works cited there. On legal strategies available even to nonnoble Frenchmen for consolidating patrimonies in senior male lines (a privilege usually reserved by custom to noble families alone), see Ralph E. Giesey, "Rules of Inheritance and Strategies of Mobility in Prerevolutionary France," *American Historical Review,* 82 (1977): 271–89.

the Old Regime, genealogical historians urged their readers to notice the "marks" or "points" of "honor" or "glory" that distinguished the houses they were writing about: antiquity of noble extraction, wealth, marriage "alliances," service to the king, offices and dignities held, "beautiful actions" performed—anything that might put a house or its members on the lighted stage of history in order to "illustrate" that house and cover it with "glory."[25]

These panegyrical uses of noble genealogical history could (though they did not have to) sustain its pedagogical functions. For according to the highly conventional rhetoric of genealogists and writers on nobility, *noblesse* did indeed *oblige:* the "glory" of a noble house called attention to its members and obliged them to "sustain" their inherited "quality" with "personal virtue" or else suffer a "dishonor" commensurate with "the rank and elevation of their houses."[26] With such rhetoric, the genealogical historian could trap the young in webs of obligation and expectation that tied them to their lineages and to the larger aristocratic society to which they belonged. The genealogical historian might even warn the young that they lived under the critical gaze of dead ancestors. Consider the following lines, written in 1751 by a father addressing his own family history to his sons: "All your ancestors have fixed their gaze upon you, anxious to acknowledge you as their true descendants if they see that your sentiments are affable, generous, noble . . . , but also well prepared to reject you [if you follow] contrary paths. Remember that it is by a wise conduct, by *moeurs* that are pure and well regulated, by virtue, finally, that one recognizes the *gentilhomme*."[27]

From this brief analysis, the two leading principles of genealogical consciousness may be identified: first, the assumption that noble "birth" fosters a noble "virtue" in the wellborn, by giving them good ancestral "examples" to follow; and second, the conviction that noble "birth" *obliges* the wellborn to cultivate their "virtue" and sustain or augment

[25]For example, André Duchesne, *Généalogie de l'ancienne et illustre maison de La Rochefoucauld* (Paris: Edme Martin, 1622), "Au lecteur" (unpaginated) on the house's "diverse marks of honor and grandeur." In the eighteenth century, royal genealogists used this same language in appraising families and recommending them for "the honors of the court"; see Bluche, *La Vie quotidienne de la noblesse,* 16; and François Bluche and Pierre Durye, *Les Honneurs de la cour,* 2 vols. (Paris: Les Cahiers Nobles, 1957).

[26]Gilles-André de La Roque, *Traité de la noblesse,* 3d ed. (Rouen: Pierre Le Boucher, 1735), "Préface" (unpaginated): ". . . personal virtue is necessary to *gentilshommes,* so that they might sustain their quality. The greater the rank and elevation of their houses, the heavier the dishonor they bear and the deeper the precipice they fall into by their lack of merit." La Roque's *Traité* was one of the Old Regime's most authoritative treatises on nobility. Its author was also a major genealogical historian of the late seventeenth century. See esp. his massive *Histoire généalogique de la maison d'Harcourt,* 4 vols. (Paris: Sebastien Cramoisy, 1662).

[27]Vipart, *Généalogie de la maison de Vipart,* v.

their family's "glory" with their own. These were Boulainvilliers' principles in 1700. Writing for his sons, he insisted that "a truly generous noble must imitate his ancestors and like them march in the paths of honor and virtue."[28] He invited his sons to read about their "illustrious ancestors" who set "examples" for "virtues of all kinds." He declared confidently that "whatever manner of life [my successors] may wish to embrace they can set before themselves excellent models."[29] He reproached nobles, among them "relations" of his own, for forgetting their ancestry and for having "made it their capricious vanity to ignore who they were." He continued, "Heaven preserve my children from such an indignity! When one believes that one owes much to the name and the blood to which one is born, one rarely assumes sentiments that will dishonor them."[30] Dissolving self-knowledge into ancestral pride and fusing respect for one's self with a respect for one's forebears, Boulainvilliers piously celebrated his lineage's glory and sought vigorously to sustain it. To that end he mounted in his family history a vigorous defense of his house's traditional claims to exalted extraction, that is, to direct masculine descent from the French-Burgundian House of Croy and, through that house, from ancient Hungarian royalty.[31] To that same end he encouraged his sons to cultivate their own virtue and pursue their own glory. Predictably, in a letter to his elder son written in 1700, Boulainvilliers wrote, "Take care of your glory and I shall take care of the rest."[32]

So far little distinguishes Boulainvilliers' genealogical history from the others that have been considered. Willful and optimistic language about "birth," "virtue," and "glory" flowed from his pen as easily as it did from Duchesne's when he wrote massive genealogical histories for great houses. In neither case were genealogical history and consciousness symptoms of noble marginalization. Rather, they expressed a noble activism and competition for renown that Boulainvilliers showed no sign of renouncing.

Yet there were clouds on Boulainvilliers' horizon. As he urged his sons to pursue glory he could not forget that he had failed to do so himself. In his own youth, Boulainvilliers had quit his military career (probably because his father had failed to subsidize it adequately),[33] thus failing to

[28]*Essais*, 8.
[29]*Essais*, iv–v.
[30]*Essais*, vi.
[31]See Ellis, "Genealogy, History, and Aristocratic Reaction," 431–33.
[32]Boulainvilliers, *Oeuvres philosophiques*, 2:41.
[33]Not because it overburdened a family fortune which, in any case, Boulainvilliers now promised to apply to his elder son's military career. See ibid., and Ellis, "Genealogy, History, and Aristocratic Reaction," 435–36.

pursue his own glory and sustain his house's. In short, he violated the principles of genealogical consciousness. In 1700, consequently, his efforts were not only pedagogical but also apologetic. In his "Dissertation" on the "old nobility" prefixed to his family history, he wrote: "I seek also to make my personal justification, which I believe I owe my family. Fortune has so prevented me from assuming employments appropriate to my birth that one might hardly refrain from blaming me . . . if one did not know the obstacles in my path—obstacles which show that fate triumphs over men's intentions—and if this work did not attest the fact that my house's glory has been as dear to me as to any of my ancestors, though they may have established that glory much more honorably."[34] Speaking now not only to his sons but to his whole "family," past, present, and future, Boulainvilliers went on to allude ominously to "bad times like those I have known," thereby implying—and this is indeed what he tried to show in his "Dissertation"—that not just biographical accidents but larger historical circumstances too might account for his failure to acquire glory.[35]

As personal apology became historical diagnosis in his "Dissertation," however, willful optimism paled before historical pessimism, for Boulainvilliers now sought to explain and deplore nothing less than the French nobility's "decadence."

Boulainvilliers' "Dissertation" was an atypical treatise on nobility. As a rule such works were topically organized and theoretically inclusive surveys of all categories of nobles and of all law and jurisprudence governing them. Historical discussions were only digressions.[36] Boulainvilliers' "Dissertation," however, was a chronological history of an exclusive social category represented in his own time by only "a small quantity of families who hardly remember their former grandeur," the "true and old nobility."[37] Moreover, by "old nobility" Boulainvilliers did not mean what French law meant, nobility at least three or (in Boulainvilliers' time) four generations old. He meant what contemporary writers and jurists did when they discovered within the legally defined old nobility a still more exalted nobility boasting "immemorial" noble

---

[34]*Essais*, v–vi.

[35]*Essais*, vi.

[36]Compare the three leading examples of Boulainvilliers' own time: La Roque, *Traité;* Père [Claude-François] Menestrier, *Les Diverses Espèces de noblesse, et les manières d'en dresser les preuves*, 2d ed. (Paris: R.-J.-B. de La Caille, 1685); and [Alexandre Belleguise], *Traité de la noblesse et de son origine*, 2d ed. (Paris: Jacques Morel, 1700), esp. 1–7 and 57–68 (an especially legalistic treatise examined in Ford, *Robe and Sword*, 23–26).

[37]*Essais*, 9–10, 227.

extraction, or feudal forebears, or even descent from the ancient Franks who presumably conquered Gaul at the end of the fifth century. Terminology might vary from author to author and jurist to jurist, but virtually all of them distinguished between a legal old nobility and an "immemorial" nobility all the more illustrious, paradoxically, because its origins were lost in the night of time, and all the more admirable because it owed its status to its birth alone and not to a recorded act of royal authority.[38] Unlike his contemporaries (at least those who took the trouble to write treatises on nobility), Boulainvilliers insisted that the "immemorial" nobility was the only nobility worthy of the name, for by calling that nobility the "true and old nobility" he implied that there was no other.

Defining such a nobility, however, was easier than writing its history. Genealogists, Boulainvilliers among them, knew that noble lineages could not be traced before the age of fiefs, when magnates appropriated their precarious benefices, turned them into hereditary fiefs, took patronyms from their new patrimonies, and began to leave documentary traces of their lineages' existence.[39] But there were ways around that impasse. Family "tradition" let Boulainvilliers trace his own lineage back to the dawn of European history.[40] Allusions in old texts to "illustrious" or "noble" men might be helpful; they still are.[41] And so might the presumption that genealogical consciousness could inspire, even in writers who denied that a noble order existed in prefeudal France: the presumption that ancestral virtue and glory spontaneously constituted

[38]La Roque, *Traité*, preface (unpaginated) and 1–31; Menestrier, *Les Diverses espèces*, 187–296; and for other examples Octave Le Maire, *L'Imprescriptibilité de l'ancienne noblesse et la dérogeance d'après la jurisprudence ancienne* (Brussels: 1953), 2–4. Belleguise, *Traité*, is exceptional in refusing to admit this distinction.

[39]For such admissions see Boulainvilliers' own 1719 "Discours sur la noblesse" (Bibliothèque de l'Institut [Paris], MS. 321, fols. 552v–553); P[ierre] Louvet, *Anciennes remarques de la noblesse beauvaisine, et de plusieurs familles de France*, 1 vol. and 80 pp. of vol. 2 (Beauvais: Veuve G. Valet, 1640), 1:1; [Robert] Hubert, *Traitté de la noblesse, où sont ajoutez deux discours, l'un de l'origine des fiefs, & l'autre de la foy et homage* (Orleans: Jean Boyer, 1681), 98–99; [Honoré Caille] Du Fourny, *Histoire généalogique de la maison de Faudoas* (Montauban: F. Descausset, 1724), preface (unpaginated); [abbé Gabriel Brizard], *Histoire généalogique de la maison de Beaumont, en Dauphiné: Tome premier, contenant l'histoire* (Paris: L'Imprimerie du Cabinet du Roi, 1779), i. Cf. Duby, *Hommes et structures*, 267–85, for similar limits to the knowledge of medieval genealogists and modern historians.

[40]B.M., Toulouse, MS. 598 (II 31), fols. 55v–83v, and (on family "tradition") fols. 10v, 13r, 85v; and Ellis, "Genealogy, History, and Aristocratic Reaction," 431–32.

[41]See, for example [Joachim d'Estaing], *Dissertations sur la noblesse d'extraction et sur l'origine des fiefs* (Paris: Gabriel Martin, 1690); Joan Martindale, "The French Aristocracy in the Early Middle Ages: A Reappraisal," *Past and Present*, 75 (May 1977): 5–45, esp. 9; Constance Bouchard, "The Origins of the French Nobility: A Reassessment," *American Historical Review*, 86 (1981): 501–32, esp. 501.

noble lineages even where no law constituted a privileged hereditary order to which they might belong.[42]

All these strategies assisted Boulainvilliers as he constituted the object of his "Dissertation," a work designed to trace the continuous history of the "true and old nobility" from Frankish antiquity through the age of fiefs and chivalry and right up to modern times.[43] Particularly helpful was his genealogical consciousness, which let Boulainvilliers presume the existence not only of a prefeudal nobility but also of a pre-Conquest "nobility" of "seniores" or "seigneurs" distinguished from the other Franks by their "birth and valor."[44] That was a remarkable move for Boulainvilliers, who is best known for arguing (even in his "Dissertation") that conquest constituted nobility and that the Frankish Conquest ennobled and "exalted" the Franks above the Gallo-Romans.[45] But that move betrays, yet again, the impress that genealogical consciousness made on Boulainvilliers' writing on the French nobility's past.

If Boulainvilliers' genealogical consciousness helped him constitute the "true and old nobility" as the subject of the history he was writing in 1700, his genealogical consciousness also helped him to conceptualize that nobility's "decadence." Unlike historians of a later time, Boulainvilliers was *not* concerned to identify a socioeconomic decline of the nobility that might be blamed on inflation, for example, or on irrational estate management. On the contrary, he blamed the nobility's "decadence" on the breakdown of its proud genealogical consciousness, and he blamed that in turn on the establishment, in the sixteenth century, of the royal court. With the court's appearance, Boulainvilliers maintained, the rules that governed the nobility's competitive game for glory changed and new means for acquiring good "fortune" began to corrupt it: "Since then men sought to advance in employments at court or in the army. They quit their country residences. They exerted themselves in every way to acquire the favor of kings or of individuals near them. Since then the path to fortune has no longer conformed to the old route. One

---

[42]Though he insisted that the Salian Franks had "no order of nobles separate from the people," Adrien de Valois admitted that there were "noble and honored men among the Franks." The abbé Dubos (Boulainvilliers' most trenchant posthumous critic) cited Valois with approval and made the same points himself. See abbé [Jean-Baptiste] Dubos, *Histoire critique de l'établissement de la monarchie françoise dans les Gaules*, 2 vols., 2d ed. (Paris: Nyon, 1742), 2:430 n. (quoting Valois, *Notitia galliarum* . . . [Paris: F. Léonard, 1675], 485), and 423. For a recent and analogous (though not identical) argument see Martindale, "French Aristocracy," 19–20.

[43]*Essais*, 16–144 (where Franks and feudatories are included in the old nobility's history).

[44]*Essais*, 20–21 and 25–27.

[45]*Essais*, 1 ("Violence has introduced distinctions of Liberty and Slavery, Nobility and Commonalty [*Roture*]"), and 17–44, esp. 21–25.

used to need an essential merit along with high birth [*dans une grande naissance*]; now one had to add an agreeable manner, then complacency, which soon degenerated into baseness and self-forgetfulness."[46] At court, the nobleman abandoned his "merit" and his "birth" to seek his "fortune" in the "favor" of kings, only to find himself on a dangerous new treadmill, competing for more and more tokens of royal "favor" against more and more parvenus who were bidding up its moral and material costs: "Formerly the nobility, faithfully attached to the kings' person by the religion of its oath and honored and loved by kings as the support of their crown, shone alone in important employments, without fearing that favor might prejudice it or that inferiors might replace it. Today the number and newness of its competitors excites its jealousy, just as the multitude of employments foments its ambition, and these two temptations have ruined its wealth and, consequently, sapped its hope by the foundations."[47] Thus if economic decline was indeed part of the story of noble "decadence," as Boulainvilliers told it, that economic decline was a consequence, not a cause, of the nobility's "decadence." And that "decadence" consisted, essentially, in the displacement of birth and virtue by royal favor and personal wealth as the ideals of elite society and as the qualities requisite for success. These ominous sociocultural transformations Boulainvilliers blamed on the royal court.

Boulainvilliers' diatribe against wealth, favor, and the royal court was traditional. It is by no means evidence of his putative marginalization or even of a reactionary antipathy to monarchy. In the early seventeenth century, for example, Jean de Saulx-Tavanes failed to acquire a marshal's baton (his father had been a marshal) and used his unwelcome leisure to reflect on how "favor" worked to exclude from royal service "generous" men like himself, men of "virtue," "merit," "valor," and "spirit." Similar language may be found in Fénelon and Saint-Simon. Its use, consequently, implies neither the marginalization of its user (Saulx-Tavanes was no marginalized *hobereau*) nor his alienation from the ideals of royal service or from the norms of France's royalist political culture, ideals and norms Fénelon and Saint-Simon embraced.[48] In 1700, Boulainvilliers too tried to embrace those ideals and norms—this is not surprising, since he sought to encourage his sons to pursue glory in royal

[46]*Essais*, 221–22.

[47]*Essais*, 229–30.

[48]Jouanna, *L'Idée de race*, 710–28 (on Saulx-Tavanes); Gallouédec-Genuys, *Le Prince selon Fénelon*, 185–214 (on the importance of "birth" and social hierarchy). Brancourt, *Le Duc de Saint-Simon et la monarchie*, 183–86 (on the importance of "birth" and "merit"). See also Pauline M. Smith, *The Anti-Courtier Trend in Sixteenth Century French Literature* (Geneva: Droz, 1963).

service. In the last pages of his "Dissertation" he suggested that the nobility's "decadence" might be reversible, because the momentary consequence of royal policy that a well-disposed prince might change. He admitted that the "needs of the state" might for a while favor the "ambition" of "new families" who claimed "preferment to old ones by virtue of their employments, their wealth—which assures to them all the dignities they can buy—or finally the favor that they believe they possess or to which they aspire."[49] He also admitted that "in our days" new ministerial families enjoyed authority and wealth once unknown even to kings, and sustained themselves by "alliances" with old families.[50] But he hated the new "political nobility" of old and new families which was emerging in his time as the governing elite, and he looked forward to the day when French princes would again prefer men of "true nobility" to ambitious clans trading on their wealth and favor.[51] With a ringing declaration of that hope, he closed his "Dissertation": "True and incommunicable nobility always subsists and cannot fail to rise up again with distinction under princes as informed and equitable as ours, when the luster of birth will be sustained by true merit."[52]

In the body of his "Dissertation," however, Boulainvilliers had already pushed his diagnosis of the nobility's "decadence" in a far more original, pessimistic, and antimonarchical direction. Despite his attempts at optimism, he was convinced that the appearance of the royal court had had fatal consequences for the French nobility. "One may say," he wrote, "that the beautiful days of the nobility are over, for it was too little concerned with thrift and with the glory of its predecessors, when the hope of a present fortune caused it to embrace the phantoms of the court and of favor, and to forget its own dignity."[53] He intensified that pessimistic reading of the court's emergence by blaming it on a still larger historical phenomenon: the decay of French feudalism. Boulainvilliers revered the feudal past. This was the glorious past to which genealogists traced the oldest lineages of France. In his "Dissertation," he wrote long and loving accounts of fief holding and chivalry and identified the "decadence" of the nobility with the decay of the feudal order that had once sustained it.[54] He deplored the reunification of great medieval fiefs to the royal domain, for it had concentrated political "grandeur" in the crown and had enhanced the importance of royal

[49]*Essais*, 300.
[50]*Essais*, 298.
[51]Pierre Goubert, *The Ancien Régime: French Society, 1600–1750*, tr. Steve Cox (New York: Harper Torchbooks, 1974), 187–88 on "political nobility."
[52]*Essais*, 300.
[53]*Essais*, 227.
[54]*Essais*, 78–94, 111–201.

"favor."[55] He lamented the substitution of paid infantry for feudal hosts, for this had secured the independence of the crown from its vassals and had established the might of the crown on ability to tax and pay commoners, not on ability to secure the service of feudatories.[56] Finally, Boulainvilliers bemoaned the modern culture of politeness and learning, for although it replaced the lamentable "ignorance" of the feudal nobility and the "barbaric" scholasticism of the medieval clergy, that new culture masked the very "passions" and "ambitions" that it aroused and thereby aided the social circulation or "confusion" that Boulainvilliers deplored.[57] Situated in this larger historical framework, the "decadence" of the nobility ceased to be the result of bad but reversible royal policy and became instead the "necessary consequence" of deeper historical transformations separating the present from the past, and separating the old nobility from the feudal order that used to sustain it.[58]

Boulainvilliers achieved a painfully acute sense of historical change, isolating the feudal past as the golden age of the nobility only to lament its loss and all but surrender his personal and familial ambitions to a dispirited fatalism. That was indeed the point to which Boulainvilliers' project of personal apology and historical diagnosis threatened to take him in 1700. Writing about his own failed career, he alluded darkly to "fate." He did so again when he compared the French nobility's "decadence" with the "fate of ancient Rome, where all the old families died out or were relegated to obscurity when the form of government changed."[59] And since he tended to identify history with "fate," he

[55]*Essais*, 230–52, esp. 231, 252.

[56]*Essais*, 253–73.

[57]*Essais*, 273–98, esp. 297–98: "By comparison with those times [the age of a "barbarous" scholasticism], how happy are the last centuries, in which the sciences have been placed within the reach of all minds and all professions. That is the advantage that we enjoy above our fathers, and that may console us for those that they enjoyed and that we have lost." He continued, "But is this advantage indeed real? Does it not consist in an ideal satisfaction rather than an effective good? The license of minds, the abuse of the sciences, the false opinions, ambition, luxury, the confusion of social conditions [*le dérangement des conditions*], are these not greater evils than simplicity and ignorance? It seems that today the most immediate effect of the sciences in which the young are instructed is to excite their passions, particularly that of ambition, and that the use of these same sciences later in life consists merely in forming a mask of virtue for iniquity and injustice." Boulainvilliers' proto-Rousseauist diatribe suggests that he may be read as a critic of the "individualist" tradition associated with France's "moralists," a tradition most recently studied by Keohane, in *Philosophy and the State in France*.

[58]*Essais*, 230: "Let us say then that the decadence in which the old nobility presently finds itself is a necessary consequence of the change that has taken place in the government, in the manner of making war, and of that which has taken place in manners [*moeurs*] and minds."

[59]*Essais*, 227. Cf. ibid., v–vi, quoted above.

tended also to identify historical study with a detached and Stoic contemplation of that fate. In fact, that is precisely the position he took in yet another text written around 1700 for his sons' education, his ancient history, where he commended the study of history for bringing "tranquil firmness" to the soul.[60]

In 1700, obviously, Boulainvilliers was sending his sons contradictory signals: brave language about the pursuit of glory, and ominous allusions to "decadence," to "fate," and, finally, to the "vicissitudes" of history which, whether favorable or unfavorable, would surround all their efforts to renew their house's glory: "It will happen, perhaps, and as for me I hope so, that one of our children will pierce through the obscurity in which we live, to restore to our name its former brilliance, and then we shall no longer complain of the vicissitudes which will lift us up after having cast us down."[61] With that prayer, one probably reaches the heart of Boulainvilliers' ambiguous reflections on the advantages and the burdens of noble birth, virtue, and glory in the last years of Louis XIV's reign.

This account of Boulainvilliers' first efforts to write French history has brought to light concerns that may be called social. He was not the race-conscious *hobereau* that Devyver supposed, but a powerful genealogical consciousness of the glory and the duties of birth into a noble lineage shaped his ambitions, and his failure to realize them fed his anxieties and informed his pessimistic historical diagnosis of the old nobility's "decadence."

Boulainvilliers never abandoned these social concerns. They were part of the ideological baggage he carried with him when he became a political writer and controversialist. He continued to look admiringly to a premonarchical past when royal "grandeur" did not yet threaten noble "glory" and genealogical pride. Despite occasional suspicions that feudalism may have contained the seeds of its own destruction, he never discarded his conviction that the "beautiful days" of the French nobility belonged to a past in which feudalism still sustained it.

That conviction committed Boulainvilliers to another project, the rehabilitation of French feudalism. He was to pursue that project diligently throughout his career as a political writer. He began it earlier, however, in a series of early texts written for his own enlightenment and revealing, in their conflicting accounts of French feudalism, the difficulties that surrounded any effort to understand it sympathetically.

[60]Bibliothèque Mazarine (Paris), MS. 1578, pp. 420–22, as quoted in Simon, *Henry de Boulainviller,* 297–98.
[61]*Essais,* 228.

The Rehabilitation of French Feudalism

"Feudalism" or "feudal government" (to use the term that Boulain-villiers and his contemporaries usually employed) preoccupied him in almost every work he wrote on French history, beginning with his 1700 "Dissertation" on the old nobility. There his admiration for French feudalism was already evident, and eventually he mounted a vigorous defense of feudalism against his contemporaries' contempt for it. Complicating that already difficult task were competing efforts to rehabilitate feudalism in order to assign a feudal pedigree to members of the titled nobility (the ducs et pairs) and justify their preeminence over the rest of the nobility. In short, Boulainvilliers' admiration for French feudalism led him onto an ideological and historiographical minefield. That treacherous terrain and Boulainvilliers' early and still private efforts to traverse it need to be charted, before his later activities as a political writer and controversialist may claim attention.

Antifeudalism in Seventeenth-Century France

Frenchmen disparaged the feudal past long before they made anti-feudalism a staple of antiseigneurial polemics in the eighteenth century.[62] For antifeudalism was a commonplace in France's essentially royalist historiography. Thanks to such Renaissance scholars as Jacques Cujas, historians knew that the hereditary fief had once been a precarious benefice, or royal grant of land and authority, whose holder had transformed it into a patrimonial estate.[63] Because of their royalist convictions, these historians quickly concluded that the fief was the product of "aristocratic usurpation" of authority and wealth properly the crown's alone. That commonplace may be traced from the work of Cujas' student, the eminent sixteenth-century historian Etienne Pasquier, into the "general histories" of France produced across the seventeenth century and into the eighteenth. Characteristically those works located the heyday of "aristocratic usurpation" and "feudal anarchy" in the ninth and tenth centuries when, under the later Carolingian kings of France, Viking invasions and civil wars dismembered the kingdom. Although these historians appreciated that feudalism eventually became part of the French political order, they explained that fact as a conse-

---

[62]J. Q. C. Mackrell, *The Attack on 'Feudalism' in Eighteenth-Century France* (London: Routledge and Kegan Paul, 1973).

[63]On Cujas see J. G. A. Pocock, *The Ancient Constitution and the Feudal Law: English Historical Thought in the Seventeenth Century* (Cambridge: Cambridge University Press, 1957), 71–77.

quence of royal weakness. As a rule, they turned to the moment in which they thought royal authority had reached its nadir—A.D. 987, when Hugh Capet ascended the throne at the end of the Carolingian decadence—to discover a weak king reluctantly or prudently ratifying the usurpations of his vassals to secure what remained of royal authority and his own possession of it. But that supposition—it rested on no document—was hardly an admission that feudalism was legitimate. Early-modern historians of the medieval past usually went on to celebrate the reunion of great fiefs to the royal domain and (if like Pasquier they wished to celebrate the achievements of French legists and magistrats) the expansion of royal jurisdiction exercised by the Parlement of Paris over the realm. For early-modern French historians, therefore, feudalism was a regrettable but passing episode in the otherwise unbroken history of the crown.[64]

Besides this royalist antifeudalism, however, Boulainvilliers also had to overcome an allodial antifeudalism before he could rehabilitate the feudal past. Allods, whether "noble" or "common," were ancient freeholds that had escaped the spread of feudal tenurial obligations in the Middle Ages. These properties were particularly numerous in the southern and eastern provinces of France where local customs based on Roman law authorized them. To jurists and historians of the sixteenth century, allods were more than local peculiarities, however, they were highly esteemed forms of landholding because they recalled Roman *proprietas* and the ancient "free allods" of prefeudal France. Beginning in the 1620s, however, the crown embarked on a sustained effort to

[64]Etienne Pasquier, *Les Oeuvres*, 2 vols. (Amsterdam: 1723), 1:46–48, 111–16, 130–31 (*Recherches de la France,* Book II, on French feudalism and the Parlement of Paris). On the "general histories" of the next century, see Tyvaert, "L'Image du roi," esp. 528–29 for Capet's accession in A.D. 987 as a nodal point in these fundamentally dynastic histories. It was usually under that date, or under the heading "Hugh Capet," that historians interrupted their narratives with accounts of the history of feudalism largely consonant with the ideas of Cujas and Pasquier. See, for example, Nicolas Vignier, *Sommaire de l'histoire des françois* (Paris: Sebastien Nivelle, 1579), 174–85, 213–14; Vignier, *La Bibliothèque historiale,* 3 vols. (Paris: Abel Langelier, 1587), 2:519–23; Scipion Dupléix, *Histoire générale de France,* 3 vols. (Paris: Laurent Sonnius, 1621–28), 1:404–8, 655–58, 2:1–17; Jean de Serres, *Inventaire général de l'histoire de France* (Paris: Guillaume Pelé, 1636), 79–89; François Eudes de Mézeray, *Histoire de France,* 3 vols. (Paris: Mathieu Guillemot, 1643–51), 1:297, 308, 353–65, 369; Mézeray, *Histoire de France,* 3 vols., 2d ed. (Paris: Denys Thierry, Jean Guignard, Claude Barbin, 1685), 1:611, 646, 2:2–3, 7–8; Guillaume Marcel, *Histoire de l'origine et des progrez de la monarchie françoise,* 4 vols. (Paris: Denys Thierry, 1686), 1:215, 255, 279; Père Gabriel Daniel, *Histoire de France,* 3 vols. (Paris: Jean-Baptiste Delespine, 1713), vol. 1, cols. 861, 879, 888–90, 989, 993–99. Daniel admitted that no "treaty" between Capet and the great feudatories of 987 survived, but tried to explain its absence: like all charters of France's early kings it remained with the king, not at a central archival depository, and was probably lost when the English ambushed the retinue of Philip Augustus in 1196 (*Histoire de la milice françoise,* 2 vols. [Amsterdam: 1724], 1:59–60).

reduce allods (or at least the richer "noble" allods) to the status of fiefs held of the crown and owing fines and quitrents to it. The costs of seventeenth-century warfare drove the crown to that expedient (an early-modern French variant of fiscal feudalism) and in the long run the crown was successful. By the end of the Old Regime, the noble allod had disappeared. But in the seventeenth century the affected provinces, notably Guyenne, Dauphiny, and above all Languedoc, mounted vigorous and sometimes successful opposition to royal efforts to reduce their allod holders to dues-paying vassals of the royal domain. Essential to their campaigns in defense of provincial privilege and property were learned treatises on local land law, the best known being Pierre Caseneuve's *Le Franc-alleu de la province de Languedoc, establi et defendu* (1645). That treatise exemplifies clearly the allodial antifeudalism with which Boulainvilliers had to contend when he wrote on the feudal past.[65]

Though concerned chiefly with provincial law and history, the allod's defenders did not abstain from larger historical and political reflections on French feudalism. Thus while Caseneuve defended Languedoc's allod basically by appealing to Languedoc's custom and its basis in Roman law, he did not hesitate to denounce the "feudal law" which he thought the crown was trying to impose on the province.[66] Feudal law was a "hateful law" that injured proprietors and sovereigns both. It established the "servitude" of proprietors to lords and weakened the king's claim to his subjects' loyalty.[67] That second point—an appeal to the royalist convictions of his contemporaries—led Caseneuve into a familiar royalist antifeudalism. He denounced feudal law as the result of

[65]Still indispensable is Emile Chénon, *Etude sur l'histoire des alleux en France* (Paris: L. Larose et Forcel, 1888), esp. 202–26 on the seventeenth- and eighteenth-century disputes about allod holding. Also valuable are the following specialized studies: E. Andt, "Sur la théorie de la directe universelle présenté par l'édit de 1692," *Revue historique de droit français et étranger*, ser. 4, 1 (1922): 604–36; Robert Boutruche, *Une Société provinciale en lutte contre le régime féodal: L'alleu en Bordelais et en Bazadais du XIe au XVIIIe siècle* (Rodez: P. Carrère, 1947), esp. 135–38, on controversies of the seventeenth and eighteenth centuries; and François Loirette, "The Defense of the Allodium in Seventeenth-Century Agenais: An Episode in Local Resistance to Encroaching Royal Power," in *State and Society in Seventeenth-Century France*, ed. and tr. Raymond F. Kierstead (New York: New Viewpoints, 1975), 180–97. For sixteenth-century writers on the allod, cf. Pasquier, *Les Oeuvres*, 1:131–32 (*Recherches de la France*, Book II, chap. 16); and (on Charles Du Moulin) William Farr Church, *Constitutional Thought in Sixteenth-Century France* (Cambridge: Harvard University Press, 1941), 181–84. For Caseneuve, see n. 66.

[66][Pierre Caseneuve], *Le Franc-alleu de la province de Languedoc* (Toulouse: Jean Bonde, 1645), first pagination, Book I, 59, 62, and esp. 2–3, 62–64, 80–82. This is an expanded version of Caseneuve's 1640 *Instruction pour le franc-alleu de la province de Languedoc* which the provincial Estates of Languedoc had commissioned as an answer to maître des requêtes Auguste Galland's statement of the crown's position: the 1629 *Contre le franc-alleu sans tiltre* and the 1637 *Du franc-alleud et origine des droicts seigneuriaux*.

[67]Ibid., first pagination, Book I, 3, 60, 63–64, 161–67, 249–56.

"anarchy" and "usurpation" under the late Carolingians. He added that feudal law was a poor foundation on which to build a stable political order. Hedged round by conditions and contingent on fief holding, the "homage" that "vassals" owed their lords was inferior to the "fidelity" that "subjects" owed their sovereigns, that is, an absolute political obligation to an absolute sovereign and, Caseneuve sought to suggest, a much more reliable basis for royal authority. Caseneuve's royalist antifeudalism did not obscure his allodial antifeudalism, however. He combined them to imply that before the age of feudal disorder France had been a community of free proprietors subject to an absolute sovereign.[68] If, under the glorious Carolingians, free proprietors coexisted harmoniously with absolute kings they might do so again, Caseneuve suggested discreetly, if modern kings would abandon the neofeudal ambitions which "our enemies, covering their malice with zeal for royalty," were trying to encourage.[69]

The learned champions of allodial landholding—for example, Caseneuve and Denis de Salvaing de Boissieu, who wrote on the usages of Dauphiny—had a measurable impact on the seventeenth-century perception of feudalism, as the work of Louis Chantereau-Lefebvre shows.[70] One of Cardinal Richelieu's first intendants—he served in Lorraine in the 1630s—and later a member of the erudite circle or "Académie Putéane" that gathered at the library of the brothers Du Puy in Paris, Chantereau wrote a Traité des fiefs that feudists at work in the early eighteenth century still remembered as one of the best available.[71] A powerful royalist and allodial antifeudalism, which recalled Caseneuve's writings, animated Chantereau. Rehearsing a familiar argument, he insisted that fiefs were merely usurped benefices that Hugh Capet sanctioned when he mounted the throne in A.D. 987.[72] Predictably, Chantereau argued that Capet's act injured monarchy and prop-

---

[68]Ibid., 97–100, esp. 97–98: Caseneuve distinguished the obligations of subjects to their sovereign from the those of vassals to their lords; using late-Carolingian capitularies as evidence, he sought to insist also that before the age of fiefs French kings insisted that individuals' obligations as royal subjects take precedence over their obligations as this or that magnate's vassals.

[69]Ibid., 62–64.

[70]Denis de Salvaing de Boissieu, De l'usage des fiefs et autres droits seigneuriales, 2d ed. (Grenoble: Robert Philippes, 1668), esp. 15–18, 47–51, 54–59, 271, 278–79, for Salvaing de Boissieu's defense of Delphine allod holding. Louis Chantereau-Lefebvre, Traité des fiefs et de leur origine, 2 vols. (Paris: Louis Billaine, 1662).

[71]On Chantereau see Dictionnaire de biographie française, 13 vols. (Paris: Letouzet et Ané, 1933–), 8, col. 397. And see Nicolas Brussel, Nouvel Examen de l'usage général des fiefs, 2 vols. (Paris: C. Prud'homme, 1727), 1:1–2, 57–70, on Chantereau's and Salvaing's treatises on fiefs as the best available.

[72]Chantereau-Lefebvre, Traité des fiefs, 1:21–42, 95–99.

erty both. Like Caseneuve, Chantereau held that ancient French kings had been absolute monarchs ruling over free and equal "subjects" (su-jets or *leudes*) who owed "fidelity" to their kings and no one else. This freedom of "subjects" derived from the freedom of their properties: unencumbered "allods" (*leudes* or *alleuds*), not dependent tenures held of feudal lords. By ratifying the "usurpations" of France's great magnates, however, Chantereau's Capet let an interloping "aristocracy" or "oligarchy" dominate the crown, pay it only conditional obedience, and force it to govern by a "council" or "assembly" of "estates" composed of "the peers and principal crown vassals." The consequence was "disorder and confusion" in government, while at the lower levels of property holding, only a few "free allods" (*franc-alleus*) escaped the entangling web of feudal tenurial obligations.[73] Yet, although Chantereau's Capet damaged the rights of monarchy and property in 987, he also laid the foundations for repairing those injuries. For though he ratified feudalism out of weakness, he ensured, by that same act, that feudalism's juridical existence depended on royal will. To drive that point home, Chantereau mobilized his considerable knowledge of Carolingian capitularies and medieval charters to argue the provocative thesis that the "fief"—word and thing both—did not exist in France before 987 when an act of royal authority constituted it.[74]

By arguing that feudal tenure depended on royal will, Chantereau was not seeking to suggest that the crown might lay claim to all property—feudal property—in the realm. He claimed to write about fiefs as they once were, that is, as tenures conferring public authority on their holders, and not about fiefs as he encountered them in his own time. Other feudists of the late seventeenth and eighteenth centuries made the same distinction between the feudal politics of the past and the feudal property of the present, in order to ignore political or constitutional questions and focus exclusively on living and litigating with feudal land law in their own time.[75]

Such disclaimers, however, did not allay fears that a feudal monarch

---

[73]Ibid., 1:12–13, 42–49, 55–73, and esp. 65, on the damage Capet did to "sovereignty." Cf. pp. 10–21, on the military threat to kings posed by great lords commanding hosts of their feudal vassals.

[74]Ibid., 1:21–42, 95–99. Chantereau's treatise is well supplied with "proofs," among them an edition of the Cartulary of Champagne. His text, like Caseneuve's, relies heavily on Carolingian capitularies.

[75]Ibid., 1:13: "The reader will be advised that I consider fiefs as they were when instituted [*dans leur institution*] and not as they are in present usage." For similar disclaimers cf. Salvaing de Boissieu, *De l'usage des fiefs*, 1; Claude Poquet de Livonière, *Traité des fiefs* (Paris: Jean-Baptiste Coignard; Angers: Pierre Foureau, 1729), 1; and in general William Farr Church, "The Decline of the French Jurists as Political Theorists, 1660–1789," *French Historical Studies*, 5 (1967–68), 1–40, esp. 25–26.

might indeed seek to impropriate the wealth of his subjects. Thus anti-feudalism took yet a third form in early-modern France: the fear of a rapacious and willful "seigneurial monarchy" or royal "despotism."[76] Jean Bodin introduced the term "seigneurial monarchy" into early-modern French political discourse in 1576, in his *Six livres de la République*. There he defined "seigneurial monarchy" as that kind of monarchy in which the monarch literally owns all persons and property subject to him. Bodin derived his model of "seigneurial monarchy" from Aristotle's *despoteia*, a regime in which a single person, like the master (*despotes*) of a household, owned all persons and properties subject to his rule.[77] To Aristotle and the Greeks, *despoteia* was a regime best suited to orientals whom the Hellenes, at war with Persia in the fourth century B.C., vilified as men by nature slaves and therefore unfit for free political life in a Greek polis. But Bodin associated *despoteia*—or "seigneurial monarchy"—not only with oriental despotism but also with the seigneurial and feudal institutions of a more recent European past.[78] To describe "seigneurial monarchy" he used the language of feudal law, which distinguished between eminent domain and usufruct (*dominium directum* and *dominium utile*), in order to suggest that by virtue of his eminent domain a European feudal monarch might absorb all property and liberty and become a "seigneurial monarch."[79] That alarming possibility, Bodin hastened to add, had long since receded, but its ominous lessons remained pertinent.[80] The French king's right to tax his subjects on his own authority and without their consent could easily be made to look like "seigneurial monarchy." That right was well established when Bodin wrote (French kings had collected the *taille*, a direct tax, on their

[76]On the history of the idea of "despotism" or "oriental despotism" see Richard Koebner, "Despot and Despotism: Vicissitudes of a Political Term," *Journal of the Warburg and Courtauld Institutes*, 14 (1951): 275–302; Richet, "Autour des origines idéologiques lointaines de la Révolution française"; Melvin Richter, "The History of the Concept of Despotism," in *Dictionary of the History of Ideas*, 4 vols. (New York: Charles Scribner's Sons, 1973), 2:1–18; Franco Venturi, "Oriental Despotism," *Journal of the History of Ideas*, 24 (1963): 133–42.

[77]Jean Bodin, *Les Six Livres de la République*, 3d ed. (Paris: 1586, repr. in facs. Aalen: Scientia, 1961), 272 (Book II, chap. 2). Especially good on Bodin's debt to Aristotle: Koebner, "Despot and Despotism," 276–77, 284–87; Richter, "History of Despotism," 2, 4.

[78]So had Aristotle's fourteenth-century translator Nicolas Oresme who observed in a gloss that "Princey despotique est princey sur serfs." Bodin owed his own term "seigneurial monarchy" to Louis Le Roy's 1568 translation of Aristotle's *Politics;* see Koebner, "Despot and Despotism," 281, 284. But neither Koebner nor other writers on the idea of despotism appreciate the feudal dimension that Bodin gave it.

[79]Bodin, *Les Six Livres*, 275 (Book II, chap. 2).

[80]Ibid., pp. 275–76, on the essentially oriental and imperfectly assimilated character of *dominium directum* which (Bodin insisted) the invading Huns or Hungarians—"nation Tartaresque"—had brought to Europe and which (he added) had since atrophied.

own authority since 1439) but Bodin was convinced that it threatened the subject's "natural" right to his property. In 1576 he insisted, in the *Six livres de la République* and in speeches at the Estates General of Blois, on the principle of consent to taxation.[81] Though he failed to establish that principle, he defined one of the basic questions that French jurists had to resolve and gave them the language with which to undertake that task. Even if, unlike Bodin, they admitted that kings could tax at will, few allowed that their kings might be "seigneurial monarchs" or "lords and masters" of their realms.[82] Already in the 1560s, Chancellor Michel de L'Hospital had insisted that the French king possessed his subjects' property only "by right of sovereign command, not by right of property": *imperio, non dominio et proprietate*.[83] Later jurists and controversialists concurred, adopting Bodin's language to deny that French kings were "seigneurial monarchs" even when they taxed their subjects at will. As Charles Loyseau explained, the king was not a "seigneurial monarch," for any sovereign could rightly claim the property of his subjects for "the very utility and necessity of the people."[84] Thus the royal right to tax became an attribute of sovereignty and a consequence of necessity, and that theory became the standard theory of seventeenth-century absolutism. Richelieu embraced it, royal intendants and publicists in his service did so too, and even Louis XIV adopted it in his *Mémoires* for the education of the Dauphin.[85] But that theory did not disarm critics of high royal taxation in the seventeenth century. During the civil wars of

[81]For sixteenth-century treatises and political debates on royal finances, and for Bodin's contributions to them, see Martin Wolfe, *The Fiscal System of Renaissance France* (New Haven, Conn.: Yale University Press, 1972), 162–68, 355–65; Wolfe, "Jean Bodin on Taxes: The Sovereignty-Taxes Paradox," *Political Science Quarterly*, 83 (1968): 268–84; and Church, *Constitutional Thought*, 165–77, 234–35, 287–90.

[82]Those who did seem to have been exceptional, in both the sixteenth and the seventeenth centuries. Church adduced only one example of a sixteenth-century writer founding the king's right to tax in his status as "lord and master of persons and properties": Jean de La Madeleine's 1575 *Discours de l'estat et office d'vn bon roy, prince ou monarque* (*Constitutional Thought*, 174, n. 130). During the Fronde, the French civil wars of 1648–1653, only two government pamphleteers dared to claim that French kings were "seigneurial monarchs" (Paul Rice Doolin, *The Fronde* [Cambridge: Harvard University Press; London: Humphrey Milford/Oxford University Press, 1935], 98–100).

[83]Church, *Constitutional Thought*, 166 n. 107: Michel de L'Hospital, *Oeuvres complètes*, ed. P. J. S. Duféy (5 vols., Paris: 1824–26), 1:392.

[84]Charles Loyseau, *Traité des seigneuries*, 3d ed. (n.p: Balthazard l'Abbe, 1613), 41–43 (chap. 3).

[85]William Farr Church, *Richelieu and Reason of State* (Princeton, N.J.: Princeton University Press, 1972), 303–4 (on Richelieu); see Doolin, *The Fronde*, 84–91, and Richard Bonney, *Political Change in France under Richelieu and Mazarin 1664–1661* (Oxford: Oxford University Press, 1978), 112–17 (on intendant and jurist Cardin Le Bret's 1632 *De la souveraineté du roi*); Jean-Louis Thireau, *Les Idées politiques de Louis XIV* (Paris: Presses Universitaires de France, 1973), 72–75, 87–88 (on Louis's *Mémoires*).

the Fronde (1648–1653), pamphleteers repeatedly accused the prime minister Cardinal Mazarin of trying to turn France into a "seigneurial monarchy."[86] Pamphleteering abated after the Fronde, but anxieties about "seigneurial" or "despotic" monarchy survived into the personal reign of Louis XIV. Efforts to reduce allod holders to dues-paying vassals of the royal domain continued, reaching a legislative climax in an edict of 1692 claiming universal eminent domain for the king.[87] These were measures of a royal government which, particularly toward the end of Louis XIV's reign, was seeking to meet the rising costs of war by increasing fiscal pressure on the realm. And if the 1690s saw no new Fronde, that decade did see renewed anxiety about the dictatorial or despotic ambitions of the monarch.[88] Thus in his *Droit publique de France*, probably completed in the 1690s for the education of Louis XIV's grandson the duc de Bourgogne, the abbé Claude Fleury defined royal "tyranny" as the realization of feudal monarchy's "seigneurial" propensities. Using Loyseau's language, Fleury described feudalism as a confusion of "public" and "private lordship": *seigneurie publique* and *seigneurie privée*, or sovereignty and property. That confusion could lead states not only to an aristocratic "anarchy" recalling the disorders of feudal France, but also to a royal "tyranny" recalling the despotisms of the Orient:

> The confusion of public and private lordship happens in two manners: (1)
> if each individual has both types of lordship, as was formerly the case in
> France, then it is anarchy; (2) if the prince alone has one and the other type
> of lordship, as is the case among the Moslems, Turks, and Moguls, then it is

[86]Doolin, *The Fronde*, 98–100; cf. Bonney, *Political Change in France*, 214–37, on "tax rebellion" in the age of the Cardinal Ministers: participants in these rebellions against royal fiscal pressure insisted on the principle of consent to taxation, thus recalling Bodin and an old tradition.

[87]Andt, "Sur la théorie de la directe universelle"; but cf. Loirette, "The Defense of the Allodium," 184–85: the crown was still prepared to relax its theoretical claims in exchange for immediate fiscal assistance. Turning from public acts performed on Louis XIV's behalf to unpublished texts written for him, one may read in his *Mémoires* for the Dauphin's education that French kings are "absolute lords" enjoying the "full and free disposition of all properties" in their realm (quoted in Thireau, *Les Idées politiques de Louis XIV*, 88). See also Herbert H. Rowen, *The King's State: Proprietary Dynasticism in Early Modern France* (New Brunswick, N.J.: Rutgers University Press, 1980), 75–81. Though sensitive to the seigneurial-monarchical implications of Louis XIV's language in the *Mémoires*, Rowen agrees with Thireau that Louis did not have despotic ambitions and successfully distinguished between owning his subjects' property and owning by dynastic inheritance the right to rule (Rowen's "proprietary dynasticism"). But cf. Paul W. Fox, "Louis XIV and the Theories of Absolutism and Divine Right," *Canadian Journal of Economics and Political Science*, 26 (1960): 134, 135, 137, 138, 140. Louis's *Mémoires*, it bears repeating, was not a public statement.

[88]François Dumont, "French Kingship and Absolute Monarchy in the Seventeenth Century," in *Louis XIV and Absolutism*, ed. Ragnhild Hatton (London: Macmillan, 1976), 77; Jean Meuvret, "Fiscalism and Public Opinion under Louis XIV," in ibid., 214.

tyranny. Among the latter, the prince is proprietor of all wealth, all his subjects are his slaves. Liberty exists where the individual enjoys an entire disposition over private rights [*Droit privé*] and where the sovereign and his officers enjoy the whole exercise of public rights [*Droit public*], whether the sovereign be the entire people as a body, or a certain assembly, or a single man.[89]

As his royalist antifeudalism and his position as subpreceptor to Louis XIV's grandson suggest, the abbé Fleury was a man at home in French monarchical political culture.[90] Yet, in describing "tyranny" for the duc de Bourgogne, he allowed himself to reflect on what earlier generations had called "seigneurial monarchy" and what his own generation— thanks to such men as Fénelon, or Jean de La Bruyère, or the anonymous author of the *Soupirs de la France esclave*—was finally learning to call "despotism."[91]

This account of the varieties of antifeudalism is only a brief survey of arguments about French history, law, and taxation which merit fuller study. My aim has been to demonstrate that Boulainvilliers set himself a difficult task indeed when he sought to rehabilitate French feudalism, which belonged to a past almost universally despised, yet traversed by the dangerous ideological crossfire of his own age.

Complicating his task still further was the fact that he was not the first to undertake it. Jean Le Laboureur had done so already on behalf of the titled nobility, the dukes and peers. And because he served aims that Boulainvilliers deplored—Le Laboureur's purpose was to assert ducal preeminence over all other nobles—he nearly led Boulainvilliers to abandon the task of rehabilitating feudalism and lapse into an antiducal antifeudalism of his own.

The Dukes and Peers and France's Feudal Past

In March 1664, France's dukes and peers formally commissioned Jean Le Laboureur to engage in historical research and writing on their behalf. Eventually he produced the "Histoire" or "Traité de la pairie de

---

[89]Abbé [Claude] Fleury, *Droit public de France*, ed. J.-B. Daragon, 2 vols. (Paris: veuve Pierres, Saillant, Veuve Duchesne, Cellot, La Combe, 1769), 1, second pagination: 5–9 (8–9 for quotation). On this work's possible uses in the duc de Bourgogne's education see A. de Boislisle, "Les Études du duc de Bourgogne," *Annuaire-Bulletin de la Société de l'Histoire de France*, 11 (1874): 59; and François Gaquère, *La Vie et les oeuvres de Claude Fleury (1640–1723)* (Paris: J. de Gigord, 1925), 94–97, 177–204, 255–73.

[90]As noted also by Church, "The Decline of the French Jurists," 12–13.

[91]See Koebner, "Despot and Despotism," 296–302, and works cited there: it was in the last twenty-five years of Louis XIV's reign that the substantive "despotism" (*le despotique* or *le despotisme*) finally entered the French language.

France" which circulated in manuscript from the 1660s until the 1740s when it finally got into print.[92] Boulainvilliers' notes on that treatise and his efforts to assimilate its arguments will be considered shortly. To begin, it is useful to examine the circumstances that led the dukes and peers to commission Le Laboureur's treatise in the first place; namely, a quarrel about ceremonial rank and precedence in the Grand'Chambre of the Parlement of Paris, where the dukes and peers and the Parlement's *présidents à mortier* (the titled elite of the sword nobility and the cream of the robe) fought a long battle for social preeminence that lasted well into the eighteenth century.

It is tempting, particularly if one seeks to appreciate the vigorous social mobility and fusion of elites during the Old Regime, to dismiss spats about ancestry, rank, and precedence as the atavistic pastimes of "diseased egos." Such conflicts seem to fly in the face of social evolution and to be little more than symptoms of maladaptation to it.[93] Hence, it has been argued, the dukes and peers resisted the rise of the robe nobility with a blindness and tenacity to be expected of men bedazzled by their own ancient extraction and their putative feudal past.[94]

But this long conflict is not so easily dismissed. Parlementaires were no less concerned than dukes and peers to exalt their own rank and ancestry.[95] Besides, the dukes and peers were themselves a modern social elite, emerging in the seventeenth century and basking in the sun of royal and ministerial favor. Rich and influential nobles of old extraction as a rule, dukes and peers owed their titles to royal letters patent "erecting" their chief estates into titled and entailed duchy-peerages held directly of the crown. Indeed, most seventeenth-century peers owed their titles to the Cardinal Ministers Richelieu and Mazarin, who had expanded the peerage to cultivate the "fidelity" of the great nobility—a carefully managed "inflation of honors" to which the notoriously rank-conscious Saint-Simon owed his own ducal title.[96] To be sure Saint-Simon exalted his order's putative feudal past when, he supposed, the

[92]Here the 1745 edition will be cited: [Jean Le Laboureur], *Histoire de la pairie de France et du Parlement de Paris*, 2 vols. bound together (London: Samuel Harding, 1745). For copies of Le Laboureur's commission see B.N., MS. Clairambault 719, pp. 627–28, and MS. Clairambault 721, pp. 407–8.
[93]Goubert, *The Ancien Régime*, 162.
[94]André Grellet-Dumazeau, *L'Affaire du bonnet et les Mémoires de Saint-Simon* (Paris: Plon, 1913). Squabbles about ceremonial precedence in the Parlement's Grand'Chambre continued into the reign of Louis XVI (see the memoranda dating to that reign: A.N., K.622[9³⁴] and [9⁴¹]).
[95]Even Grellet-Dumazeau acknowledged the genealogical *amour-propre* of great robe families such as the Mesmes (*L'Affaire du bonnet*, 243–46).
[96]Labatut, *Les Ducs et pairs*, 57–67, 80–88.

French peerage had constituted a genuine political elite.[97] But a seventeenth-century duchy-peerage was an honor or "dignity," not a political office or charge, and the seventeenth-century duke and peer bore little resemblance to the feudal magnate of the past who commanded a territorial army of vassals. In this light, ducal-parlementaire conflict in the seventeenth century appears less as a contest between the embattled remnant of a feudal class and the confident members of a new governing elite, and more as a struggle between two seventeenth-century elites, a struggle for honor and preeminence in a society that still imagined and organized itself as a society of orders.[98]

Of course, such disputes may still seem to be little more than trivial squabbles about honor and rank, for they, it may be argued, did not entail the exercise of real authority.[99] In early-modern France, however, ceremony and disputes about it had wider significance. Because ceremony made visible not only the social order but also the constitutional order, quarrels about ceremony could easily become disputes about the character and history of the French constitution, as a recent study on *lits de justice* and "royal sessions" in the Parlement of Paris makes emphatically clear.[100]

It was in fact a dispute about precedence at such assemblies—august meetings of the Parlement attended by the king, the princes of the blood royal, and the dukes and peers—that occasioned the ducal rehabilitation of feudalism in the 1660s. At issue was the order of opining: should the Parlement's first president, having taken the opinions of royal princes, turn to the dukes and peers for theirs, or should he grant the honor of opining just after the princes to the Parlement's leading magistrates, the *présidents à mortier*?[101] This quarrel first broke out on the occasion of a *lit* held in February 1662 and resumed in December 1663 when Louis XIV came to Parlement for a "royal session." On that occasion, the king requested that both sides—the dukes and peers, and the *présidents à*

[97]Carcassonne, *Montesquieu et le problème de la constitution*, 14–18. Brancourt (*Le Duc de Saint-Simon*) rightly insists that Saint-Simon adhered to the principles of French royal absolutism, but alludes only in passing (58, 64) to Saint-Simon's "Mémoire sur la renonciation" (1712), with its elaborate account of a medieval feudal polity in which the dukes and peers constituted a political elite (see chapter 4).

[98]Labatut, *Les Ducs et pairs*, 33–37, 82–87, 407–14.

[99]Ibid., 83–84; Henri Brocher, *A la cour de Louis XIV: Le rang et l'etiquette sous l'Ancien Régime* (Paris: Félix Alcan, 1934), 55–77.

[100]Sarah Hanley, *The* Lit de Justice *of the Kings of France: Constitutional Ideology in Legend, Ritual, and Discourse* (Princeton, N.J.: Princeton University Press, 1983), a study to which I am much indebted.

[101]On the precedence of the royal princes and the reasons for its establishment in the sixteenth century, see Richard A. Jackson, "Peers of France and Princes of the Blood," *French Historical Studies*, 7 (1971–72): 27–46.

mortier—sign and submit petitions to his council. He thereby engaged the parties in litigation that lasted till April 1664 and that took the form of repeated submission to the royal council of petitions and counterpetitions in which peers and *présidents* argued their own claims and rebutted their opponents'. These elaborate legal briefs appear to have circulated in manuscript while litigation lasted. And once it ended—with an *arrêt de conseil* in the dukes and peers' favor issued on April 26 in anticipation of a *lit de justice* to be held three days later—the triumphant ducal party had all the petitions collected and printed.[102] By their nature, however, these texts were appeals to the king's judgment, not the public's, and even in print they probably reached only a narrow audience.[103] Despite its narrow audience and its small stakes, however, the ducal-parlementary quarrel of the 1660s was hardly trivial. The dispute gave Louis XIV an occasion to subordinate "his" Parlement: on the advice of his minister, Jean-Baptiste Colbert, he decided against the Parlement deliberately to humiliate that body, whose *frondeur* past both men remembered and feared.[104] More important, the dispute's protagonists marshaled big arguments from French history to support their small claims to ceremonial courtesy: the dukes and peers claimed nothing less than to have inherited the mantle of the feudal peers of the past, whereas the *présidents* answered that claim with a familiar royalist antifeudalism. Thus a contest for social preeminence became a debate about feudalism and its place in the evolution of the constitutional order. That debate

---

[102]*Recueil des écrits qui ont esté faits sur le différend d'entre messieurs les pairs de France, & messieurs les présidens au mortier du Parlement de Paris, pour la manière d'opiner aux lits de justice. Avec l'arrest donné par le roy en son conseil en faveur de messieurs les pairs* (Paris: 1664). The B.N. has several copies of this 4° edition: 4° Fm 34785; Inv. F 12370; Réserve des imprimés, Recueil Thoisy, vol. 364 at fol. 105; B.N., MSS. f.f. 4319 and n.a.f. 2083 (bound *recueils factices* of printed and MS texts occasioned by Old Regime aristocratic controversy). A second edition appeared during the regency of the duc d'Orléans and will be cited here: *Recueil des écrits qui ont esté faits sur le différend entre les pairs de France & les présidens à mortier du Parlement de Paris, pour la manière d'opiner aux lits de justice, avec l'arrêt donné par le roy en son conseil en faveur des pairs en 1664* (Paris: Antoine-Urbain Coustelier, 1716) (see pp. 1 and 67 on MS circulation of petitions in Paris in 1664, and pp. 1–4 for a general account of the conflict). For copies of this edition see A.N., K.619(43); K.622(10); U.907; and B.N., f° Fm 5247; f° Fm 17325(3); Réserve des imprimés, Recueil Thoisy, vol. 67 at fol. 47. For copies bound into Old Regime *recueils factices* see B.N., MSS. f.f. 7502; n.a.f. 7417; Clairambault 720; and Bibliothèque de l'Assemblée Nationale (Paris), MS. 336. For still later editions see n. 105.

[103]The dukes and peers claimed that unlike manuscript copies their printed edition would not be marred by copiests' errors (*Recueil des écrits* [ed. 1716], 1), thus implying that the printed edition would reach the same narrow audience as manuscripts. For yet clearer indications of the narrow audience for aristocratic controversy in the regency see chapter 5.

[104]Albert N. Hamscher, *The Parlement of Paris after the Fronde, 1653–1673* (Pittsburgh: University of Pittsburgh Press, 1976), 57.

would not be forgotten. Controversialists and historians reprinted and cited the petitions of 1664 until the end of the Old Regime.[105] Le Laboureur wrote to sustain the ducal position. And Boulainvilliers, in his own encounters with ducal claims, had to to contend with arguments first developed in the 1660s. Those arguments merit attention here.[106]

When the dukes and peers appealed to their putative feudal past in 1662–64, they were obeying the implications of early-modern French historical scholarship. Beginning with Jean Du Tillet, who worked in the middle of the sixteenth century, historical scholars and writers recognized in peerage an institution ultimately feudal in origin: peers, it was agreed, were originally fellow vassals of a common lord, and fellow members of his court where they kept their feudal obligation to advise him and help him dispense justice.[107] It is true that Frenchmen also thought that Charlemagne created the peerage when he created the "paladins" of medieval romances. But Du Tillet dispatched that myth by observing that when Charlemagne ruled, fiefs were not yet hereditary.[108] It is also true that Frenchmen identified the peerage with the consecration of kings, a rite traditionally performed at Rheims cathedral by six clerical and six lay peers.[109] But that ceremonial function of the

[105]For the second edition of 1716, see n. 102. A third edition in 1720 appears to be the 1716 edition reissued with other ducal prints of the regency, with a new title page: *Mémoires concernant les pairs de France avec les preuves* (Paris: Antoine-Urbain Coustelier, 1720) (B.N., Réserve des imprimés, F 323). For a fourth edition see *Recueil des ecrits qui ont été faits sur le différend d'entre messieurs les pairs de France, & messieurs les présidens au mortier du Parlement de Paris, pour la maniere d'opiner aux lits de justice. Avec l'arrêt donné par le roi en son conseil en faveur de messieurs les pairs* (Paris: 1771) (B.N., 4° Fm 23658[23]). For the abbé Mably's use of the 1664 petitions see Gabriel Bonnot de Mably, *Oeuvres complètes*, 12 vols. (London: 1789), 3:342–64 (*Observations sur l'histoire de France*).

[106]For detailed descriptions of the course of litigation, see *Recueil des écrits* (1716 ed.), 1–4; Harold A. Ellis, "Boulainvilliers Ideologue, and Publicist: Ideologies of Aristocratic Reaction and the Uses of History in Early-Eighteenth-Century France" (Ph.D. Diss., Washington University, St. Louis, 1981), 237–55; Hamscher, *The Parlement of Paris*, 54–57; Labatut, *Les Ducs et pairs*, 407–14. See also Hanley, *The Lit de Justice of the Kings of France*, 325 and n. 41.

[107]Jean Du Tillet and Jean Du Tillet, *Recueil des roys de France, leur couronne et maison. Ensemble, le rang des grands de France, par Iean du Tillet, sieur de La Bussière, protonotaire & secrétaire du roy, greffier en son Parlement. Plus une chronique abbrégée . . . par M. I. du Tillet, evesque de Meaux, frères* (Paris: Barthélemy Macy, 1607), first pagination, 362–78, esp. 362–63 (the 1563 *Recueil des roys* by Jean Du Tillet, *greffier*). Cf. the similar account by the seventeenth-century *érudit* and lexicographer Charles Du Fresne, sieur Du Cange, *Glossarium mediae et infimae latinitatis*, ed. G. A. L. Henschel, L. Favre, 10 vols. in 5 (Graz: Akademische Druck- und Verlagsanstalt, 1954), s.v. "par." And see Labatut, *Les Ducs et pairs*, 45.

[108]Du Tillet, *Recueil des roys*, first pagination, 363.

[109]See Labatut, *Les Ducs et pairs*, 48–52, on the medieval peerage's evolution and the twelve ceremonial peers. The six clerical peers were the archbishop-duke of Rheims, the bishop-duke of Laon, the bishop-duke of Langres, the bishop-count of Beauvais, the bishop-count of Noyons, and the bishop-count of Châlons. The six lay peers were the

peerage, however important, did not shake the conviction of early-modern French historians that peerage was ultimately a feudal institution. Some, like Pasquier, tried to assimilate the feudal and ceremonial peerages, by tracing them to a common origin in Hugh Capet's putative ratification of feudal "usurpations" in A.D. 987.[110] Others appreciated the difficulties inherent in that strategy, thanks largely to the labors of Jean Du Tillet who collected as much record evidence as he could on royal consecrations in the Middle Ages and found that the twelve ceremonial peers acquired their feudal titles and their monopoly on officiating at royal consecrations much later in their history.[111] For Du Tillet and for later writers and scholars, however, the feudal provenance of the peerage was never in doubt. Accordingly, narrative historians of the sixteenth and seventeenth centuries usually dismissed the Charlemagne myth (an easy and obligatory display of disabused erudition) and then proceeded to sketch out the histories of both ceremonial and feudal peerage.[112]

In 1662–64, the dukes and peers appropriated these historical ideas to defend their own claims to precedence at *lits de justice*. Abundant marginal references attest their debt to Du Tillet, a selective debt, admittedly, for unlike Du Tillet the dukes and peers identified feudal with ceremonial peerage to inscribe them both within a single glorious past.[113] But the dukes and peers had feudal peerage uppermost in mind when they demanded precedence at *lits de justice*, for on those occasions they claimed to constitute a royal *cour des pairs*, a feudal court of peers not to be confused with the Parlement of Paris in which *lits* happened to take place. In effect, the dukes and peers looked at a single institution— the Parlement of Paris in its various sessions—and claimed to see two. In ordinary sessions, the Parlement was a royal law court staffed by professional magistrates and (the dukes and peers conceded) presided over by *présidents à mortier* representing the king's justice. But at *lits de justice* or royal sessions, the Parlement became a *cour des pairs* or *Cour du Roy* or *Cour de France* in which dukes and peers took precedence over *présidents*

---

dukes of Normandy, Burgundy, and Guyenne and the counts of Flanders, Toulouse, and Champagne. By the sixteenth century the lay peerages had either escheated back to the crown or (in the case of Flanders) had been lost to the Empire, so that other princes or dukes now "represented" the "old" lay peers at royal consecration ceremonies.

[110]Pasquier, *Les Oeuvres*, 1:95–106 (*Recherches de la France*, Book II, chaps. 9 and 10).

[111]Du Tillet, *Recueil des roys*, first pagination, 262–63, 364.

[112]For example, Bernard de Girard Du Haillan, *De l'Estat et succez des affaires de France*, 2d ed. (Paris: 1571), fols. 108–112v; Du Haillan, *L'Histoire de France* (Paris: 1576), 162–65, 229–32, 700; Vignier, *Sommaire*, 175–77, 260; Dupléix, *Histoire générale*, 1:404–8; 2:40, 186; Mézeray, *Histoire* (1643–51 ed.), 1:173, 369, 434–35; and his *Histoire* (1685 ed.), 2:2–3, 7–10, 83–84.

[113]*Recueil des écrits* (1716 ed.), 5, 26, 38, 72, 94–96, 107.

à mortier—now mere *assesseurs* of the dukes and peers—and deliberated on "important" or "great affairs of state."[114]

Such language suggests that the dukes and peers were seeking to share in the exercise of sovereign authority—an authority that monarchical political tradition assigned to the king alone. With predictable zeal, the Parlement's *présidents* leapt to the defense of royal authority, deploying a familiar royalist antifeudalism to discredit the feudal *cour des pairs* as an usurpation at the king's expense, a corruption of his "parlement" by feudal nobles who "established in the monarchy an aristocracy independent of royalty . . . and lifted themselves even above the king." Happily, the *présidents* added, fourteenth-century kings rendered their court sedentary at Paris, staffed it with professionals of their own choosing, and restored its true character as the *Cour du Roy* or *Cour de France* where, the *présidents* added, they rightfully presided in the king's name.[115]

The antimonarchical implications of the dukes and peers' appeal to the feudal past are undeniable, but in 1662–64 they entertained no political ambitions. They were claiming precedence, not power. They appreciated (and the *présidents* reminded them of this juridical fact) that they were dignitaries obliged to the crown for their status, not independent potentates like the great feudatories of old. But the dukes and peers sought to insist that "old" or feudal peers had also been royally created dignitaries and that any honors which the "old" peers had enjoyed ought still to be enjoyed by the "new" peers on whom their dignity had devolved. Thus the feudal past to which the dukes and peers appealed in 1662–64 was a past at least partly cleansed of its antimonarchical implications, a past that might safely be used to defend ducal preeminence in the reign of Louis XIV.[116]

It was not possible, however, to ignore the troublesome age of "feudal anarchy" or "aristocratic usurpation" which French historians usually identified as the seedbed of French feudalism. To their predictable charge that feudal peerages were "usurpations at the expense of royalty," the *présidents* added a second, that feudal peerages were usurpations at the expense of the entire nobility, whose ancient right of peerage, had the medieval peers not monopolized it, might now be the right of some 20,000 "peers" holding of the crown. That second charge may

[114]Ibid., pp. 5–6, 24–27.
[115]Ibid., 11–22, esp. 11–12.
[116]*Recueil des écrits* (1716 ed.), 9–10, 35–41, 43, 48, 52. Contemporary jurists commonly described the duchy-peerage as a "dignity" (Labatut, *Les Ducs et pairs*, 82–88). See chapter 5 for the genuinely political aspirations of the dukes and peers during the regency, when they reprinted the petitions of 1662–64.

have been an effort to arouse the jealousy of the untitled nobility against the dukes and peers, though there is no independent evidence of such antiducal sentiment in 1662–64.[117] In any case the dukes and peers thought the charge sufficiently grave to merit formal refutation—even after they had won their case against the *présidents*. In a set of "Réflexions" appended to the petitions which they collected and printed in 1664, the dukes and peers tried to dissipate the *présidents*'s clever mirage of an ancient peerage to which all nobles once belonged.[118] Carefully the dukes and peers distinguished a peerage of headvassals from a nobility of rearvassals who held of them. The feudal peers became "a separate order" from the "nobility" and "highly elevated" above it, while the "new" peers or dukes and peers who were the "successors of the old peers" continued to enjoy "preeminence . . . over all the rest of the nobility, the peers being its leaders, first lords, and natural judges."[119] These were grand assertions indeed, but they were only assertions. The "Réflexions" did not provide that careful account of feudalism's early history which alone might have answered the *présidents*' charges that feudalism and feudal peerage were usurpations at the expense of royalty and nobility alike.

Jean Le Laboureur attempted—with mixed success, it will be apparent—to provide that account in his "Traité" or "Histoire de la pairie de France."[120] He began by defining peerage as an "office" and the peer as an "officer of the state, constituted by the king," and empowered to judge peers and nobles, counsel their royal lord, and act as "natural judges of the succession to the crown."[121] That peer-officer enjoyed a more clearly defined political vocation than the peer-dignitary of the 1664 petitions, but he had the same impeccably royal pedigree: the feudal peers, Le Laboureur maintained, were not usurpers since they owed their status to the crown. Turning directly to the peers' feudal past, however, Le Laboureur encountered the "feudal anarchy" and "aristocratic usurpation" to which French historians commonly assigned the fief's origins, and he all but conceded what he sought to refute. "Fiefs," he observed, were originally "pure benefactions" of kings,

[117]*Recueil des écrits* (1716 ed.), 72. Labatut holds that the "tradition of union" binding peerage and untitled sword nobility together was still intact (*Les Ducs et pairs*, 371–79). But ducal pretensions strained that "tradition" and during the regency it collapsed altogether (see chapter 5).

[118]*Recueil des écrits*, 79–108, and (on the composition of the "Réflexions"), 4.

[119]Ibid., 96, 99, 107.

[120]He may have already helped to compose the ducal petitions just examined. Grellet-Dumazeau assigned them all to him (*L'Affaire du bonnet*, 27), but the dukes and peers claimed them for members of their own body (*Recueil des écrits* [1716 ed.], 2–4).

[121][Le Laboureur], *Histoire* (1745 ed.), 1:1–20, esp. 10.

whereas feudal peerage owed its existence to "a manner of usurpation."[122] He admitted that the magnates who elected Hugh Capet king in 987 acquired their prominence and power under the late Carolingians, when "hereditary fiefs" and their "subordination" one to another had arisen.[123] Le Laboureur even confessed that the feudal peers had monopolized a right originally enjoyed by all members of the ancient Frankish "nation": due to feudalism and subinfeudation, he wrote, an ancient and widely shared "personal" right had become a "real" (that is, a tenurial) right restricted to a diminished circle of the crown's tenants in chief.[124]

Despite these remarkable admissions, Le Laboureur sought to assign a legitimate pedigree to the fief. That task led him to write a history of allods, benefices, and fiefs in pre-Capetian France and to confront the rich legal and historical literature on those forms of landholding. "Whole volumes" had been devoted to the allod, he knew, and the learned Louis Chantereau-Lefebvre had written on fiefs. Although he claimed to admire Chantereau's learning, however, he dismissed Chantereau's *Traité des fiefs* as ill-digested, too quickly written, and in any case unfinished.[125] Against Chantereau and the allod's learned champions, Le Laboureur propounded a counterthesis designed to disarm their royalist and allodial antifeudalism.

That counterthesis was willful in the extreme, as Le Laboureur admitted that fiefs were benefices usurped by their holders under the later Carolingians. But now he denied that fiefs were usurped benefices. On the contrary, he insisted, fiefs derived from the "allods" of the ancient Franks. To sustain his counterargument, however, he had to identify feudal with prefeudal France and minimize the palpable differences that Chantereau and Caseneuve discovered between a medieval France where feudatories wielded their own authority over their own vassals and a Frankish France where the crown's beneficed officers wielded the crown's authority over the crown's free and propertied subjects. Performing that task required verbal sleight-of-hand, but Le Laboureur was eminently capable of it. To represent the governing officers of Frankish kings as propertied magnates, Le Laboureur simply observed that those dukes and counts (*duces* and *comites*) were also called *leudes* or (in Gaulish) *druds* or (later) "barons." And like those feudal barons, the Frankish

[122]Ibid., 1:29–30, 99.
[123]Ibid., 1:20–27 (on the seven lay peerages, including Capet's duchy of France) and 1:37–71 (on the six ecclesiastical peerages which, Le Laboureur admitted, owed their emergence to other factors besides the development of feudalism).
[124]Ibid., 1:1–2; 2:51–52.
[125]Ibid., 1:33, 60–61.

leudes were "great landholders." They were powerful men, Le Laboureur reasoned, and power could have no other source than land: "that [holding power] was impossible without great estates." To complete the ancient *leude*'s transformation into a propertied magnate comparable to a feudal baron, Le Laboureur claimed that the "charters" (that is, the capitularies) of Frankish kings alluded repeatedly to their *fideles:* according to Le Laboureur that term recurred over and over again in the formula *omnibus regni fidelibus.* Because, Le Laboureur argued, *fidelis* was another term for *leude;* because, he added, ancient chroniclers described the fidelis as a powerful supporter of the crown; and because, he reminded his readers, power presupposed property, it followed (once again) that the fidelis or duc or leude was a great proprietor—in short, the possessor of a leud or alleu or "allod."[126] Having collapsed the distinction between the feudal baron and the prefeudal leude or fidelis, Le Laboureur could now collapse the distinction between the fief and the allod. In his pages, the fief virtually became a free property like the allod, its putative ancestor.

But the fief was also a military tenure, so Le Laboureur could not stop at allodializing the medieval fief. He also had to militarize the ancient allod. He began with the *franc-alleu* or free allod, which he identified with the "Salic land" defined in the celebrated Title 62 of the Salic Law (the ancient law code of the Salian Franks) as a patrimony that might be inherited only by males. A late medieval tradition had sought to use Title 62 to argue that the French crown could not pass by inheritance to princesses or their male descendants, but Le Laboureur appreciated that Title 62 governed the hereditary transmission of property, not royal authority. He inferred from its provisions, however, that the "Salic land" or free allod was not a pure freehold but rather a tenure acquired and held by military service: "It is not so much a land which is held of no lord but which is absolutely free, like a freehold [*terre franche*]; rather it is the share of an ancient Frank and the recompense of his military service, and so it is a Salic land."[127] As each conquering Frank's portion of the conquest—like the *Sortes Wandalorum* and *Sortes Gothicae* of the Vandal and Gothic conquerors of Spain and Italy—the Frank's "Salic land" was a tenure won and kept by the sword.[128] So was his "allod," which Le

---

[126]Ibid., 1:61–64. On the *omnibus regni fidelibus* formula that Le Laboureur claimed to discover in ancient texts see chapter 3, n. 76.

[127]Ibid., 2:33. On efforts to apply the ancient Salic Law to the royal succession see Ralph Giesey, "The Juristic Basis of Dynastic Right to the French Throne," *Transactions of the American Philosophical Society*, n.s., 51, no. 5 (1961): 17–22.

[128][Le Laboureur], *Histoire* (1745 ed.), 2:99–100.

Laboureur explicitly identified with the fief of a later time: "From the fact that the terms fief and allod imply that the men who hold those lands must be faithful to the lord of whom they hold them, I conclude that there was a sort of hereditary fief, possessed by these ancient *leudes* and *fideles* of our first kings."[129]

Le Laboureur knew that his account of the ancient allod or free allod was highly unusual.[130] Yet he was convinced that he had discovered in his militarized allod the fief's true origins, thus laying to rest any doubts about the fief's antiquity and legitimacy. He probably had Chantereau's *Traité des fiefs* in mind when he wrote, "one will no longer say that fiefs are as modern as several individuals have said . . . , despite the fact that there is no difference between fiefs and ancient allods except the name."[131] Thus Le Laboureur summed up the provocative counterthesis that he developed to disarm the royalist and allodial antifeudalism of his contemporaries.

Le Laboureur's history of land tenure in Frankish and feudal France is woefully obscurantist and would not merit the attention given it here were it not part of a larger and influential effort to rehabilitate feudalism and use it to assert the dukes and peers' preeminence over the rest of the nobility. To that end, Le Laboureur turned from allodializing fiefs and militarizing allods to defending tenurial hierarchy. The hierarchy of fiefs was integral to the feudal past to which the dukes and peers had appealed in their "Réflexions" in 1664, a past in which a feudal peerage of headvassals was clearly distinguished from a nobility of rearvassals. To explain that feudal hierarchy's emergence, Le Laboureur had to redeploy the conventional argument that fiefs were benefices usurped in the ninth and tenth centuries by the great governing officers of early French kings: the dukes and counts. Now he once again distinguished institutions that he had equated elsewhere, differentiating dukes and counts from a larger body of Frankish leudes or "ancient barons and great lords of France" from which the dukes and counts had been recruited. Belonging to, yet rising above the mass of Frankish leudes, the dukes and counts now became a protopeerage from which a genuine feudal peerage eventually evolved while the rest of the ancient leudes became the feudal peerage's vassals. Unfortunately for Le Laboureur, reviving the conventional account of the origins of fiefs to explain the origins of feudal hierarchy had its disadvantages. He seems to have recognized them, for he had to admit that peerage established itself by

---

[129]Ibid., 1:62.
[130]Ibid., 2:33.
[131]Ibid., 2:109–10.

"a manner of usurpation" not only at the crown's expense but also, and above all, at the nobility's expense. He wrote:

> They [the ancient barons and great lords], although they were not dukes and counts, were not of lesser quality as far as birth was concerned. One can even say, to their advantage, that in antiquity they may have been something yet more distinguished; the dukes and peers later acquired precedence over them only by a manner of usurpation. To speak properly, the barons were the ancient *leudes* who were descended from the Salians and who for centuries had possessed their *Sortes Salicae* or their portions of the conquest of Gaul which they held solely of the king until the dukes and counts, taking advantage of our kings' weakness, made themselves into proprietary lords of the lands they governed. These dukes and counts were originally of this species of nobles [the barons], among whom there were men who possessed great expanses of land and who, far from coveting the quality of duke or count, held it an honor to call themselves lords of their lands, for so they were in effect and by virtue of a legitimate succession, like the lords of Bourbon, Beaujeu, Montmorency, Coucy, Sully, and an infinity of others.[132]

At this point one can pronounce Le Laboureur's "Traité" only a mixed success, for he failed to answer the charges that the *présidents à mortier* had leveled against the peers in 1664, charges that that body owed its existence to the usurpation, by medieval feudatories, of rights properly the crown's or even the entire nobility's. Le Laboureur did argue at length that the fief was not a usurped benefice but rather a legitimate descendant of the ancient allod, but since the dukes and peers had already grounded their claims to preeminence in the grandeur once enjoyed by the the great vassals of medieval kings, Le Laboureur had to build feudal hierarchy and the subinfeudation that produced it into his "Traité." Hence his admission that feudal hierarchy (if not the fief itself) had indeed arisen by "a manner of usurpation." That admission was inopportune, however, for it exposed Le Laboureur's "Traité" to precisely the antiducal antifeudalism which, it is tempting to suppose, the *présidents à mortier* had tried to arouse in the untitled nobility in 1664.

The mixed success with which Le Laboureur implemented his ideological program may explain why his "Traité" never got into print until the 1740s. Peers and présidents continued their quarrels about marks of ceremonial courtesy throughout the balance of Louis XIV's reign and into the regency.[133] But Le Laboureur's "Traité," a dubious history and

---

[132]Ibid., 2:99–100.

[133]See Grellet-Dumazeau, *L'Affaire du bonnet*, 27–80. Cf. Hamscher, *The Parlement of Paris*, 58–60, on [François Bertaut de Fréauville], *Les Prerogatives de la robe* (Paris: Jacques Lefebvre, 1701), a major parlementary polemic of the period.

an inadequate polemic, circulated only in manuscript to elicit only iso-
lated and private responses from its readers—among them Henri de
Boulainvilliers.

The larger interest of Le Laboureur's "Traité" and the aristocratic
controversies that led him to write it should not be forgotten, however.
The contests about ceremonial courtesy that divided the robe and sword
elites in the 1660s led them to engage in elaborate (if sometimes obscurantist) debates about the monarchy's constitution, their own places in it,
and the role of feudalism in its history. In the course of those debates,
they adumbrated political ambitions and encouraged social antagonisms
destined to become far more powerful later, during the regency, than
they were at the dawn of Louis XIV's personal reign. The problematic
character of feudalism, however, was fully apparent to the peers and the
présidents as they pursued their quarrels in the 1660s. Here, later
polemics had little to add to the arguments just examined.

Boulainvilliers and the Problem of French Feudalism

It is now possible to rejoin Boulainvilliers, whose fine sensitivity to the
implications of genealogical consciousness and erudition had led him in
1700 to embark on his own efforts to defend French feudalism against
the contempt of his contemporaries. The difficulty of his task should
now surprise no one. Nor should his interest in Le Laboureur's earlier
efforts to perform it. Boulainvilliers' response to Le Laboureur was by
no means a simple one, however. Reading the ducal antiquarian led him
to lapse into an antiducal antifeudalism before he finally managed to
apply Le Laboureur's ideas in his own nobiliaire rehabilitation of French
feudalism.

Exactly when and why Boulainvilliers read Le Laboureur's "Traité"
remains unknown, but he had not yet done so in 1700 when he wrote his
"Dissertation" on the "true and old nobility," a work that betrays no
acquaintance with Le Laboureur's and develops arguments antithetical
to it. In Boulainvilliers' "Dissertation" a leude—or "Leuth"—was not a
Frank or magnate but a "subject man" and an "allodial" land was merely
his taxable and therefore "subject" property.[134] If Boulainvilliers believed that the Franks had private property, he said little about it in

[134]*Essais*, 171, 178, 180. In taking these positions, Boulainvilliers aligned himself with
authoritative scholars such as the seventeenth-century lexicographer Du Cange or the
sixteenth-century historian Pasquier (whom Boulainvilliers claimed to admire). Cf. Du
Cange, *Glossarium*, s.v. "Leudes" (defined as "Vassali, subditi"), "Leuda" (tax), and "Leud-
abilis" (taxable); Pasquier, *Les Oeuvres*, 1:125–34, esp. 131–32 (*Recherches de la France*,
Book II, chap. 16); Boulainvilliers, "Lettre à Mademoiselle Cousinot sur l'histoire et sa
méthode (1707)," in Simon, *Un Révolte du grand siècle*, 80 (on Pasquier).

1700. He wrote only of the "benefices" and "honors" that a grateful "nation" conferred upon its elder warriors in recognition of their "wounds" and "services." Carved out of the old Roman fisc which the Franks had expropriated when they conquered Gaul, those "benefices" and "honors" were precarious tenures: their holders were "to possess them by title of benefice or recompense for life only, and as a property of the nation, not of the crown or as a fief in dependent tenure. These terms," Boulainvilliers added, "are posterior by several centuries to the usages of the earliest times."[135] Thus the society to which Boulainvilliers consigned his ancient Franks was emphatically prefeudal. It knew no fiefs, or fief-allods as Le Laboureur described them, that is, it knew no hereditary military tenures held by free, yet tenurially obliged Franks.

Boulainvilliers hardly wished to read the fief out of French history as he recounted it in the "Dissertation." On the contrary, that work exudes his sympathy for feudalism. But in 1700, he still had unclear ideas about the fief's origin and did not trace it back to the Franks and their putative Conquest. At one place Boulainvilliers described the fief as a "northern" (that is, Germanic) institution which the Lombards brought to Italy and which the Saxons may have brought to France when Charlemagne conquered them and transported them into the Frankish heartlands in 785.[136] That supposition had its advantages: it let Boulainvilliers derive the emerging feudalism of late Carolingian France from ancient Germanic institutions—not from the "feudal anarchy" and "aristocratic usurpation" in which early-modern French historians usually detected the origins of feudalism. Elsewhere in the "Dissertation," however, Boulainvilliers restated that authoritative view, describing the fief as an "usurpation" of royal domain lands and of "benefices" held of the "nation." In defense of the feudal nobility, Boulainvilliers claimed that circumstances, not aristocratic ill will, led to that "usurpation": weak royal authority, Viking invasions, and civil war all forced local populations to seek the protection of local lords.[137] But in the "Dissertation," the fief remained a usurped benefice. Thus, in the very work in which Boulainvilliers committed himself to the rehabilitation of feudalism, he gave an account of it that remained dangerously exposed to the antifeudalism of his contemporaries.

Eventually, Le Laboureur's "Histoire de la pairie de France" showed Boulainvilliers how to construct a less objectionable history of the fief's origins. In his first encounter with that ducal tract, however, he was hardly sympathetic. An antiducal animus, already visible in the "Disser-

[135]*Essais*, 172, 173.
[136]*Essais*, 102.
[137]*Essais*, 102–4, 104–10.

tation," dominates his "Extrait d'un manuscrit de M. l'abbé Le Laboureur intitulé: De l'origine de la pairie de France."[138]

Borrowing selectively from Le Laboureur to refute him, Boulainvilliers asserted the primordial equality of all the ancient "leudes" or "Leuth," terms Boulainvilliers (like Le Laboureur) now assigned to free Franks, not to "subject" Gallo-Romans: "By . . . [leudes] I understand all Franks [François] in general because the word Leuth means men, comrades of Frankish kings, each Frank distinguishing by this term his nation from the Gaulish just as one would say today, 'These are our men.'" He continued, "Let not the author [Le Laboureur] say that this term applies only to the grandees of the state for at that time no individual of the nation distinguished himself from others by birth or dignities. Everything was common, the power to judge, to assemble in *parlements* and to decide all affairs of state. No Frank was or could be excluded."[139] Having asserted the equality of the ancient Franks, Boulainvilliers went on to assert the equality of their "allods" and to trace the later inequalities of feudal hierarchy to the usurpations by magnates of the precarious benefices entrusted to them: "Allodial possessions were inheritable by males according to the provisions of the Salic Law, and benefices were simply granted for life; the two were not confused. When benefices were usurped by the powerful families who held them during the decline of the Carolingian dynasty, the subordination that had existed with regard to jurisdiction was changed into feudalism."[140] Stressing the Franks' equality, Boulainvilliers rejected Le Laboureur's claims that their tenures or their positions in a tenurial hierarchy of allods or fiefs might assign them different ranks in a hierarchy of nobility.[141] Borrowing once again from Le Laboureur to refute him, Boulainvilliers derived equality of nobility from the equality of Frankish birth:

[Le Laboureur] concludes that . . . nobility comes from possession of fiefs and that it is divided into three different classes [peers, knights, squires]. . . . This . . . is entirely false. Nobility's origin is prior to the possession of fiefs. Nobility really comes from the Frankish [françoise] nation as the nation that conquered Gaul: no distinction of class in the early nobility—all designated by the word Leuth. It is true that in the second age, there did exist distinctions within the nobility because of feudalism. But that was

[138]Two MSS survive: B.N., MSS. f.f. 7504, and 7508, fols. 1–55v; see Bibliographical Appendix, Part 2. Cf. *Essais*, 247–48: a complaint that sixteenth-century kings "erected duchy-peerages for the richest men and for courtiers with the most credit."
[139]B.N., MS. f.f. 7504, pp. 16–17.
[140]Ibid., pp. 21–22.
[141]After describing allod holding or fief holding among the ancient Franks, Le Laboureur wrote: "One will understand more clearly by this succinct account of the earliest usages of the kingdom that nobility comes from fiefs" (*Histoire* [1745 ed.], 1:68).

clearly a corruption of the [nobility's] original state. The author here abused his own erudition and the credulity with which others accept his teaching; it is not true that nobility comes from possession; rather possessions were usurped by certain families and were at first assigned and ceded to the nobility along with jurisdiction as precarious benefices. As for the first form of government of the kingdom, it ceased.[142]

Face to face with Le Laboureur's ducal rehabilitation of the feudal past, Boulainvilliers intensified his own nobiliaire egalitarianism. He even lapsed into a powerful antiducal and nobiliaire antifeudalism that might surprise readers of his 1700 "Dissertation."

Yet Boulainvilliers' debt to Le Laboureur is obvious. For Le Laboureur provoked Boulainvilliers to insist, far more strenuously than he had in the "Dissertation," on the equality of all the ancient Franks.[143] Le Laboureur himself gave Boulainvilliers the means to do so. In the "Dissertation," it will be recalled, Boulainvilliers' "leudes" were Gallo-Romans and his "allods" were their servile and taxable lands. In the notes on Le Laboureur, however, Boulainvilliers' "leudes"—like Le Laboureur's—had become Franks. And Boulainvilliers' "allods"—again like Le Laboureur's—had become free properties that Franks enjoyed. In response to Le Laboureur, Boulainvilliers revised his ideas on landholding and personal status in Frankish antiquity.

In fact Boulainvilliers sought to incorporate his new ideas into his "Dissertation" when, again for reasons that remain unknown, he returned to that text to revise it.[144] There, in one of his two substantive (rather than stylistic) changes, Boulainvilliers transformed his Franks into "Leuth" who held "free" and "allodial" patrimonies. His Gauls, meanwhile, lost their "allodial" properties and acquired "servile *mas* and *mansions*" instead. All that remained of the original account of land tenure and personal status in Frankish antiquity was the admission—an important one, to be sure—that the Franks also enjoyed "benefices" carved out of the old Roman fisc expropriated at the Conquest.[145]

---

[142]B.N., MS. f.f. 7504, pp. 20–21.

[143]Cf. *Essais*, 20–21, 25–27, and n. 44 of this chapter, on Boulainvilliers' earlier effort to discover a nobility of "seniores" of "birth and valor" *among* the ancient Franks.

[144]"Dissertation sur la noblesse françoise servant de préface aux mémoires de la maison de Croï et Boulainviller," in Devyver, *Le Sang épuré*, 501–48 (Appendix). Also see Bibliographical Appendix, Part 2.

[145]Devyver, 513–14:
Though the right of conquest had given the Franks [*François*] the power to dispose of lands and properties and all their new subjects, one must not suppose that all the indigenous inhabitants of Gaul were dispossessed of their patrimonies at that time. [. . .] They seized only the domains of the Romans—be they the domains of the fisc or of individuals—and left to the indigenous population practically all their hereditary

It might now appear that reading Le Laboureur led Boulainvilliers to abandon the project to which he had committed himself when he first composed his "Dissertation," the rehabilitation of French feudalism. Reading Le Laboureur certainly led Boulainvilliers to lapse into an antiducal antifeudalism. The rehabilitation of feudalism remained on his agenda, however, even in the revised "Dissertation," where he retained the original text's sympathetic accounts of chivalry, feudalism, and the historical circumstances—civil war, the invasions of Northmen, the weakness of the later Carolingian kings—surrounding the nobility's "usurpation" of its benefices and their transformation into fiefs. In the second of his two substantive revisions, he even added an expanded account of feudal hierarchy—despite his vigorous insistence on the equality of all ancient Franks and all modern nobles of ancient birth.[146]

Only in his first major historical work—the "Mémoire historiques" prefixed to his *Etat de la France*—did Boulainvilliers finally and fully assimilate Le Laboureur's ideas and use them to defend feudalism against its modern detractors. Only in his "Mémoires historiques" did Boulainvilliers follow Le Laboureur and assimilate fief and allod, interpret the allod as a military tenure, and permit military command to introduce "different degrees of vassalage" among allods and their holders, so that the later emergence of a mature feudalism might seem to grow naturally out of ancient French institutions.[147]

The text of the "Mémoires historiques" is examined in the next chapter. When Boulainvilliers wrote it, he had become a political writer working for the duc de Bourgogne and the men around him, and probably brought his *Etat de la France* to near completion—he never really finished it—in 1711. Even when writing for princes, Boulainvilliers pursued concerns of his own, ideological and historical concerns that he first acquired while writing French history for his sons' education or his own edification.

It has been the aim of this chapter to identify those concerns and to watch Boulainvilliers acquire and pursue them in his earliest works. In 1700, his familial circumstances and his sensitivity to the demands of genealogical consciousness and the implications of genealogical erudi-

---

possessions, in the state in which they found them. They nevertheless imposed on those possessions certain tributes and servitudes. On this basis there arose the classification of all properties in the kingdom into servile *mas* and *mansions* which were the patrimonies of the Gauls, free or allodial properties which were possessed freely and hereditarily by Frankish individuals (who, as has been said, called each other *Leuth* or companions), and fiscal properties divided into royal domains and benefices. By the general name, Salic Lands, one understood all those which belonged to the Franks.

[146]Ibid., 515–30, 523–24.
[147]*Etat*, 1, "Mémoires historiques" (separate pagination): 24–26, 113–14, 152.

tion all led Boulainvilliers to assume the task he would pursue for the rest of his life. His first efforts at rehabilitating French feudalism, however, reveal his intellectual and ideological difficulties. He thought and rethought his ideas on ancient land tenure, personal status, and early feudalism. Only after considerable effort did he finally embrace the ideas of the ducal antiquarian Le Laboureur. As a result, Boulainvilliers' ideas on French feudalism were to become as obscurantist as Le Laboureur's, but he developed those ideas because he had an ideological agenda: exalting the ideals of genealogical consciousness; celebrating the birth, virtue, and glory of the "old nobility"; deploring the obstacles that the modern monarchy placed on the noble's path to glory; and celebrating an earlier age of feudalism in which those obstacles—the court, royal favor, new wealth, promiscuous social circulation, open competition for "glory," and the preeminence of a favored and titled nobility of dukes and peers—did not yet exist. Boulainvilliers did not forget that agenda when he began to write French history for princes as a client, counselor, and controversialist; rather he sought to discover possibilities for its realization in the problems of the monarchy and in the goodwill of French princes.

3

Boulainvilliers and
the Burgundy Circle

Boulainvilliers' first piece of political writing was a bulky compilation on the condition and history of France that appeared posthumously in 1727 as the *Etat de la France*. There is little doubt that Boulainvilliers wrote it for Louis XIV's grandson and heir the duc de Bourgogne, and for the men around him.[1] But the aims of the Burgundy Circle and Boulainvilliers' connections with it are less than clear. Were the prince's friends aristocratic constitutionalists or liberals? Or were they neofeudal reactionaries? Did they lead an aristocratic "opposition" to Louis XIV and inaugurate an Enlightenment critique of Bourbon absolutism? Or were they at home in the Sun King's monarchy? Historians have already raised these questions. Another may be added to the list here: Did Bourgogne really commission the *Etat de la France*, as Boulainvilliers suggested when he described the king's grandson as the "great prince who placed the pen in my hand"? Bourgogne's eighteenth-century biographer had his doubts, and claimed that whether or not the prince commissioned Boulainvilliers' work Bourgogne disavowed it when he saw it.[2]

The aim of this chapter is to answer these questions. The nobiliaire ideological commitments of the Burgundy Circle's members—Fénelon and Saint-Simon were preeminent among them—will not be denied. Nor will the constitutionalist or even liberal implications of their

---

[1] *Etat;* see Bibliographical Appendix, Parts 2 and 5. Keohane, *Philosophy and the State in France,* 332–57; and Tréca, *Les Doctrines et les réformes.*

[2] *Etat,* 1, "Préface" (separate pagination): xviii. Abbé [Liéven-Bonaventure] Proyart, *Oeuvres complètes,* 17 vols. (Paris: Mequignon fils, 1819), 7:277 (*Vie du dauphin, père de Louis XV*). Proyart, who wrote well after the events he recounted, may have wanted to dissociate the legendary Bourgogne from the controversial Boulainvilliers, but Proyart also had access to papers of Bourgogne's now lost.

thought. Yet the duc de Bourgogne's entourage arose at the court of Louis XIV and operated within the constraints of the Old Regime monarchical political culture. It will be argued here (as others have argued elsewhere) that the prince's friends did not roundly reject the principles of absolutism, a troublesome term here used to denote the tendency to assign all power in the state to the king's men. In this environment, at once nobiliaire and absolutist, Boulainvilliers made his first efforts at writing history for princes—for he did indeed write for the Burgundy Circle even if a commission from the prince amounts to no more than a fiction. In this same environment, Boulainvilliers continued to pursue his task of rehabilitating French feudalism—for he invited Bourgogne and his friends to discover in French "feudalism" the principles of a French "constitution."[3] Writing for a court coterie as committed to absolutist values as it was wedded to nobiliaire ideals, Boulainvilliers had taken on an awkward task. The difficulties that arose when he presented his work to his first readers are not surprising.

The Duc de Bourgogne's Entourage and Its Activities

It has long been argued that the disastrous wars at the end of Louis XIV's reign emboldened his aristocratic critics, preeminent among them the men in his grandson's entourage. Lionel Rothkrug restated and refined that thesis in his *Opposition to Louis XIV* (1965), a searching study of mercantilist and antimercantilist thought in early-modern France. Rothkrug argued that the "unprecedented scale" of Colbert's bellicose mercantilism called forth an "opposition" of merchants and nobles who, armed with a "fully matured political ideology," formed a powerful "movement for reform" by the end of Louis XIV's reign. These "ideological movements of political opposition" were strong enough to force concessions from the crown, notably the formation in 1700 of a merchant-dominated Council of Trade critical of the crown's mercantilist policies. No less important was an aristocratic "opposition" led by the Burgundy Circle. In Rothkrug's pages, the prince's coterie became "a conspiratorial shadow government," a "shadow government growing up around the Duke of Burgundy." No mere court cabal, the Burgundy Circle led an aristocratic "opposition to Louis XIV," to his "administration," to his "government," and indeed to "all the values traditionally associated with the *ancien régime*."[4]

[3]*Etat*, 1, "Préface": xx (on the "constitution"); 1, "Mémoires historiques": 180 (on "feudalism" [*féodalité*]).
[4]Lionel Rothkrug, *Opposition to Louis XIV: The Political and Social Origins of the French*

That the members of the Burgundy Circle deplored the crown's Colbertist policies, not to mention its wars, is undeniable. "Mercantilism" may be a far more elusive phenomenon than Rothkrug supposed, but he rightly located Fénelon and his friends in an old French tradition—dating back at least to Cardinal Richelieu's *dévot* critics in the 1620s—which opposed war and demanded peace and "reform."[5] At the end of Louis XIV's reign, Rothkrug has reminded us, the men in the Burgundy Circle revived that tradition, to blame the "misery and economic distress" in France "rightly or wrongly" on Colbert's mercantilism and on Louis XIV's wars.[6]

It may be misleading, however, to enroll the Burgundy Circle in an "opposition" to "Louis XIV" and the *ancien régime,* or to place it at the head of independent "ideological movements of political opposition" inspired by clear-eyed antimercantilism and forcing concessions from the crown. Even when Rothkrug wrote, it was clear that the antimercantilism of the merchants, as it may be found in their memoranda for the Council of Trade established in 1700, was ambiguous, for the merchants continued to embrace mercantilist assumptions too. And it has since been established that the Council of Trade itself was not a concession but an initiative taken by Louis XIV's administration.[7] Moreover, such noble antimercantilism as may be found in sources outside the Burgundy Circle was hardly widespread enough to suggest an independent "movement" of "opposition": in Rothkrug's account only two pamphlets—one from the 1660s, the other from the 1680s—provide evidence of it. Given Rothkrug's admission that no means existed in late-seventeenth-century France for shaping or expressing "public opinion," broad "independent

---

Enlightenment (Princeton, N.J.: Princeton University Press, 1965), 35, 242; chaps. 5, 6, and 7. See ibid., 423; 174, 448; 349; 423, 434; 349, 386; and 261 n., 328.

[5]Ibid., 7–85, 234–86 (on sixteenth- and seventeenth-century celebrants of piety, peace, and trade, and on the "Christian agrarianism" of Fénelon and the abbé Claude Fleury), and esp. 64 (on Fénelon). Cf. Richard Bonney, *The King's Debts: Finance and Politics in France, 1589–1661* (Oxford: Clarendon Press, 1981), 115–58; and J. Russell Major, *Representative Government in Early Modern France* (New Haven, Conn.: Yale University Press, 1980), 487–518 (on *dévot* opposition to Richelieu in the 1620s). On "mercantilism" and its problems as a historical concept see D. C. Coleman, "Editor's Introduction," in *Revisions in Mercantilism,* ed. D. C. Coleman (London: Methuen, 1969), 1–18.

[6]Rothkrug, *Opposition to Louis XIV,* 35. These diagnoses should not obscure the evidence now being assembled for incipient economic recovery at the end of Louis XIV's reign. See Thomas J. Schaeper, *The Economy of France in the Second Half of the Reign of Louis XIV,* Interuniversity Centre for European Studies Research Report 2 (Montreal: Interuniversity Centre for European Studies, 1980).

[7]Charles Woolsey Cole, *French Mercantilism, 1683–1700* (New York: Columbia University Press, 1943), 235–40; Warren G. Scoville, "The French Economy in 1700–1701: An Appraisal by the Deputies of Trade," *Journal of Economic History,* 22 (1962): 231–52. Thomas J. Schaeper, *The French Council of Commerce, 1700–1715: A Study of Mercantilism after Colbert* (Columbus: Ohio State University Press, 1983), chap. 1.

movements of political opposition" are hard to imagine.[8] Turning to the prominent reform writers and critics active in the last years of Louis XIV's reign—Burgundy Circle members Fénelon and Saint-Simon, or men outside or on the group's margins such as Marshal Vauban or Pierre Le Pesant de Boisguilbert—one finds little evidence that they sought to coordinate their recommendations with each other or with the principles of a concerted "opposition." On the contrary, these writers and critics advanced a rich and uncoordinated variety of ideas and proposals and shared only the assumption that their task was to counsel their king or persuade his advisers.[9] This deference to the authority and person of a king does not suggest an "opposition" to the "values" of the *ancien régime*. Nor does the concern, highly visible in the writings of the Burgundy Circle members, to restore France's old nobility to preeminence in society and government.[10] In short, Louis XIV's critics remained men of the Old Regime. They were social conservatives who understood their society as a hierarchy of orders. They were political conservatives, too, who understood their polity as an absolute monarchy. The king alone, they agreed, was sovereign. He alone, they insisted, enjoyed ultimate political responsibility in France.[11] However ardent their condemnations of Louis XIV's "despotism"—Fénelon's were ardent indeed—they did not seek to discredit the king in the eyes of a hostile public opinion.[12] They sought to advise him, to persuade

[8]Rothkrug, *Opposition to Louis XIV*, 200–203, 223. See also p. 419—a surprising conclusion to an account of "the growth of public opinion, 1695–1700" (pp. 392–419).

[9][Louis de Rouvroy], duc de Saint-Simon, *Projets de gouvernement du duc de Bourgogne*, ed. P. Mesnard (Paris: Hachette, 1860), xxv et seq. (Mesnard's introduction); Werner Gembruch, "Reformforderungen in Frankreich um die Wende vom 17. zum 18. Jahrhundert: Ein Beitrag zur Geschichte der Opposition gegen System und Politik Ludwigs XIV.," *Historische Zeitschrift*, 209 (1969): 274; Sanford B. Kanter, "Archbishop Fénelon's Political Activity: The Focal Point of Power in Dynasticism," *French Historical Studies*, 4 (1965–66): 320–34.

[10]A concern that Rothkrug noted (*Opposition to Louis XIV*, 278 n. 58 [on Fénelon], and 342–51 [on Charles-Paul Hurault de l'Hôpital, seigneur de Belesbat]), but failed to comment on.

[11]See Gembruch, "Reformforderungen"; Georges Lizerand, *Le Duc de Beauvillier 1648–1714* (Paris: Les Belles Lettres, 1933), 364–75; Françoise Gallouédec-Genuys, *Le Prince selon Fénelon;* Brancourt, *Le Duc de Saint-Simon et la monarchie;* Roland Mousnier, *La Dîme de Vauban*, Les Cours de Sorbonne (Paris: Centre de Documentation Universitaire, 1969).

[12]As did for example, exiled Huguenots or foreign pamphleteers who supported the efforts of Louis XIV's enemies; see Guy Howard Dodge, *The Political Theory of the Huguenots of the Dispersion: With Special Reference to the Thought and Influence of Pierre Jurieu* (New York: Octagon, 1972); Hubert Gillot, *Le Règne de Louis XIV et l'opinion publique en Allemagne* (Paris: Honoré Champion, 1914); P. J. W. van Malssen, *Louis XIV d'après les pamphlets répandus en Hollande* (Amsterdam: H. J. Paris; Paris: A. Nizet and M. Bastard, 1937). For Fénelon's denunciations of Louis XIV's wars and "despotism" see [François de La Mothe Salignac-]Fénelon, *Ecrits et lettres politiques,* ed. Ch. Urbain (Paris: Bossard, 1920), 143–56, 170–83. These texts were not public or printed utterances but private letters, one ad-

him, to reshape his policies, or, and this was especially important for the Burgundy Circle, to influence his heir.[13]

The aristocratic and corporatist ideals of the Burgundy Circle recall the ideals of earlier noble activists, the conspirators who plotted against Richelieu, Mazarin, and even Louis XIV in the first half of his personal reign.[14] But Burgundy Circle members were servants of the crown, not plotters against it. These critics of Louis XIV's policies belonged to the world of Louis XIV's absolutism. Indeed, the duc de Beauvillier's political career—Paul de Beauvillier was the coterie's effective leader—demonstrates that the Burgundy Circle owed whatever influence it enjoyed to royal favor and ministerial connections. Louis XIV launched Beauvillier's career in 1685 by naming him head of the Council of Finances. And the king advanced Beauvillier's career in 1689 when, on August 16, he named him duc de Bourgogne's governor. Within two weeks Beauvillier had organized the seven-year-old prince's household and provided for his education, naming Fénelon preceptor and the abbé Claude Fleury as subpreceptor. Two years later, in 1691 when the war minister François-Michel Le Tellier, marquis de Louvois died, Louis XIV crowned Beauvillier's career by calling him to the Conseil d'en haut, the king's inner council of ministers. Beauvillier was the first (and only) "old" noble whom Louis XIV called to the ministry and his elevation may appear to be the first step in a resurgent old nobility's reconquest of ministerial posts. In fact, Beauvillier's elevation was the last step in the Colbert family's conquest of ministerial ascendancy over the Le Tellier clan. Like Charles-Honoré d'Albert, duc de Chevreuse, another leading figure in the Burgundy Circle, Beauvillier was a son-in-law of the great Colbert (who had died in 1683), and until his own death in 1714, Beauvillier continued to cooperate with *colbertiste* ministers and royal servants. However paradoxical it may seem for a connection critical of Louis XIV's wars and mercantilism, the Burgundy Circle depended vitally on the fact that Beauvillier (and Chevreuse) enjoyed royal confidence and *colbertiste* connections—not to mention the goodwill of Louis XIV's mistress or morganatic wife, Madame de Maintenon, who herself supported the Colbert clan into the 1690s.[15]

---

dressed in 1694 to the king (but probably meant for Madame de Maintenon and the duc de Beauvillier [Rothkrug, *Opposition to Louis XIV,* 269 n. 46]), the other addressed in 1710 to the duc de Chevreuse. See esp. Fénelon, 178–79, on the need to persuade (not oppose) the king.

[13]Gembruch, "Reformforderungen," 271, 274, 310, 317.

[14]Klaus Malettke, *Opposition und Konspiration unter Ludwig XIV.: Studien zu Kritik und Widerstand gegen System und Politik des französischen Königs während der ersten Hälfte seiner persönlichen Regierung* (Göttingen: Vandenhoeck und Ruprecht, 1976), esp. 333.

[15]On Beauvillier's career and *colbertiste* connections see Lizerand, *Le Duc de Beauvillier,*

Thanks to royal favor and ministerial connections, Beauvillier and his friends took charge of the duc de Bourgogne's education and the kingdom's "reform." In Bourbon France, the education of a prince was a political matter of the highest order. A prince's education, it was assumed, let the men entrusted with it shape the political future by shaping a future king, and the Burgundy Circle members shared that assumption.[16] Royal favor and ministerial connections also let the Burgundy Circle plan to "reform" and revive a France exhausted by the War of the League of Augsburg (1688–97).

Both ends, pedagogical and reformist, informed the famous inquest, very likely modeled on an earlier inquest conducted by Colbert in 1664, which Beauvillier launched in 1697. Even before the Peace of Ryswick formally ended the war (September–October 1697), Beauvillier sent a questionnaire to France's thirty-two intendants, asking them to send to Versailles, by the end of the year, "ample and detailed" memoranda on their *généralités*. (In fact, memoranda continued to arrive at Versailles for the next three years.) Beauvillier explained that these reports were to acquaint Bourgogne with "the interior of the kingdom." In the plans for his education, the prince was scheduled to study French geography in 1700, so the intendants' memoranda may well have served the prince's education. Their use in the kingdom's "reform" was destined to be postponed, for the War of the Spanish Succession (1702–13) soon forced Beauvillier to defer "reform" until the new war's conclusion.[17]

In the last years of that war the Burgundy Circle's hopes for "reform" rose once again, not only because of the approach of peace but also because of the imminence of the succession of the duc de Bourgogne to the throne. In March 1711 Bourgogne's father (the "Grand Dauphin," son of Louis XIV) died and Bourgogne became Louis XIV's direct heir. In the heady months that followed, Fénelon and Chevreuse drafted their "Plans de gouvernement" (or "Tables de Chaulnes"), and Saint-Simon held his long conversations with the duc de Bourgogne, whose putative content the little duke recorded in his *Projets du gouvernement du*

45–50, 87–107, 167–89; and Jean Meyer, *Colbert* (Paris: Hachette, 1981), 342, 345. Aware of these connections, Rothkrug admitted that the Burgundy Circle was "in part an expression of family-faction rivalries at Court" (*Opposition to Louis XIV*, 259), but he wrongly insisted that Beauvilliers' hostility to *colbertiste* mercantilism led him to break his alliance with the Colbert clan (262). In any case other members of the clan were equally dubious of its founder's economic and administrative convictions, as Rothkrug observed (260–62).

[16]Chartier, Compère, and Julia, *L'Éducation en France*, 175–77.

[17]Louis Trénard, *Les Mémoires des intendants pour l'instruction du duc de Bourgogne (1698): Introduction générale* (Paris: B.N., 1975), 19–23 and 89–91 ("Annexe 3. Questionnaire du duc de Beauvillier [1697]"). On Colbert's 1664 inquest see also James E. King, *Science and Rationalism in the Government of Louis XIV 1661–1683* (Baltimore: Johns Hopkins Press, 1949), 126–40.

duc de Bourgogne.[18] In this context it is likely that Beauvillier once again planned to use the intendants' memoranda to plan for the kingdom's "reform." Once again, the Burgundy Circle was to be disappointed. In January 1712, ten months after his father's death, the duc de Bourgogne too went to his grave, victim of an outbreak of measles that also killed his wife and elder son.

In 1711–12, the Burgundy Circle may have resembled a "conspiratorial shadow government" "growing up around the duc de Bourgogne" and spinning projects rich in "liberal" or "constitutionalist" implications.[19] Yet even the historian who seeks to emphasize its contribution to "constitutionalist" thinking in France can admit that the Burgundy Circle embraced an "old vision of a king governing in a formally unlimited fashion, making the final decision on all issues, relying on the institutionalized help of representatives of various parts of his kingdom."[20] Even Fénelon, who sought to defend the "interest" of the French "nation" against that of the dynasty that governed it, is no exception to this rule.[21] At home in the traditionally monarchical political culture, the Burgundy Circle members were also at home in the world of Bourbon absolutism. Despite their traditionalism, they sought not to subvert but to serve absolutism, by ensuring its reliance on the service and counsel of a revived French nobility.[22] Dependent themselves on ministerial connections, royal favor, and (one may now add) such dynastic contingencies as the need to educate a prince or plan for his anticipated reign, the Burgundy Circle members did not yearn for a

[18]Fénelon, *Ecrits politiques*, 97–124: "Plans de gouvernement concertés avec le duc de Chevreuse pour être proposés au duc de Bourgogne (Novembre 1711)," prepared by Fénelon and Chevreuse at the latter's estate at Chaulnes (whence the alternate title "Tables de Chaulnes"). Saint-Simon, *Projets du gouvernement;* Brancourt, *Le Duc de Saint-Simon*, 146.
[19]Denis Richet, *La France moderne: L'esprit des institutions* (Paris: Flammarion, 1973), 144–46; Keohane, *Philosophy and the State in France*, 343–46.
[20]Keohane, *Philosophy and the State in France*, 345, 346.
[21]See Fénelon, *Ecrits politiques*, 170–83 (letter to the duc de Chevreuse, Cambrai, August 4, 1710). Writing during the War of the Spanish Succession, Fénelon proposed that kings consult an assembly of notables before taking up arms, and he denounced the practice of "hazarding France without consulting her" (171). He added: "It would be necessary that there spread throughout our nation a deep and abiding persuasion that it is the whole nation itself that supports, for its own interest, the weight of this war, just as the English and the Dutch are persuaded that it is by their own choice and for their own interest that they go to war" (173). But when he proposed (in the 1711 "Plans de gouvernement" for example [ibid., 102–5]) that general and provincial estates be revived, he limited their roles to consultation and administration (Gallouédec-Genuys, *Le Prince selon Fénelon*, 129–36).
[22]In addition to works by Brancourt and Gallouédec-Genuys already cited, see Roger Mettam, "The Role of the Higher Aristocracy in France under Louis XIV with Special Reference to the 'Faction of the Duke of Burgundy' and the Provincial Governors" (Ph.D. Diss., Cambridge University, 1967), 5–6, 9, 67–114.

preabsolutist or feudal past. A royalist antifeudalism preserved them against that nostalgia (despite the ducal pride to which Beauvillier and especially Saint-Simon were susceptible) and only the most pressing dynastic difficulties impelled or permitted them to overcome that royalist antifeudalism. It will be no surprise, then, if it shall appear that Boulainvilliers' search for a French "constitution" in the feudal past met with a cool reception among the men in the Burgundy Circle.

The *Etat de la France:*
The Author, His Book, and His Readers

There is ample evidence of Boulainvilliers' difficulties with the first readers of the *Etat de la France*. They belonged no doubt to the Burgundy Circle, though no record confirms Boulainvilliers' claim that the duc de Bourgogne ordered him to take up his pen. Boulainvilliers had long since been acquainted with the duc de Beauvillier. In August 1689, only a few days after being named the young Bourgogne's governor, Beauvillier did Boulainvilliers the honor of witnessing his contract of marriage with Marie-Anne Hurault du Marais. So did Charles d'Albert duc de Luynes, the duc de Chevreuse's father. It is likely, therefore, that Beauvillier was a patron of Boulainvilliers' in 1689.[23] It is no less likely that Beauvillier later asked Boulainvilliers to prepare the *Etat de la France*.

There is no way of knowing, however, when Boulainvilliers began it. In the "Préface" he gave several accounts of how he started the work. In one he claimed that he began digesting the intendants' memoranda of 1697–1700 "to shorten the immense task that he [the duc de Bourgogne] would have had to perform to read each of the intendants' treatises."[24] That remark suggests that Boulainvilliers may have begun his work early enough to finish it in time for the prince's studies on French geography in 1700, but no other evidence confirms that possibility. Efforts to fix the date at which Boulainvilliers set to work remain conjectural.[25]

[23]A.N., M.C., CII, 148 (August 20, 1689) (marriage contract). In Parisian marriage contracts of the eighteenth century, witnesses of higher rank than the spouses tended to be their patrons and protectors (Adeline Daumard and François Furet, *Structures et relations sociales à Paris au milieu du XVIIIe siècle* [Paris: Armand Colin, 1961], 83).

[24]*Etat*, 1, "Préface" (separately paginated): xviii ("Avertissement").

[25]A. de Boislisle suggested that Boulainvilliers began in 1705 if not earlier: "Note sur les mémoires dressés par les intendants en 1697 pour l'instruction du duc de Bourgogne," *Annuaire-Bulletin de la Société de l'Histoire de France*, 10 (1873): 155. He cited no evidence, but may have had in mind a marginal note by Boulainvilliers' posthumous editor Philippe

It is clear that Boulainvilliers was still at work in and after 1709—if not on abridging the intendants' reports, then at least on drafting his massive introduction to them—for in his "Préface" Boulainvilliers alluded to his sons' deaths which had occurred in 1709.[26] Thus, if Boulainvilliers began his *Etat de la France* as a text for the duc de Bourgogne's education, he probably continued it as an aid or blueprint for the reforms that the Burgundy Circle was planning, in 1711–12, in preparation for Bourgogne's anticipated succession to the throne. Indeed, Boulainvilliers may have still been working on the *Etat de la France* when Bourgogne died in January 1712.

The bulk of the *Etat de la France* consists of Boulainvilliers' digests of the intendants' reports of 1697–1700—digests, unfortunately, that are misleading and unreliable. In fact, Boulainvilliers' editorial work has elicited serious scholarly criticism. Deploring his hatred for the intendants, his contempt for their work, his additions and interjections, and the carelessness of his posthumous editors and printers, modern historians have rightly urged their colleagues to ignore the *Etat de la France*, to rely instead on the original intendants' reports, and to prepare critical editions of them.[27] These charges are legitimate. In Boulainvilliers' defense all that can be said is that he is not guilty of them all.

Mercier, in which Mercier dated Boulainvilliers' digest of Lamoignon de Bâville's report on Languedoc to 1705 (*Etat*, 2:527). Like many men at Paris in the first decade of the eighteenth century, Boulainvilliers was a harsh critic of Bâville's repression of the Huguenot Camisard rebellion in the Cévennes in 1702–4. In his abridgment of Bâville's report, Boulainvilliers interpolated his own comment on the intendant's campaign against the rebels: "The Albigensian War was scarcely more tragic; but what is truly deplorable is the fact that these movements are not yet over." Although that statement led Mercier to date Boulainvilliers' digest of Bâville's report to 1705, it could just as easily lead one to date it to 1709 or after, for the Camisard rebellion continued to smolder and to alarm Bâville as late as 1709 (Jean-Robert Armogathe, Philippe Joutard, "Bâville et la guerre des Camisards," *Revue d'histoire moderne et contemporaine*, 19 [1972]: 52).

[26]*Etat*, 1, "Préface": iii ("Première partie"); Moréri et al., *Le Grand Dictionnaire historique*, 2:133.

[27]Boislisle, "Note sur les mémoires," 152–55; Boislisle, "Introduction," *Mémoires des intendants sur l'état des généralités, dressés pour l'instruction du duc de Bourgogne*, vol. 1, *Mémoire de la généralité de Paris*, ed. Boislisle (Paris: 1881), i; Edmond Esmonin, *Etudes sur la France des XVIIe et XVIIIe siècles* (Paris: Presses Universitaires de France, 1964), 114–17; Trénard, *Les Mémoires des intendants*, 53–54; Hervé Hasquin, "Introduction," *L'Intendance de Hainaut en 1697: Edition critique du mémoire pour l'instruction du duc de Bourgogne*, ed. Hasquin (Paris: B.N., 1975), 50; Jean Bérenger and Jean Meyer, "Introduction," *La Bretagne de la fin du XVIIe siècle d'après le rapport de Béchameil de Nointel*, ed. Bérenger, Meyer et al. (Paris: C. Klincksieck, 1976), 2; Louis Trénard, "Introduction," *L'Intendance de Flandre Wallonne en 1698: Edition critique du mémoire rédigé "pour l'instruction du duc de Bourgogne"*, ed. Trénard (Paris: B.N., 1977), 32, 52, 55; François Moreil, "Introduction," *L'Intendance de Languedoc à la fin du XVIIe siècle: Mémoire pour l'instruction du duc de Bourgogne*, ed. Moreil (Paris: Comité des Travaux Historiques et Scientifiques, 1985), 59; Gérard Hurpin, "Introduction," *L'Intendance de Rouen en 1698: Mémoire rédigé par l'intendant pour l'instruction du duc de Bourgogne*, ed. Hurpin (Paris: Comité des Travaux Historiques et Scientifiques, 1985), 216

In any case, for the student of Boulainvilliers' career as political writer and controversialist, the chief interest of the *Etat de la France* resides not in its digests of the intendants' reports but in the mass of introductory material prefixed to them. There one finds Boulainvilliers' original contribution to the Burgundy Circle's efforts and evidence of the difficulties he encountered when he submitted his work to that princely coterie.

The "Preface": An Author's Difficulties

In the "Préface de l'auteur" to the *Etat de la France* one finds no less than three different accounts of how and why Boulainvilliers began his project. That peculiar fact suggests that the "Préface" that Philippe Mercier, Boulainvilliers' posthumous editor, printed in 1727 may not be the preface Boulainvilliers intended. Manuscript evidence confirms this and reveals that Mercier printed together, one right after the other, different versions of a preface distinguished by their different accounts of how and why the author undertook his task. The "Préface de l'auteur," consequently, is a bad edition of Boulainvilliers' work. Yet it is a good record of his difficulties as a political writer working for the Burgundy Circle, for it contains his repeated attempts at representing himself, his readers, and his reasons for addressing them.

Before we turn to the fictional self-portraits-of-the-author-at-work that Boulainvilliers composed for his *Etat de la France* it is necessary to examine the text in which they appear: the "Préface de l'auteur" that Philippe Mercier printed in 1727. A reader opening these volumes first encounters Mercier's own dedication to the British king.[28] A map of France follows, and then the text of a "Memorandum which His Majesty commanded to be sent to Messieurs the Masters of Requests, Commissioners, posted in the Provinces, in 1697."[29] Finally, the reader encoun-

---

and passim (as indexed under Boulainvilliers). See also Abel Poitrineau, "Introduction," *Mémoire sur l'état de la généralité de Riom en 1697 dressé pour l'instruction du duc de Bourgogne par l'intendant Lefèvre d'Ormesson*, ed. Poitrineau, Publications de l'Institut d'Etudes du Massif Central (Clermont-Ferrand: 1971); and François-Xavier Emmanuelli, "Introduction," *L'Intendance de Provence à la fin du XVIIe siècle: Edition critique des mémoires "pour l'instruction du duc de Bourgogne"*, ed. Emmanuelli (Paris: B.N., 1980); these two editors refrain from deploring Boulainvilliers' bad work.

[28]Boulainvilliers' posthumous editor was probably the Philippe Mercier whom George II had engaged as his principal painter in 1727 and later as his librarian at Leicester Fields (*The Dictionary of National Biography*, 22 vols. [London: Oxford University Press, 1949–50], s.v. "Mercier, Philippe").

[29]*Etat*, 1, "Mémoire Que sa Majesté a ordonné être envoyé à M^{rs}. les Maitres des Requêtes, Commissaires, departis dans les Provinces, en 1697" (separately paginated): 1–14.

ters Boulainvilliers' own texts: the "Préface de l'auteur" consisting of some introductory paragraphs, a "Première partie," an "Avertissement," and a "Seconde partie"; next the "Mémoires historiques" or "Memorials on the History of the Government of France, from the Beginning of the Monarchy, by Monsieur le Comte de Boulainvilliers"; and then, following that "histoire raisonnée" as Boulainvilliers described it, the abridged intendants' reports, which occupy the larger part of the first volume of the *Etat de la France* and the whole of the second.[30]

The disposition of texts just described was not Boulainvilliers'. It was Philippe Mercier's, and Mercier was a careless editor indeed. The "Memorandum to the Masters of Requests," for example, was *not* the circular that Beauvillier had sent to the intendants in 1697 but rather a circular that Colbert had issued to the intendants in 1664, on the occasion of an earlier, similar, but in fact less successful inquiry. Beauvillier may have dispatched Colbert's circular with his own in 1697, but no competent editor should have confused the two documents. That error, often imputed to Boulainvilliers, was in fact Mercier's, for no manuscript copy consulted of Boulainvilliers' digests of the intendants' reports includes the text of the 1664 circular.[31]

Equally careless was Mercier's handling of Boulainvilliers' own texts. The "Préface de l'auteur" that Mercier printed does not answer Boulainvilliers' own description of it. Boulainvilliers' preface (like Mercier's) was to consist of two parts: the first on why and how Boulainvilliers abridged the intendants' memoranda, the second on the history of French government from the beginning of the monarchy to the present.[32] But the

---

[30]*Etat*, 1, "Préface" (separately paginated): i–xxvii. See i for the introductory paragraphs, i–xvii for the "Première partie," xviii for the "Avertissement," and xix–xxvii for the "Seconde partie." Ibid., 1, "Mémoires historiques" or "Mémoires sur l'Histoire du Gouvernement de France, dès le Commencement de la Monarchie. Par Monsieur le Comte de Boulainvilliers" (separately paginated): 1–182. See ibid., 1, "Préface": xxii ("Seconde partie"), on this history as an "histoire raisonnée." For another abridged edition of it in 1727, see Bibliographical Appendix, Part 5.

[31]Boislisle, "Note sur les mémoires," 155–57; Esmonin, *Etudes sur la France*, 116; Trénard, *Les Mémoires des intendants*, 54. For MS copies of Boulainvilliers' digests consulted, see Bibliographical Appendix, Part 2. Some MSS of the original intendants' reports do include copies of Colbert's circular (e.g. A.N., MM. 923, fols. 1–23v, and B.N., MS. f.f. 4282, fols. 1–22v), an error frequently made by copyists (Boislisle, "Note sur les mémoires," 157). Further evidence that Mercier, not Boulainvilliers, mistook Colbert's circular for Beauvillier's may be found in Mercier's marginal notes, which abound in the *Etat de la France* (e.g. *Etat*, 1, "Mémoires historiques": 5, 41, 48). At p. 13 of the "Memorandum to the Masters of Requests," where to the end of Colbert's circular Mercier added what was actually the Paris intendant's introduction to his report (cf. *Mémoires des intendants*, 1, *Mémoire de la généralité de Paris*, 1–2), Mercier commented, "I believe that what follows is an addition to the memorandum [to the intendants] by the late Monsieur le Duc de Bourguogne [sic]." Boulainvilliers, who knew and abridged the original report on Paris, could not have made that mistake.

[32]*Etat*, 1, "Préface": i. For Boulainvilliers' abandoned plans for an even more ambitious four-part preface, see below, p. 89.

"Seconde partie" of Mercier's "Préface de l'auteur," despite some pointed comments on the history of French government, is not such a history itself. And its final pages on Frankish history really belong to the beginning of the "Mémoires historiques," and that is where one finds them in manuscripts. Mercier misplaced the "Avertissement," too, for in manuscripts one finds it not with Boulainvilliers' prefatory material but at the head of his abridgments of the intendants' reports.[33] In effect, instead of printing the two-part preface that Boulainvilliers designed— it was to contain a denunciation of the intendants' work followed by a history of French government—Mercier fabricated a two-part preface out of what were actually two alternative versions of Boulainvilliers' prefatory diatribe against the intendants. They are never found together in manuscripts of the abridged intendants' reports. In fact, two separate manuscript copies of a "Discourse on the intendants" (Mercier's "Première partie") bear a remark clearly identifying it as a text rejected and replaced by another: "This preface was suppressed, because it was found too lively and because it did not suit the present time. The author substituted another for it, not as long, and more moderate, which however says just about the same thing."[34]

In short, the "Préface de l'auteur" printed by Mercier in 1727 is a pastiche that Boulainvilliers would not have recognized as his own work. The elements of that pastiche, however, record his successive attempts to respond to criticisms from his first readers in the Burgundy Circle and reveal his difficulties as a political writer.

Boulainvilliers did not write the *Etat de la France* in isolation. He showed his work to readers and their criticisms left clear marks on the surface of his text. In the "Avertissement," for example, he defended the procedure he had followed in digesting the intendants' reports: condensing each report and, where he thought it necessary or possible, interjecting critical comments and "refutations" into his abridgments. To "censors" who had wanted a synthesis of the reports' contents Boulainvilliers replied that no one could command the "thorough and uniform knowledge of the kingdom's provinces" required for such a task. Besides, he added, the "faults" and "errors" of the intendants' reports made such a task impossible.[35]

Critics also left their mark on Boulainvilliers' prefatory diatribe

[33] Ibid., xxiii–xxvii ("Second partie"). For MS copies consulted of the "Mémoires historiques" and of the abridged intendants' reports see Bibliographical Appendix, Part 2.

[34] Boulainvilliers, "Discours sur les intendans" (B.M., Dijon, MS. 682 [409¹]), esp. fol. 2 ("Avertissement") for the quotation. See also B.M., Angoulême, MS. 23, pp. 241–306, for another copy.

[35] *Etat,* 1, "Préface": xviii ("Avertissement").

against the intendants: indeed they obliged him to rewrite it. Doubtless one reason was the harshness of his vituperation. Adhering to the values of genealogical consciousness and deploring what he took to be the replacement of "birth," "virtue," and "merit" by "wealth," "favor," and "ambition" as the qualities that promoted men to prominence in France, Boulainvilliers wrote a bitter jeremiad against modern French society and the intendants who administered it. Men of all "conditions," he wrote, had been "corrupted" by "ambition" and by "the immoderate thirst for riches and the fury to dissipate them." Such corruption, he added, was most dangerous where money was most important—in acquiring "dignities" and offices. Predictably he denounced the venality of office in the magistracy and above all in the royal council, where the posts of *maîtres des requêtes* were bought up not only by former magistrates but also by "subjects lately arrived from the lowest conditions, sons of merchants, of clerks [*greffiers*], of procurators, and—this is still more deplorable for its consequences—sons of tax farmers [*partisans*]." From the vile body of the *maîtres des requêtes*, he argued, the most ambitious stepped forward to procure intendancies by "these *mouvemens intriguans*" and by "these secret practices that lead to fortune by routes that are justly suspect." Disinclined to think that men driven by ambition, money, and favor might be men of capacity and experience, Boulainvilliers proceeded to castigate the intendants' "inapplication," "fear," "pride," and "ambition" and to denounce the putative uselessness of their reports. He even resorted to direct attacks on individuals.[36] He took these liberties, he explained, because with the exception of Languedoc's no intendant whose work he deplored remained at his post— and also because the intendants, by having made their reports public ("*en les mettant au jour*"), invited criticism.[37] But so did Boulainvilliers, of course. And in his rewritten diatribe against the intendants he discarded his attacks on individuals and abbreviated his attacks on the putative ambition and incompetence of the intendants.[38]

Yet Boulainvilliers' vituperation of the intendants was probably not what most offended his first readers in the Burgundy Circle. After all, Saint-Simon, Fénelon, and even Bourgogne himself would have liked to see intendancies abolished and old nobles preferred for royal service.[39]

[36]Ibid., viii–xvii ("Première partie"). Predictably, Boulainvilliers pilloried the intendant in Languedoc, Bâville (xvii).

[37]Ibid., xv. This was a remarkable comment, given Beauvillier's assurance in his 1697 letter to the intendants that "what you shall send me is not to become public" (Trénard, *Les Mémoires des intendants*, 89).

[38]*Etat*, 1, "Préface": xix–xxiii, esp. xxi ("Second partie").

[39]Brancourt, *Le Duc de Saint-Simon*, 68, 122–44, 183–86; Gallouédec-Genuys, *Le Prince selon Fénelon*, 137–47, 161–69, 186–98; Proyart, *Oeuvres complète*, 7:277–334, esp. 292–93 (on Bourgogne's preference for old nobles).

Besides, in rewriting his prefatory remarks on the intendants Boulain-villiers actually expanded his argument, already undertaken in his first draft, that intendancies were dangerous innovations in French government with no warrant in the kingdom's ancient practices and serving instead as pillars of a new and dangerously "arbitrary" and "despotic" power.[40]

Other, more significant differences can be detected between the two versions of the prefatory diatribe against the intendants and between those texts and Boulainvilliers' "Avertissement," notably his divergent self-portraits-of-the-author-at-work. In the "Avertissement" (the brief notice that Boulainvilliers prefixed to his abridgments of the intendants' memoranda) he stated that the duc de Bourgogne "placed the pen in my hand."[41] In both versions of the diatribe against the intendants, however, the prince's initiative disappears while Boulainvilliers' reasons for writing the *Etat de la France* and Bourgogne's likely response to it become problematic. In the second and final version of the diatribe Bourgogne and his entourage reemerge only at the end of the text, where Boulain-villiers proclaimed his "sincere wishes" that the prince might find his work "agreeable" and devote himself to becoming "the best of our kings."[42] That circumspect account of his association with the prince must have pleased Boulainvilliers' first readers, for in writing it he suppressed a far more elaborate and probably far more offensive account which he had written in the first draft of his preface.

There, Boulainvilliers began by presenting his connection with Burgundy as a happy accident. "In the depths of my solitude and in the provinces," Boulainvilliers wrote, he learned of the prince's "renown," his "rare qualities," and his laudable plans to collect reports on all of France's *généralités* from their intendants.[43] Boulainvilliers obtained copies of those reports, but only when they "fell into my hands." He began to abridge them, but only for his sons' education, not Bour-gogne's (a not implausible claim given Boulainvilliers' activities in about 1700 as a paternal pedagogue). After his sons' deaths Boulainvilliers continued his work, but only because his "ideas about the public good" impelled him to do so.[44] Boulainvilliers carefully refrained from sug-

[40]*Etat*, 1, "Préface": xxi–xxiii ("Seconde partie" or second version). Cf. Ibid, v, xiii–xiv ("Première partie" or first version).

[41]Ibid., xviii ("Avertissement").

[42]Ibid., xxii–xxiii ("Seconde partie"): "I shall here add sincere wishes that my work may become agreeable to him [Bourgogne] and that, my ideas supporting his first and just designs, he may apply himself one day with all his heart and mind to becoming the best of our kings and to rendering this state the most prosperous of all Christian kingdoms!"

[43]Ibid., i–ii ("Première partie").

[44]Ibid., iii.

gesting a direct association with the duc de Bourgogne, and for good reason. After maligning the intendants as the enemies of "liberty" and the "public good," Boulainvilliers raised the banner of the Fronde against them: "It is necessary to recognize that the opposition raised by practically all the peoples of the monarchy to this novelty was the last effort of French liberty, and after the light and useless resistance they offered to it, the wounds by which we are afflicted have succeeded one another almost year by year and have finally reduced us to our present oppression."[45] Praising the Fronde was an unlikely move in a work presumably destined for Louis XIV's grandson and heir. But Boulainvilliers went on to observe that he was *not* writing for Bourgogne. He even dared to express doubts about Bourgogne's "habits" and "maxims." Then, in a remarkable passage that deserves to be quoted at length, he allowed himself to hope that "Providence" might convey his work to men near the prince who might instill its lessons in him:

> I do not flatter myself . . . that my work could ever merit the prince's attention. I even think that at present it would be not only useless but perhaps dangerous if he saw it, and here is my reason. As far as the [intendants'] memoranda are concerned, most of the information they contain is hardly worth retaining, thanks to the intendants who wrote them. This preface is designed to extract their essence, to reduce facts to maxims of government, to seek in historical reality truths attested by experience [*des véritez éxpérimentales*] which might be applied to our present condition. These truths will be set forth without adulation, without [any concern for] personal interest, and even without fear of displeasing. Now these qualities in a work—although the only qualities that are just and worthy of a good citizen's intention—are they suited to the taste of a prince already prejudiced by other ideas, a prince already mature and settled in an opposite habit? Here one can only count on his good nature, which has directed him since his childhood, or on the piety which seems to determine his entire conduct.
>
> I shall not elaborate my thoughts on that subject. It is enough to confine the idea of my work's utility to speculation. Perhaps Providence will extract from it other fruits. . . .
>
> But if one must think, though with regret, that my work will be of no direct use to the prince for the end he proposed, can I not flatter myself that my work might become useful to him by some indirect route [*par une voye indirecte & réfléchie*]? In effect, if it is necessary, in the interests of his glory and his conscience, that the prince know the precise detail in which I see the principle of a fruitful administration [*hûreuse oeconomie*] and a good govern-

---

[45]Ibid., v. On the Fronde's unsuccessful efforts to abolish the intendants, see Bonney, *Political Change in France under Richelieu and Mazarin*, 57–75.

ment, it is no less necessary for those individuals whose birth and condition let them approach the prince. With this knowledge, they will be better prepared to please him and to converse with him, to respond well to his intentions, to execute his orders ably, to suggest correct ideas to him as occasions allow. And if these individuals have merit enough to enter his councils, then they shall better understand the matters discussed in them, they shall find themselves well informed where others are perfectly ignorant, and, finally, they shall be able to give advice based on certain truths to which princes and their ministers hardly ever pay attention. This advice, heard by a wise and judicious monarch, will certainly carry more weight than the advice which ignorance, passion, or prejudice all too often utter in the presence of kings. How happy my design, how happier still my work, if it shall ever serve the instruction of some men whom fortune shall lift high enough to let them act, following my principles, to the advantage of the public good![46]

In these revealing lines, Boulainvilliers completed his original account of how and why he wrote the *Etat de la France*. Having proclaimed his nostalgia for the Fronde, he now betrayed his doubts about Bourgogne's conventionally royalist and absolutist convictions and established an elaborate fictional distance that redoubled the ideological distance that separated him from the men in the Burgundy Circle.[47]

Boulainvilliers did his best to work within the constraints of the Old Regime's monarchical political culture and to respect the Burgundy Circle's absolutist sentiments. Even in the lines just quoted he understood his task as giving counsel, if not to the prince (or the prince's heir apparent) then to the men around him. And when they rejected the first version of his prefatory diatribe against the intendants, he wrote a second in which he suppressed his nostalgia for the Fronde, swallowed his doubts about Bourgogne, and professed unimpeachably absolutist sentiments: "My views . . . are as respectful of the government under which we live as they are loyal in the discussion of what can be done to render that government as durable as it is absolute."[48]

In the final version of his prefatory diatribe against the intendants Boulainvilliers suppressed his misgivings about the prince he sought to serve. It is remarkable that he confessed them, however, and it is reasonable to ask why he entertained them. To answer that question one may turn at last to the history of French government that Boulainvilliers prefixed to his abridgments of the intendants' reports: the "Mémoires historiques." There we may find what was probably the fundamental

[46]*Etat*, 1, "Préface": vi–vii ("Première partie").
[47]See Lizerand, *Le Duc de Beauvillier*, 364–71 on Bourgogne's convictions.
[48]*Etat*, 1, "Préface": xx ("Seconde partie").

reason for his problems with the Burgundy Circle, that is, his determination to discover in feudalism the foundations of a French "constitution."

The "Mémoires historiques" and France's Feudal Constitution

The second half of Boulainvilliers's two-part preface was to have been a history of French government from its beginnings to the present.[49] He never finished that history—the "Mémoires historiques" ends with Hugh Capet's accession to the throne in 987—and his reasons for cutting his history short will need to be considered. Nevertheless the "Mémoires historiques" may be read (as Boulainvilliers no doubt intended) as a finished work. Because it was a moment of dynastic change, Capet's accession was a nodal point for French historians writing in the seventeenth century.[50] The year 987, consequently, was a logical time for drawing a narrative to a close. Thus Boulainvilliers finished the "Mémoires historiques" with a formal peroration preceded by a concluding account of "feudalism" designed to pull together the political lessons that he wanted French history to teach.[51] Once again he was trying to rehabilitate feudalism, not just to defend it against the antifeudalism of his contemporaries but also to mine it for the principles of an "ancient economy" or "constitution" of French government, principles he sought to expound for the edification of the duc de Bourgogne and his entourage.[52]

Boulainvilliers' search for a feudal constitution runs like a red thread through the "Mémoires historiques." Yet that work is so full of minutiae about kings, battles, and civil wars that it seems odd that Boulainvilliers called it a "histoire raisonnée": that is, a history in which fact and narrative were supposed to take second place to reasoning, argument, and analysis.[53] Boulainvilliers lifted his reharbative detail from the 1685 edition of Mézeray's *Histoire de France* and from the learned abbé de Longuerue's disquisitions on Frankish and early French history and chronology, which Boulainvilliers consulted in manuscript. From these works, he prepared lengthy notes or "extracts" cast in his own prose which he then transferred, barely altered, into his "Mémoires historiques."[54] That practice may explain why Nicolas Fréret, writing shortly

[49]Ibid., i (introductory paragraphs).
[50]Tyvaert, "L'Image du roi," 528–30.
[51]*Etat,* 1, "Mémoires historiques": 178–82.
[52]*Etat,* 1, "Préface": xv ("Première partie") and xx ("Seconde partie") for the "ancient economy"; and xxi ("Seconde partie") for the "constitution."
[53]Ibid., xxii ("Seconde partie"); Phyllis K. Leffler, "The '*Histoire Raisonnée*' 1660–1720: A Pre-Enlightenment Genre," *Journal of the History of Ideas,* 37 (1976): 219–40.
[54]See Bibliographical Appendix, Part 2. On Boulainvilliers' use of "extracts" see also

after Boulainvilliers' death, remarked that "his works flowed almost perfect from his pen."[55] In any case, when one subtracts from the "Mémoires historiques" the passages that Boulainvilliers took from Mézeray and Longuerue, only some 85 of the text's 182 pages contain original writing by the author—writing in which he sought to pursue his own political and historical program and to discern in the past the feudal lineaments of a "constitution" that might be restored in the present.[56]

Boulainvilliers claimed that his project, extracting political lessons from the historical past, was part of the project the intendants had been asked to undertake in 1697–1700. Ascribing the intendants' instructions to the duc de Bourgogne, Boulainvilliers wrote:

> My aim in this abridgment is to follow as closely as possible the prince's idea, which he made public in the plan which he gave the intendants for organizing their memoranda. There one sees that the prince wants to be informed not only on the details concerning the situation, nature, and forces of each province, not only on the details concerning the different orders of subjects, but also on local antiquities [*Antiquitez particulieres*], ancient and modern usages, the means by which the different provinces were reunited to the crown, and the form of government to which they were subjected in diverse times. Above all he wants to be able to compare the practices of the past with those of our own time, in order to form a plan favorable to his future subjects.[57]

Accordingly, Boulainvilliers planned in the historical part of his preface (the "Mémoires historiques") to "extract" from the intendants' reports an "essence" that was palpably historical: "to reduce facts to maxims of government, [and] to discover in the reality of history truths attested by experience [*des véritez éxpérimentales*] which might be applied to our present condition."[58]

Boulainvilliers may have exaggerated history's importance in the original Burgundy inquest, but he did not invent it. He erred in ascribing the

---

Moréri et al., *Le Grand Dictionnaire,* 2:132. Boulainvilliers' work habits were not exceptional. Early-modern narrative historians characteristically "compiled" their works by borrowing from their predecessors—a practice that allowed motifs from medieval chronicles to pass into the new humanistic narratives of the sixteenth and seventeenth centuries; see Ariès, *Le Temps de l'histoire,* 160–4; and Wilfred Hugo Evans, *L'Historien Mézeray et la conception de l'histoire en France au XVIIe siècle* (Paris: Librairie Universitaire J. Gamber, 1930), 13–14, 99–100.

[55]Fréret, "Lettre de M. Fréret," 203. On dating Fréret's "Lettre," see chapter 1, n. 3.
[56]*Etat,* 1, "Mémoires historiques": 11–49, 74–76, 88–89, 93–94, 102–103, 113–15, 117–19, 127–28, 141–46, 150–64, 174–82.
[57]*Etat,* 1, "Préface": xix–xx ("Second partie").
[58]Ibid., vi ("Première partie").

intendants' instructions to the prince, but ascribing initiatives to kings and princes was a polite political fiction commonly employed in the Old Regime and he may have been doing no more than using that fiction once again. Beauvillier's 1697 circular to the intendants made no mention of history; nor did Colbert's 1664 circular which Beauvillier may have dispatched with his own.[59] But history may well have been a prominent theme in the model memorandum on Auvergne that Beauvillier also sent to the intendants along with his circular. Certainly it figured prominently in the majority of the intendants' reports submitted in response: twenty-four out of thirty treated history, eight devoting at least 20 percent to it.[60]

Predictably, however, Boulainvilliers deplored the intendants' uses of French history and sought to put it to uses of his own. The intendants, he complained, "professed to recognize no other principle of government than that of a pure despotism in the prince and his ministers and a blind obedience on the part of his subjects, cruelly suppressing the very names of liberty of persons and property of goods."[61] Against these dangerous men and their dangerous ideas, Boulainvilliers made his own appeal to history: "I call to my assistance the example of past ages, not because I am prejudiced in antiquity's favor beyond the bounds of reason, but because it would be willfully blind to deprive a monarchic regime of the means which have maintained it for thirteen centuries, in order to adopt new means which are commendable only for introducing a despotic power more proper to the spirit of oriental peoples like the Persians or the Turks than to our constitution."[62] Thus he announced his plans to demonstrate, in the "Mémoires historiques," what French political and historical writers had long since sought to demonstrate, that France was *not* a seigneurial monarchy or despotism.

To perform that task—to discover a French "constitution" in the historical past—Boulainvilliers returned once again to his studies of feudalism and its origins, in other words, to historical problems and possibilities which had concerned him long before he became a political writer for the Burgundy Circle. Once again, "leudes" and their "allods," "benefices" and "fiefs" absorbed Boulainvilliers' attention. Once again, he had to account for the late appearance of feudal patrimoniality and

[59]*Etat*, 1, "Mémoire Que sa Majesté a ordonné être envoyé à M^rs. les Maitres des Requêtes, Commissaires, departis dans les Provinces, en 1697" (separately paginated): 1–14 (Colbert's circular); Trénard, *Les Mémoires des intendants,* 89–91 (Beauvillier's circular).
[60]*L'Intendance de Provence,* 47 (introduction by Emmanuelli). Beauvillier's memorandum has not been identified with certainty, but see Trénard, *Les Mémoires des intendants,* 20–22, and works cited there.
[61]*Etat,* 1, "Préface": xx ("Seconde partie").
[62]Ibid.

hierarchy under the later Carolingians. Once again—but now in a single text—he sought to deny, to deplore, and to explain the emergence of a noble elite, lifted by monarchical favor above the noble corps and threatening the solidarity of that noble "nation." Most important, Boulainvilliers once again sought to discover in the feudal past a viable "nation," sustained by its own social and political institutions, and not yet subordinated to the "grandeur" of its kings.

Boulainvilliers drew political lessons from French history at two points in the "Mémoires historiques": toward the beginning, in a long section on the "State of the Frankish Nation [*Nation françoise*]" after its establishment in Gaul; and toward the end, in an account of "feudalism" on the eve of Hugh Capet's accession in 987. In Frankish Gaul, he sought to discover the "essential and primordial law [*droit*]" and the prototype for "the administration [*police*] and the political order that the nation has followed since."[63] The Frankish *champs de mars*, he wrote, was a "parlement" or "general assembly of the nation" empowered to legislate, to deliberate on administrative questions and on matters of state, to declare war, to elect civil and military officers, and to constitute a court of peers wherein every Frank might be judged by his fellows. In that assembly he located supreme political authority among the Franks because, he was convinced, they acknowledged no "master" or "sovereign."[64] This freedom from masters was of course an exclusive freedom, for the Franks were themselves the masters of the Gauls whom they had enserfed at the time of their putative Conquest.[65] Boulainvilliers' chief aim, however, was not to distinguish noble Franks from their Gaulish serfs, though he certainly did that.[66] His chief aim was to insist on the Franks' liberty and equality and draw political lessons from them. In the Franks' assembly he saw precedent for "noble participation in our monarchy's administration." In that assembly's right and duty to declare war he saw a check on bellicose princes and their appetite for

[63]*Etat*, 1, "Mémoires historiques": 15–49 (on Frankish Gaul) and 179–82 (on feudalism); 24 (for quotations).

[64]Ibid., 26–27, 29–30, 46–47; and 25: "The diverse [Frankish] individuals, who had no master, at least found in the common assembly of the the nation's members that superiority without which no external or internal administration [*police*] could subsist." Cf. ibid., 26, 42: In receiving justice from their peers, not from a superior authority surrounded by men of arms, war trophies, and the insignia of "sovereignty," Boulainvilliers' Franks differed from their Gaulish subjects who did indeed receive justice from their Frankish lords in the summary manner just described—that is, "souverainement."

[65]Ibid., 17–19.

[66]He could report the serfs' eventual enfranchisement without deploring it, observing simply that the freed serfs became a Third Estate and joined the Frankish "nation" or nobility in the "state" (*Etat*, 1, "Mémoires historiques": 17).

"glory," a "glory" always purchased, he noted, with the "lives and property" of the "people."[67] And in the Franks' property rights to their own portions of conquered Gaul (booty, land, and serfs) he found evidence that no French king, not even the rapacious Clovis who in a celebrated incident laid claim to a costly vase that had fallen to one of his soldiers, enjoyed "despotic authority" and the right to tax at will.[68] These last lessons were especially important to Boulainvilliers, who drew them again when he wrote about French "feudalism" on the eve of Hugh Capet's accession to the throne. Private property, he said, rested securely in France on foundations established by the Frankish Conquest. But, he added, private property derived still firmer support from French "feudalism."[69] Against a long line of historians and feudists, he insisted that feudal property was not a concession by sovereigns to their subjects. Fiefs, he wrote, were not usurped benefices that Capet confirmed in 987 to secure his newly acquired crown.[70] Against a "crowd of modern flatterers" he argued that "feudalism"—la féodalité—bound kings and their subjects together by "convention" and "reciprocal faith" and secured the property of individuals. In the last pages of the "Mémoires historiques," he intended "to show, by detailing the state of the kingdom at the advent of Kings Hugh and Robert [Hugh Capet's son, who succeeded with him], that this right of property of goods was not created by them, that they found it well and solidly established, and were given the crown only on condition that they maintain it."[71]

Doubtless, the men in the Burgundy Circle would have taken no exception to Boulainvilliers' hatred of "despotism," or to his plea for "aristocratic participation in the administration of the kingdom," or to his remark that kings all too often purchased their "glory" with the "lives and property" of the "people." Yet even in these simple lessons extracted from French history, it is possible to detect tendencies in Bou-

---

[67]Ibid., 25, 46.

[68]Ibid., 15, 21. On the Soissons vase incident, destined to inspire pages of commentary by eighteenth-century historians, see Henri Duranton, "L'Épisode du vase de Soissons vu par les historiens du XVIIIe siècle: Quelques aspects de la pensée historique sous l'Ancien Régime," Revue de synthèse, 96 (1975): 283–316.

[69]Etat, 1, "Mémoires historiques": 179–80.

[70]For that thesis and its exponents see chapter 2. One of Boulainvilliers' cribs (the 1685 edition of Mézeray's Histoire de France) included a statement of that thesis and Boulainvilliers took pains to refute it in his "extracts" on Mézeray's work. See François Eudes de Mézeray, Histoire de France, 2d ed., 2:2–3; B.N., MS. n.a.f. 11091, fols. 161v–163r. Cf. the "Remarques tirées de l'histoire de France" at the end of the B.N.'s MS copy of Boulainvilliers's "extracts" on Longuerue [MS. n.a.f., 11077]). And see Bibliographical Appendix, Part 2.

[71]Etat, 1, "Mémoires historiques": 182 (on "flatterers"); and 180: "Feudalism, which has convention for its principle and the reciprocal faith of the parties for security, obliges kings to us as it obliged us to them, with the one difference that force is on their side."

77

lainvilliers' thought clearly at variance with Fénelon's, for example, or with Saint-Simon's or Beauvillier's. The men in the Burgundy Circle distinguished "despotism" from a legitimate form of absolute monarchy; Boulainvilliers tended to identify "despotism" *with* absolute monarchy while distinguishing them both from polities where no "sovereignty" existed at all, or where it resided in "assemblies" of a (Frankish) "nation" or in the provisions of the "feudal law" which (as Boulainvilliers described it at the end of the "Mémoires historiques") let feudatories not only own but also "govern" their provinces.[72]

Once again, one finds Boulainvilliers constituting as his object of study a French "nation" independent of the crown. In fact (remarkably in a work written for Louis XIV's heir apparent), Boulainvilliers' histories of the French "nation" and monarchy turn out to be mutually antagonistic histories. And their conflict turns on feudalism.

Feudalism stands at the heart of Boulainvilliers' historical and political argument in the "Mémoires historiques." And at the heart of Boulainvilliers' history of feudalism stands Jean Le Laboureur's account. Le Laboureur's "Traité" or "Histoire de la pairie de France" had already attracted Boulainvilliers' sustained attention. A stern critic of Le Laboureur, and of the ducal aspirations to preeminence over the rest of the nobility which Le Laboureur sought to defend, Boulainvilliers nevertheless learned from him too, often borrowing from him to refute him. Boulainvilliers already had absorbed many of Le Laboureur's ideas about land tenure and personal status in Frankish France when he composed his "Mémoires historiques." In that work he at last acknowledged the ducal antiquarian, whom he now called "a very capable modern," as his guide.[73]

A reader acquainted with Boulainvilliers' earlier reflections on Frankish France and on Le Laboureur's "Traité" will not be surprised to read in the "Mémoires historiques" that the ancient Franks were all free and equal "peers" or *leudes* or *fideles*. Le Laboureur had said as much, and Boulainvilliers already had seized upon that admission to refute Le Laboureur's argument for ducal preeminence over the rest of the French nobility.[74] Boulainvilliers did so again in the "Mémoires histori-

[72]Ibid., 180: "As for Flanders, we have seen that Charlemagne granted its care to a count who took the title of Forester and who governed it so well that despite the ravages of the Northmen it became one of the most considerable provinces of France, having repopulated itself within less than a century." On the traditional royalism and absolutism of the Burgundy Circle see works cited in n. 11.

[73]*Etat*, 1, "Mémoires historiques": 155, for the quotation. See [Le Laboureur], *Histoire de la pairie*, and chapter 2 on that work and its earlier impact on Boulainvilliers.

[74]See [Le Laboureur], *Histoire de la pairie*, 2:99–100; see also chapter 2.

ques." He carefully eliminated from his account of the Frankish past anything suggesting a legally constituted and hereditary order superior to the Frankish "nation" as a whole. Hence "seigneurs" of "birth and valor," encountered in the 1700 "Dissertation," become "seniores" and chosen "elders" in the "Mémoires historiques."[75]

Boulainvilliers added two new dimensions to his thinking on Frankish France, however. One was his claim that Frankish France was *not* a monarchy or despotism (virtual synonyms in Boulainvilliers' political lexicon), for he held that free and equal Franks could never have been "subjects" of a royal "master" enjoying "sovereign, monarchic, or despotic" authority over them.[76] The other was a willingness to *feudalize* Frankish France. Like Le Laboureur, Boulainvilliers placed his free and equal Franks in a web of effectively feudal relationships. Their allods were still free properties, yet they were military tenures too, for all of Boulainvilliers' Franks were military men, they had to serve in the "nation"'s armies, and if they refused then the "common assembly of all the members of the nation" might take their allods from them.[77] The *leude*'s allod thus became "a continuation of the militia because it was the price and recompense of military service" and just as there was a hierarchy of military command so too there was a hierarchy of allods, ranked

[75]*Etat,* 1, "Mémoires historiques," 24, 40–43, 47, on *seigneurs, thungins, or centeniers,* chosen by each "hundred" for their age and experience to be military leaders, presiding judges (Boulainvilliers applauded the ancient Franks' refusal to divide political labor between "men of war" and "men of the robe"), and spokesmen for each hundred at legislative "assemblies" of the "nation." Cf. *Essais,* 20–21, 25–27; also see chapter 2, p. 26.

[76]*Etat,* 1, "Mémoires historiques": 16–17:

It is absolutely contrary to the truth and to the spirit of the ancient Franks to imagine that among them royal authority was sovereign, monarchic, or despotic, so that individuals were subject to it for life, property, liberty, honor, and fortune. On the contrary . . . all the Franks were free and therefore they were not subjects. . . . They were all companions and so they were called *leudes,* from the German word *Leuth,* which they used among themselves; it means compatriots, people of the same society and condition. Translated into Latin, this term was *fidelis* and that is why kings used it in the salutations of their most ancient ordinances: *omnibus regni fidelibus,* to all the *Fidelles* [sic] of the kingdom. . . . kings treated the Franks (who were their inferiors in dignity and authority) as they [the Franks] treated each other. They were all reciprocally *leudes, fideles,* companions, and not subjects. Indeed, could one believe that the Franks, freeborn and sovereignly jealous of this quality, would have employed their blood and effort to make a conquest, simply to give themselves a master rather than a king? Could one believe that the Franks would have sought to acquire slaves simply to become slaves themselves?

One of Boulainvilliers' first posthumous critics failed to find the *omnibus regni fidelibus* formula in ancient texts. In fact Boulainvilliers had found it in Le Laboureur's *Histoire de la pairie,* 1:63. See Etienne Laureault de Foncemagne, "Examen critique d'une opinion de M. le comte de Boulainvilliers sur l'ancien gouvernement de la France" (paper read April 22, 1732), in *Mémoires de littérature, tirez des registres de l'Académie Royale des Inscriptions et Belles Lettres,* vol. 10 (Paris: Imprimerie Royale, 1736), 539.

[77]*Etat,* 1, "Mémoires historiques": 15, 20, 21, 25–26.

according to their "different degrees of vassalage."[78] Boulainvilliers detected this hierarchy in the Franks' "assemblies" as well. On the *champs de mars,* he wrote, the "state" organized itself in military units ("hundreds" or *centaines*) within which the members of the "nation" deliberated.[79] By feudalizing the Franks' allods and assemblies Boulainvilliers endowed Frankish antiquity with a protofeudalism anticipating the classical feudalism of the Middle Ages. The only difference was that among Boulainvilliers' Franks a "nation," not a king or "suzerain," stood at the pinnacle of the hierarchy and constituted the ultimate object of political loyalty. Frankish kings and generals, Boulainvilliers claimed, were merely officers elected by the "nation," thus ascribing to the Franks in sixth-century Gaul arrangements that the Roman historian Tacitus had claimed to discover among the barbarians in second-century Germany.[80]

Assigning a kind of protofeudalism to the Franks had its ideological advantages for Boulainvilliers, a man committed to the rehabilitation of feudalism. This strategy let him escape the allodial antifeudalism that deplored the insecurity and dependency of feudal tenure, for by feudalizing the allod, he implicitly allodialized the fief and turned it into a secure property. In this way, he also sought to disarm the royalist antifeudalism that traced feudalism to aristocratic "anarchy" and "usurpation": by feudalizing the allod, he gave the fief an ancient and legitimate ancestor.

Boulainvilliers knew that French feudalism had emerged slowly, however, owing to political disintegration under the later Carolingians and to the "usurpation" by great magnates of the "benefices" entrusted to them. He knew that French feudalism matured fully only in the ninth, tenth, and eleventh centuries. He had embraced that conventional (and correct) interpretation in earlier works and continued to embrace it in the "Mémoires historiques."[81]

Yet, to tell that story, Boulainvilliers again began in Frankish antiquity, with an account of the "benefices" that the first kings of France granted to their servants. The benefice, of course, was the fief's true

[78]Ibid., 24.

[79]Ibid., 24 (on the army) and 47 (on the assembly).

[80]Ibid., 16, quoting Tacitus in the *Germania:* "Reges ex nobilitate, duces ex virtute sumunt. . . ." On the basis of other evidence, Le Laboureur (*Histoire de la pairie,* 2:18–19) had already advanced a similar "opinion"—that kings and generals were separate "dignities" among the ancient Franks—but Le Laboureur let *his* Franks elect only their generals. See also Boulainvilliers' 1700 "Dissertation" (*Essais,* 48–51) for the analogous (and peculiar) arguments that a "palace" was an "army" and that the Merovingians' "mayor of the palace" was a military commander distinct from the Frankish king himself.

[81]*Etat,* 1, "Mémoires historiques": 137, 138, 142, 142–43, 144–45, 164.

institutional ancestor, and so Boulainvilliers' decision to begin this alternative account of fief's history with the Franks' benefices was by no means an arbitrary one. But in the "Mémoires historiques" the benefice became a source of grave disorders destined to afflict Merovingian and Carolingian France. The benefice, according to Boulainvilliers, belonged to an "exterior administration" or *police extérieure* that his Franks had imposed on regions of Gaul south of the Seine, where they had settled too thinly to impropriate all the territory and its inhabitants. There, in "Aquitaine," the Franks established what was in effect government by an occupying army. There they garrisoned troops supported by local tribute stored in "public storehouses" or *magasins publics*, and they installed magistrates called "dukes," "counts," and "vicars" sustained by local land grants called "benefices."[82] Boulainvilliers' sources for his account of an "exterior administration" remain uncertain, though his propensity to schematize may be partly responsible for it.[83] In any case, these *seigneurs bénéficiés* or "beneficed lords" entered French history, as Boulainvilliers wrote it in his "Mémoires historiques," to subvert Frankish liberty and equality. These "beneficed lords" were dangerous men, especially after their introduction into the Frankish heartlands of the north, for they owed their offices and lands not to the "nation" but to the ambitious king who created and awarded their magistracies: Clovis.[84] To enhance his own power, already magnified because he had combined the Franks' kingship with supreme military command over their armies (functions usually entrusted to two separate individuals), Clovis corrupted the ancient Franks.[85] Extending beneficed magistracies throughout Gaul and using them as plums of royal patronage, he taught the Franks to disdain "the possession of a mediocre heritage," prescribed by "common law" but far less impressive that the government of several towns. Thanks to Clovis, the Franks lost the "sentiment of the common interest" that had once animated them. Now "ambition" guided them as they followed new and dangerous routes to

[82]*Etat*, 1, "Mémoires historiques": 23–24.

[83]Boulainvilliers remarked, "No author has given us a detailed description of it [the exterior administration]; but it seems that everything that I have said about it is sufficiently based on historical facts that few ignore" (ibid., 24). Mézeray, whom he cites on the Franks' divisions of lands in Gaul (22–3), may have given him some of his ideas: in the *Abrégé chronologique, extraict de l'Histoire de France* (first published in 1667–68), Mézeray referred to the Franks' "Magazines for the subsistence of their Forces" (*A General Chronological History of France*, tr. John Bulteel [London: 1683], 17). Boulainvilliers probably localized the "exterior administration" in Aquitaine because, he was convinced, in northern France where the Franks settled densely they constituted a landed army whose soldiers lived off the proceeds of their own estates (see *Etat*, 1, "Mémoires historiques": 101, 113–14).

[84]*Etat*, 1, "Mémoires historiques": 10–15, esp. 11, and 34–37.

[85]Ibid., 16.

"fortune," routes, Boulainvilliers remarked ominously, which resembled those available to ambitious men in his own time: "The ways or means of fortune were practically the same as they are in our day, with the exception of the venality of employments." Soon, "the great men of the state" distinguished themselves from the "ordinary men" and excluded those "ordinary men" from the "nation's" assemblies. And an aristocratic democracy—Boulainvilliers described it as "a sort of aristocracy" whose members were all free and equal—became a "monarchy" sustained by an ambitious oligarchy of grandees: "We may say that the principle of union, which established the monarchy on the ruins of a sort of aristocracy that had been its cradle, was nothing but the misguided ambition of individuals."[86]

It may by now be apparent that Boulainvilliers recounted *two* histories of feudalism in the "Mémoires historiques." One was a history of liberty, equality, and feudalized allods held of a "nation," and the other a history of inequality, ambition, and rich benefices granted by a "monarchy" and eventually "usurped" by the "great men" to whom they had been entrusted. That second history runs throughout his narrative, and in it "beneficed lords" were plainly the villains. Under the successors to Clovis, "beneficed lords" monopolized the assemblies of the "state," pursued their own "particular interest," sacrificed to it the "interest of the state," and plunged that "state" into the civil wars endemic in Merovingian France.[87] Carolingian France, too, was a France dominated by ambitious magnates bent on the "usurpation" of the benefices entrusted to them.[88]

Like his first history of feudalism, Boulainvilliers' second had ideological functions. His account of "beneficed lords" and their "ambition" recalls his attacks on the intendants and *their* ambition; it may be one more polemic against those servants of modern absolutism. More likely, however, it was a polemic against the dukes and peers. To assert their corporate preeminence over the nobility, the seventeenth-century peerage claimed as its institutional ancestors the great feudal vassals of medieval kings, and the dukes and counts of ancient Frankish monarchs. Boulainvilliers, because of his close reading of Le Laboureur's "Traité," was well acquainted with those claims and had already sought to rebut them formally in his notes on Le Laboureur. In effect, he was doing so again in his "Mémoires historiques," with what amounts to a cautionary tale about the dukes and peers' putative corporate ancestors:

[86]Ibid., 34; and 16, 20, 37 (on "venality"), and 47–48.
[87]Ibid., 49–103, esp. 88–89: a long indictment of the eighth-century *grands* who had "practically no principle but their ambition and natural ferocity."
[88]Ibid., 137, 138, 142, 142–43, 144–45, 164.

the villainous "beneficed lords." That cautionary tale was also an indictment of "monarchy," however. For just as his account of feudalized
allods held of a "nation" belonged to his history of that "nation," so too
his account of benefices, "beneficed lords," and their "usurpations" was
integral to his history of the French "monarchy," and of the "ambition"
and "interest" disfiguring it and the elites that served it, used it, and
derived their being from it.

The establishment by Clovis of "monarchy" on the "ruins" of "aristocracy" seems to be the dramatic climax of French history as Boulain-
villviers wrote it. With Clovis, it appears, French liberty died an early
death while the ambition of kings, the egoism of their clients, and the
heedlessness of their subjects now determined the course of French
history.[89] Boulainvilliers' reading of French history was not so simple,
however. His mythical Charlemagne and the conceptual and rhetorical
functions performed by that commanding figure in the "Mémoires historiques" have yet to be considered.

French history as Boulainvilliers wrote it in his "Mémoires historiques"—particularly in his original sections on Carolingian mayors and
monarchs or on early Capetian kings—was a dreary tale of ambition and
neglect. Like another Clovis, Boulainvilliers' Charles Martel (the celebrated early-eighth-century mayor of the palace) crushed Frankish liberty and equality by destroying Frankish assemblies and armies and by
installing troops of his own on confiscated church lands.[90] French liberty
fared no better under Martel's son Pepin, the first Carolingian king: he
revived the Franks' assemblies, Boulainvilliers admitted, but packed
them with prelates to regain their favor, enlist their "credit" with the
"people," and secure their aid in dethroning the "do-nothing" Merovingians and installing his own house in their place.[91] The mid-eighth-
century Franks whom Pepin ruled, Boulainvilliers insisted, no longer
resembled their free and glorious ancestors. "These are no longer the
freeborn and independent Franks, more attached to their ancient laws
than to their own lives, who elected their kings and generals in perfect

[89]Henry St. John, Viscount Bolingbroke interpreted Boulainvilliers in precisely this
fashion for his English readers in the 1720s (*The Works of Lord Bolingbroke*, 4 vols. [New
York: Augustus M. Kelley, 1967]: 2:133–34 [Bolingbroke's "Dissertation on Parties"]).
[90]*Etat*, 1, "Mémoires historiques": 59, 65, 66, 69, 88–90, 93–94, 102–3. Here Boulainvilliers relied on Mézeray who, writing on Martel's use of confiscated church lands to
support his army, even suggested that Martel founded the feudal nobility: "It is certain
that one can call Martel the institutor of the nobility, since he gave it fiefs and enfeoffed
tithes" (*Histoire de France, depuis Faramond jusqu'à maintenant*, 3 vols. [Paris: Matthieu
Guillemot, 1643–51], 1:139; see 1:125–47 for Mézeray's account of Martel).
[91]*Etat*, 1, "Mémoires historiques": 101–2, 105, 108.

freedom, and who enjoyed in glory and tranquillity a conquest which they owed to their valor and perseverance in an infinitely difficult enterprise. They were conquered in turn not by a foreign nation but by a particular family, like the others in origin, [but one] which was more ambitious and which knew how to take advantage of all the events that occurred and of all the circumstances that arose across a century."[92]

Like his Carolingians, Boulainvilliers' Capetians were usurpers who profited from their predecessors' decadence and their subjects' corruption. Thanks to "address," "subtlety," and, indeed, a deliberate act of "usurpation" consummating the ambitions of his clan, Hugh Capet mounted the throne in 987.[93] Boulainvilliers argued, and not without reason, that no proper Frankish assembly or "parlement" elected Capet. Arguing against Mézeray (whose *Histoire*, it will be remembered, was one of his cribs), he claimed that no such assembly could have gathered in the short interval between the death of the last Carolingian on May 22 and the consecration of Hugh at Rheims on July 3. That Hugh had indeed called an assembly at Noyon at the end of May Boulainvilliers did not deny. But, like the assembly or "parlement" that had named Pepin king of the Franks two centuries earlier, the Noyon assembly, once Hugh Capet had purged it, was little more than a gathering dominated by "his own principal feudatories," a judgment modern historians would not deny.[94]

These were remarkable assertions for an author addressing (at least ostensibly) the grandson and heir of Louis XIV, and Boulainvilliers tried to mitigate them. The Capetians, he claimed, were an "illustrious race" of "princes great and worthy of an eternal veneration," and he professed to admire "the particular successes of the branch of the Bourbons and . . . the glory of the two last reigns, which one may regard as the summit of this family's prosperity." The Bourbons, he added, could take pride and comfort in the "constant possession of a single throne across more than 700 years," in the "providence" that sustained their house, and in the "fidelity, the "constant obedience" and the "oaths" of their subjects.[95] Yet Boulainvilliers refused to ascribe any electoral or hereditary legitimacy to the three "races" of French kings.

[92]Ibid., 108.

[93]Ibid., 175, 176. Cf. ibid., 159–63, 165–67, on the earlier Capetian (or "Robertian") kings Eudes (reigned 888–893) and Robert (reigned 922–923).

[94]Ibid., 175–76. Boulainvilliers relied on a "famous letter" of Gerbert of Rheims printed by Duchesne but ignored by Mézeray. For Mézeray's account of Capet's accession and for Boulainvilliers' earlier refutations of it see sources cited in n. 70. Cf. Laurent Theis, *L'Avènement d'Hugues Capet: 3 juillet 987* (Paris: Gallimard—N.R.F., 1984), 14–17, relying on Richer's *Histoire de France* dedicated to Gerbert.

[95]*Etat*, 1, "Mémoires historiques": 159, 174, 179.

For although myths of dynastic continuity captivated French historians and their readers in the seventeenth and eighteenth centuries,
Boulainvilliers dismissed such claims as tissues of "entirely absurd facts,
[fabricated] in the thought of meriting well of the reigning house," and
he resolutely deprived the Capetians of Carolingian and Merovingian
ancestors.[96] Predictably, he had no use for the elaborate and articulate
tradition of dynastic throne right, with its myths about the Salic Law,
immutable dynastic custom, and the "rights of blood."[97] He recognized
the Capetians' right to rule, but on patently nondynastic and plainly less
mysterious grounds, and only after having reduced the French monarchy's history to a history of usurping dynasties. Not surprisingly, one
of Boulainvilliers' earliest posthumous critics, the impeccably royalist
academician Etienne Laureault de Foncemagne, rose to refute his antimonarchical account of the monarchy's origins and character.[98]

There is, however, a striking exception to Boulainvilliers' dreary history of French monarchs in his portrayal of Charlemagne. Boulainvilliers created nothing less than a myth of Charlemagne and placed it at
the conceptual and rhetorical center of his "Mémoires historiques."[99]
The memory of Charlemagne had long been shrouded in legends about
his creation of the peers or "paladins," for example, or his establishment
of fiefs. Despite the critical acumen of Renaissance scholars, these legends survived in the work of narrative historians who characteristically
borrowed their materials from their predecessors. Thus Boulainvilliers
took from Mézeray who had himself borrowed it from earlier authors
the fanciful notion that Charlemagne, having found feudalism in Lombardy when he conquered that Italian kingdom in 774, imported it into

[96]Ibid., 159–63, 159 for quotation. Cf. Tyvaert, "L'Image du roi," 527–29; and Henri
Duranton, "Le Mythe de la continuité monarchique chez les historiens français du
XVIIIème siècle," in *Modèles et moyens de la réflexion politique au XVIIIe siècle: Tome troisième:
Débats et combats idéologiques* (Lille: Université de Lille III, 1979), 203–26. Seventeenth-
century *érudits* also sought to establish the Carolingian ancestry of the Capetians in order
to defend their dynastic preeminence and territorial claims against the House of Habsburg
(Nathan Edelman, *Attitudes of Seventeenth-Century France toward the Middle Ages* [New York:
King's Crown Press, 1946], 49–50).
[97]Giesey, "The Juristic Basis of Dynastic Right to the French Throne."
[98]Foncemagne, "Examen critique d'une opinion de M. le comte de Boulainvilliers,"
526–36. Foncemagne exposed serious weaknesses in Boulainvilliers' accounts of ancient
French history, notably the use, in the "Mémoires historiques," of the second-century
Tacitus as a source for fifth- and sixth-century Franks. He also refuted the claim, in the
1700 "Dissertation," that mayors of the palace (actually household officers) were military
commanders similar to the *duces* of the Germans in Tacitus. See n. 80.
[99]Not, however, because of any "inadequacy" that Boulainvilliers may have discovered
in his Frankish Conquest myth; cf. Price, "Boulainvillier and the Myth of the Frankish
Conquest of Gaul," 155–85, esp. 157–58.

some of his Frankish dominions.[100] Boulainvilliers expanded that habitual commonplace into an admiring portrait of Charlemagne as a beneficent innovator who instituted French feudalism and thereby laid the foundations for a sound political, military, and fiscal order:

> It is apparent that Charlemagne altered this disposition [the Merovingian order], he who innovated in so many other matters of government and who laid it on entirely new foundations. We have seen that the Lombard administration [*police*] appeared to him so beautiful that he adopted much of it and . . . if one considers the disposition of manners and affairs at the time, and even if one considers the matter abstractly, nothing is so good and commodious as the order of fiefs. It establishes a revenue fixed and yet subject to necessary augmentation; it establishes a military service of effective troops, always ready as occasions arise [and] which, similarly, can be augmented in numbers according to need. Besides, this order, by making men owners of their goods, interests them in the conservation of the whole, and employs to this end the liveliest passions that exist in nature: love of oneself and of one's well-being, and love of one's family and kin.[101]

In these lines, Boulainvilliers completed his rehabilitation of feudalism. Here he finally allodialized the fief: feudalism makes men "owners of their goods." Above all he secured for feudalism the approval of kings. True, he still admitted that fiefs were benefices usurped by their holders under the later Carolingians.[102] But he could now represent those usurpations as acts consonant with royal will. Accordingly, he described Charles the Bald's capitulary of Kiersy or Quiercy-sur-Oise (877)—that act conceded the heredity of counties under carefully specified circumstances—as a full royal authorization of feudal patrimoniality, "something that appeared in no other public act."[103] Similarly,

[100]*Etat*, 1, "Memoires historiques": 113–14. Mézeray, *Histoire de France* (1685 ed.), 1:398. One of Mézeray's own sources was the sixteenth-century historian and scholar Bernard de Girard Du Haillan, who knew and appreciated Renaissance scholarship (Donald R. Kelley, *Foundations of Modern Historical Scholarship. Language, Law, and History in the French Renaissance* [New York: Columbia University Press, 1970], 233–38) and yet preserved the myth that Charlemagne instituted fiefs in France. Indeed, Du Haillan pronounced it the most widely adopted view on the origin of fiefs (*De l'estat et succez des affaires de France*, fol. 28v; see also his *L'histoire de France*, 229–32). See n. 54.

[101]*Etat*, 1, "Mémoires historiques": 152.

[102]Ibid., 137, 138, 142, 142–43, 144–45, 164. See esp. 138: an observation that great fiefs became hereditary only during the troubled reign of Charles the Simple (893–923). This was a commonly held view when Boulainvilliers wrote; cf. Marcel, *Histoire de l'origine et des progrez de la monarchie françoise*, 1:190n.: "It is . . . the most common opinion that fiefs did not begin to become patrimonial until the reign of Charles the Simple."

[103]*Etat*, 1, "Mémoires historiques": 143–45. This is an early instance of that eighteenth- and nineteenth-century myth of the Edict of Quiercy as a constitutional charter surveyed and demolished in Emile Bourgeois, *Le Capitulaire de Kiersy-sur-Oise (877): Etude sur l'état et*

Boulainvilliers transformed the impropriation and subinfeudation of benefices—the "aristocratic usurpation" and "feudal anarchy" commonly deplored by the historians and jurists of early-modern France—into the natural consequences of Charlemagne's decision to introduce fiefs into some regions of France and "sow the seeds of feudalism [*la féodalité*], which bore their fruit in their own time, though nourished among the thorns of the cruelest divisions."[104]

In the legendary Charlemagne, Boulainvilliers reconciled his antagonistic histories of "monarchy" and "nation." A magnanimous prince and legislator, Boulainvilliers' Charlemagne rose above the ambitions of ordinary monarchs to establish feudalism and thereby secure the "nation"'s well-being. For these reasons Charlemagne occupies the conceptual center of the "Mémoires historiques."

For these same reasons Charlemagne occupies the rhetorical center of that narrative. Although the "nation" acquired its own history in that work, Boulainvilliers wrote it for a prince and his advisers. As a rhetorical performance, therefore, it may be included among the crown-centered narrative histories of France typical of the Old Regime, dynastic histories which performed the same pedagogical and panegyrical functions that aristocratic family histories typically performed and which spoke to living kings and princes by speaking about dead ones.[105] In the "Mémoires historiques" Boulainvilliers spoke to the duc de Bourgogne by speaking about Charlemagne, the "greatest king the French monarchy ever had" and therefore the finest model for the duc de Bourgogne to emulate.[106]

This explains Charlemagne's reappearance in the last pages of the "Mémoires historiques" despite Boulainvilliers' refusal to include him among Bourgogne's own ancestors. At the end of the "Mémoires historiques" Boulainvilliers had no more reverence for the dynastic mystique than he had had before, and he insisted once again that the reigning house "does not descend from Charlemagne."[107] He acknowledged its throne right; he even hinted that it might rest on French dynastic custom (the "Salic Law"). Jurists commenting on that custom typically claimed that kings acquired their crown from the law, not from their ancestors as if it were a family property. Boulainvilliers echoed those jurists when he wrote, "kings and peoples err equally in imagining that

le régime politique de la société carolingienne à la fin du IXe siècle d'après la législation de Charles le Chauve (Paris: Hachette, 1885), esp. 155–205, on the myth's history (Boulainvilliers is one of its earliest proponents).

[104]*Etat*, 1, "Mémoires historiques": 152.
[105]Ranum, *Artisans of Glory*, 3–17, on "Dynastic History and Service."
[106]*Etat*, 1, "Mémoires historiques": 117.
[107]Ibid., 180.

crowns are patrimonial."[108] Yet Boulainvilliers did not ground the Capetians' right to rule in dynastic custom—rather he grounded it in "possession," in the "supereminent rule of Destiny," and above all in the respect for their subjects' "property in their goods" that distinguished, or ought to have distinguished, the Capetian monarchs. He wrote: "If I believe fully and from the bottom of my heart in the perfectly incontestable right of the royal house, I have no less firm an opinion of that of the peoples to property in their goods, whether one considers it at the beginning, that is at the first Conquest [of Gaul], or during the decadence of the monarchy under the second race."[109] Royal respect for property was "a principle no less sacred for them [kings] than that which teaches among us the necessity of obedience."[110] Indeed, kings had to respect their subjects' property rights, Boulainvilliers insisted, for these derive from Scripture, from conquest (be it Israel's conquest of Canaan or the Franks' conquest of Gaul), and above all from the feudalism that developed "during the decadence of the monarchy under the second race."[111] Proclaiming feudalism "our best title," he embarked on a brief survey of France in A.D. 987—when the duc de Bourgogne's ancestors, "kings Hugh and Robert," mounted the throne—to demonstrate that "this right of [feudal] property in goods was not instituted by them, that they found it well and solidly established, and that the crown was given to them only on condition that they maintain it [this right]."[112] Even as he wrote about the kings who had established Bourgogne's own house on the throne, however, Boulainvilliers remembered the earlier monarch who had established the conditions for their rule by introducing into France the "feudal law" which had been "consecrated by the esteem in which Charlemagne held it."[113]

At the end of the "Mémoires historiques," Boulainvilliers thanked "heaven" that French kings "abhor . . . the maxims of Mohammedanism and the barbarous law of the Orient which annihilates property in goods." And he praised the "education" of French "princes" which taught them to prefer "naive truth" to "a flattering and dissembling history."[114] Those remarks suggest a writer anxious to remind Bourgogne that France was not a "seigneurial monarchy" or "despotism" and

---

[108]Ibid., 179; Giesey, "The Juristic Basis of Dynastic Right." For the position that Boulainvilliers criticized see Rowen, *The King's State.*
[109]*Etat*, 1, "Mémoires historiques": 179.
[110]Ibid., 180.
[111]Ibid., 179; for the conquest of Canaan see 180.
[112]Ibid., 180–82, 180 for the quotation.
[113]Ibid., 180.
[114]Ibid., 182.

that his duty was to eschew the rampant fiscalism of his grandfather.[115] They also reveal a writer anxious to count on Bourgogne's goodwill, for (he sought to suggest) a less well-educated and well-disposed prince might not find the "naive truth" of the "Mémoires historiques" pleasing. When one recalls that for Boulainvilliers feudalism was a matter of politics as well as of property, it is tempting to detect here one more indication of Boulainvilliers' difficulties as an author writing for Louis XIV's heir and his entourage.

Boulainvilliers and the Burgundy Circle

No record survives, unfortunately, of the reception with which the intended readers of the "Mémoires historiques" greeted it. In fact, they may have never laid eyes on it, for Boulainvilliers never finished it. He closed it with a carefully orchestrated conclusion, but he had originally intended to carry his history of French government beyond the accession of the Capetians and down to the present.[116] Moreover, some manuscript copies of his work contain plans for a still more ambitious preface to the *Etat de la France*. After the sections on the intendants and on the history of French government, there were to have been two further sections, one designed "to examine politically and even philosophically the causes of the present ills and to attempt to discover remedies for them," and the other intended to collect Boulainvilliers' "many genealogical researches and a considerable number of ennoblements which are worth conserving, particularly when one has taken so much trouble to assemble them." No trace of these texts survives.[117] It is inviting to suppose that Boulainvilliers reduced the scope of his project as he worked to finish it between March 1711 and January 1712: the Burgundy Circle's short *annus mirabilis* when nothing stood between Bourgogne and the crown but the aging Louis XIV, and when Bourgogne's friends hastened to plan the "reforms" they hoped he would implement upon mounting the throne. It is equally tempting to suspect that Boulainvilliers abandoned his project unfinished when Bourgogne died in January 1712.[118] In either case, Boulainvilliers' history of French

[115]Ibid., 180, 182 (against "despotism" and the "despotic maxims" of modern flatterers").
[116]*Etat*, 1, "Préface": i.
[117]See, for example, B.N., MS. f.f. 8137, pp. 4–5; B.M., Angoulême, MS. 23, pp. 246–47; B.M., Dijon, MS. 682 [409¹], fols. 4r–v. No trace survives of this elaborate preface, unless one includes the notes on provincial nobility extracted from the intendants' reports of 1697–1700: Bibliothèque de l'Ecole de Médecine de Montpellier, MS. H.193 ("Recherches généralles de la noblesse en France, par M. de Boulainvilliers").
[118]As Nicolas Fréret suggested in 1722 ("Lettre de M. Fréret," 202); see chapter 1, n. 3.

government seems to have been a project overtaken by events and abandoned by its author until new political circumstances led him to return to it.[119]

Although one cannot know how the men in the Burgundy Circle responded to the "Mémoires historiques," it is likely that if they did see it they deplored it—and not because of its account of the Frankish Conquest. That account raised a celebrated controversy after Boulainvilliers' death, because he harshly insisted that when the Franks conquered Gaul, they reduced the Gallo-Romans dwelling there to servitude.[120] In all other respects his account of the Conquest was conventional—his contemporaries commonly traced the origins of the French monarchy and nobility to the ancient Franks—and in fact he cribbed his pages on the Conquest itself from earlier writers.[121] Besides, Boulainvilliers did not systematically exalt free Franks over enserfed Gauls: his learning prevented that.[122] But he consistently asserted the liberty and equality of his conquering Franks and consistently identified aggrandizing kings

[119]There is, admittedly, a remark in Boulainvilliers' "Préface" that seems to disallow this hypothesis; namely, that, of all the intendants who had submitted reports in 1697–1700, only the intendant of Languedoc—namely Bâville—was still at his post (*Etat*, 1, "Préface": xv ["Première partie"]). That comment is troubling because in 1711–12 not only Bâville but also Gaspard Le Gendre, intendant at nearby Montpellier, still held the posts they had occupied in 1697–1700. But Bâville's notoriety could easily have led Boulainvilliers to overlook Le Gendre. Besides, Boulainvilliers often revised his works (Moréri et al., *Le Grand dictionnaire*, 2:133) and could have added his remark about Bâville in 1715–16, that is, after Le Gendre's resignation in 1713 but before Bâville's in 1718 (see lists of intendants in *Almanach Royal* [Paris: d'Houry, 1700–1792], for 1711 to 1718) and at a moment when Boulainvilliers or men near him were trying (unsuccessfully) to publish the "Mémoires historiques" (*Nouvelles littéraires, contenant ce qui se passe de plus considérable dans la rèpublique . . . des lettres*, 4 [1716]: 156–57; and see chapter 1, n. 7). Perhaps this explains the abridged versions of the "Mémoires historiques" to be found in MSS omitting the passages cribbed from Longuerue and Mézeray (e.g. Bibliothèque du Sénat, Paris, MS. 258) and (even more severely abridged) in *Histoire de l'ancien gouvernement de la France, avec XIV. lettres historiques sur les anciens parlements ou états généraux de la France*, 3 vols. (Amsterdam and The Hague: 1727), 1 (for this edition see Bibliographical Appendix, Part 5).

[120]*Etat*, 1, "Mémoires historiques": 17–19.

[121]*Etat*, 1, "Préface": xxiii–xxvii, and "Mémoires historiques": 1–10. See Bibliographical Appendix, Part 2. For Old Regime writing on the Franks see Barzun, *The French Race;* Lombard, *L'Abbé Du Bos*, pt. 2. Hardly an original historian of Frankish antiquity like his young acquaintance Fréret, he probably had less influence on him than has been supposed. See Nicolas Fréret, "De l'Origine des français et de leur établissement dans la Gaule," in *Mémoires de l'Institut Impérial de France: Académie des Inscriptions et Belles-Lettres*, vol. 23 (Paris: Imprimerie Impériale, 1868), pt. 1, pp. 323–559 (read at the Académie on November 14 and December 11 and 14, 1714); and Simon, *Nicolas Fréret, académicien*, 18–20 and 130–39, esp. 133–38 (an argument for Boulainvilliers' influence on Fréret).

[122]Acquainted with the text of the ancient Salic Law, and with Jerome Bignon's commentaries on it, he appreciated that there were free as well as servile Gauls or Gallo-Romans in the Frankish dominions, although he sought to sink these Gaulish freemen (*ingénus* or *ingenui*) into the "subjected nation" because they paid taxes (*Etat*, 1, "Mémoires historiques": 32).

and their clientèles of ambitious grandees, lords, and royal servants as the enemies of that liberty and equality. Here, in the antagonism between the Frankish "nation" and the monarchy lies the drama of French history as Boulainvilliers wrote it.

And here, in his suspicions of kings and the great elites that arose to serve them, lie some of the likeliest reasons for his difficulties with the Burgundy Circle, difficulties visible in his efforts to write and rewrite his prefatory diatribe against the intendants. Doubtless, Bourgogne and his friends shared Boulainvilliers' antipathy to the intendants. Doubtless, too, they shared the "tender and compassionate concern [*distinction*] for the old nobility" that Boulainvilliers claimed to admire in the prince.[123] They did not share Boulainvilliers' suspicions of kings, however, and could not possibly have shared his antiducal animus which may be also be detected in the "Mémoires historiques." Beauvillier, Chevreuse, and Saint-Simon were all dukes and peers, and proud of it.[124] Finally, it is likely that they did not share his admiration for feudalism, despite the ducal pride that animated such men as Beauvillier and Saint-Simon. The men in the Burgundy circle were loyal servants of their absolute king, not "neo-feudal types."[125] Only the most unusual dynastic conjunctures would lead such men to look to the feudal past for means to solve problems arising in the present.

Despite his connections with Beauvillier, therefore, a deep ideological chasm separated Boulainvilliers from his readers in the Burgundy Circle and accounts for the uncertain rhetoric he used to represent himself and his work to them: the fictional distance between the prince and the historian who wrote for him, the prayer that "Providence" would bring his message to the prince's attention by some "indirect route," and the passing allusions to the "public" character of the intendants' reports of 1697 or the instructions to which they responded, as if a public space were necessary to accommodate the ideological gap that divided the prince and his entourage from the nobleman who wrote French history to counsel them. For despite these uneasy fictions, Boulainvilliers' "Mémoires historiques" and the *Etat de la France* to which it belonged were not public utterances but discreet acts of counsel communicated by manuscript to his first readers and badly designed to please them.

[123]*Etat*, 1, "Préface": i ("Première partie"); see also sources in n. 39.
[124]See Lizerand, *Le Duc de Beauvillier*, 363–64.
[125]Mettam, "Role of the Higher Aristocracy," 66.

4

Boulainvilliers and the Duc d'Orléans:

Toward the Regency

The duc de Bourgogne's death in January 1712 dashed the hopes of his friends. It also raised dynastic, diplomatic, and political questions that threatened to prolong the War of the Spanish Succession. Happily, France and her enemies managed a year later to make peace at Utrecht. But dynastic difficulties and the political problems they entailed continued to trouble France, for Bourgogne's was not the only death in the royal house. His father, the "Grand Dauphin," preceded him to the grave in 1711. In 1712, not only Bourgogne but also his wife and older son succumbed to measles. And two years later, in 1714, death claimed Bourgogne's youngest brother the duc de Berry. Only two of Louis XIV's legitimate masculine descendants now survived. One was Bourgogne's younger son, born in 1710 and destined to become king Louis XV of France. The other was that child's uncle (and Bourgogne's surviving brother), the duc d'Anjou, who in 1700 had become King Philip V of Spain. A regency—traditionally an occasion for political instability—was now imminent. And for reasons that will be explained presently, it was expected that the regency would devolve on Louis XIV's nephew, Philippe, duc d'Orléans.

Historians have long since appreciated the Bourbons' dynastic difficulties at the end of Louis XIV's reign. And they are well acquainted with the efforts of the king to restore his house's dynastic fortunes by adding his bastards, the duc du Maine and the comte de Toulouse, to the order of royal succession along with their legitimate descendants. Those acts of a doting father and anxious dynast were to occasion a celebrated controversy during the regency, the *affaire des princes* (see chapter 6). Less well known, perhaps, though no less serious were the quarrels about the anomalous position that the Spanish king Philip V occupied in the order of succession to the French throne. By birth and dynastic custom, Philip was heir apparent to the future Louis XV and therefore a likelier candidate for the regency than the duc d'Orléans. Only Philip's absence in Spain permitted Orléans to assume the regency in 1715. But—to complicate this tangled dynastic web still further, and to return to the dynastic, diplomatic, and political questions that the duc de Bourgogne's death had raised in 1712—Philip V had renounced his right to succeed to the French throne. France's enemies had insisted on that act as a preliminary to the Treaty of Utrecht—the English particularly sought to ensure that the Spanish and French kingdoms would never be united—and Louis XIV embodied Philip's renunciation in French law as a royal declaration registered by Parlement in 1713. The validity of that act remained dubious, however, for Frenchmen believed that an inviolable dynastic custom regulated the succession to the French crown, and that neither reigning kings nor solemn peace treaties could alter that custom. The Bourbon beyond the Pyrenees, consequently, was to complicate Orléans' political position within France and inspire (when he did not lead) malcontents during the regency. Despite the Treaty of Utrecht, then, the dynastic, diplomatic, and political questions that had arisen in 1712 continued to trouble French affairs.[1] These "problems of the regency" aggravated its notorious political instability and led the kingdom's aristocratic elites to lodge conflicting claims of their own to regulate regencies and the royal succession and to judge disputes about them. To defend those claims, the aristocratic elites engaged in sustained debates about an unwritten French constitution and their own places in it. Dynastic conflicts, therefore, generated aristocratic constitutional controversies in early-eighteenth-century France.

It is one aim of this chapter to watch those controversies begin. Yet another is to watch Boulainvilliers' first efforts to engage in them as he moved, during the last years of Louis XIV's reign, from the entourage of the duc de Bourgogne into the entourage of the duc d'Orléans. The

[1]The *affaire des princes* is discussed in chapter 6. For an excellent recent summary of these "problems of the regency" see J. H. Shennan, *Philippe, Duke of Orléans, Regent of France, 1715–1723* (London: Thames and Hudson, 1979), 17–23. Jean Meyer, too, acknowledges their importance in *La Vie quotidienne en France au temps de la Régence* (Paris: Hachette, 1979), 63–74, and in *Le Régent* (Paris: Ramsay, 1985), 75–78, 131–33. Older works remain valuable, however: [Marie-René-Roussel,] marquis de Courcy, *Renonciation des Bourbons au trône de France* (Paris: E. Plon, Nourrit, 1889) (an *orléaniste* tract); Alfred Baudrillart, *Philippe V et la cour de France*, 5 vols. (Paris: Firmin Didot, 1890–1901), 1:463–542, 692–95, 2:146–228, 326–402; Sixte de Bourbon [prince de Parme], *Le Traité d'Utrecht et les lois fondamentales du royaume* (Paris: Honoré Champion, Edouard Champion, 1914) (a Bourbon-legitimist argument, very sensitive to the demands of French dynastic custom which the Treaty of Utrecht violated). See too the chapters on the foreign policy of Orléans in Henri Leclercq, *Histoire de la Régence pendant la minorité de Louis XV*, 3 vols. (Paris: Honoré Champion, 1923).

competing aristocratic constitutionalisms to be examined shortly may deserve to be called reactionary, yet they cannot be dismissed as myths for marginalized nobles because they arose in the highest reaches of Louis XIV's court and council and in the circles of royal princes. In those same milieus, Boulainvilliers pursued his own career as a client and counselor seeking to serve Orléans while vesting in him his highest hopes as a nobiliaire ideologue. For Boulainvilliers did not forget his own antiducal animus, his hopes to revive the old nobility's preeminence, and his desire to reanimate the "nation" by reviving its assemblies of Estates. This agenda may be detected in his earliest memoranda for Orléans, written to assist that prince and defend his tenuous position against all critics.

The Renunciation Crisis and the Duc de Saint-Simon

The duc de Bourgogne's death had the impact that it did because of the war it threatened to prolong. That war was a modern war for trade and empire. But the War of the Spanish Succession was also a dynastic war, precipitated by dynastic events and accidents and very nearly prolonged by them too. Before his death in 1700, King Carlos II of Spain signed a testament bequeathing his kingdom to a French prince, the youngest of Louis XIV's three grandsons, the duc d'Anjou, who duly became King Philip V of Spain at the end of the year. Carlos and his advisers hoped thereby to enlist France's might in protecting Spain against powers bent on dismembering her empire. Carlos carefully sought to prevent a dynastic union of Spain and France, however. He stipulated that if Anjou returned to France to exercise his rights to succeed to the French throne, he would forfeit his Spanish kingdom. Louis XIV's enemies feared such a union nonetheless and after further provocation by Louis XIV—the king chose to recognize the claims of the Stuart "Pretender" to the English throne and proclaim Philip V's rights to the French throne—the Allies took up arms in 1702 to place an Austrian Habsburg (the archduke Charles, later Emperor Charles VI) on the throne of his Spanish cousins.[2]

Just as dynastic accidents precipitated the war they governed efforts to

[2]For a concise account of the dynastic as well as commercial and imperial origins of the war see Derek McKay and H. M. Scott, *The Rise of the Great Powers 1648–1815* (London: Longman, 1983), 54–58. See also Rowen, *The King's State*, 93–101; and John B. Wolf, *Louis XIV* (New York: W. W. Norton, 1968), 491–532. Like Wolf (510–15), Pierre Goubert appreciates the role that Louis XIV's provocations played in starting the war (*Louis XIV and Twenty Million Frenchmen*, tr. Anne Carter [New York: Pantheon, 1968], 234–38). It will be noted, however, that the king's acts were assertions of dynastic claims.

end it, even after 1710 when a Tory administration committed to peace took office in Britain. The Tories were prepared to live with a Bourbon Spain, not least of all because the Habsburg claimant to the Spanish throne had become Emperor Charles VI in 1711, thus making a dynastic union between Spanish and Austrian might a dangerous possibility. Because of deaths in the French royal family in 1711–12, however, a dynastic union between Spain and France was barely less likely. After Bourgogne and his elder son died, therefore, Britain demanded that the Bourbon princes make a series of reciprocal renunciations: that Philip V of Spain renounce his right to succeed to the French throne (a redundant act, since the testament left by Carlos II stipulated that Philip abdicate the Spanish throne should he mount the French); that Philip's brother the duc de Berry renounce his rights to the Spanish throne (rights that had been acknowledged by the will of Carlos); and, finally, that the duc d'Orléans renounce his own rights to the Spanish succession (rights resting on the marriage between his grandparents, Louis XIII of France and the Spanish princess Anne of Austria, and confirmed in 1703 by Philip V of Spain).

The Bourbon princes agreed to these demands, but new problems arose over arrangements for ratifying Philip of Spain's renunciation in France. To perform that act, the British demanded the convocation of an Estates General. Predictably Louis XIV and his chief negotiator, Colbert de Torcy, refused. The Estates General, they argued, was no longer part of French political usage and would not be revived. Thus a dynastic problem and its diplomatic and political consequences precipitated a crisis in 1712–13: the Renunciation Crisis, which brought the British minister, Henry St. John, Viscount Bolingbroke, to Versailles on a secret mission in July 1712.[3]

The Renunciation Crisis also preoccupied the men in the erstwhile Burgundy Circle, like the English Tories committed to peace between France and her enemies and determined to secure it now that it was at hand. The duc de Beauvillier and his friends met informally to discuss the problems of ratifying Philip V's renunciation and the duc de Saint-Simon, a leading participant in their meetings, later described them in his *Mémoires*.[4] "From the beginning of the difficulty," Saint-Simon

[3]See, in addition to works cited in n. 1, McKay and Scott, *Rise of the Great Powers*, 63–66; Wolf, *Louis XIV*, 582–95; and, for a rich account of Torcy's conjoined propaganda and diplomacy in 1712–13, Joseph Klaits, *Printed Propaganda under Louis XIV: Absolute Monarchy and Public Opinion* (Princeton, N.J.: Princeton University Press, 1976), 246–90, esp. 267–70.

[4]For what follows see Saint-Simon, *Mémoires*, 23:122–56. Beauvillier rarely participated in efforts to direct the War of the Spanish Succession, but after 1709 he consistently supported negotiations for peace (Lizerand, *Le Duc de Beauvillier*, 261, 263–83).

wrote, he conferred with Beauvillier and Chevreuse. Soon three more dukes and peers joined them: Noailles, Humières, and Armand II de Béthune, duc de Charost. Because (Saint-Simon wrote) he alone had sufficient leisure and inclination to devote himself to study, Beauvillier and his friends deferred to him and adopted his ideas on how to ratify Philip V's renunciation. They resolved that a memorandum embodying those ideas be drawn up and that Beauvillier and Chevreuse, one a royal minister, the other a trusted royal confidant, assume the delicate task of presenting its argument to a monarch jealous of his authority. Although the memorandum was to contain Saint-Simon's ideas, its preparation fell to the duc de Noailles who had volunteered to draft it. Having acquired an intense dislike for Noailles by the time he wrote his *Mémoires,* Saint-Simon was pleased to describe the duke's poor performance. Noailles had promised to finish his memorandum before the court left Versailles for Fontainebleau in midsummer. He failed to meet his deadline and continued his work at Fontainebleau, where it was discovered that he was keeping a stable of hack writers in the rooms above his apartment and rewriting what "his unknowns in his attic" had written already. Confronted by his friends, Noailles was "most embarassed." But he did not abandon his task and no one asked him to do so. Secretly, however, Beauvillier urged Saint-Simon to draft à memorandum. He willingly assumed that task despite the difficulties surrounding it, difficulties described with self-serving zeal in the *Mémoires:* the lack of books, the ubiquity of court spies, the demands of a court routine that required that one appear preoccupied by nothing else. As a result, by August 1712 Beauvillier and his friends had two memoranda to consider: the "fairly short memorandum" that Noailles eventually finished and Saint-Simon's "Succinct Memorandum," which despite its title occupies 300 pages of print in its modern edition.[5] It was resolved that the dukes and peers meeting with Beauvillier would debate the merits of the two memoranda in his presence and then adhere to his decision between them. He chose Saint-Simon's text and presented it to the king.

That was a remarkable decision, for Saint-Simon's constitutional proposals were ill-calculated to please Louis XIV. Saint-Simon admitted that in France "the legislative and constitutive power [was] in the hands of the king alone," but he deplored "those who have sought to argue, by remarks more appropriate to the court than to the state or to persons learned in our history, that laws can only be made by kings alone when

[5][Louis de Rouvroy, duc de] Saint-Simon, *Ecrits inédits,* ed. P. Faugère, 8 vols. (Paris: Hachette, 1880–92), 2:181–408: "Mémoire succint sur les formalités desquelles nécessairement la renonciation du roy d'Espagne tant pour luy que pour sa postérité doit estre revestue en France pour y estre justement et stablement validée. Aoust 1712."

there is a recognized king in France."⁶ Indeed, he devoted the bulk of his "Succinct Memorandum" to proving that "the legislative and constitutive power" really belonged to the peerage which, he concluded, should be assembled along with simple dukes and officers of the crown to ratify Philip of Spain's renunciation. Thus a dynastic emergency prompted Saint-Simon to abandon his customarily orthodox absolutism and to reshape ducal ideology into a blueprint for a ducal-monarchical constitution.⁷

To develop his thesis Saint-Simon reviewed the entire history of French government, the history of a government "always identical to itself" and so, Saint-Simon believed, a consistent record of the peerage's political authority. Predictably, he sought continuity rather than change in the national past: "one single chain of identity" identifying the *"leudi* [sic] and *fideles"* and "great feudatories" of Merovingian antiquity with the "peers" and *"grands"* who, Saint-Simon wrote, elected Hugh Capet king in A.D. 987.⁸ Locating the origins of French feudalism at the dawn of French history—he discovered not only "great feudatories" but also "lordship and vassalage" in Merovingian France—Saint-Simon managed to identify fiefs with benefices, to admit that magnates impropriated them, to concede that Hugh Capet ratified those "usurpations," and yet insist that only their names distinguished Frankish *leudes* from feudal peers and *grands*. All, Saint-Simon insisted, held the same "legislative and constitutive power."⁹ And they all enjoyed it to the exclusion of their vassals: for as Saint-Simon described them the *"placita"* (assemblies) of the ancient Franks were assemblies of great lords alone. Clearly recalling the late-ninth-century account of Charlemagne's government written by Hincmar of Rheims, Saint-Simon described the Merovingians' *placita* as assemblies dominated by a preeminent "order" of *"leudi* and *fideles"* while the "multitude" or "crowd" of their vassals (a separate "order" of knights [*milites*] later called "the nobility") remained outside to acclaim by shouts of "Vivat!" the resolutions taken by their virtual representatives within.¹⁰ Saint-Simon deigned to notice only one signif-

⁶Saint-Simon, *Ecrits inédits*, 2:204 and 315.

⁷Jean-Pierre Brancourt makes a convincing case for Saint-Simon's commitment to a formal royal absolutism, but refers only in passing to the "Mémoire succinct" (*Le Duc de Saint-Simon et la Monarchie* [Paris: Cujas, 1971], 64).

⁸Saint-Simon, *Ecrits inédits*, 2:189–204, 210, 234.

⁹Ibid., 2:204–5, 206, 210.

¹⁰Ibid., 2:197–98; Saint-Simon's "knights" took themselves "to be represented and consulted, to be persuaded in the person of their lords in whom resided . . . the legislative and constitutive power." Cf. Hincmar of Rheims, *De ordine palatii*, ed. and tr. Maurice Prou (Paris: F. Vieweg, 1884), 70–95, esp. 72–75 and 92–93 for Hincmar's distinction between the *multitudo* or *minores* and the *seniores* or *comites* or *principes* or *maiores* at general assemblies. It was willful in the extreme to use Hincmar's *De ordine palatii*, a nostalgic account of

icant change in the history of ancient French or Frankish government: Hugh Capet's decision to add his own vassals from his duchy of France to the great magnates, in order to check their influence.[11]

Pursuing this history of French government into the age of the Capetians, Saint-Simon continued to insist on the peers' exclusive enjoyment of "legislative and constitutive power." Medieval "parlements," he maintained, were assemblies of barons not to be confused with the tribunals that later assumed the same name. The Parlement of Paris, he explained, was called "court of peers" only because peers sat in it when judging each other. It was really a law court, nothing else, and when peers and barons exercised their "legislative and constitutive power" they did so elsewhere.[12]

Doubtless, Saint-Simon was indebted to the ducal memoranda of the 1660s and to Jean Le Laboureur's "Traité" in seeking to distinguish peerage from Parlement and nobility alike. Doubtless, too, he learned from his predecessors when he went on to claim that modern dukes and peers enjoyed the same "dignity," if not the same "power" and "sovereignty," that feudal peers used to enjoy. He reinforced that claim, however, with an ingenious argument of his own: because ecclesiastical peers enjoyed no less an authority than lay peers during the Middle Ages, that authority could only derive from their "dignity," for their "fiefs" were manifestly not great feudal principalities like those of the lay peers.[13] With that argument Saint-Simon obscured the feudal foundation that he was trying to give the French dukes and peers, but he did not diminish his claims on their behalf. Rather he detected in their role at royal consecrations and in the magnificent language in royal letters of erection establishing their lands as duchy-peerages held immediately of the crown (*laterales Regis, Tuteurs des Rois et de la Couronne, les soustiens de l'Estat, une portion de la Royauté*) evidence that modern dukes and peers continued to hold public authority and to cooperate with kings in exercising it.[14] Moreover, Saint-Simon revived his argument from the dukes and peers' supposed feudal past when he described those dignitaries as members of the king's body politic. According to Saint-Simon, the duke and peer's "dignity," composed of his head-fief and of the "office" that he exercised at royal consecrations, *lits de justice,* and, in-

Charlemagne's already legendary reign (ibid., xviii–xx [Prou's introduction]), as a source for Merovingian political practice.

[11]Saint-Simon, *Ecrits inédits,* 2:203–4, on the *"Hauts Barons du Duché de France"* and (later) *"Hauts Barons de France."*

[12]Ibid., 2:209–15.

[13]Ibid., 2:234–35. For Le Laboureur, the ducal memoranda of the 1660s, and the definition of peerage as a "dignity," see chapter 2.

[14]Saint-Simon, *Ecrits inédits,* 2:216–48.

deed, "everywhere," accounted for "this summit of inherence in king and crown" that exalted him above all other Frenchmen. He was literally *pars corporis principis,* part of the prince's body (politic), and he shared the king's duty to exercise kingship.[15]

On these grounds, Saint-Simon recommended that the dukes and peers be assembled to ratify Philip V's renunciation, for that extraordinary departure from French dynastic custom required equally extraordinary "formalities" for its ratification as French law. But it was singularly difficult to locate a modern institution in which the duke and peer might exercise his exalted political functions, except for the *lit de justice* which ducal statements of the 1660s had identified with the "court of the peers." Saint-Simon rejected the *lit,* however, along with the Parlement of Paris: these were mere tribunals. He also rejected the Estates General: a mere petitioning body.[16] He proposed instead a special assembly—it was to consist of dukes and peers, simple dukes (recalling the *Hauts Barons de France* admitted to medieval "parlements" by Hugh Capet) and officers of the crown (whose signatures were necessary for the validity of royal acts)—wherein the dukes and peers might exercise their "legislative and constitutive power."[17] Once again he ransacked French history for evidence that such assemblies had indeed been called in the past. He found "four very striking examples" which all concerned regencies and the royal succession, dynastic problems just like that confronting France during the Renunciation Crisis in 1712. And in each example, Saint-Simon claimed, peers resolved those problems. In 1314, he wrote, peers and barons awarded the regency of the kingdom (claimed by the late Louis X's widow on behalf of her unborn son) to the late king's brother. In 1328, Saint-Simon added, peers upheld the "Salic Law" and awarded the crown to Philippe de Valois, passing over Edward III of England who had claimed the crown through his wife, the late king's sister. In 1374, Saint-Simon continued, Charles V asked peers, barons, and officers of the crown to ratify his edict reducing the age at which French kings attained majority from twenty-five to fourteen, a seemingly absurd regulation, Saint-Simon observed, but properly ratified and so a stable part of French law. Finally, Saint-Simon wrote, the future Henri IV appealed to the peers of

---

[15]Ibid., 2:256–57. On corporate or office theories of kingship in France see Ernst H. Kantorowicz, *The King's Two Bodies: A Study in Mediaeval Political Theology* (Princeton, N.J.: Princeton University Press, 1957), 409–37; Ralph E. Giesey, *The Royal Funeral Ceremony in Renaissance France* (Geneva: Droz, 1960); and Hanley, *The* Lit de Justice *of the Kings of France.* Such theories coexisted with proprietary or private-law notions of royal authority and its transmission, examined in Rowen, *The King's State.*

[16]Saint-Simon, *Ecrits inédits,* 2:186–87, 209–13.

[17]Ibid., 2:257–68.

France when the Estates General stripped him of his right to succeed to the French crown, an appeal, Saint-Simon noted, whose legitimacy no historian ever impugned. Saint-Simon stated: "Nothing concludes with so much evidence the diverse proofs of the legislative and constitutive power of the peers, and of their right to judge matters regarding the crown, as these four very striking examples."[18]

Saint-Simon's political claims for the peerage were dazzling. He claimed for his order nothing less than an exclusive right to regulate disputes about the royal succession and regencies: "their right to judge matters regarding the crown." He even suggested that peers should participate in all royal legislation, for he derided the "court" doctrine that kings alone might make law.[19] Peers, he declared, "alone constituted the body of the state."[20] And if royal law were to enjoy "stability" then the peers must consent to it, for like the *"leudi* and *fideles"* of Merovingian France, dukes and peers virtually represented their inferiors: "The other subjects . . . count themselves consulted in the person of these great subjects." Failure to consult those "great subjects," according to Saint-Simon, would arouse their "jealousy," injure their *"amour-propre,"* and increase the "fragility" of laws by increasing the chances that they would be disobeyed.[21]

Saint-Simon was not proposing that dukes and peers become a legislature permanently associated with the crown, a sort of English Parliament without a House of Commons. He admitted that as a rule kings alone made laws in France, but he called such laws "private ordinances of kings," claimed that they tended to be unstable, and warned against their use for "great sanctions of the kingdom."[22] For these "great sanctions," he argued, prudence dictated approval by dukes and peers, dukes, and officers of the crown.

If Beauvillier and his friends hoped that Louis XIV would consent to Saint-Simon's scheme, they were to be disappointed. Louis rejected the proposals contained in the "Succinct Memorandum" and explained to him by Beauvillier and Chevreuse. Nor did he call an Estates General to ratify Philip of Spain's renunciation, despite the insistence of the British negotiators. The renunciation became French law as a simple royal declaration registered as any other piece of royal legislation by the Parlement of Paris on March 15, 1713. The British accepted that procedure and the Treaty of Utrecht, embodying the Bourbon princes' mutual renunciations in its text, was signed on April 11.

[18]Ibid., 2:287–306, and 306 for quotation.
[19]Ibid., 2:204–5.
[20]Ibid., 2:321.
[21]Ibid., 2:313–14.
[22]Ibid., 2:320.

It is not hard to imagine why Louis XIV rejected Saint-Simon's proposal. By following it he would have relinquished his monopoly on legislative sovereignty. Rather more remarkable is the fact that Saint-Simon made his proposal at all and that Beauvillier supported it, for both men believed that France was a formally absolute monarchy in which kings alone made law and decisions and in which an inviolable fundamental law summoned those kings to the throne and obliged their subjects to obey them. In 1712, however, they seriously contemplated calling an assembly of peers, recognizing its "legislative and constitutive power," and giving it the task of modifying the fundamental law to exclude the Spanish Bourbons from the French throne. Because Louis XIV refused to follow that procedure, Saint-Simon never recognized the validity of Philip V's renunciation, although in 1712 he imagined that an assembly of peers could have rendered it "stable."[23] Saint-Simon's and Beauvillier's conduct in 1712 attests the unsettling impact of dynastic uncertainties on France's monarchical political culture, and the new political possibilities imaginable in moments of dynastic crisis.

Boulainvilliers' "Réflexions" and the Duc d'Orléans

The ideas that Saint-Simon developed in his "Mémoire succinct" displeased not only Louis XIV but also the comte de Boulainvilliers, who prepared a short and sharply critical memorandum of his own to refute Saint-Simon's: the "Réflexions et considérations sur le mémoire des formalités nécessaires pour valider la renonciation du roi d'Espagne."[24] It is not hard to date that text or to identify its purpose, for Boulainvilliers's conclusion makes these emphatically clear:

> I finish these reflections written amidst the confusion of a departure and without the assistance of any books. I am persuaded that they may usefully be expanded to support the justice of the royal declaration given in consequence of the renunciation of the king of Spain, a declaration which establishes an order of succession to the crown, which cannot be impugned except by those insufficiently acquainted with our history, and which will suffer no contradiction if, after the king's death which, however sorrowful it shall be to us, must nevertheless be regarded as inevitable, one takes the

---

[23]Bourbon, *Le Traité d'Utrecht*, 95–102, recognizes (to reject it) Saint-Simon's ascription of constitutional authority to the peers. On Saint-Simon's and Beauvillier's generally orthodox commitment to royal absolutism see Brancourt, *Le Duc de Saint-Simon*, and Lizerand, *Le Duc de Beauvillier*, 364–75.

[24]Printed by Nicolas Lenglet-Dufresnoy in his edition of [chevalier de Piossens], *Mémoires de la Régence: Nouvelle édition, considérablement augmentée*, ed. Lenglet-Dufresnoy, 5 vols. (Amsterdam: 1749), 2:231–88. For MSS see Bibliographical Appendix, Part 2.

necessary precaution of assembling the Nation to secure its consent, a consent which it cannot refuse to execute the last wishes of a monarch so wise and so well intentioned.[25]

Boulainvilliers wrote well after Saint-Simon, since he referred to Louis XIV's royal declaration which the Parlement of Paris registered on March 15, 1713. Very likely, Boulainvilliers wrote in August 1715, because he alluded to the king's "inevitable" death, which, after an illness of two weeks, occurred on September 1. One of Boulainvilliers' aims was implicit in his suggestion that the "nation" be assembled to "consent" to Philip V's renunciation. This was an antiducal and no-biliaire riposte to Saint-Simon's claim that the peerage represented the "nation" and could ratify Philip's renunciation on its behalf. Boulain-villiers' clearest aim, however, was to defend the validity of Louis XIV's declaration which had already ratified the Spanish king's renunciation. In short, Boulainvilliers was not only a nobiliaire ideologue seeking to restore the assemblies of the "nation," but also an *orléaniste* ideologue seeking to defend and advise the duc d'Orléans. The "Réflexions," as the lines just quoted suggest, was a piece of high-level political advice and a short defense of the future regent's dynastic and political position in France that could be "usefully expanded" into a more elaborate state-ment on his behalf.

For whom exactly did Boulainvilliers write the "Réflexions"? Orléans himself is a likely candidate. Boulainvilliers' devotion to the prince during the regency is well attested, and not only by his efforts to write on French history and politics for Orléans. In 1719, Boulainvilliers de-scribed himself as "zealous servant" of the regent."[26] Three years later, when Boulainvilliers was dying, Orléans sent him his own doctor and later assigned his widow a handsome pension of 1,000 *écus*.[27] Boulain-villiers may have been one of the many individuals, therefore, who had ingratiated themselves with Orléans—hitherto in disrepute because of his libertinage, his ambition, and his (ill-deserved) reputation as a man who may have poisoned Bourgogne and his family to increase his chances of succeeding to the throne—as the regency approached.

[25][Piossens], *Mémoires de la Régence* 2:287–88. It will be apparent that Lenglet wrongly dated this text to 1717.

[26]See "Mémoire touchant la taille réelle et proportionnelle," printed in Boulainvilliers, *Mémoires présentés à Monseigneur le duc d'Orléans, contenant les moyens de rendre ce royaume très-puissant, & d'augmenter considérablement les revenus du roy & du peuple,* 2 vols. (The Hague and Amsterdam: 1727), 1:87. On this text, on the collection to which it belongs (Boulain-villiers may not have written all the pieces in it), and on editions and manuscripts of it, see Bibliographical Appendix, Part 4.

[27]Marais, *Journal et mémoires,* 2:227, 228.

The young duc de Noailles was another possible recipient of the "Réflexions." Like Orléans, Noailles was a patron of Boulainvilliers. On several occasions he came to Boulainvilliers' assistance, and an engraved portrait of the duke adorned Boulainvilliers' study when he died.[28] The likelihood that Boulainvilliers wrote his "Réflexions" for Noailles increases, however, when we recall the efforts of Noailles during the Renunciation Crisis. Like Saint-Simon, Noailles penned a memorandum in 1712 on the formalities required to ratify Philip V's renunciation in France. In his *Mémoires* Saint-Simon wrote that Noailles' memorandum "agreed on the principal and the essential" with his own, but he went on to note significant differences between the two texts.[29] In his own memorandum, Saint-Simon had proposed that after an assembly of dukes and peers, dukes, and officers of the crown ratified Philip V's renunciation, the nobility might do so too: by swearing oaths to adhere to it, either individually or through presidents of the noble "order" at meetings of provincial estates or an Estates General. But such oaths, he insisted, would add nothing to the already well-established juridical status of the renunciation's ratification by the peers, for those great lords, like the *grands* at Merovingian *placita*, virtually represented their inferiors. The oaths that Saint-Simon proposed for the noble "order" in 1712, therefore, were of no greater importance than the shouts of *Vivat!* with which, he wrote, the Merovingian "nobility" acclaimed the resolutions of its lords.[30] In his memorandum Noailles assigned a far greater role to the nobility in 1712. He proposed that in the persons of *nonducal* representatives, namely provincial governors and knights of the Order of the Holy Spirit, the nobility might participate directly in the extraordinary assembly planned to ratify Philip V's renunciation. That proposal, Saint-Simon complained in his *Mémoires,* was a bold attempt to cultivate the favor of the "nobility."[31] He may have had the noisier ducal-noble conflicts of the regency in mind, since he was writing many years later. Even in the last years of Louis XIV's reign, however, ducal-noble enmity may be detected, notably in Boulainvilliers' "Réflexions," a work critical of Saint-Simon's memorandum, reminiscent of Noailles' memorandum, and for that reason among others possibly written for Noailles.

[28]A.N., M.C., XIV, 255 (February 13, 1722) (postmortem inventory). On Noailles' assistance to Boulainvilliers see A.N., M.353, no. 21 (for which see Simon, *Henry de Boulainviller,* 32 n. 75); and B.N., MS. f.f. 6929, fol. 231v.

[29]Saint-Simon, *Mémoires,* 23:135. On Noailles' memorandum see also Bourbon, *Le Traité d'Utrecht,* 95.

[30]Saint-Simon, *Ecrits inédits,* 2:383–85.

[31]Saint-Simon, *Mémoires,* 23:136–37.

Boulainvilliers' antiducal animus was powerful indeed. Against Saint-Simon, he insisted that kings did not share "legislative and constitutive power" with the peerage. Not that he defended "despotic power—I who have so often shown its abuses and inconvenience as well as its unsuitability to French *moeurs.*" Equating "despotic power" with unmixed monarchical authority (this was to become one of his abiding habits) Boulainvilliers insisted that kings did indeed share their "legislative power," but with the "nation" assembled in Estates. And in that body— here Boulainvilliers' position recalls that taken by Noailles in 1712—not peers but provincial governors took precedence.[32]

Boulainvilliers claimed an acquaintance with French history that was "the fruit of long work" and therefore superior to Saint-Simon's.[33] Nevertheless, he equivocated massively when writing about the monarchy and its history. Having insisted that kings share power, he also admitted that kings alone had made law in France, at least since 1300 when they began with impunity to issue laws harmful to the feudal nobility.[34] Against Saint-Simon, however, Boulainvilliers claimed that even in the sixteenth century the Estates General, not the peerage, regulated the royal succession. In 1589, Boulainvilliers argued, Henri IV succeeded to the throne because in 1576 the Estates General had already confirmed the preeminent rank and dynastic status of French princes of the blood.[35]

Boulainvilliers' comments on royal legislative sovereignty may have been equivocal, but not his antiducal animus. Here his use of Hincmar of Rheims, whose *De ordine palatii* Saint-Simon had already used to describe Frankish assemblies, is revealing. Boulainvilliers refused to admit that those legislative "parlements" might be assemblies of great feudatories. He knew that Hincmar had distinguished "lords" who deliberated within them from the "multitude" that awaited their decisions outside, but he thought it "natural" that "the most experienced and wise" deliberate to the exclusion of the rest. Thus he identified Hincmar's "lords" or "seniores" with the "seniores" of his own "Mémoires historiques," who were chosen "elders," not the great feudatories whom Saint-Simon sought to distinguish from a "nobility" of their "vassals."[36]

So powerful was Boulainvilliers' antipathy to the peerage that he lapsed once again into the antiducal antifeudalism to which he had

---

[32][Piossens], *Mémoires de la Régence,* 2:238 and 271–76.
[33]Ibid., 2:265.
[34]Ibid., 2:233–38, 246.
[35]Ibid., 2:274–75. On their rank and the dynastic reasons for its establishment in 1576 see Jackson, "Peers of France and Princes of the Blood."
[36][Piossens], *Mémoires de la Régence,* 2:239–54, esp. 241–42, 250, 239–54.

succumbed in his notes on Le Laboureur's "Traité" or "Histoire de la pairie de France." Indeed, Boulainvilliers now reversed the position he had carefully taken in the "Mémoires historiques." He deplored "feudal law" (*le droit des fiefs*) and the "too excessive" authority of "parlements." Further, he complained that feudalism distracted the Franks from public affairs. Too preoccupied with their own fiefs, they abdicated political responsibility to kings who found increased power in increased work.[37] That argument may recall his harsh indictment of "beneficed lords" and their egoism in the "Mémoires historiques." In the "Réflexions," however, Boulainvilliers indicted not only the egoism of the great but also the feudalism that sustained them, and even the legendary architect of feudalism, Charlemagne: "Truly Charlemagne introduced feudalism [*la féodalité*] into all the lands he subjected to his arms. But he did not force the Franks [*les François*] to receive it, for that would have required abolishing the common law under which he had been born himself, and he contented himself with sowing the seeds which later bore, contrary to his intentions, a quantity of bitter fruits among the good, for this feudalism established itself without method, since kings in that time failed to understand their greatest interest."[38] Boulainvilliers' indictment of Charlemagne was a mild one, for he proceeded to deny that the great Carolingian destroyed Frankish equality by instituting peerage. That, Boulainvilliers wrote, was a myth propagated by medieval romances and deserving no credit.[39] Still, he insisted that feudalism was to blame for the emergence of a peerage in France. Convinced that prefeudal Franks were equals and that peerage was originally "a right common to all the Franks [*François*]," Boulainvilliers blamed the rise of an exclusive peerage on the rise of feudalism.[40]

At this point Boulainvilliers introduced yet another motif into his antifeudalism, that is, the "subtlety of legists" whose commentaries on feudal law introduced the tenurial distinctions inimical to the Franks' equal "distinction of blood." Now an antilegist antifeudalism redoubled Boulainvilliers' antiducal antifeudalism! Legists, he complained, were descendants of enfranchised serfs who had purchased their liberty from kings misled by their financial needs.[41] A familiar Boulainvilliers emerges here, the Boulainvilliers consumed by hatred for the robe

---

[37][Piossens], *Mémoires de la Régence*, 2:253–54, 256.

[38]Ibid., 2:240.

[39]Ibid., 2:240–41.

[40]Ibid., 2:255, 256. Boulainvilliers ascribed the opinion that ancient Franks were equal to a "great man"—doubtless Le Laboureur to whom he owed a similar argument in the "Mémoires historiques."

[41]Ibid., 2:258–60, 262–64.

nobility and for the monarchy that facilitated its rise to power and preeminence.

In the "Réflexions," however, the rise of a peerage remained the chief threat to the old nobility and Boulainvilliers did not hesitate to denounce the nobility's willingness to let a peerage emerge within it. This was an egregious example of the nobility's "inattention," which he never ceased to deplore as he contemplated the nobility's history: He noted the "strange inattention of the noble Frenchman who, to console himself for his true losses, later thought to form a fiction of peerage outside himself and to attribute it to lands most of which were usurped and held illegitimately; he completely forgot what he was, and what he ought to have been."[42]

This was not the last time that Boulainvilliers' antipathy to the titled nobility would push him to adopt an antiducal (or for that matter an antilegist) antifeudalism, but it was the first time he wrote to sustain the dynastic and political position of the duc d'Orléans. This position was complicated by the dubious validity of Philip V's renunciation of his rights to succeed to the French crown and (later) by Philip's active encouragement of malcontents in France during the Orléans regency. Even before the end of Louis XIV's reign, however, Boulainvilliers had become an *orléaniste* ideologue. And he was to remain an *orléaniste* ideologue to the end of his life, pursuing his own nobiliaire agenda in works designed to sustain or shape the regent's. Like the duc de Saint-Simon whose work he criticized in the "Réflexions," Boulainvilliers' political imagination took flight when dynastic and political questions let it. Like Saint-Simon's, Boulainvilliers' projects for an aristocratic constitutionalism owed their existence to the monarchy's difficulties and to the efforts of its aristocratic servants to resolve them. These projects may have been reactionary, but they were not the dreams of decayed nobles rotting in the provinces.

Early Memoranda for the Regent: *Noblesse* and Nation

After Louis XIV's death Boulainvilliers continued to pursue his nobiliaire ideological agenda in two additional memoranda for the duc d'Orléans. One urged the prince to establish a "General Chamber of the Nobility" charged with compiling a *nobiliaire* or catalog of the kingdom's *noblesse*. The other sought to persuade Orléans to assemble the Estates

[42]Ibid., 2:263–64.

General and entrust to it the task of retiring Louis XIV's massive debts.[43] Neither memorandum had any impact on the regent's conduct, but they reveal Boulainvilliers' great expectations of the new regime, for in them he detailed his nobiliaire agenda for the regency: restoring the old nobility's preeminence and reviving the assemblies of the "nation."

Like his early "Dissertation" on the old nobility, Boulainvilliers' plea for letting a "General Chamber of the Nobility" catalog the order's members bespeaks his genealogical consciousness. Genealogical consciousness, it will be recalled, consisted in a body of assumptions about the social meaning of noble birth. Noble birth, it was assumed, imparted several things to the wellborn individual: the "glory" of his house; the duty to "sustain" it with his own; and ancestral "examples" of "virtue" to emulate in the pursuit of his personal "glory." Boulainvilliers shared those assumptions. He understood nobility, consequently, as a genealogical attribute constituted by "birth," "virtue," "glory," and social esteem for these qualities. In short, Boulainvilliers may be said to have understood nobility as a social elite constituted by its own social self-consciousness and by the comportments that it authorized. For that reason, he was finely sensitive to threats to that social self-consciousness and to the nobleman's obligation to realize his "virtue" and acquire "glory." In the "Dissertation," Boulainvilliers identified these threats with social circulation, with increased and therefore increasingly costly competition for "glory," with the royal court, and ultimately with the decay of French feudalism. In his memorandum for Orléans he turned his attention to another threat to the old nobility and its proud genealogical consciousness: Louis XIV's celebrated *recherches de faux nobles* and the fundamentally legalistic concept of nobility with which the commissioners charged with those *recherches* operated.

It has been argued that many legitimate nobles welcomed Louis XIV's *recherches*, for they were designed to purge the nobility's ranks of usurpers.[44] Boulainvilliers condemned them nevertheless. They were mere

[43]Boulainvilliers, "Mémoire présenté à son altesse royale Mgr. le duc d'Orléans dans le commencement de sa régence pour la construction d'un nobiliare général" (Bibliothèque du Sénat [Paris], MS. 990). For other MSS see Bibliographical Appendix, Part 2. "Mémoire sur la convocation d'une assemblée d'états géneraux," in Boulainvilliers, *Mémoires presentés*, 1:1–15.

[44]Doyle, "Was There an Aristocratic Reaction in Pre-Revolutionary France?" 99. For Louis's *recherches* and their antecedents see [H.] Bourde de La Rogerie, "Etude sur la réformation de la noblesse en Bretagne (1668–1721)," *Mémoires de la Société d'Histoire et d'Archéologie de Bretagne*, 3 (1922): 237–312; Jean-Marie Constant, "L'Enquête de noblesse de 1667 et les seigneurs de Beauce," *Revue d'histoire moderne et contemporaine*, 21 (1974): 548–66; Edmond Esmonin, *La Taille en Normandie au temps de Colbert (1661–1683)* (Paris: Hachette, 1913), 202–24; Jean Meyer, *La Noblesse de Bretagne au XVIIIe siècle* (Paris:

fiscal expedients, he complained (and not without reason), undertaken by tax farmers and intendants "as barely conversant with the knowledge of families as they were barely informed of the nature of nobility."[45] True, the *recherches* were also social measures designed to purify the nobility's ranks. The results were supposed to be recorded in an official "catalog" of nobility, but no such catalog ever appeared during Louis XIV's reign and the inability of many families to amass documents attesting their noble status to an intendant's satisfaction cast doubts upon the equity of the *recherches,* the wisdom of the men who conducted them, and the value of their findings.[46] Louis XIV's *recherches* no doubt imposed an unsettling bureaucratic "rationalization" on social status, especially where no *recherches* had been undertaken before.[47] Moreover, the unkept promise to compile a "catalog" of nobility probably haunted nobles who wanted to see their order's composition stabilized and their own status secured. In fact, when Louis-Pierre d'Hozier and his nephew Antoine-Marie d'Hozier de Sérigny (they were Louis XV's *juges d'armes*) undertook the publication of their massive *Armorial général,* they claimed that they were realizing at last Louis XIV's project for a definitive "catalog" of French nobility.[48]

Boulainvilliers' project for a "catalog" of nobility must not be confused with Louis XIV's, however, or with the other catalogs it inspired. The legalistic concept of nobility with which Louis XIV's commissioners operated during the *recherches* violated the mystique of immemorial nobility and the ideals of genealogical consciousness dear to Boulain-

---

S.E.V.P.E.N., 1966), 29–73; Roland Mousnier, *Les Institutions de la France sous la monarchie absolue: 1598–1789: Tome I: Société et état* (Paris: Presses Universitaires de France, 1974), 111–14; D. J. Sturdy, "Tax Evasion, the *Faux Nobles,* and State Fiscalism: The Example of the *Généralité* of Caen, 1634–35," *French Historical Studies,* 9 (1975–76): 549–72; Wood, *The Nobility of the Election of Bayeux,* 20–42. Louis *recherches* were the first undertaken throughout the kingdom.

[45]Bibliothèque du Sénat (Paris), MS. 990, fol. 1. Cf. *Etat,* 1, "Préface": v ("Première partie"), for an earlier and similar complaint addressed to the Burgundy Circle. Historians of the *recherches* appreciate the fiscal concerns behind them, especially those of the 1690s.

[46]On the March 22, 1666, *arrêt de conseil* inaugurating the *recherches* and promising a "catalog" of their results, see Mousnier, *Les Institutions de la France,* 113. Some alphabetically arranged provincial catalogs did appear, based largely on the results of the *recherches.* For a list see B.N., *Catalogue de l'histoire de France,* 16 vols. (Paris: B.N., 1968), 9:117–29. For complaints against the *recherches* see Père Toussaint de Saint-Luc, *Mémoire sur l'état du clergé et de la noblesse de Bretagne* (Paris: 1691), 290, quoted by Meyer, *La Noblesse de Bretagne,* 48; [Sautour], *A Messeigneurs les états généraux de Bourgogne* (n.p.: n.d.), 1–2 (on the 1664–72 *recherche*); and the critical marginalia in B.N., MS. f.f. 15467, fols. 1–6v (a draft royal edict composed during the War of the Spanish Succession and proposing that intendants compile a "catalog" of nobility).

[47]Meyer, *La Noblesse de Bretagne,* 27, 49–51, 53.

[48][Louis-Pierre d'Hozier and Antoine-Marie d'Hozier de Sérigny], *Armorial général de la France,* 6 registers in 10 vols. (Paris: Jacques Colombat, 1738–68), 1:i–viii.

villiers and, doubtless, to other nobles besides. The king's commissioners had been instructed to "presume" that since only kings could create and confer nobility, all nobles owed their status to the crown.[49] That "presumption," it is true, was an obligatory dogma in the age of Louis XIV and contemporary writers on nobility normally embraced it.[50] Still, they refused to agree with Louis XIV's commissioners that all nobles were alike, all equal members of a single *ordre* created by the crown. Instead, they insisted that "illustrious" nobility and immemorial nobility (*gentilshommes de nom et d'armes*) differed fundamentally from nobility created by the crown, whether freshly ennobled or already at least four generations old (the legal definition of "old" or "perfect" nobility).[51] A Frenchmen holding these principles might readily deplore Louis XIV's *recherches* and the provincial catalogs of nobility that they inspired, especially since their compilers mixed all nobles indiscriminately in their alphabetically arranged lists. Boulainvilliers' complaint—that the intendants who conducted Louis XIV's *recherches* were "as barely conversant with the knowledge of families as they were barely informed of the nature of nobility"—is hardly surprising for a man of his social convictions.

Nor is his proposal to the duc d'Orléans that he wrest the work of reforming and cataloging the nobility from the intendants and entrust it to a permanent "General Chamber of the Nobility" at Paris. Not altogether a die-hard reactionary, Boulainvilliers admitted that the chamber might include commissioners from the "Magistracy of Paris" as well as from the "High Nobility." He admitted too that princes and peers might take precedence within it, just as they did (he wrote) at *lits de justice*. And he sought to accommodate royal authority, for he proposed that a chair and canopy symbolize the king's presence and presidency.

---

[49][Belleguise], *Traité de la noblesse et de son origine*, 1–7, 57–68. On Belleguise, one of the commissioners for Louis XIV's *recherches*, see Ford, *Robe and Sword*, 23–26.

[50]La Roque, *Traité de la noblesse*, 43–92, 178, 189–91. See also Menestrier, *Les Diverses espèces*, 215–96 (on ennoblement as a royal monopoly). This was, in fact, a position traditionally taken by early-modern jurists writing on nobility: see André Tiraqueau, *Commentarii de nobilitate et iure primigeniorum*, 3d ed. (Lyon: "apud Guliel. Rouillium," 1559), "Tractatus de nobilitate" (separately paginated), 66, 100; André Brejon, *André Tiraqueau, 1488–1558* (Paris: Recueil Sirey, 1937), 349–52.

[51]See Menestrier, *Les Diverses espèces*, 187–296, esp. 187–90; and above all La Roque, *Traité de la noblesse*, 12, and esp. 15: "He who is newly ennobled [*anobli*] may with time become a *gentilhomme;* but never a *Gentilhomme de nom & d'armes*, since he hasn't the antiquity [of extraction] for that. It is this antiquity that makes the difference between the *Gentilshommes de nom & d'armes*, those of extraction [*race*—i.e. nobility of less than immemorial extraction but more than four generations old], and the new *Anoblis*." See also Octave Le Maire, *L'Imprescriptibilité*, 2–4, for other examples. For the working principles of Louis XIV's commissioners, cf. Belleguise, *Traité de la noblesse et de son origine*, 52: ". . . order admits neither the more nor the less. . . ."

As for the chamber's catalog, Boulainvilliers allowed that new nobles (*anoblis*) might be listed in it, but he insisted that they be distinguished clearly from old nobles—"nobility by privilege" from "nobility by right."[52] He proposed, moreover, that *anoblis* be relegated to the lowest in a carefully graduated hierarchy of noble ranks to which houses would be assigned according to the antiquity of their extraction and the "illustriousness" of their members' service, religion, alliances, and dignities.[53]

Boulainvilliers wanted a catalog of nobility built on the assumptions of genealogical consciousness, not on the legalistic principles of royal commissioners ill-prepared to make fine distinctions between families according to their antiquity or illustriousness. In addition, Boulainvilliers wanted to entrust that catalog's compilation to men likely to share the assumptions of genealogical consciousness: the members of his "General Chamber of the Nobility." Convinced that noble status was a product of "birth," "virtue," "glory," and social esteem for them, he wished to commit its maintenance to the community that constituted it in the first place—the noble community—by restoring that community's autonomy.

Boulainvilliers was no less concerned to restore the autonomy of the "nation" by reviving its assemblies of Estates. In the second of the two memoranda that he submitted to Orléans at the beginning of the regency, Boulainvilliers urged him to assemble the Estates General at Bourges in August 1716 to let it retire Louis XIV's debts.[54] Saint-Simon had lately made a similar proposal, that Orléans summon the Estates to let it declare a partial bankruptcy and take the blame for it.[55] Boulainvilliers, however, was far more anxious to protect the king's creditors and enhance the credit of the Estates. True, he cared little about France's financiers, as echoing a long tradition, he called them "cruel bloodsuckers of the state." He showed them no sympathy as the regency's (equally traditional) Chambre de justice tried and mulcted them for peculation in 1716.[56] He sought nevertheless to protect the interests of rentiers and recipients of state wages and demanded that only the Estates could assume the task of retiring Louis XIV's debts without troubling the "confidence" in royal "wisdom" and "probity" on which the monarchy's finances depended.[57] Boulainvilliers was a rentier him-

[52]Bibliothèque du Sénat (Paris), MS. 990, fols. 1v–2, 2v–3, 3v–4v, 5v–6.
[53]Ibid., fols. 3v–4v.
[54]Boulainvilliers, *Mémoires presentés*, 1:13–4.
[55]Leclercq, *Histoire de la Régence*, 1:99, 154–55, 187–88.
[56]Boulainvilliers, *Mémoires présentés*, 1:13, 10. And see works cited in notes 65 and 69.
[57]Boulainvilliers, *Mémoires presentés*, 1:8. For the debts that Boulainvilliers wanted the Estates to retire and the creditors to whom they were owed, see ibid., 1:9–10: "The

self, but the interest of his argument is not exhausted when the personal interest that it may have served is identified.[58] He refused to countenance even a partial bankruptcy—even if it were said to be in the "public interest," he wrote, such a measure would despoil the "public" since the "public" consisted of the individuals who composed it.[59] He was proposing therefore that the French royal debt be assumed and managed by the Estates and transformed into a public or national debt like that lately established in England, where a sovereign and credit-worthy Parliament guaranteed the nation's debt to its creditors.[60] Boulainvilliers' financial ideas are not unsophisticated, but his financial concerns must not be exaggerated. He made few detailed recommendations of his own, and he urged the Regent to seek further advice elsewhere, by asking "everyone" to propose remedies which "several wise persons" would then screen, digest, and present for his consideration.[61] Boulainvilliers' own concerns were chiefly political. He sought to seize the opportunity that the fiscal problems created for reviving the Estates General and with it the autonomy of the "nation."

In the memoranda just considered Boulainvilliers pursued aims at once nobiliaire and national, reactionary and constitutionalist. He hoped to revive the old nobility's preeminence, and at the same time to end the "annihilation" and "slavery" to which Louis XIV had reduced the French.[62] Indeed, he now abandoned all deference for the dead king and opened his memorandum on calling the Estates by proclaiming: "Never has a government been so dear to France as that of His Royal Highness [the duc d'Orléans]. It follows a despotic, money-minded, very long and consequently odious reign."[63] At the beginning of the regency Boulainvilliers had high hopes indeed and he vested his hopes in the regent's goodwill. Boulainvilliers did not write solely to persuade him, however. He wrote also to serve him. A nobiliaire ideologue, Boulain-

---

liberation of the king's revenues has been carried to a considerable point by the revocation of assignments on anticipated receipts; but it does not appear that one can ever hope to extinguish charges on land, *rentes* on the [Hôtel de] Ville [of Paris], wages for useless offices, *rentes* constituted on the *aides, tailles* and *gabelles,* etc., without deliberation by the Estates General."

[58]Part of his family's fortune was invested in *rentes* on the *aides* and *gabelles* (Ellis, "Genealogy, History, and Aristocratic Reaction," 451).

[59]Boulainvilliers, *Mémoires presentés,* 1:4–5.

[60]P. G. M. Dickson, *The Financial Revolution in England: A Study in the Development of Public Credit: 1688–1756* (London: Macmillan; New York: St. Martin's Press, 1967). Cf. Meyer, *Le Régent,* 172–87, 220–35, and esp. 178, for John Law's French "financial revolution" which (while it may well have been Orléans's central concern and achievement) resembled neither England's nor Boulainvilliers'.

[61]Boulainvilliers, *Mémoires presentés,* 1:6–7, 9.

[62]Ibid., 1:2, 7.

[63]Ibid., 1:1.

villiers was also an *orléaniste* ideologue seeking to overcome the problems—their weight cannot be underestimated—which beset the Orléans regency and which may be traced to the dubious validity of Philip V's renunciation.

Philip of Spain's Renunciation and
the Problems of the Regency

Regencies, it has been argued, were usually *temps faibles* for the French monarchy.[64] The regency of Orléans appears to have been no exception, for during his first three years as regent, his concessions and experiments seem calculated to dismantle Louis XIV's machinery of government, reverse his policies, and promote what may be called aristocratic reaction. Louis had limited the size of his high council and had usually kept great nobles out of it. Orléans expanded his regency council into a "Polysynody" or system of colleges, each assigned its special function and each dominated by nobles. Louis had abolished the Parlements' right to remonstrate against royal legislation before registering it. Orléans, in one of his first acts as regent, restored that right. Louis had persecuted the Jansenists and secured a papal bull (*Unigenitus* or the celebrated "Constitution" [1713]) declaring their doctrines heretical. Orléans favored the Jansenists and named a leading Jansenist prelate (Cardinal Louis-Antoine de Noailles) president of the Polysynody's Council of Conscience. Finally, Louis had relied on financiers to fund his wars and collect his taxes. Orléans terrorized them, reenacting in March 1716 (and for the last time) one of the Old Regime's traditional political rituals, by establishing a Chambre de justice to try financiers for peculation, to fill the king's coffers with fines levied on them, and (incidentally) to discourage great nobles from making lucrative marriage "alliances" with them.[65]

Despite his experiments and concessions, however, Orléans was no champion of aristocratic reaction. On the contrary, he conducted him-

[64]Richet, *La France moderne*, 69–77.

[65]For these measures see Leclercq, *Histoire de la Régence*, 1:97–205, 295–313. On the *Chambre de justice* see also J. F. Bosher, "*Chambres de Justice* in the French Monarchy," in *French Government and Society 1500–1850: Essays in Memory of Alfred Cobban*, ed. Bosher (London: University of London Athlone Press 1973), 19–40; and above all Claude-Frédéric Lévy, *Capitalistes et pouvoir au siècle des Lumières*, vol. 2, *La Révolution libérale* (Paris: Mouton, 1979), 37–53, 83–105; see 86–91 on memoranda and speeches prepared for the Polysynody's Council of Finance in March 1716 when it established the Chambre and expressing its architects' hopes to discourage noble "misalliances" with financiers' daughters.

self as a prince determined to preserve intact the absolute royal authority entrusted to him.[66] The Polysynody, though inspired by Saint-Simon (who was inspired in turn, he claimed, by the duc de Bourgogne), was no more than an expansion of the Royal Council, not a fundamental change in its nature. Like the councils of Louis XIV, Orléans' councils were purely consultative, a "façade" behind which he continued to rely on the professional secretaries of state and their bureaus. Eventually, in 1718, he abolished the Polysynody altogether.[67] His concessions to the Parlements and the Jansenists turned out to be equally insubstantial and he qualified or withdrew them in the course of the regency.[68] The financial reforms with which the regency began fared no better. The Chambre de justice procured only limited profits; after 1718 Orléans turned away from the cautious policies of the Polysynody's Council of Finance, led by the duc de Noailles, to the brilliant but disastrous experiments of the Scottish adventurer John Law.[69] Regencies may have been *temps faibles* for the French monarchy, but the regency of Orléans fared better than most, thanks in fact to the administrative institutions that the monarchy had developed and that Orléans, despite his experiments and concessions, sought to maintain.[70]

During the regency, however, contemporaries could not foresee its outcome any more than they could read the regent's mind as they contemplated that artful dissembler's "pragmatic" accommodations to the shifting circumstances in which he found himself.[71] And Orléans himself seems to have been no less uncertain about his political fortunes.

[66]Shennan, *Philippe, Duke of Orléans*, 33–50.

[67]Ibid., 33–43; Michel Antoine, *Le Conseil du roi sous le règne de Louis XV* (Geneva: Droz, 1970), 77–100; Leclercq, *Histoire de la Régence*, 2:189–207; Meyer, *La Vie quotidienne en France au temps de la Régence*, 74–75, 85–87. On Saint-Simon as the architect of the "Polysynody," see Brancourt, *Le Duc de Saint-Simon*, 13, 147–62.

[68]Leclercq, *Histoire de la Régence*, 2:25–50, 129–87, 3:105–25. For conflicts between Orléans and the Parlement of Paris see J. H. Shennan, "The Political Role of the Parlement of Paris, 1715–1723," *Historical Journal*, 8 (1965): 179–200; Shennan, *The Parlement of Paris* (Ithaca, N.Y.: Cornell University Press, 1968), 285–96; and also James D. Hardy, Jr., *Judicial Politics in the Old Regime: The Parlement of Paris during the Regency* (Baton Rouge: Louisiana State University Press, 1967).

[69]Leclercq, *Histoire de la Régence*, 1:179–205; 2:99–127, 385–407, 459–81. On the financial history of the regency see also Guy Chaussinand-Nogaret, *Gens de finance au XVIIIe siècle* (Paris: Bordas, 1972), 9–37; Edgar Faure, *La Banqueroute de Law: 17 juillet 1720* (Paris: Gallimard, 1977); Lévy, *Capitalistes et pouvoir*, 2 *La Révolution libérale*; idem, *Capitalistes et pouvoir au siècle des Lumières*, vol. 3, *La Monarchie buissonnière 1718–1723* (Paris: Mouton, 1980). According to Jean Meyer, Orleans' greatest achievement was sustaining Law's experiment with paper money and a central royal bank (*Le Regent*, 172–87, 220–35), although that experiment ended in speculative fever and bankruptcy in 1720.

[70]Richet, *La France moderne*, 75, 76. Shennan, *Philippe, Duke of Orléans*, 139–43.

[71]Meyer, *Le Régent*, 29–32, 133–34; Shennan, *Philippe, Duke of Orléans*, 135.

When Breton nobles rose against his rule at the end of 1719, in a rebellion rightly dismissed as a negligible threat to his authority, Orléans suppressed it with 15,000 troops and executed four of its seven leaders within two hours of their conviction. Such alacrity suggests nagging fears of a new Fronde.[72] It also suggests genuine anxieties about his dynastic and political position in France, for behind the Breton conspiracy and inspiring its participants stood Philip V of Spain.[73] It is appropriate, then, to return to the dynastic, diplomatic, and political questions that first arose in 1712 when the duc de Bourgogne died and when Philip V renounced his rights to succeed to the French throne.

Philip's renunciation, or rather its dubious validity, was at the heart of the problems besetting Orléans during his regency. Since 1560 it had been French practice to assign the regencies of minor kings to their mothers. But French dynastic custom continued to authorize the assumption that regencies properly belonged to the heirs of minor kings, that is, to the princes destined to succeed to their throne should they die.[74] Inasmuch as Louis XV's mother was dead it was clear that his regent would be the prince next in line to the throne. According to dynastic custom, that prince was Philip V and the regency would have been his had he returned from Spain. No one forgot, of course, that in 1712 Philip had renounced his and his heirs' rights to succeed to the French throne. But Frenchmen could question that act's validity. Despite his devotion to Orléans, Saint-Simon did question it, for he believed that only ratification by the peerage would have legitimized Philip's renunciation. At the beginning of the regency he told Orléans that the French would be obliged to obey Philip V as regent were that prince to return from Spain.[75] Saint-Simon was not alone: Louis XIV and the duc d'Orléans himself agreed that Philip V's renunciation was an invalid breach of the inviolable and fundamental law of the royal succession in France.[76] Contemporaries could easily believe, therefore, that Orléans was regent only because Philip V was absent in Spain.

[72]Meyer, *Le Régent*, 215–18.
[73]Baudrillart, *Philippe V et la cour de France*, 2:326–402, esp. 372–402; Leclercq, *Histoire de la Régence*, 2:331–64.
[74]Despite his conviction that precedents were contradictory and prince regents dangerous, the seventeenth-century *érudit* and apologist for the Cardinal Ministers, Pierre Dupuy, subscribed to that view in his *Traité de la majorité de nos rois, et des régences du royaume*, 2 vols., 2d ed. (Amsterdam: Jansons à Waesberge, 1722), 1:16–151, esp. 49–50. On French dynastic custom and debates about female regencies in the seventeenth century see Giesey, "The Juristic Basis of Dynastic Right to the French Throne"; and Harriet Lightman, "Queens and Minor Kings in French Constitutional Law," *Proceedings of the Annual Meeting of the Western Society for French History, 1981*, 9 (1982): 26–36.
[75]Saint-Simon, *Mémoires*, 23:145–56, 322–47.
[76]Shennan, *Philippe, Duke of Orléans*, 21.

Louis XIV's bastards posed another threat to Orléans. The late king had long since sought to enhance the credit of his sons by Madame de Montespan, the duc du Maine and the comte de Toulouse. By his Declaration of May 5, 1694, he legitimated them. By his Edict of May 1711 regulating the peerage Louis gave his bastards an "intermediate rank" above the dukes and peers and below the legitimate princes of the blood. To those acts by a doting father may be added two others by an anxious dynast concerned (since death had claimed all but two of his legitimate male descendants between 1711 and 1714) to maintain his house on the French throne. By the Edict of July 1714, the king added Maine and Toulouse and their legitimate male descendants to the line of succession, after the legitimate princes of the Orléans and Condé houses. Finally, by his Declaration of May 23, 1715, Louis conferred on Maine and Toulouse the title or "quality" of "prince of the blood."[77] By enacting this legislation Louis XIV confused bastardy and legitimacy, he disrupted court hierarchy, he demeaned the dukes and peers' rank in it by creating a new rank above theirs and filling it with his bastards, and he appeared to extend his own sovereign will over the French royal succession which, it was assumed, an inviolable dynastic custom regulated. It is not surprising that his legislation angered rank-conscious contemporaries, preeminent among them Saint-Simon and his fellow dukes and peers, or that it eventually occasioned a noisy controversy during the regency.[78] But Louis XIV's legislation also enhanced his bastards' credit, particularly the duc du Maine's, and encouraged the creation around that prince of a party rivaling the coterie surrounding Orléans. Louis XIV's testament had the same effect.

The king drafted his last will and testament at Versailles on August 2, 1714, and entrusted it to the first president and procurator general of the Parlement of Paris three weeks later. Only the king knew the document's contents, but contemporaries could surmise that it concerned the approaching regency and the relative positions in it of the duc du Maine and the duc d'Orléans. After the duc de Berry's death early in 1714, no one doubted that the regency would devolve on Orléans. That eventuality dismayed influential persons at court and the king too, who all deplored the libertinism of Orléans, his interest in alchemy, and his ambition (as noted earlier, it was rumored that he had poisoned Bourgogne and his family in 1712). In the eyes of a suspicious court that had

[77]For this legislation see the contemporary printed editions listed in B.N., *Catalogue général des livres imprimés de la Bibliothèque Nationale, Actes royaux*, 7 vols. (Paris: B.N., 1910–60), nos. 18320, 24561, 25605, 25882.
[78]See Labatut, *Les Ducs et pairs*, 340–50; Emmanuel Le Roy Ladurie, "Auprès du roi, la cour," *Annales. E.S.C.*, 38 (1983): 21–41; see chapter 6 on the *affaire des princes* of 1716–17.

effectively ostracized him, Orléans was too dangerous a man to be entrusted with the regency and government of a minor king. In his testament, consequently, Louis XIV imposed a regency council of his own choosing on Orléans and required that decisions taken by a majority of its members bind him. In addition, Louis assigned control over the future Louis XV's education and the royal household troops to the duc du Maine. Louis seems to have appreciated that the testaments of French kings had never bound their successors in the past (his own father's testament had been quashed shortly after his death and so would his own). He drafted his testament nevertheless, doubtless bowing to pressure from his court and above all from Madame de Maintenon and the duc du Maine. It was inevitable, then, that the regency would begin with a contest for influence between Maine and the regent, whose first act, it will be remembered, was to go to Parlement on September 2, 1715, and have the late king's testament opened, read, and nullified.[79]

Philip V's renunciation remained at the heart of this tangled knot of dynastic problems, however, for the claim of Philip V to succeed to the French throne preempted that of Orléans, weakened Orléans' hold on the regency, and inspired malcontents—not only *frondeur* nobles of Brittany but also the duc du Maine's party at Paris—alienated by his regime.[80] Hence the regent's "pragmatic" experiments and concessions of 1715–18. Hence too his innovative diplomacy in that same period. With the aid of his minister the abbé (and later cardinal) Guillaume Dubois, Orléans sought to isolate Philip V; align France with Austria, the United Provinces, and Hanoverian Britain; and thereby reinforce his tenuous political position in France. When the Quadruple Alliance of 1718 finally crowned his efforts, he abandoned the "pragmatic" concessions of 1715–18 to embark on other experiments promoted by John Law.[81]

[79]For Louis XIV's testament and the position of the duc d'Orléans at court at the end of his reign see Faure, *La Banqueroute de Law*, 70–71, 77; Leclercq, *Histoire de la Régence*, 1:1–32; Meyer, *Le Régent*, 112–15, 122–23; Shennan, *Philippe, Duke of Orléans*, 11–17 Wolf, *Louis XIV*, 615–16. In 1712, after the duc de Bourgogne's death, men in and out of favor reflected in memoranda for the king or his advisers on the possibility of "excluding" the duc d'Orléans from a future regency. See Fénelon, *Ecrits et lettres politiques*, 125–30, esp. 125; and André Picciola, "Sur l'établissement de la Régence: Mémoire inédit du chancelier de Pontchartrain," *Dix-huitième Siècle*, 8 (1976), 306 (Picciola hesitates to believe, however, that Pontchartrain's "exclusions" concerned Orléans). In 1712, of course, the princes likely to be regent were the duc de Berry or his older brother the king of Spain, not Orléans.

[80]Baudrillart, *Philippe V et la cour de France*, 2:326–48; Leclercq, *Histoire de la Régence*, 2:247–81, 305–64; Meyer, *Le Régent*, 188–219.

[81]This thesis is argued at length by Leclercq, *Histoire de la Régence*. (On the formation of the "Anglo-French *entente*" in 1716–18 see also McKay and Scott, *Rise of the Great Powers*,

In fact, the problems raised by Philip V's doubtful renunciation of his rights to the French throne continued to trouble French politics, complicate the kingdom's diplomacy, and inspire treatises and polemics until 1729, when at last an heir to Louis XV was born.[82] Yet even before those treatises and polemics had begun to appear in 1718–19—when the war against a now-isolated Spain first occasioned their publication—the French succession and Philip V's renunciation had already exacerbated the conflicts among the aristocratic French elites.[83] It may be argued that the dynastic difficulties besetting the French monarchy in the early eighteenth century had two consequences. First, they raised the pos-

---

106, 108–15.) Jean Meyer has suggested another though not incompatible reason for the suppression of the Polysynody in 1718: the *vieille cour* attachments of many of its members, a possible source of trouble for the Regent now engaged in isolating Spain and aligning France with Louis XIV's former enemies (*Le Régent*, 160–67). It will be noted that Philip V had a firm supporter in the Polysynody's foreign minister, Nicolas du Blé, marquis and maréchal d'Huxelles.

[82]For these later developments see Baudrillart, *Philippe V et la cour de France*, 2:7–8, 3:276–344, 455–78; Bourbon, *Le Traité d'Utrecht*, 216–24; Courcy, *Renonciation des Bourbons d'Espagne*, 297–302. See Baudrillart, 2:7–8 and 3:456–57, for Père Poisson's unpublished *orléaniste* tract (ca. 1723) and for the abbé Joachim Legrand's rigorous vindication of French fundamental law, the *Traité de la succession à la couronne* (Paris: Gabriel Martin, 1728). During the War of the Spanish Succession Legrand wrote for Colbert de Torcy to defend Philip V's dynastic claims to Spain and (later) to resist Allied proposals that he renounce his succession rights in France (Klaits, *Printed Propaganda under Louis XIV*, 246–72). Despite a French rapprochement with Spain in the late 1720s, Legrand's treatise was suppressed. Legrand was not the only *érudit* to discuss the French royal succession and Philip V's renunciation. To begin see the critique of French historians and scholars written by the English Hanoverian apologist Pierre Rival, *Examen d'une partie de la dissertation de M. l'abbé de Vertot, qui a pour titre "Sur l'origine des loix saliques", etc.* (London: frères Vaillant, 1722; 2d ed. Amsterdam: Pierre Humbert, 1726). Rival was chaplain in the British king's French chapel at Saint James. The abbé René de Vertot whom he sought to criticize was a member of the Académie des Inscriptions. His "Dissertation" antedates the regency but was printed during it: "Dissertation sur l'origine des loix saliques, et si c'est précisément en vertu de l'article LXII. paragraphe 6. que les filles de nos rois sont excluës de la succession à la couronne," in *Memoires de littérature tirez des registres de l'Académie Royale des Inscriptions et Belles Lettres, depuis le renouvellement de cette Académie jusqu'en M.DCCX.: Tome second* (Paris: Imprimerie Royale, 1717), 651–68. A careful study of research and writing on French history in the early-eighteenth-century Académie is badly needed.

[83]The leading *orléaniste* tract was by the Jansenist Plantavit de la Pause, abbé de Margon, *Lettres de Monsieur Filtz-Moritz, sur les affaires du temps & principalement sur celles d'Espagne sous Philippe V. & les intrigues de la princesse des Ursins. Traduites de l'anglois par Monsieur de Garnesai. Seconde Edition augmentée d'une reponse à ces Lettres* (Amsterdam: Du Villard & Changuion, 1718). The "Réponse" in this edition was by the abbé Brigault, a client of the duc and duchesse du Maine's and party to their plots against Orléans in 1718 (Leclercq, *Histoire de la Régence*, 2:255, 262, 265, 269). His "Réponse" first circulated in MS; a copy is bound into one of the B.N.'s copies of the first edition of "Filtz-Moritz" (*cote* 8° Lb[38] 127 A). For later *orléaniste* (or *orléaniste*-Hanoverian) contributions see *L'Europe savante*, 11, no. 1 (May 1719): 3–47; [Thémiseul de Sainte-Hyacinthe], *Entretiens dans lesquels on traite des entreprises de l'Espagne, des prétentions de M. le Chevalier de S. George. Et de la renonciation de Sa Majesté Catholique. O.D.A.* (The Hague: A. de Rogissart, 1719); and Anon., *Conférence d'un anglois & d'un allemand sur les Lettres de Filtz-Moritz* (Cambrai: P. Secret, 1722).

sibility that dynastic custom might be abrogated or modified. That possibility was alien to the traditional notion of fundamental laws constituted by custom, constitutive of the monarchy, and superior to the will of monarchs. Yet when Louis XIV adding his bastards to the royal succession, or when Saint-Simon proposed that an assembly of peers exclude the king of Spain from it, or, finally, when an *orléaniste* or Hanoverian publicist defended Philip V's renunciation as a departure from French fundamental law required and guaranteed by international law and treaty, early-eighteenth-century Frenchmen were forced to imagine that the realm's basic principles might deliberately be altered.[84] Second, if the realm's basic principles might be altered, then one had to determine by whom: a distinction, it will be argued in the next two chapters, that France's quarreling aristocratic elites sought to claim for themselves and to the exclusion of each other during the *affaire du bonnet* and the *affaire des princes*. At bottom, those quarrels were about nothing less than the authority of the duc d'Orléans and the roles that the aristocratic elites might play in securing or assigning it to him.

Boulainvilliers participated actively in those quarrels, as an *orléaniste* controversialist and as a nobiliaire ideologue vesting his hopes in the prince he sought to serve. Boulainvilliers' hopes were destined to be dashed and here he was not alone. The regent, it bears repeating, did not care to preside over an aristocratic reaction or over any constitutional experiment that really threatened Ludovican absolutism. Yet the aristocratic quarrels of 1715–17 and Boulainvilliers' contributions to them merit attention, for they reveal the political possibilities imaginable among members of the noble elites as the French monarchy traversed its dynastic crisis at the beginning of the eighteenth century.

[84]Thus [Saint-Hyacinthe], *Entretiens*, or Anon., *Conférence*.

5

The *Affaire du Bonnet* (1715–1716) and Boulainvilliers' Hopes

On September 1, 1715, Louis XIV died. Early the next morning, the duc d'Orléans went to the Parlement of Paris, where the late king's testament was to be opened and read. Keeping its promise to Orléans, the court quashed the testament, thus lifting the restrictions that Louis had sought to impose on the regent's authority. Now Orléans would enjoy the fullness of royal authority unhampered by a regency council of the late king's choosing or by the duc du Maine's command of the royal household troops. On September 15, a grateful duc d'Orléans kept a promise of his own and restored the Parlements' right—Louis XIV had suppressed it in 1673—to remonstrate against royal legislation before registering it.

The bargain that began the regency is justly celebrated, for it set the stage for the eighteenth century's repeated confrontations between the king and "his" sovereign courts.[1] Less familiar is the aristocratic controversy about an unwritten French constitution that also began on September 2. At first glance, the *affaire du bonnet* hardly seems capable of bearing the weight that will be assigned to it here. Although it might be tempting to dismiss that dispute as merely another, albeit noisy episode in a long contest about rank and precedence that had opposed dukes and peers to the great magistrates of the Parlement of Paris since the early seventeenth century (and until the end of the Old Regime), the *affaire du bonnet* must be taken seriously.[2] It engaged the robe and sword

---

[1] Jean Egret, *Louis XV et l'opposition parlementaire 1715–1774* (Paris: Armand Colin, 1970), 10; Ford, *Robe and Sword*, 79–104.

[2] See Grellet-Dumazeau, *L'Affaire du bonnet,* for a useful account of ducal-parlementaire conflicts in the seventeenth and early eighteenth centuries despite its tendency to dismiss the dukes and peers as social throwbacks blindly hostile to the rise of the robe. Cf. A.N., K.622 (9³⁴ and 9⁴¹) (ducal memoranda against parlementaire breaches of courtesy dating to Louis XVI's reign).

elites in a quarrel for social preeminence coveted by all and it led them to support their (only apparently small) claims to preeminence with big arguments about the history of an unwritten French constitution and their own places in it.[3] After Louis XIV's death, the quarrel between parlementaires and peers acquired an explicitly political dimension, for it unfolded amidst doubts about the regent's dynastic right to the authority that he had assumed. Now the *affaire du bonnet* became a debate about regencies and the royal succession recalling the debates that had already taken place in court and princely circles even before Louis XIV's death. During the *affaire* those debates became "public" debates, as parlementaires and above all peers appealed to a "public" whose size and character remain to be determined but whose existence—as audience and as rhetorical postulate—shifted the conflict into a "public sphere" that had not existed under Louis XIV.[4]

In this context Boulainvilliers continued to write the history of France, not only as a princely client and counselor but also (and for the first time) as a princely controversialist: he began writing his "Lettres sur les parlements ou états généraux" on the duc d'Orléans' orders.[5] In this same context Boulainvilliers continued to write history as a nobiliaire ideologue. Nevertheless, as untitled nobles gathered in assemblies and entered the *affaire* to press claims of their own—here was yet another novelty of the conflict as it developed during the regency—he did not add his voice to theirs.[6] His commitment to Orléans prevented that (especially when the noble assemblies fell under the duc du Maine's influence) and so did his own convictions as a nobiliaire ideologue. His commitment to the ideals of genealogical consciousness, it will be argued in this chapter and the next, clearly distinguished his position from that taken by the assembling nobles. Yet Boulainvilliers' hopes as a nobiliaire ideologue were never higher than during the *affaire du bonnet*. During that aristocratic controversy about regencies, the royal succession, and the provisions of an unwritten French constitution, Boulainvilliers wrote history not only to defend Orléans' authority but also to invite him to use it—as Charlemagne had once used his—to restore a noble civic order that the French monarchy had destroyed in the course of its long history.

[3]See Labatut, *Les Ducs et pairs,* 401–27; also see chapter 2.
[4]The term "public sphere" is that of Jürgen Habermas; see n. 48 of chapter 1.
[5]Fréret, "Lettre de M. Fréret," 202.
[6]As other historians have sought to insist; see Lassaigne, *Les Assemblées de la noblesse,* 137, 143 (on Boulainvilliers as "the brain of these assemblies"), 146; and above all Devyver, *Le Sang épuré,* 258–60. These judgments rest on the faulty ascription to Boulainvilliers of a single pamphlet issued by the assembling nobles during the *affaire des princes;* see chapter 6, n. 64.

It is no exaggeration to say that the *affaire du bonnet* is one of the more remarkable chapters in the history of aristocratic ideologies of the Old Regime—and in the history of Boulainvilliers' own career as a nobiliaire ideologue and historian.

Dynastic Conflict and Aristocratic Constitutionalism

The *affaire du bonnet* had a long history. As early as 1643 the first president of the Parlement of Paris had neglected to remove his hat (his *bonnet*) when asking for the opinions of dukes and peers accompanying the king to Parlement for *lits de justice* and "royal sessions." But no peer objected to such breaches of respect for the ducal dignity until 1681, when the new bishop-count of Châlons (Louis-Antoine de Noailles, the future cardinal) came to Parlement for his reception. On that occasion, the duc d'Uzès (Emmanuel II de Crussol, by right of seniority the first lay peer of the realm) angrily put his hat back on when the first president failed to take his off. That event was immortalized in the hypersensitive memories of the peers, Saint-Simon's above all, and a spat about formal courtesy became an *affaire:* the *affaire du bonnet.*

Despite its name the *affaire du bonnet* was not only about the putting on and taking off of hats. Also at issue was the order of opining at *lits de justice* and "royal sessions," so important in the 1660s and still a matter of contention between peers and the Parlement during the regency. Another source of conflict was the court's practice of seating ordinary councillors at the ends of the high benches of the Grand'Chambre, supposedly reserved to the peers. Thus the *affaire du bonnet* was a long and many-sided contest between peerage and Parlement fought on one of the Old Regime's leading ceremonial battlefields, *lits* and "royal sessions" in the Parlement's Grand'Chambre.

A contest for social preeminence, the *affaire du bonnet* was a constitutional conflict too. Even before the regency, the polemics it occasioned could raise constitutional questions—perhaps inevitably, given the rich constitutional meanings that attached to *lits de justice* and "royal sessions" in the Grand'Chambre.[7] During the regency, dynastic conflicts and the political questions they raised further enhanced the constitutional significance of the *affaire,* and now that Louis XIV was dead it easily became a sustained constitutional debate among the aristocratic elites.[8]

[7]Hanley, *The* Lit de Justice *of the Kings of France.*
[8]Among earlier studies of the *affaire,* Lassaigne's is most sensitive to the dynastic conflicts behind it; see *Les Assemblées de la noblesse,* 130–32, 146–47.

Even before Louis XIV's death dynastic conflicts could exacerbate the *affaire,* as the duc du Maine sought to embroil the peerage in conflict with Parlement to weaken ducal resistance to his own newly exalted rank.[9] Only after the king's death, however, did the peers and magistrates manage to ignite their quarrel. Indeed it may be said to have begun on the same occasion that launched the regency: the September 2 session of the Parlement of Paris.

That celebrated session, it has been observed, was an anomaly. It had become customary to launch the reigns of minor kings by bringing them to Parlement for "inaugural" *lits* demonstrating that royal legislative authority continued undiminished even during minorities. On September 2, however, the king was absent and he was not to come to Parlement for his "inaugural" *lit* until September 12. On September 2, therefore, not the king but the persons present in the Parlement's Grand'Chambre inaugurated the regency.[10] This ceremonial innovation raised the Parlement's credit. Orléans enhanced it further by declaring that while he owed the regency to his dynastic status he would be "flattered" to receive the "suffrages" and "approbation" of the assembly's members.[11] At the "inaugural" *lit* of September 12, the Parlement's *gens du roi* repeated that language, but subtly transformed Orléans' "suffrages"—an added but constitutionally unnecessary vote of confidence graciously requested of the September 2 assembly—into a necessary constitutive act performed by the Parlement and literally "conferring" the regency upon him.[12]

[9]For these preliminary skirmishes see Grellet-Dumazeu, *L'Affaire du bonnet,* 158–75; and (for contemporary ducal accounts) A.N., K.622 (9³); A.N., K.648 (32); Archives du Ministère des Affaires étrangères (Paris), Mémoires et documents, France, MS. 205, fols. 195–97v; and *Recueil de pièces concernant les différends des pairs de France avec les présidens à mortier du Parlement de Paris* (Paris: Antoine-Urbain Coustelier, 1716), 1 ("Mémoire des pairs de France présenté au roy à Marly le [blank] novembre 1714") (several copies in A.N., K.648 [76] and at the B.N.; for the latter see B.N., *Catalogue des factums et d'autres documents judiciaires antérieures à 1790,* 10 vols. [Paris: Imprimerie Nationale, 1890–1936], 4:103). Maine's rank is discussed in chapter 4.
[10]Hanley, *The Lit de Justice of the Kings of France,* 333–35. For a fuller description of the September 2 session see Leclercq, *Histoire de la Régence,* 1:1–32, 82–83, 97–126.
[11]A.N., U.907 (2): *Procez verbal de ce qui s'est passé au Parlement, le lundy deuxieme septembre mil sept cens quinze* (Paris: Veuve Hubert Muguet, Louis Denis de Latour, 1715), 7: "I am . . . persuaded that according to the laws of the kingdom, according to what has been done in similar conjunctures, and according to the very intention [*destination*] of the late king, the Regency belongs to me; but I shall not be satisfied if to so many titles joined in my favor you do not join your suffrages, and your approbation, which shall flatter me no less than the Regency itself."
[12]A.N., U.907 (4): *Extrait des registres de Parlement. Du jeudy douziéme septembre mil sept cens quinze, de relevée* (Paris: Veuve Fr. Muguet, Hubert Muguet, Louis Denis de Latour, 1715), 7, 9: "Nature, our laws, and our suffrages have conferred [*ont deferé*] the Regency of your kingdom . . . upon Monsieur le Duc d'Orléans whom we regard as the guardian angel of the state"; " . . . a perfect unanimity has joined all the wishes of this company to confer [*déferer*] the Regency upon a prince whom birth and merit summoned to it" (the first

Orléans probably did not intend to compromise his dynastic right to the regency by exalting the "suffrages" of persons present in the Parlement's Grand'Chambre on September 2, but he had solicited those "suffrages" nonetheless. That act, no less than the revival of the Parlement's right to remonstrate, encouraged the court to claim that it had "declared" the regency and to pursue its old ambition to be legislative tutor to minor kings and their regents.[13]

The ceremonial innovations of September 2 and the rhetoric surrounding them had yet another consequence: they exacerbated the *affaire du bonnet* by raising its stakes. The dukes and peers were not surprised, of course, when the Parlement's first president once again failed to remove his hat when taking their opinions. In fact they had already agreed to Orléans' request not to disrupt the September 2 session by insisting on the *bonnet*. In return, he allowed them to prepare notarized "protestations" against Parlement's "usurpations" and he promised the dukes and peers a judgment on the *bonnet* within fifteen days. But while the dukes and peers planned to put the *affaire du bonnet* on ice on September 2, the Parlement escalated the conflict. Early that morning, the court assembled to prepare a procedural decree or *arrêté* stipulating that if the peers failed to observe procedure that the court deemed correct, their votes would not be counted. The peers fell into the trap. They refused to uncover their heads since the first president failed to do so. They even refused to utter their opinions, claiming that they had done so already when the princes of the blood (next to whom they sat on the Grand'Chambre's high benches) had given theirs. Predictably, the court refused to count the peers' votes and even omitted from its record of the September 2 session the traditional formula for indicating the peers' presence: "the court sufficiently garnished by peers," *la cour suffisamment garnie des pairs*. Because of a spat about ceremonial courtesy, the peers lost their political voice. And they lost it on what contemporaries took to be a great and extraordinary state occasion.[14]

Regaining that political voice was at the top of the dukes and peers'

---

president's and the king's advocate's speeches, respectively). The chancellor's speech on the same occasion betrays his reservations about the Parlement's right to "confer" the regency, for he mentioned only Orléans' "birth," that is, his dynastic status, when commenting on his right to be regent: "His [the king's] authority shall be exercised by a prince regent, to whom this title is due by his birth" (ibid., 6).

[13]Hanley, *The* Lit de Justice *of the Kings of France*, 333–41.

[14]Grellet-Dumazeau, *L'Affaire du bonnet*, 209–16; Leclercq, *Histoire de la Régence*, 1:100, 101, 104, 124–26; *Recueil de pièces*, 3–4: "Protestations des Pairs faites au Parlement le 2. septembre 1715. Luës par l'archeveque de Reims, & reçües par S. A. R. M. le duc d'Orléans, Regent."

agenda when, after waiting in vain for Orléans' promised judgment on the *bonnet*, they assembled on December 15 to draft and submit two petitions to the king and one to Orléans.[15] In their petition to the regent they asked for the speedy judgment on the *bonnet* that he had promised them.[16] In their petitions to the king they made still weightier demands. Claiming to be the "necessary judges" of "public affairs," the dukes and peers declared that their presence alone gave Parlement "that preeminence of legislation and dignity that it claims over all the other parlements of the kingdom." Accordingly they demanded that the formula attesting their presence—"that sacred formula of our ancestors: *la Cour sufisament garnie des Pairs*"—be restored in all "acts which regulated at Parlement the most important affairs of state like the succession to the crown and the government of the kingdom." Omitting that formula, they warned, compromised the "validity" of such acts.[17] And because they were the "only" persons in the kingdom competent to be "judges" of "public affairs," the peers also asked that the Parlement's September 2 *arrêté*—the procedural decree which had deprived them of their constitutional voice that day and which they pronounced "in contempt [*attentatoire*] of your authority [and] contrary to all laws"—be "crossed and rubbed out" of the court's registers.[18] Again they insinuated that constitutional acts performed without their participation might be invalid, including the measures taken on September 2 to inaugurate the Orléans regency:

[15]*Recueil de pièces,* 5–16. For ducal assemblies during the regency (there were to be more) see Labatut, *Les Ducs et pairs,* 393–400, 414–19, and A.N., K.648 (5–56): assembly minutes kept by the peers' secretary Antoine Lancelot and related documents (notably drafts, final texts, and printed editions of ducal petitions and memoranda). In A.N., K.648 (21), there is a polished and shortened version of the minutes for the assemblies occasioned by the *affaire du bonnet* which sometimes clarifies obscurities in the original set: "Extrait des assemblées de MM. les ducs et pairs de France."
[16]*Recueil de pièces,* 5–6.
[17]Ibid., 10–11:
It would matter little if the presidents remained there [with their ceremonial usurpations at the peers' expense]. The peers alone would find themselves injured by these enterprises, but the most ancient usages are violated by the innovation that they have lately introduced in seeking ambitiously [*en affectant*] to suppress in acts which regulated at Parlement the most important affairs of state like the succession to the crown and the government of the kingdom that sacred formula of our ancestors: *La Cour sufisamment garnie des Pairs,* A formula repeated so often in old acts. A formula which, expressing the presence of the peers in the Parlement, established the right that they had on these occasions to speak on public affairs. A formula whose absence compromises the validity of the most solemn acts. A formula, finally, that the presidents have suppressed in recent times, in order to confuse peers with councillors [of the Parlement], whose presence is not expressed in the wording of the decree because, not being necessary judges, they were not invited, as were the peers.
[18]Ibid., 14–15.

The presidents have tried to exclude the peers from the Parlement on an occasion when, since it was a matter of ruling on the most important affairs of state, assuring the form of government during Your Majesty's minority, and conferring [*conférer*] the regency upon the prince to whom the law of blood assigned [*déféroit*] it, the peers alone truly had the right to judge while the Parlement of Paris held its right to speak on this occasion only from the presence and only by the agreement of these same peers.[19]

Clearly, the *affaire du bonnet* was about the dynastic and constitutional problems of the regency and the responsibility for solving them which, the peers imagined, was theirs alone. They were already claiming that responsibility in January 1715 when, in an unsubmitted petition to Louis XIV, they pronounced Philip V's renunciation invalid because the Parlement omitted the *cour suffisamment garnie* formula when registering it.[20] A year later, Saint-Simon himself told Orléans that the fundamental issues of the *affaire* were its constitutional issues: the September 2 *arrêté*, the *cour suffisamment garnie* formula. Such issues as the "chapeau aux audiences," Saint-Simon declared, were merely "matters whose brilliance dazzles though solidity is not to be encountered in them" (*choses dont l'éclat éblouisse si le solide ne s'y rencontre pas*).[21] In their *Mémoire des pairs de France contre les présidens à mortier du Parlement de Paris* published in March 1716, the dukes and peers gave pride of place to constitutional argument. In the last pages of the *Mémoire,* they complained that by effectively excluding the peers from the proceedings of September 2, the Parlement had prevented them from performing their "essential functions," which were "to counsel and assist the king in his most high, great, and important affairs." They added, "In this assembly of September 2, 1715, it was necessary to open the late king's testament, and to declare the regency. This right to declare the regency has always belonged to the barons, that is, to the princes of the blood, the peers, and the high nobility. And history shows that before 1610, not only did Parlements not involve themselves in conferring the regency, they were not even consulted on these occasions."[22]

Yet despite their massive doubts about the validity of the September 2

[19]Ibid., 14.
[20]A.N., K.622 (9⁴), fols. 3v–4.
[21]Archives du Ministère des Affaires étrangères (Paris), Mémoires et documents, France, MS. 205, fols. 192–94, esp. 193 ("Mémoire secret sur le bonnet à S.A.R.").
[22][Louis-Silvestre de Sacy], *Mémoire des pairs de France, contre les présidens à mortier du Parlement de Paris* (Paris: Antoine-Urbain Coustelier, 1716), 15–16 (copies in A.N., K.648 [77, 78]; for the B.N.'s copies see B.N., *Catalogue des factums*, 4:103). A rough draft of this *Mémoire* was ready on February 22, but rewriting it, securing the peerage's approval of it, and correcting printers' errors in it delayed its distribution until March 22 (A.N., K.648 [24, 28, 31, 33]). On the *Mémoire*'s author see n. 27.

proceedings, the dukes and peers did not wish to impugn Orléans' authority or to shake the already wobbly dynastic foundations on which it rested. On the contrary, they insisted that the Parlement's magistrates "want to recognize no superior authority during the minority."[23] At the same time they claimed that "regents have always been vested with the totality of sovereign power to judge all contestations."[24] The peers defended the regent's authority because they were appealing to the regent's judgment, not only in the *affaire du bonnet* but also in the *affaire Richelieu* which coincided with it. In that second dispute they sought to persuade Orléans to "evoke" the duc de Richelieu's trial for dueling from the Parlement, which the dukes and peers were boycotting because of the *bonnet,* to a special commission which the peers might attend and where Richelieu might enjoy the (in fact poorly established) ducal privilege to be tried by his peers.[25] Consistently, the dukes and peers asserted the regent's royal authority because they were appealing to it.

The dukes and peers came remarkably close to victory in the *affaire du bonnet.* While the Parlement sought to stall the conflict—the court questioned the regent's competence to judge it, protested the "violence" of the peers' demand that the September 2 *arrêté* be "crossed and rubbed out" of the court's registers, and refused to answer the peers' petitions with proper counterpetitions of its own—the peers plied Orléans with memoranda and deputations urging him to "force the Parlement to respond" to their petitions in writing and thus break the procedural deadlock.[26] Very likely the regent wished to avoid alienating either party by deciding between them but he intervened nonetheless, albeit not to "force" the Parlement to answer the peers' December petitions but to urge the peers to let Louis-Antoine de Sacy, the celebrated lawyer and man of letters, draft a new one on their behalf. The peers complied, adopted Sacy's text in assembly on February 12, and presented it Orléans the next day.[27] Little distinguished Sacy's petition or his later

[23]A.N., K.648 (18): a January 31, 1716, memorandum to the regent.
[24]A.N., K.648 (22): a February 13, 1716, memorandum to the regent.
[25]These events may be followed in A.N., K.648 (25, 27, 29, 36, 38, 41–44, 46–47, 50, 52). See also *Requeste du duc de Richelieu . . . présentée à sa majesté le 26 mars 1716* and *Requeste des pairs de France . . . présentée à sa majesté le 28 mars 1716* (a single publication; Paris: Antoine-Urbain Coustelier, 1716); and *Mémoire des pairs de France, servant de preuve à leur requeste du 28 mars 1716, sur l'affaire de M. le duc de Richelieu* (Paris: Antoine-Urbain Coustelier, 1716) (copies in A.N., K.619 [9³, 9⁴], and in Bibliothèque de l'Assemblée Nationale (Paris), MS. 336). On the ducal privilege of trial by peers see Labatut, *Les Ducs et pairs,* 85, 87.
[26]See A.N., K.648 (11–13, 16–22, 24–29, 31, 33). For Parlement's arguments and tactics see A.N., K.648 (17) (the dukes' syndics learned of the court's complaints against their "violent" language on January 27), and A.N., K.648 (11, 25, 26, 29).
[27]A.N., K.648 (19–22). Sacy's text was adopted over one prepared by the duc de La Force, but modified to include some of its arguments. Cf. marquise de Balleroy et al., *Les*

Mémoire des pairs from earlier ducal statements, for he too insisted that the Parlement's September 2 *arrêté* be expunged from the court's registers.[28] And little had changed in the Parlement's conduct, for the court still refused to answer the peers' petitions with anything more than verbal reports to the regent and explanatory decrees on its September 2 *arrêté* consigned to its own registers. But the regent was now prepared to decide the *affaire* in the dukes and peers' favor. On March 20, a triumphant Saint-Simon reported to the dukes and peers' syndics what he had learned in conversation with Orléans: "We shall have a council decree which quashes [the Parlement's *arrêté*]." Putting an end to weeks of alarming rumors he added, "The matter of the *affaire* will not be postponed to the king's majority."[29] And on March 22, the very day that the dukes and peers began to distribute copies of Sacy's *Mémoire*, Orléans issued his decree. Borrowing the "violent" language that the dukes and peers had used in December, he ordered the Parlement "to cross and rub out" of its registers the September 2 *arrêté* along with subsequent decrees explaining it. And he wiped the slate clean of precedents back to September 1, the day Louis XIV died.[30] Thus the regent repaid the dukes and peers' faith in the fullness of his royal authority.

The regent's resolve quickly evaporated, however. Since he hesitated to send his council decree to Parlement for registration, the peers took matters into their own hands and on March 27 they resolved in general assembly to "signify" the council decree to the Parlement just as victorious litigants customarily brought judgments in their favor to the attention of their vanquished opponents.[31] The next day the Parlement sent a deputation to the regent, to protest that act as an insult to a supreme public body like their own. And in the presence of the court's deputies Orléans withdrew his March 22 council decree, tore it up, and proclaimed his desire to remain on the best of relations with the court. A grateful Parlement opened its doors to the public on March 30, for a speech by the first president thanking Orléans for sparing the court the

Correspondants de la marquise de Balleroy d'après les originaux inédits de la Bibliothèque Mazarine, ed. Edouard de Barthélemy, 2 vols. (Paris: Hachette, 1883), 1:75 (? to the marquise de Balleroy, February 8, 1716): "The *affaire* of the dukes against the *présidens à mortier* is hotter than ever. M. le duc d'Orléans had ordered M. de Sassy [sic], the celebrated lawyer, to work on the dukes' brief [*factum*]; it is said that the Parlement does not wish to respond and that it wishes to hold to its possession [of its ceremonial precedence]; it is doubted that the regent wishes to judge the *affaire*."
[28]A.N., K.648 (22). For the *Mémoire* see above at n. 22.
[29]A.N., K.648 (33); for the rumors see A.N., K.648 (30).
[30]A.N., K.648 (33), contains two copies of the council decree.
[31]A.N., K.648 (36). On "signification" see *Encyclopédie méthodique: Jurisprudence*, 10 vols. (Paris: Pancoucke; Liège: Plomteux, 1782–91), 7:601–2.

"affront" of the peerage's "signification" and the need to resort to disagreeable means to contest it.[32]

The *affaire du bonnet* was not yet over, but the end was now in sight.[33] Ducal efforts to reverse Orléans' course were in vain,[34] and on April 30 a dismayed duc de La Force (Henri-Jacques-Nompar de Caumont) informed a general assembly of the peerage that the regency council was preparing a royal declaration to end the *affaire* in the Parlement's favor. Despite visits to the regent by the entire peerage,[35] Orléans issued his dreaded declaration on May 10—the Parlement registered it two days later—postponing any decision on the ducal petitions until Louis XV should choose to render one and-forbidding any opposition.[36] Disappointed and in disarray, the peers could not even get their collective "protestation" against the May 10 declaration notarized. Slowly, they broke their boycott of the Parlement and returned to their benches in the Grand'Chambre to attend, at last, Richelieu's trial.[37]

Despite the peerage's defense of the regent's authority and despite the Parlement's ambition to exalt itself as legislative tutor to minor kings and their regents, the sovereign court was clearly the victor.[38] The Parlement, not the peerage, was the body whose support Orléans felt he most needed. The outcome of the *affaire,* therefore, was one more sign of the Parlement's rising political credit during the regency.[39]

Orléans' remarkable reverses during the *affaire du bonnet* have yet other lessons. His oscillating position between the contending parties to the dispute may be traced not only to their arguments about his own authority but also to the movement of a public opinion that even he

[32]A.N., K.648 (27, 38); Philippe de Courcillon, marquis de Dangeau, *Journal . . . avec les additions du duc de Saint-Simon,* ed. Eud. Soulié et al., 19 vols. (Paris: Firmin Didot, 1854–60), 16:351–52 (March 28, 29, 30, 1716).

[33]One regency memorialist actually ended his account of the *affaire* with Orléans' retraction of his March 22 council decree: [Piossens], *Mémoires de la Régence,* 1:88–92.

[34]A.N., K.648 (39, 41).

[35]A.N., K.648 (45).

[36]*Declaration du Roy, donnée à Paris le 10. May 1716. Registrée en Parlement le 12. May 1716* (Paris: Veuve François Muguet, Hubert Muguet, Louis Denis de la Tour, 1716) (copy in A.N., K.648 [46]).

[37]A.N., K.648 (46–52). The original signed copy of the peers' "protestation" is in A.N., K.648 (50). The peers had to sign it secretly and keep individual copies of it as personal testaments.

[38]The anonymous parlementary author of the *Gazette de la Régence* rightly celebrated the May 12 declaration as a victory for the Parlement: Anon., *Gazette de la Régence, janvier 1715–juin 1719,* ed. E. de Barthélemy (Paris: Charpentier, 1887), 77–78 (May 15, 1716): "It is not stated [in the declaration] that the decision is remitted the king's majority, but to whenever it should please the king: one of the most delicate and able and advantageous expressions [*places*] for the Parlement. . . . In a word we have won our trial and the dukes have lost it."

[39]Leclercq, *Histoire de la Régence,* 2:97.

could not ignore. For the *affaire du bonnet* overflowed the boundaries of decorous litigation before the regency council and became a truly public debate about the regent's shaky authority and the provisions of an unwritten constitution for securing it.

On December 15, the dukes and peers sent their first petitions of the *affaire du bonnet* not only to the regent and to Louis XV but also to the printer.[40] Thus they appealed not only to the crown's authority but also to the public's and began an open contest before the tribunal of public opinion. But who constituted the "public" whose "opinion" they sought to persuade?

To answer that question, one may look first to the debates, memoranda, and pamphlets of the dukes and peers, who first brought the *affaire du bonnet* to the attention of a "public." They were finely sensitive to its opinions, even its opinions about the literary "style" of their petitions.[41] The dukes and peers attached still greater weight to the "opinion" that the "public" held of their petitions' substance. When the regent ordered them to stop printing their petitions on December 16, they implored him to let them proceed. No doubt Orléans had wanted to contain the public debate that the peers were trying to start, but he rescinded his order and asked only that they distribute no copies of their petitions before consulting him.[42] Consult him they did, for until he finally let them distribute their petitions at the beginning of January,[43] they lobbied him ceaselessly with deputations and memoranda. Among them was an illuminating memorandum explaining why they wanted their petitions to "become public by print."[44] Erroneous and provocative versions of their petitions printed by the Parlement, they explained, might be "capable of raising against us [*révolter contre nous*] the most disinterested readers." Were the peers to circulate their petitions in manuscript, they added, copyists' errors might mar them. "The public," the peers continued, might take any delay in publication to mean that the regent favored the Parlement. Already, they complained, rumors were circulating "in society"—*dans Le Monde*—that the dukes and peers' assemblies displeased the regent. It is clear that the dukes and peers understood "public" opinion as malleable, exposed to the thrust and

[40]A.N., K.648 (7).
[41]A.N., K.648 (10): A January 3 decision not to alter the text of the November 1714 petition to Louis XIV before printing it, although the "public" deplored its "style." The publication in question here is *Recueil de pièces*, containing peerage's November 1714 and December 1716 petitions.
[42]A.N., K.648 (7).
[43]A.N., K.648 (9, 10).
[44]A.N., K.648 (7): a December 17 memorandum to the regent.

parry of public argument in an ideological world no longer bound by a universal and authoritative consensus.[45] It is also clear that the "public" addressed by the dukes was tiny indeed, a "public" that might be reached not only by print but also by manuscript or by rumors circulating "about town"—*par tout Paris*, as they put it in a memorandum to the regent at the end of January.[46] That impression is confirmed by surviving evidence about the print runs and distribution of ducal pamphlets in 1716. When Orléans finally let the dukes and peers distribute (not sell) printed copies of their petitions, they proceeded to give each peer twelve copies to pass on to his friends. Thus they probably distributed little more than 420 copies in all.[47] The dukes and peers followed the same procedure for distributing Sacy's *Mémoire des pairs de France* at the end of March.[48]

[45]Cf. Klaits, *Printed Propaganda under Louis XIV*, 9, for whom only the Enlightenment would make such a public opinion possible.

[46]A.N., K.648 (18). Note too that the "public" had been assessing the "style" of ducal petitions even before they were printed (see above at n. 41).

[47]A.N., K.648 (9, 10). The minutes of the ducal assemblies, it is true, contain ambiguous information on the printing and distribution of the petitions (*Recueil de pièces*). Under December 27 the ducal secretary Lancelot reported that the petitions were now ready and wrote in the margin, "There are 28 of them" (A.N., K.648 [9]). In the abridged version of the minutes he again reported that 28 or 30 copies of the petitions were ready on December 27 (A.N., K.648 [21]: "Extrait des assemblées de MM. les ducs et pairs de France," fols. 2 and 2v). But these improbable figures represent only the copies at the peers' disposal around Christmastime, for in the minutes for January 3 Lancelot reported that the regent had finally permitted the peers to distribute printed copies of their petitions, that the peers prepared MS copies for the princes of the blood ("to pay them greater respect"), and that the peers then distributed 12 copies to *each* duke and peer for personal distribution. "Having paid this mark of respect to the princes," Lancelot wrote, "packets of 12 copies each were prepared to be sent to all M. M. les Pairs. These parcels were sent out on Saturday and Sunday" (A.N., K.648 [21]: "Extrait," fols. 3r, 3v). Still later, under January 8, Lancelot reported "a second dispatching of 12 copies the following Wednesday and Thursday" (A.N., K.648 [21]: "Extrait," fol. 3v). That remark may suggest that each peer actually received 24 and not 12 copies for distribution, but other evidence in the minutes (see n. 48) indicates that the dukes and peers adhered to the rule of sending each member of their order 12 copies of each pamphlet for distribution to his friends. There were more than seventy dukes and peers in 1715–16, but at most thirty-five seem to have been active in their order's general assemblies during the *affaire du bonnet* (see lists of participants and absentees who formally excused themselves for the December 15, February 12, and March 27 assemblies in A.N., K.648 [6, 21, 36]; the level of participation in the other general assemblies held during the *affaire*—for which see A.N., K.648 [28] [March 2], [42] [April 20], [44] [April 30], [45] [May 1], [47] [May 14], [49] [May 17], and [52] [May 25]—was consistently lower, running between twenty-seven and thirty-three). Thus only 420 copies of the peers' prints may have been distributed in 1716. The dukes and peers' "public" was tiny indeed, even by contemporary standards. Compare the average print run for seventeenth-century books (1,000 to 1,500 copies) or the observation by a mid-seventeenth-century *érudit* that "good" books (scholarly, philosophical, or mathematical publications) enjoyed print runs of between 500 and 750 (Martin, *Livre, pouvoirs et société*, 377–78 and 378 n.).

[48]As the following note to Lancelot indicates: "Monseigneur the bishop-duke of Coislin has charged Madame the duchess of Sully to ask you, monsieur, for twelve [*douz(e)*] copies of the last petition which MM. the dukes have just printed, since all MM. the dukes have

They probably followed that same rule when they distributed their other prints as well, their petitions to the regent concerning the *affaire Richelieu,* and above all their new edition of the ducal and parlementary petitions submitted to Louis XIV in 1662–64.[49] The dukes' "public" may have been a small one, but they made elaborate efforts to reach and persuade it. They plied it with magnificent folio editions of their memoranda and petitions, they regaled it with the massive historical arguments that they had marshaled in the 1660s, and they were still seeking to compile for its edification a monumental collection of documentary "proofs" supporting their claims when the regent brought the *affaire du bonnet* to an end in May.[50]

The dukes and peers' extensive efforts to publicize their constitutional claims and their historical arguments for them did not go unanswered. On the contrary, claims that had been anodyne at the beginning of Louis XIV's personal reign turned out to be inflammatory at the beginning of the Orléans regency, their weight enhanced by their applicability to his dynastic and political problems.[51] Not surprisingly, they provoked an outburst of hostile parlementary and noble propaganda in April 1716 which, it will be argued, led the regent suddenly to reverse his decision to end the *affaire* with a decree in the dukes' favor. The Parlement, it is true, had no petitions and memoranda of its own to print and publish, for the court refused to answer the dukes' petitions in writing. But it could open its doors to the public for speeches by its first president. And it could resort to manuscript pamphleteering. At the end of April Parisians began acquiring copies of a short "Mémoire pour le Parlement contre les ducs et pairs présenté à monseigneur le duc d'Orléans, Régent." As its

received as many. She prays you to send them to her by the present porter" (in A.N., K.648 [35], minutes for March 25, 1716). The "petition" in question is probably Sacy's *Mémoire des pairs,* which the dukes and peers had begun to distribute on March 22 (A.N., K.648 [33]).

[49]See n. 25, and *Recueil des écrits qui ont esté faits sur le différend entre les pairs de France & les présidens à mortier du Parlement de Paris, pour la manière d'opiner aux lits de justice, avec l'arrêt donné par le roy en son conseil en faveur des pairs en 1664,* 2d ed. (Paris: Antoine-Urbain Coustelier, 1716) (copies in A.N., K.619 [43], K.622 [10], U.907; Bibliothèque de l'Assemblée Nationale [Paris], MS. 336; and at the B.N., for which see B.N., *Catalogue des factums,* 4:100).

[50]The peers finally got permission to print their *preuves* on June 24, 1716 (A.N., K.648 [50, 51, 66]), but they seem not to have published them until 1720, when they collected all their pamphlets of the *affaire du bonnet* and the *affaire Richelieu*—petitions, memoranda, and the enormous body of *preuves*—and published them with a new title page as *Mémoires concernant les pairs de France avec les preuves* (Paris: Antoine-Urbain Coustelier, 1720), a rare publication to be consulted in the B.N.'s Réserve des imprimés (*cote* F.323). A copy of the printed *Preuves des mémoires concernant les pairs de France*—801 folio pages of documentation concerning the period 1015–1461—is also bound into Bibliothèque de l'Assemblée Nationale (Paris), MS. 336.

[51]On ducal claims and Louis XIV's decision to grant them in 1664, see chapter 2, n. 104.

title suggests, this pamphlet was tricked out as a formal petition to
Orléans, but it also included thumbnail genealogical sketches on ducal
families and these little essays in genealogical character assassination
earned the pamphlet another title: the "libelle généalogique."[52]

As a contribution to political and constitutional debate in 1716 the
"libelle" was negligible. Although the author challenged the dukes and
peers' exclusive claims to "declare" regencies and although he requested
that the regent postpone a judgment on the *bonnet* until Louis XV's
majority, he left all other ducal claims and arguments unchallenged. He
made no counterclaims for the Parlement and carefully described the
plea for a postponed decision as nothing more than "a likely [*spécieux*]
pretext to leave matters undecided."[53]

As a social polemic, however, the "libelle" was powerful indeed and
herein lies its significance as a contribution to the *affaire du bonnet*. The
"libelle" vilified ducal ancestries.[54] It asserted the equality of robe and

[52]"Mémoire pour le Parlement contre les ducs et pairs présenté à monseigneur le duc
d'Orléans, Régent," printed in Moufle d'Angerville, *Vie privée de Louis XV*, 4 vols. (London:
John Peter Lyton, 1781), 1:235–50, and reprinted in [Edmond-J.-F.] Barbier, *Chronique de
la Régence et du règne de Louis XV (1718–1763) ou Journal de Barbier, avocat au Parlement de
Paris, nouvelle édition complète*, 8 vols. (Paris: G. Charpentier, 1885), 8:386–96. Moufle
claimed to print the "Mémoire" from MSS though there are some small discrepancies
between his text and that given in MSS consulted (B.N., MSS. n.a.f. 9724, fols. 179–83,
and n.a.f. 9726, fols. 46–53v; A. N., K.619 [10] and K.622 [7³⁷, 39, 40, 42]): Moufle
printed "Boulainvilliers" where manuscripts read "Beauvillier" (Barbier, 8:395). There
was a near contemporary printing of the "Mémoire" (bound in B.N., MS. Clairambault
721 at p. 869), but the pamphlet reached the public chiefly by MS circulation, as contemporaries observed: for example, Dangeau, *Journal*, 16:371–72 (April 19, 1716); and
Nouvelles littéraires, contenant ce qui se passe de plus considérable dans la république des lettres, 4
(1716): 167–68 (issue of August 22). Contemporaries speculated about the author of the
"Mémoire," attributing it to the Parlement's first president (Jean-Antoine de Mesmes), to
Jean-François-Paul Le Fèvre (or LeFebvre), abbé de Caumartin (later bishop of Blois), or
to the *président à mortier* André III Potier de Novion (B.N., MS. n.a.f. 9726, fol. 54; B.N.,
Clairambault 721, p. 869). But the author was probably Claude Blanchard, advocate at
Parlement and author of a short memorandum prepared in February for the *président à
mortier* Chrétien II de Lamoignon on the dukes and peers' petitions of December (*Recueil
de pièces*). In that memorandum Blanchard wrote short genealogies of ducal houses which,
albeit in less inflammatory terms than the "libelle généalogique," also vilified their ancestry: "Reflexions Sur le Memoire presenté au Roy par les Pairs de France au mois de
Novembre 1714. Les assemblées qu'ils firent à l'instant du deces de ce Prince le premier
Septembre 1715. Et la nuit du meme jour, Et la protestation que L'archeveque de Reims
lut dans L'assemblée du Parlement du deux du meme mois, Et Sur les trois Requestes qu'ils
ont presentées au Roy, Et a Son Altesse Royale Monsieur Le Duc d'orleans Regent" (A.N.,
K.622 [9³] and B.N., MS. Clairambault 721, pp. 579–64, copies that date the text and
ascribe it to Blanchard). On Blanchard's later activities as a parlementary pamphleteer
during the regency see chapter 6.

[53]Barbier, *Chronique de la Régence*, 8:386–88.

[54]Ibid., 8:393–96. Some examples: "We conserve in the precincts of the Palais [de
Justice] the ennoblements of the first two dukes. Gérault Bastel was ennobled by the
bishop of Valence in 1304. He was the son of Jean Bastel, apothecary of Viviers who, in

sword as two "professions" equally "illustrious" and equally noble.[55] Most important, it sought to arouse the antiducal jealousies of untitled nobles. Barely visible in the 1660s, except perhaps in the Parlement's efforts to encourage and exploit them, those jealousies were now much in evidence. On the day that Louis XIV died, the dukes and peers sought to persuade Orléans to lead them separately to greet the new king. With the encouragement of the duc de Noailles—not for the first time Noailles was seeking to curry noble favor by resisting ducal ambitions— untitled nobles at Versailles mobilized rapidly to torpedo that project. They were successful: Orléans led peers and nobles *pêle-mêle* to greet the five-year-old boy who was now king.[56] No one forgot that encounter, and the author of the "libelle généalogique" exploited it skillfully during the *affaire du bonnet:* "But perhaps they [the dukes and peers] will enlist the nobility in their party? One knows how they have alienated it by their ridiculous *hauteur* on all occasions, and especially when they wanted it to march after them on the day of the king's death."[57] The author of the "libelle" had touched a raw nerve.

The dukes and peers knew that they had to mollify noble antagonism even before the appearance of the "libelle généalogique" in April. Meeting in assembly on January 27, they acknowledged that their exclusive claim to "declare" regencies and to be the "only" or "necessary" judges of "public affairs" could offend nobles as well as magistrates. They planned a reply to noble criticism should it arise: the dukes and peers, they reasoned, enjoyed a right that the entire "high nobility" used to enjoy until the Parlement deprived them of it.[58] At the end of March, the

1300 according to the same register, bought the land of Crussol from the heirs of that house" (393). "Luynes, Brantès, and Cadenet were three brothers who had but one cloak, which they wore by turns to go to the Louvre" (394). "The duc de Saint-Simon is of nobility and fortune so recent that everyone knows it" (394). "The Noailles come from a domestic of Pierre Roger, count of Beaufort, viscount of Turenne, who ennobled them and erected as a fief a little corner of the land of Noailles whence they sprang" (395). "The duc d' Harcourt issues from a bastard of a bishop of Bayeux" (395).

[55]Ibid., 8:392–93. The author added: "There is but one sort of nobility, [though] it is acquired by different means: by military employments and by employments in the magistracy; but its rights and prerogatives remain the same."

[56]Dangeau, *Journal*, 16:137; Marais, *Journal et mémoires*, 1:177; and—on the role of the duc de Noailles—Archives du Ministère des Affaires étrangères (Paris), Mémoires et documents (France), MS. 205, fols. 197r–v.

[57]Barbier, *Chronique de la Régence*, 8:839.

[58]A.N., K.648 (17): "The assembly agreed . . . that should one day the occasion arise for explaining the term 'only judges' it would be necessary to do so in such a way that one might avoid all the jealousy that people [*on*] were trying to raise against MM. the peers on this subject; that one would make clear that one sought to say only that in this conjuncture of declaring the regency the peers alone had the right to attend; that if the high nobility used to share with the peers the right to decide affairs of the crown, it was the Parlement that had deprived it of that prerogative to take its place, etc."

dukes and peers deployed that argument publicly when, in their *Mémoire des pairs,* they blamed the loss of the nobility's right to trial by peers on the Parlement.[59] In short, the dukes sought to defuse the antagonism of untitled nobles by presenting themselves as the embattled heirs of rights and privileges once shared by all nobles but now, thanks to Parlement's ambition, reserved to dukes and peers alone. The dukes and peers were not successful, however. On April 1, nonducal nobles at Paris began to gather in assemblies of their own; by April 11, the dukes and peers' syndics confronted the delicate task of answering the nobles' *Requête . . . contre les fausses prétentions de messieurs les ducs et pairs.*[60]

It has been argued that the assembling nobles of regency Paris were the vanguard of an impoverished "noble proletariat" vegetating in the provinces, anxious for "aristocratic reaction," and animated by a protoracist egalitarianism of noble "birth."[61] Nothing could be further from the truth. There were provincial movements of the nobility under the regency, but their connections with the assembling nobles in the capital were tenuous.[62] And the men in the Parisian assemblies were hardly

---

[59][Sacy], *Mémoire des pairs de France,* 12: "It was more or less around the time of this last decree [a 1315 decree of the Parlement of Paris just cited] that the right to be judged by one's peers and, reciprocally, to judge them (a right which in its origin was essentially common to the entire nobility) began to be restricted to the peers of France alone. The preeminence of their dignity always maintained them in that right, and if the high nobility can ever regain the enjoyment of its primordial right, it will be to the peers of France that it owes its preservation, since the peers alone in the body of the nobility have prevented that right from being lost [*prescrit*] and from falling into oblivion."

[60]A.N., K.648 (38) (on April 1 Saint-Simon informed the peers' syndics "of the assembly of the nobility [and the] dangerous consequences of this assembly") and A.N., K.648 (39). On the noble assemblies of the regency see Lassaigne, *Les Assemblées de la noblesse,* 129–52. The *Requête de la noblesse contre les fausses prétentions de messieurs les ducs et pairs* circulated in print and MS in and after April 1716. It is reprinted in Lassaigne, *Les Assemblées de la noblesse,* 230–43.

[61]Devyver, *Le Sang épuré,* 247–62, 392–97.

[62]True, Saint-Simon wrote of the assembling nobles that "they caballed in the provinces to encourage deputations . . ." (Saint-Simon, *Mémoires,* 31:197). It is equally true that the regency council's May 14, 1717, decree, which finally suppressed the noble assemblies, mentioned "a great number of *gentilshommes* not only in Paris but also in the provinces" participating in them (text in Lassaigne, *Les Assemblées de la noblesse,* 247). But that council decree probably magnified the assemblies' proportions to justify their suppression. Saint-Simon, writing his *Mémoires* long after the regency had ended, probably mistook the noble assemblies that did gather in the provinces as satellites of the Parisian assemblies, although the provincial noble assemblies of the regency seem to have been most concerned to protest the regent's continued collection of Louis XIV's *dîme* and *capitation,* hated war taxes against which they organized tax strikes calling those of the mid-seventeenth century. In their official correspondence for the Polysynody's Council of Finances, Orléans and Noailles (the council's president) roundly condemned those provincial assemblies and insisted on prompt payment of taxes (B.N., MSS. f.f. 6932, pp. 36–37; 6934, fols. 31–2v; 6938, fols. 9v–12; 6942, fols. 83v–9v; see also Bonney, *Political Change in France,* 214–37, for earlier tax strikes). The Parisian assemblies, on the other hand, began with the regent's permission and at his princely residence, the Palais Royal, in the apartments of his captain

hobereaux. Social and ceremonial life at court and capital commanded their attention. They could mobilize at a moment's notice against ducal projects.[63] On occasion they could be as rank-conscious as the dukes and peers and no less contemptuous of any "little *gentilhomme* in simple orders" who might claim to equal them.[64] In a word, they were a small body of court nobles.[65] And although they asserted a nobiliaire egalitarianism against the dukes and peers, its inspiration was not protoracist but legalistic. Like the author of the Parlement's "libelle généalogique" the assembling nobles' *Requête* against ducal "pretensions" asserted the equal dignity of robe and sword. And like the royal commissioners who had conducted the *recherches de faux nobles* of Louis XIV, the assembling nobles admitted the equality of *anoblis* and old nobles: that is, an equality within the second order between nobles "whom their fathers' services or their virtue placed in it" and nobles "whose ancient line lost, in the course of many centuries, the knowledge of its first origin." "Nobility once recognized admits no internal distinction," the assembling nobles insisted. They continued, "One *gentilhomme* is not more of a *gentilhomme* than another; it is a character that does not admit the greater or the lesser. In France all nobles are equal, as far as nobility is concerned; it is this equality that forms its courage and force and which till this day has

---

ot the guards, Alexis-Henri, marquis de Châtillon (Lassaigne, *Les Assemblées de la noblesse*, 148). That the duc and duchesse du Maine and their clients soon sought to manipulate noble movements in both Paris and the provinces is undeniable. So is the fact that the provincial movements could evolve into rebellions (notably in Brittany in 1718–19) (ibid., 130–32; Leclercq, *Histoire de la Régence*, 2:129–34, 331–64, esp. 337–38; Meyer, *Le Régent*, 195–99, 212–15). There is however no independent evidence of collusion between the assembling nobles in Paris and those in the provinces at the height of the *affaire du bonnet*.

[63]See sources in n. 56. Saint-Simon, in his *Additions* to Dangeau's *Journal*, blamed antiducal sentiment among the nobility on the ceremonial "confusion" that reigned in regency Paris, where princes ceased to insist on observing the marks of rank—who sat on what, when, and in whose presence—to let everyone sit comfortably at the gaming tables, gambling having become a more fashionable pastime than ever (Dangeau, *Journal*, 17:66–68).

[64]Cf. Balleroy, *Les Correspondants de la marquise de Balleroy*, 2:187. On July 21, 1717, Caumartin de Boissy wrote the marquise about the marquis de Châtillon (in whose apartments in the Palais Royal the nobles had assembled during the *affaire du bonnet*): "The other day, the gentle marquis attempted a lively defense of the nobility's interest against the dukes and peers before M. de Brancas [a duke and peer] who, wounded by what he said, [and] pretending to share his interests, told him that the subordination between different degrees must be maintained and said, for example, 'Would you wish that a little *gentilhomme* in simple orders [*de simple tonsure*] claim equality with you?' The marquis agreed with what the duke said. The duke said to him, 'You are right, for there is as great a difference between him and you as between you and me.' The response stunned him and closed his mouth."

[65]Mousnier, *Les Institutions de la France sous la monarchie absolue*, 161. Lassaigne pronounced the assembling nobles "de fort bonne noblesse" and said nothing of their poverty (*Les Assemblées de la noblesse*, 141–43), although Devyver claimed he did (*Le Sang épuré*, 258–60).

maintained the monarchy."[66] Given their court connections and their legalistic conception of nobility, the assembling nobles of the regency cannot be described as marginalized and racist *hobereaux.*

This evidence—the social and ideological character of the assembling nobles, the dukes and peers' carefully constrained print publicity, the continued importance of rumor, the persistence of manuscript pamphleteering—all suggests that the audience of the *affaire du bonnet* was narrow indeed and largely coterminous with the robe and sword elites of Parisian and court society. Yet the *affaire*'s publicists addressed that audience as a "public" and exalted its "opinion." They continued to appeal to the crown's authority, it is true, but they did not confine themselves to counseling or petitioning a prince. They appealed to "public opinion" and notably by print. Manuscript, they still believed, was a medium of official communication and "respect" especially suitable for addressing princes. Thus the dukes and peers sent manuscript copies of their December 1715 petitions to the princes of the blood: "to pay them greater respect."[67] Print, however, was the medium for reaching "public opinion." Because the Parlement routinely printed its records of its own proceedings, the dukes and peers claimed, it wielded enormous influence over "public opinion."[68] Hence their determination that their own petitions against the Parlement "become public by print."[69] But all parties to the dispute cultivated "public opinion" aggressively, thus turning the *affaire* into a quarrel pursued in public. That transformation of aristocratic controversy—quite evident when the ducal parlementaire conflict of 1715–16 is compared with that of 1664—was especially significant because during the regency, Orléans' tenuous claim to his authority invited the squabbling aristocratic elites of Paris to make conflicting claims to judge disputes about regencies and the royal succession. The *affaire du bonnet,* consequently, was a public dispute about an unwritten French constitution and the roles that peers, parlementaires, or nobles might play in it.

Given the dynastic questions surrounding Orléans' claim to authority, ducal "pretensions" to be the "only" or the "necessary" judges of "public

[66]*Requête de la noblesse* in Lassaigne, *Les Assemblées de la noblesse,* 241–42.
[67]A.N., K.648 (21): "Extrait," fol. 3. See also Church, *Richelieu and Reason of State,* 364.
[68]*Recueil de pièces,* 10 (second petition to the king, December 15, 1715), against the Parlement's "affectation to mark the success of their enterprises [their ceremonial usurpations at the dukes and peers' expense] within the Parlement in these accounts of the assemblies attended by the peers that they have lately taken upon themselves to make public, less to give information on the matters there under deliberation than to establish for themselves a kind of possession in [the eyes of] public opinion." Cf. the Parlement's publications cited in notes 11 and 12.
[69]A.N., K.648 (7): a December 17 memorandum to the regent.

affairs" were bound to be provocative. No less provocative were the Parlement's attempts at genealogical character assassination in the "libelle généalogique." In April and May 1716, these provocations led to complex and contradictory interventions in the *affaire du bonnet* by untitled nobles at Paris. Here may be detected, at last, the movements of "public opinion" to which peers, parlementaires, and the regent himself were so attentive.

In their petitions and memoranda the peers had defended their "pretensions" by deriving them from rights which, they supposed, great feudatories used to enjoy. Against these historical arguments the assembling nobles deployed a familiar royalist antifeudalism in their *Requête*. There they bemoaned once again the feudal anarchy that let ancient dukes and counts usurp royal authority delegated to them by Carolingian kings. The assembling nobles held that dukes and peers could exercise public authority—but only by the king's will, not by virtue of fiefs held of the crown—and they warned the king against dangerous ducal dreams "of participating in sovereignty, which will submit the nobility, all the estates of the realm, even your majesty and the princes of your blood to the aristocracy of the peers."[70] The charge of "aristocracy" was natural to inhabitants of the Old Regime monarchical political culture (even if they happened to be nobles) and for that reason it was a potent reply to the oligarchical ambitions of the peers.

Ardent defenders of the crown against the peers, the assembling nobles nevertheless had constitutional aspirations of their own. Against ducal "pretensions" to be the "only" or "necessary" judges of "public affairs," the assembling nobles claimed that the right to regulate disputes about regencies and the royal succession belonged to the "nation":

---

[70]Lassaigne, *Les Assemblées de la noblesse*, 233–36; and 231:
The dukes and peers form (if one wants to believe them) a separate body in the state; they make themselves the mediators between kings and the people; they are the only judges of the succession to the crown; it is their task to assure the form of government during the minority of kings; only peers truly have the right to judge the right to the regency. The Parlement of Paris in which one wanted to include them in confused fashion as councillors only enjoys the right to pronounce on these great occasions by virtue of the peers' presence alone.

From them alone this company received its preeminence in legislation; the peers' dignity, conserving the political hierarchy, forms and maintains this intimate and necessary union between your majesty and the lesser orders of the realm which you govern. . . .

Thus, the peers, taking flight with a limitless grandeur, openly proceed toward the usurped power of the sovereign peers [i.e., the great feudal peers of the past], of which happily they [i.e., the modern peers] are today only the image.

Thus, the idea, so loudly declared, of participating in sovereignty, which will submit the nobility, all the estates of the realm, even your majesty and the princes of your blood to the aristocracy of the peers.

France, Sire, knows but one power, that of Your Majesty, and when the crown becomes the object of agitations, when the fate of regencies is doubtful, it is not to the peers but to the entire state that the right to decide belongs. It is to the suffrages of the entire nation that the choice is given, and not to a portion of the nobility which would change its right to sit in Parlement into a prime ministership and which would transform itself from councillors in Parlement into the arbiters of the state and the crown.[71]

That "nation," the assembling nobles added, performed its exalted functions when assembled in Estates.[72] With this observation they came close to pleading for that body's revival. They would actually do so a year later, during the *affaire des princes*. During the *affaire du bonnet*, however, they sought not to press their own claims but to oppose the peerage's claims and confined themselves to asking that the king reject them.[73]

The assembling nobles were not the only nobles to enter the *affaire du bonnet*, however. There were yet others who, scandalized by the Parlement's "libelle généalogique," sought to refute it and even (albeit reluctantly) to support the dukes against the sovereign court. This movement of opinion is barely discernible. One must follow it in manuscript pamphlets that began to appear in April and that continued to circulate throughout the summer.[74] Like the author of one untitled attack on the

---

[71]Ibid., 236.

[72]The nobles proceeded to adduce historical evidence of disputes about regencies resolved, they sought to insist, by the Estates General:

But if the peers participate in public power in the tribunal of the Grand'Chambre [of the Parlement], without excluding from it the nobility, they may also take part in the general assembly of the estates of the kingdom, wherein the nobility forms a body that cedes only to the respect due to religion and its ministers, this body, the soul and the force of the two others, [and] forming with them the three estates.

There the dukes and peers, who have never had the power to decide alone any public or private affair, will find the power they seek to judge of the rights of kings and regencies.

There they will see the regency conferred [*déférée*] on Philip the Tall after the death of Louis Hutin, that which was given to the Count of Valois after the death of Charles the Handsome, that of Charles V after his father King John had been taken prisoner at the battle of Poitiers, they will find the regency of Charles VIII debated [*agitée*] in the Estates General held at Tours, and the regency conferred on Catherine de Medici in the Estates General of Orléans after the death of François II. (Ibid., 238)

[73]Ibid., 236–41.

[74]See, for example, "Lettre de M^r . . . à un de ses amis" (MS copies consulted: A.N., K.622 [7¹] [dated June 8]; B.N., MS. Clairambault 720, pp. 203–17 [dated May 16 and ascribed to the abbé de Vertot]). Part of the text was printed: see *Réponse au libelle injurieux, qui attaque les maisons des ducs et pairs* (n.p.: [1716]) (B.N., *cote* 8° L1³9). Predictably the "Lettre" smeared the genealogical character of the Parlement's magistrates: "Since the Parlement became sedentary there have been very few *gentilshommes* in it. Most [magistrates] arose from the dregs of the people" (A.N., K.622 [7¹], fol. 1v). See also "Réflexions sur le mémoire des présidens au mortier du Parlement de Paris contre les ducs et pairs de France" (MS copies consulted: A.N., K.622 [7⁴¹] [dated July 1]; B.N., MS. Clairambault

"Parlement's libelle," the writers of these pamphlets might deplore the "foolishness of the dukes" (the *sotises des ducs*); nevertheless they endorsed the dukes' claims against the Parlement as "reasonable."[75]

Particularly ambitious was the "Mémoire d'un homme de condition au corps de la noblesse sur ses véritables interests dans l'affaire des pairs contre le Parlement," a tract that began to circulate in April.[76] The author conceded the nobility's "interest" in preventing the peerage's elevation into a "fourth body separate from and superior to it," but he reminded the nobility that it had other "interests, more pressing still," to back the peers against the Parlement. "In effect," he asked, "what noble . . . is not interested in the degrading manner in which the Parlement . . . has tried to treat those among the nobility invested with the greatest dignity to which it can attain?" Bearers of the nobility's highest "dignity," the peers were heirs to the nobility's erstwhile power too, now all but entirely usurped by a Parlement responsible for the nobility's "decadence." Once resplendent and powerful in the "parlements" of Merovingian and Carolingian antiquity (where only clergy but no "third estate" could join it), the nobility had now long since lost its "deliberative voice in matters of government" to the Parlement: "From the institution of the monarchy the high nobility was in well established possession of [the right] to be the principal body with deliberative voice in matters of government. Yet what have we seen this past century? The Parlement of Paris which puts itself in possession of [the right] not to decide with it [the nobility] but to decide alone and to its exclusion."[77]

By a patent "reversal of order," the author complained, the Parlement

---

720, pp. 121–68 and 169–76 [two undated copies]). There were still later rejoinders (the "libelle généalogique" was provocative indeed): an undated letter to Saint-Simon about "an unknown *Gentilhomme* of Picardy" who "could not read without an extreme indignation the injurious memorandum that circulated in Paris last summer" and who planned a genealogical work to reply to it (MS copies consulted: A.N., K.622 [7²]; B.N., MS. n.a.f. 9726, fol. 67); a 1720 riposte appended to a MS *nobiliaire* or catalog of Norman nobility (B.N., MS. f.f. 32309 [Cabinet des titres 483], fols. 698–746v); and [Louis] Chasot de Nantigny, *Les Généalogies historiques des rois, empereurs, etc., et de toutes les maisons souveraines qui ont subsisté jusqu'à présent*, 4 vols. (Paris: P.-F. Giffart, 1736–38), 3:162.

[75]MSS consulted: B.N., MS. n.a.f. 9726, fols. 61–66 (dated July 28), and B.N., MS. Clairambault 720, pp. 179–88.

[76]MS copies consulted: Archives du Ministère des Affaires étrangères (Paris), Mémoires et documents (France), MS. 204, fols. 173–182v; A.N., K.619 (3²); B.N., MSS. n.a.f. 9730, fols. 263–71v, and Clairambault 720, pp. 191–200. The second and third MSS listed here bear the indication "copied on April [blank] 1716." The last MS listed is dated May 1716. Nothing on the MSS confirms Devyver's ascription of this text to Saint-Simon (*Le Sang épuré*, 282–83), although the first MS listed here belongs to a collection of texts some of which may be his (*Inventaire sommaire des Archives du Département des Affaires Etrangères: Mémoires et documents*, 3 vols. [Paris: Imprimerie Nationale, 1883–96], 1:26–27). The content of the "Mémoire" is hardly consonant with Saint-Simon's ideas.

[77]B.N., MS. n.a.f. 9730, fols. 263r–v; 263v; 264–266v; 266v–267; 267r–v.

had pretended to represent the "estates" and the "nation" and, "in the last three regencies," to assume their authority.[78] And now, to consummate its ambitions to disfranchise the nobility and to be legislative tutor to minor kings and their regents, the Parlement staged its procedural coup of September 2, whereby it effectively excluded the dukes and peers from inaugurating the regency.[79] The peers, however, were the only members of the nobility still able to resist the usurpation of its political rights by the "third estate," and the author closed by urging nobles to support the peers' efforts to force the Parlement to rescind the fatal *arrêté* of September 2.

> Let it [the nobility] not believe that in this matter its interest is separate from the interest of those among it who hold the dignity of peers. The peers defend only the sad remains of its ancient rights, rights of which its has already been stripped. . . . There remains only this head to lop off and the entire nobility will be undone. It will soon occupy the third estate's place in the nation, and the third estate will succeed in taking the nobility's. Only the peers, by their union and credit, can stop the torrent.[80]

Because the dukes and peers stood little chance of stopping the torrent of parlementaire ambition while untitled nobles were encouraging it, they attempted to persuade the assembling nobles to reverse their antiducal course.[81] To that end, the dukes' syndics gathered on April 11 to prepare a careful letter to the regent answering the nobility's *Requête* and speaking a language recalling that of the manuscript pamphlets just considered. The peerage's cause was the nobility's too, according to the ducal letter, for the peerage's rights had been the entire nobility's until the Parlement usurped them: "The prerogatives that we defend against the Parlement are prerogatives which it has insensibly stripped from the nobility." Claiming that "the quality dearest to us is that of being *Gentilshommes*," the ducal syndics declared: "We would never be able to believe that one could impute to us the idea of wishing to separate ourselves from the body of the nobility, still less the idea of attributing to ourselves alone the right to decide [matters] concerning the crown." These assertions marked an undeniable retreat from claims lodged in 1664 and revived in 1716, claims that the dukes were indeed "a separate body" or *corps à part*, distinguished from mere nobles as headvassals had

[78]Ibid., fols. 267v–268.
[79]Ibid., fols. 268v–269.
[80]Ibid., fol. 270.
[81]A.N., K.648 (38, 39).

once been distinguished from rearvassals.[82] The dukes' capacity for conciliation had its limits, however, for they continued to claim that they were "the only judges" of disputes about regencies and the royal succession, and they sought to defend that claim, not to mitigate it.[83] Their efforts were plainly contradictory and after further attempts to debate, revise, and approve the April 11 letter, the dukes and peers left it unsent.[84]

Determined to bring their case to the "public" in December, the dukes and peers were overtaken by "public opinion" in April and May. They failed to get sympathetic spirits to prevail among the assembling nobles to subdue their jealousy. Instead, the "tradition of union" that once bound peers and nobles together in shared antagonism to the robe crumbled.[85] In its place arose an alliance of parlementaires and untitled nobles angered by ducal "pretensions" and proclaiming identical concepts of nobility: nobility for the magistrates and the assembling nobles alike was membership in a legally defined order created and populated by a royal sovereign and admitting no distinctions of rank between robe and sword or titled (ducal) and untitled. Of course, this social and ideological "regrouping" of aristocratic elites in regency Paris cannot be explained by ducal "pretensions" alone, for in 1715–16 those "pretensions" were not new: they may be found in the peerage's petitions and memoranda of the 1660s.[86] In 1715–16 exclusive ducal claims to regulate matters "concerning the crown" (as the ducal letter of April 11 described them) were provocative because matters "concerning the crown" seemed to be in immediate need of regulation. The regent's dynastic and political problems—Louis XIV's testament, the duc du Maine's credit, and above all the dubious validity of Philip V's renunciation—account for the intensity of aristocratic controversy in 1715–16 and for the remarkable shifts in aristocratic social self-consciousness that may be detected during the *affaire du bonnet*.

Those same problems account for the constitutional projects floated

---

[82]A.N., K.648 (40). Cf. *Recueil des écrits* (1716 ed.), 107: "Since the peers formerly possessed the only royal fiefs, or fiefs held immediately of the crown, the whole kingdom was composed of only three parts: the king who was the head and sovereign, the peers who were his first vassals, and all the others who held of the peers [they in turn] in the dependance of royalty." For the nobility's response to that claim (quoted in n. 70) see *Requête de la noblesse* in Lassaigne, *Les Assemblées de la noblesse*, 231.

[83]A.N., K.648 (40).

[84]A.N., K.648 (41, 42, 43). One copy of the letter bears the indication "was never presented" (A.N., K.619 [3¹]).

[85]Labatut, *Les Ducs et pairs*, 371–79.

[86]See chapter 2. On the "regrouping" of aristocratic elites in the regency see Ford, *Robe and Sword*, 173–87.

by the competing aristocratic elites in 1715–16. The dukes and peers sought to assert the regent's authority, certainly, for they appealed to it against the Parlement. Yet they insinuated that their participation was no less necessary for "declaring" regencies than for ratifying renunciations to the crown, and thereby cast doubt on Orléans' right to the authority in his hands. Further, the assembling nobles upheld the king's authority and deplored ducal dreams of "aristocracy" and "prime ministership." Yet they claimed that the "nation" assembled in "Estates" should judge disputes about regencies and the royal succession, thus directing against ducal ambitions a project—assembling the Estates General—traditionally used by nobles against the authority of the Parlement of Paris.[87] The *affaire du bonnet's* public was exiguous and its protagonists' constitutional proposals easily dismissed as velleities. Some contemporaries had trouble taking the *affaire* seriously, satirizing its participants and all but ignoring their quarrel in their own memoirs and histories of the regency.[88] Others, however, appreciated that the *affaire* was a historical debate about an unwritten French constitution conducted before the bar of "public opinion" in Paris.[89] It is obvious that Orléans actively sought to test if not to direct the course of "public opinion." He ended the *affaire* with a council decree against the dukes when they had plainly lost its support. He probably encouraged the assembling nobles for they gathered in his own residence, the Palais Royal, and in the apartment of his captain of the guards, the marquis de Châtillon.[90] Finally, Orléans even sponsored polemical contributions to

[87]See Gerard Francis Denault, "The Legitimation of the Parlement of Paris and the Estates General of France 1560–1614" (Ph.D. diss., Washington University, St. Louis, 1975), 131, 320–32.

[88]See the satirical "Requeste des ducs et duchesses à S. A. R. Mgr. le duc d'Orléans régent" (MS copy consulted: B.N., MS. n.a.f. 9730, fols. 260–62 [dated April 1716]) and its bowdlerized edition (based on another MS) in E. Fyot, "L'Affaire du bonnet avec deux documents inédits," *Annales de l'Académie de Mâcon, Société des Arts, Sciences, Belles-Lettres et Agriculture de Saône-et-Loire*, ser. 3, vol. 6 (1901): 222–25. A pornographic squib, this "Requeste" concerned precedence in bed: how noble but nonducal lovers of duchesses should conduct themselves with their mistresses. Mathieu Marais ignored the quarrel (*Journal et mémoires*) and the chevalier de Piossens dismissed it as "an incident which distracted somewhat the attention of individuals from public affairs" (*Mémoires de la Régence*, 1:88). Jean Buvat promised to include pieces on the *affaire* in his *Journal* but neglected it nevertheless (*Journal de la Régence*, 1:33).

[89]For example, Anon., *Nouvelles littéraires, contenant ce qui se passe de plus considérable dans la république des lettres*, 4 (The Hague: Henri de Sauzet, 1716): 156–57 (August 22, 1716): "MM. the dukes and peers' suit against MM. the *Présidens à Mortier* brings us pieces from the former which illuminate very curious points of history, it is M. Lancelot [the dukes' secretary], a man learned [*consommé*] in our history, who has played the largest part in [composing] these pieces." Clearly on the dukes' side, this Dutch journal's Parisian correspondent went on to denounce the Parlement's "libelle généalogique" as "a bloody piece [*Ecrit*]" in which "the best houses of the kingdom . . . are attacked."

[90]Lassaigne, *Les Assemblées de la noblesse*, 148.

the *affaire*, for he ordered Henri de Boulainvilliers to begin work on his own contribution to it in 1716. The text of the "Lettres sur les parlements ou états généraux" attests the weight Orléans attached to the constitutional and political debates of the *affaire du bonnet*. It also bears witness to the high hopes for the revival of the "nation" that Boulainvilliers vested in the regent.

The "Lettres sur les parlements": Orléans and the French Nation

Shortly after Boulainvilliers' death in 1722, Nicolas Fréret wrote a letter on his life and works, among them his "twelve letters on the government of France containing, principally, the history of the Estates General or assemblies of the free orders of the Nation." "This work," Fréret continued, "had been undertaken by order of His Royal Highness the Regent. It was intended to be printed, but since circumstances changed, M. de Boulainvilliers interrupted a work too tiring, because of the researches upon which it engaged him, for a state of health like his, a work which he could sustain only in the hope of being useful to his fatherland."[91] Fréret was alluding to Boulainvilliers' "Lettres sur les parlements ou états généraux," an unfinished collection of twelve letters on Capetian France composed in 1716.[92] Boulainvilliers described his "Lettres" as a sequel to "what I already wrote on the history of the first two families of our kings."[93] That work, the "Mémoires historiques" originally written for the men in the Burgundy Circle, was also to have been printed in 1716, as a contemporary journalist reported, adding, "there is great eagerness here [at Paris] for this work, above all among people of condition . . . for this work is beyond the reach of the vulgar."[94] Once again, however, changing circumstances frustrated Boulainvilliers' efforts to get into print.

Boulainvilliers intended both publications as contributions to the *affaire du bonnet*. As an untitled nobleman who gave measured support to the dukes and peers, he met with their syndics on April 11 and urged them to respond to the assembling nobles' *Requête* against ducal "pretensions" with a conciliatory letter. The "Lettres sur le parlements," how-

[91]Fréret "Lettre de M. Fréret," 202.
[92]*Etat . . . Tome III*, 1–189. For MSS and other editions see Bibliographical Appendix, Parts 2 and 5, where evidence for dating the first twelve "Lettres" (there were to be two more) is also given.
[93]*Etat . . . Tome III*, 2 (Letter 1).
[94]*Nouvelles littéraires, contenant ce qui se passe de plus considérable dans la république des lettres*, 4 (1716): 156 (August 22, 1716).

ever, is Boulainvilliers' chief contribution. A learned piece—Boulainvilliers' "researches" for it may well have been as "tiring" as Fréret claimed—the "Lettres" was above all a polemic addressing the issues that the *affaire du bonnet* raised.[95] To begin, the "Lettres" was a brief for the regent, defending his dynastic right to his office. The "Lettres" was also a plea for the dukes, urging the nobility to support them against the Parlement. Above all, the "Lettres" was an appeal to Orléans, inviting him, in the course of a history of the Estates General, to revive the assemblies of the "nation." Boulainvilliers pursued all these aims in his "Lettres," orchestrating them in an impressively complex performance. The "Lettres" was his most strenuous effort at writing French history as a princely client, counselor, and controversialist. The "Lettres" was also his masterpiece.

A Brief for the Regent

Even in its unfinished state, Boulainvilliers' "Lettres" was a vigorous defense of Orléans' authority. Neither the Parlement nor the peerage, Boulainvilliers insisted, enjoyed the right to confer authority upon regents during royal minorities or to judge contests about the royal succession. True, he said nothing about the proceedings of September 2, which had exercised the parties to the *affaire du bonnet,* and he never mentioned Philip V's renunciation or Louis XIV's testament. Instead, Boulainvilliers gave his readers a careful account of regencies and dynastic disputes in the fourteenth century, addressing the political and constitutional problems of 1715–16 by writing about events that had taken place in 1316–18, 1328, 1355, 1374, and 1407. He could expect his readers to appreciate his meaning, however, for other polemics of the *affaire du bonnet,* notably the assembling nobles' *Requête* against ducal "pretensions," were appealing to those same fourteenth-century events to make points of their own.[96]

The fourteenth century was fertile terrain indeed for eighteenth-century debates about the royal succession and the rights of regents, for laws and precedents governing the French royal succession dated to that period. In the fourteenth century, France's dynastic principle or "Salic

---

[95]On the documentation that Boulainvilliers amassed to prepare his "Lettres" see Bibliographical Appendix, Part 2. For his meeting with ducal syndics see A.N., K.648 (40): "M. de Boul[ainvilliers] was there and gave his advice. He was for the letter." Cf. A.N., K.648 (21), "Extrait," fols. 20r–v: "I [the ducal secretary, Lancelot] read several drafts which had already been prepared. M. le comte de Boulainvilliers who was present at this assembly gave his advice. I was charged with preparing this letter."

[96]Lassaigne, *Les Assemblées de la noblesse,* 238 (see n. 72).

Law" was established, excluding princesses and their descendants from the throne and summoning princes to it by primogeniture. The Salic Law was a myth, of course, for it was not the ancient and immutable custom of hereditary monarchy that early-modern Frenchmen supposed. On the contrary, the Salic Law was a weapon of dynastic conflict forged during the Hundred Years' War by French propagandists seeking to justify the succession of Philip of Valois to the throne as Philip VI in 1328 and the exclusion of the English king Edward III from it because he claimed it through his mother (a French princess and sister to the late Charles IV). Fifteenth-century writers perfected the Salic Law myth by applying to the French royal succession the principle, laid down in the ancient law code of the Salian Franks, that females and their descendants might not inherit "Salic" lands. Thus an ancient and forgotten provision of private law became a principle of constitutional or public law.[97] Of course, the Salic Law myth was exposed to historical criticism and by the end of the sixteenth century scholars had reduced it to rubble. The dynastic principle itself, however, now was firmly established, not as a law enshrined in texts (though some persisted in referring to the "Salic Law" of the royal succession) but as an ancient and immutable custom "engraved on the hearts of Frenchmen."[98]

In his brief for the regent, Boulainvilliers appealed to that dynastic custom. Nevertheless, he rejected its antiquity along with the Salic Law myth. Reviewing the events of the early fourteenth century, he discovered no dynastic principle or "Salic Law" governing them. Instead, he found historical contingencies, political conflicts, and princely coups which, together, laid down the foundations for the French law of royal succession. No one remembered a "Salic Law," he declared, when Louis X died in 1316 and a league of nobles formed to "defend" his widow, pregnant with his male heir. No "Salic Law" inspired France's peers and nobles, Boulainvilliers noted, when upon the early death of that heir (King Jean I in the French canon of kings) they prepared to award the crown to Louis X's widow rather than to his brother Philip. And Philip reigned as Philip V (1317–22) not because a "Salic Law" called him to the throne but because he seized it. According to Boulainvilliers, he arranged a hasty consecration at Rheims followed by an equally hasty

[97]See Giesey, "Juristic Basis," 11, 17–22; John Milton Potter, "The Development and Significance of the Salic Law of the French," *English Historical Review*, 52 (1937): 235–53. See also P. S. Lewis, *Later Medieval France: The Polity* (London: Macmillan; New York: St. Martin's Press, 1968), 32–42, 59–77.

[98]H. B. P. [Jerome Bignon], *De l'excellence des roys, et du royaume de France* (Paris: Hiérosme Drouart, 1610), 265–66, 284–317, esp. 284–85. And see Giesey, "Juristic Basis," 40–42.

assembly of Estates at Paris, where pliant deputies swore oaths of fidelity to him thus binding his subjects to obey him.[99] Turning to 1328 and the Valois succession, Boulainvilliers again failed to find evidence of a Salic Law calling Philip VI to the throne and denying it to Edward III. Boulainvilliers rejected the notion that the rival princes argued their cases before a court of peers which then invoked the Salic Law and decided for Philip. That story, Boulainvilliers wrote, was a "fiction" [*une espèce de roman*] invented by humanist historians ("later rhetoricians like Paulus Aemilius") along with the elegant speeches they put in the mouths of their putative royal litigants.[100] Philip, Boulainvilliers argued, owed his throne not to a "Salic Law" or to French peers or nobles, but simply to the precedent of 1316–17. Boulainvilliers concluded:

> What likelihood is there . . . to base the exclusion of daughters from the succession to the crown upon the Salic Law, which says nothing on the subject and which had been neither known nor followed for more than 700 years? Let us admit—for it is true—that it [the exclusion of females] is the effect of a simple usage which began with Philip the Tall [Philip V], which continued with his brother Charles IV, and which was perfected with Philip of Valois, surnamed for this reason The Most Fortunate, so that it later became a fundamental and incontestable law—all the more so since the kings of England contested it for a hundred years and finally lost their case . . . at least by the force of events.[101]

Boulainvilliers' account of events in 1316–17 and in 1328 had clear lessons for his readers in 1715 and 1716. By making French dynastic custom the product of contingencies, conflicts, and coups in the early fourteenth century, Boulainvilliers pushed that custom beyond the reach of aristocratic elites or bodies claiming to be its guarantors or judges. In the heat of the *affaire du bonnet,* his remark that peers and nobles had played no such role in the fourteenth century was an argument that they should play no such role in the eighteenth, either.

Boulainvilliers drew two further lessons from the events of 1328. These lessons concerned not the royal succession but the designation of regents, a matter no less timely at the beginning of Orléans' regency. In 1328, Boulainvilliers wrote, Charles IV died survived by a pregnant

[99]*Etat . . . Tome III,* 88–89 (Letter 8).

[100]Ibid., 94 (Letter 8): Boulainvilliers observed that the *Trésor des chartes* conserved no records concerning the Valois succession or Philip's and Edward's putative debate before the French peers. Philip and Edward did indeed conduct a formal dispute for the succession—but in 1338 not 1328; Latin chroniclers, not humanist historians, changed its date (Giesey, "Juristic Basis," 18–19).

[101]*Etat . . . Tome III,* 94–95 (Letter 8), 95 for quotation.

widow. Only when she bore her child, a daughter excluded from the throne, did Philip of Valois succeed as Philip VI. But during the short interregnum of 1328, he had been the unborn child's regent, and that regency arrested Boulainvilliers' attention. By what right, he sought to ask, did Philip assume the regency? Writing in the late fourteenth century, the chronicler Jean Froissart asserted that Philip owed his regency to Charles IV's testament. Writing in the early eighteenth century, Boulainvilliers demurred. He had consulted that testament and its codicil at the *Trésor des chartes,* he wrote, and had found no mention of a regency in either document. He took this to be evidence of Charles IV's wise forebearance, pausing to observe that the testaments of dying kings were "all too often" dictated by "favorites, mistresses, and confessors." Even testaments containing "the wisest provisions," he added, tended to be quashed by "force, address, [and] popular favor."[102] Such remarks were oblique criticisms of Louis XIV's testament, but by deflating the authority of royal testaments, Boulainvilliers also deflated the authority of the bodies that quashed them, notably that of the Parlement of Paris which had nullified the testament of Louis XIV on September 2, 1715. Writing about the regency of Philip of Valois Boulainvilliers defended the regency of Philip of Orléans and rejected the Parlement's claim that it had played a constitutionally significant role in establishing it. Once again, Boulainvilliers sought to lift Orléans' authority beyond the reach of the contending robe and sword elites.

Boulainvilliers' brief for the regent was vigorous indeed. He nearly compromised it, however, when he drew his second lesson from the 1328 regency: that the right to judge disputes about regencies belonged not to peers or Parlement but to the "barons" or "high nobility" of the kingdom. Boulainvilliers held that just such a dispute had erupted in 1328 when, he argued, both Philip of Valois and Edward of England claimed the regency and appealed to the judgment of the "lords of the kingdom." No document recorded that contest, Boulainvilliers admitted, but he professed to find evidence of it in Thomas Rymer's *Foedera* which had begun to appear in 1704, and in contemporary French chronicles as well.[103] One in particular, that of the "True Continuator of Nangis," was especially useful to Boulainvilliers, who quoted a telling passage from it: "Upon King Charles' death, the barons gathered to discuss the government of the kingdom and said to the Englishman . . . [Boulainvilliers's elision]. In this decision, many experts in canon and

---

[102]Ibid., 95–96 (Letter 8), 96 for quotations.
[103]Ibid., 96 (Letter 8): Boulainvilliers cited the chronicles but only mentioned Rymer's compilation as "the acts of the kingdom of England, printed several years ago."

civil law agreed, and by this decision, which was accepted by the wiser among them and approved by the barons, the government of the kingdom was given to Philip. . . . And he was then called regent of the kingdom, [and] others called him king."[104] After quoting the chronicle, Boulainvilliers concluded,

> The regency of the French state, during minorities or pregnancies of widowed queens, belongs incontestably to the heir apparent or presumptive: . . . should a contest or legal difficulty arise, it is only in very recent times that one has thought to consult men of the law: the right of the *grands* or barons of the kingdom in this regard can be questioned only because of new ideas, according to which one would make all orders equal and destroy the natural advantages of the nobility. Indeed, Philip of Valois owed much to the fact that the rights of the first body of the state were not yet altered or misunderstood; for if the jurists and canonists had been believed, the crown of France doubtless would have passed to the king of England. Thus one may say that the nobility contributed to maintaining the reigning house on the throne, no less by its attachment to ancient French law—which legists have weakened, mutilated, and finally reduced to the state we see it in today—than by the sacrifice of its blood and its wealth.[105]

Read in the context of the *affaire du bonnet,* that commentary on a medieval chronicle becomes a political and constitutional argument, an argument that dynastic status alone confers regencies on princes, that neither peerage nor Parlement must "declare" them, and that the nobility alone might judge disputes about them. Not surprisingly, Boulainvilliers called the decision taken by the "barons" in 1328 "the most important and solemn decree that the lords of the kingdom have ever rendered."[106]

Nevertheless, Boulainvilliers did not seriously weaken his brief for the regent. Though he embedded within it an argument that "nobles" or "barons" or "lords" should adjudicate regency disputes, the argument was a weak one which he proceeded to qualify rather than to pursue. In their April 1716 *Petition,* the assembling nobles claimed that an Estates General had judged a regency contest in 1328 and might do so again.[107] In Boulainvilliers' pages, the "barons" alone acted, not an Estates Gen-

---

[104]Ibid., 97 (Letter 8): my translation from the Latin text quoted by Boulainvilliers. Cf. Guillaume de Nangis, *Chronique latine de Guillaume de Nangis de 1113 à 1300 avec les continuations de cette chronique de 1330 à 1368,* ed. H. Géraud, 2 vols. (Paris: Jules Renouard for Société de l'Histoire de France, 1843; repr. New York: Johnson Reprint Corporation, 1965), 2:82–84.

[105]*Etat . . . Tome III,* 97 (Letter 8).

[106]Ibid., 94 (Letter 8).

[107]Lassaigne, *Les Assemblées de la noblesse,* 238 (quoted in n. 72).

eral whose "third estate," he remarked contemptuously, had recently risen from servitude.[108] He went on, it is true, to exalt the Estates General, including the Third Estate, as the "representative body of the whole nation."[109] But he also sought to argue that the authority of both nobility and Estates waned as the French dynastic principle established itself. In 1358, he claimed, dynastic custom, not the nobility, called the future Charles V to the regency while the English held his father captive.[110] In 1374, Boulainvilliers observed, Charles V asked the Parlement, not the nobility, to approve his ordinance establishing that French kings reach their majority in their fourteenth year. Though "malcontents" challenged that ordinance in 1560—it was, they said, improperly enacted—Boulainvilliers insisted that events had confirmed it, for its provisions were followed in the minority of Charles IX, who mounted the throne in 1560, and again in the minorities of Louis XIII and Louis XIV.[111] Thus, Boulainvilliers concluded, a king effectively made constitutional law in 1374 without the nobility's cooperation, thereby monopolizing a right to legislate that once belonged to medieval "parlements" of feudal "peers" or "barons" or, later, to Estates General.

One cannot deny . . . that the acceptance then made [of the ordinance] failed to satisfy the most important formality, that is, acceptance by the Estates General or at least by the peers of France, on the principle that they participated in legislation—since it was a matter of knowing whether or not the nation wished to assign its own government to a thirteen-year-old child naturally incapable of so great a function. Nevertheless, it is certain that no one made the least mention of either body in the [Parlement's] registration, and this must lead us to believe that the essential right of peerage had already been forgotten; that right consisted less . . . in titles and in particular and arbitrary prerogatives granted by the king, as is the case today, than in the high nobility's effective jurisdiction over all matters of government and over the promulgation of law which, denuded of its suffrages, would not have had sufficient authority.[112]

[108]*Etat . . . Tome III*, 96–97 (Letter 8). This was an answer to Jean Savaron, *Chronologie des estats généraux, où le tiers estat est compris, depuis l'an MDCXV. iusques à CCCCXXII* (Paris: Pierre Chevalier, 1615), under the date 1328. Deputy and spokesman of the Third Estate at the Estates General of 1614–15, Savaron prepared this inverse chronology to establish that the Third Estate was as ancient as the first two, and therefore as worthy of esteem. Nobiliaire ideologue as well as better historian, Boulainvilliers rejected that thesis here and throughout his "Lettres."
[109]*Etat . . . Tome III*, 128–29 (Letter 10).
[110]Ibid., 119–22, 140 (Letters 10 and 11).
[111]Ibid., 128–29 (Letter 10). For the disputes of 1560 to which Boulainvilliers referred see Hanley, *The* Lit de Justice *of the Kings of France*, 116–18; and Kelley, *Foundations of Modern Historical Scholarship*, 224–26.
[112]*Etat . . . Tome III*, 129 (Letter 10). Boulainvilliers' history of French representative bodies in his "Lettres" is discussed later.

Boulainvilliers vigorously sustained his thesis that French kings had monopolized a right to make law that had once belonged to the nobility or to the Estates. Commenting on Charles VI's regency ordinance of 1407, Boulainvilliers confined his remarks to the order of precedence observed at the "lit de justice" that registered it. He said nothing about the legislative authority that the nobility might still have enjoyed on that occasion.[113] To be sure, he refused to admit that the Parlement of Paris ever inherited it. Elsewhere in the "Lettres" he wrote that "it does not follow that the Parlement, abusing the name it retained and to which in fact it succeeded, rightly arrogates to itself by this simple title the government of the state, the tutelage of minor kings, and the participation, with major and able kings, in validating ordinances."[114] But if the Parlement never acquired legislative competence, according to Boulainvilliers, the nobility had certainly lost it. What remained was a powerful monarchy whose autonomous laws and customs secured the rights of kings and regents to their authority, and placed that authority beyond the reach of nobility, peerage and Parlement alike.

Built on a series of remarkable refusals to countenance any of the constitutional claims lodged by conflicting aristocratic elites during the *affaire du bonnet,* Boulainvilliers' brief for the regent was powerful indeed. Yet it was subversive too, for Boulainvilliers violated the myth of the dynastic monarchy's antiquity. That monarchy, he argued, was an innovation dating to the fourteenth century, which in his pages became the seedbed of a modern political order radically unlike the order that had preceded it and plainly inferior to it. Boulainvilliers had said as much in earlier works. In his "Lettres," too, he deplored the costs of France's dynastic monarchy. Exalting kings above their subjects, it made kings insensible to "the misery of the people." Worse still, it invited "despotic power."[115] Boulainvilliers' brief for the regent, therefore, was also an indictment of dynastic monarchy and the "despotism" it entailed.

That indictment of dynasticism and despotism was essential to Boulainvilliers' appeal to Orléans for the Estates' revival. Before examining that appeal, however, it is necessary first to turn to Boulainvilliers' plea for the dukes, a plea that the nobility support them against the Parlement in the *affaire du bonnet.* Here, too, the dramatic discontinuity that Boulainvilliers introduced into the course of French history is of central importance.

[113]*Etat . . . Tome III,* 135–36 (Letter 11). Like most Old Regime Frenchmen, Boulainvilliers thought *lits* to be ancient usages. In fact they date to the early sixteenth century (Hanley, *The* Lit de justice *of the Kings of France,* chaps. 1–4).
[114]*Etat . . . Tome III,* 66 (Letter 6).
[115]*Etat . . . Tome III,* 92–93 (Letter 8).

A *Plea for the Dukes*

Plainly jealous of the dukes, and purportedly the "brain" of the nobles assembling to resist their "pretensions," Boulainvilliers called nevertheless for ducal-noble solidarity against the Parlement of Paris. Hence his collusion with the peers' syndics on April 11.[116] Hence too his plea for the dukes, a plea made in the course of his history of the aristocratic elites carefully developed in the "Lettres sur les parlements."

Boulainvilliers did not, however, abandon his powerful antiducal animus. In the "Lettres," he still insisted on the equality of all the ancient Franks. "Accidental dignities," he wrote, "never altered the inner character attached to a Frankish [*François*] birth."[117] He still refused to identify the "seniores" or "maiores" of Carolingian "parlements" (as Hincmar of Rheims described them) with an exclusive and exalted peerage.[118] Reflecting on the French medieval experience, he declared that dividing the nobility with "distinctions and ranks" was no less damaging than diluting it with "popular families": "Thus one attacked the nobility by the head, by establishing, in violation of ancient usage, distinctions and ranks for those who were richest or who were allied or related to kings. And thus one attacked the nobility by the tail, by securing entry into it for popular families lately risen from servitude."[119]

Predictably, Boulainvilliers' history of the peerage was less than flattering. Ducal spokesmen contemplating the peers' functions at royal consecrations exalted the peers as royal electors. Boulainvilliers reduced those ceremonies and the peers' role in them to devices for enhancing the dynastic character of the Capetian monarchy. He added that the ceremonial peerage that shone alone at consecrations disappeared when a broader and more powerful feudal peerage gathered in baronial "parlements." Never, not even after 1216 when (he admitted) records begin to distinguish peers from other barons, did the twelve peers enjoy a separate rank in French baronial assemblies. There they always voted as equals with the other barons. Boulainvilliers concluded that a "new definition" of peerage was necessary, a definition associating it not with royal consecrations but with feudal assemblies, not with a few royal dignitaries but with a broad feudal nobility, not with ceremonies but with the right to make law.[120]

[116]See n. 6 and n. 95.

[117]*Etat . . . Tome III*, 14 (Letter 2).

[118]Ibid., 15–19 (Letter 2): a long quotation from Hincmar of Rheims, *De ordine palatii*, and a long discussion of it recalling Boulainvilliers' "Réflexions et considérations."

[119]*Etat . . . Tome III*, 93 (Letter 8).

[120]Ibid., 47–48 (Letter 5, on Boulainvilliers' "new definition" of peerage), 122, 127 (Letter 10). For a ducal account of the consecration ceremony with which Boulainvilliers

Boulainvilliers was not the first writer to associate peerage with feudalism or with a broad feudal nobility.[121] What made his "definition" of peerage "new" was his claim that peers, that is, the broad feudal nobility assembled in "parlements," enjoyed legislative competence. He assigned his feudal nobility or peerage a grand political patrimony indeed; moreover, he accused the ceremonial peers and the modern dignitaries whom he associated with them of having sacrificed that political patrimony in a weak effort to secure privileges and distinctions of their own. In short, the "Lettres" delivered a stinging indictment of the dukes and peers' corporate egoism.

Boulainvilliers delivered that indictment in the course of a clever account of two *lits de justice* repeatedly adduced by ducal ideologues as precedents for ducal privileges, notably the right to trial by peers. One of those *lits* was the duc de Bretagne's trial on December 9, 1378. Here, peers did indeed serve as judges. The other *lit* was the comte d'Alençon's trial on March 2, 1386. Here, not peers but officers of the crown tried the accused, but ducal ideologues cited this *lit* as precedent anyway because, they argued, the king had promised the peers royal letters affirming their privileges and disclaiming any intention to set precedent contrary to them.[122] Boulainvilliers had little to say on the 1378 *lit* beyond acknowledging its existence. His account of the 1386 "lit" was sly indeed, for he reminded his readers that King Charles VI (1380–1422) never expedited his promised letters! Thus the peers failed to defend their cherished privileges. Worse, in 1378 and 1386 they did not even try to defend what really mattered—not the right to trial by peers, but the "right to legislation pure and simple."[123] Having lost their legislative competence in the course of the fourteenth century, the peers made no effort to reclaim it. "It is easy to see," wrote Boulainvilliers, "the point to which the peers restricted their rights, however great and powerful they

was acquainted see Saint-Simon's "Mémoire succinct" of 1712, in Saint-Simon, *Ecrits inédits*, 2:216–33. Convinced that the Capetians were usurpers, Boulainvilliers exaggerated their lack of legitimacy in the High Middle Ages and their use of coronation ceremonies to solidify their dynastic claims to the throne (cf. *Etat*, I, "Mémoires historiques": 175–76). On the elective and dynastic implications of the coronation ceremony and their sometimes fortuitous development see Giesey, "Juristic Basis," 4–5, 10; Richard A. Jackson, *Vive le Roi! A History of the French Coronation from Charles V to Charles X* (Chapel Hill: University of North Carolina Press, 1984); Andrew W. Lewis, "Anticipatory Association of the Heir in Early Capetian France," *American Historical Review*, 83 (1978): 916–27; Gabrielle Spiegel, "The *Reditus Regni ad Stirpem Karoli Magni:* A New Look," *French Historical Studies*, 7 (1971–72): 145–74, esp. 151–58.

[121]See chapter 2, note 107, and [Le Laboureur], *Histoire de la pairie*, 1:1–2, 2:51–52.

[122]Cf. Ibid., 1:147–52; *Requeste des pairs de France*, 9–10; *Mémoire des pairs de France*, 9–10. On *lits* see n. 113.

[123]*Etat . . . Tome III*, 129 (Letter 10).

may have been at the time. This justifies once again . . . that among us ignorance has caused the ruin and destruction of all conditions, the greatest as well as the mediocre, and that it is true that kings have always sought, whether by their own efforts or their ministers', to profit from the faults, mistakes, and inattention of all subjects."[124] In short, in vain pursuit of their own privileges the peers betrayed the feudal nobility.

In the "Lettres sur les parlements," Boulainvilliers' sympathy for the feudal nobility extended to feudalism itself. Once again, he sought to rehabilitate it. Once again, Boulainvilliers described fiefs as "northern" institutions imported from Lombardy to France by a farsighted Charlemagne, who thus sowed the "seeds" of a feudalism that matured "a few years after Hugh Capet." Boulainvilliers added new arguments too: arguments that feudal kings governed France as a "great fief," respected the nobility's "rights" and "liberties," and engaged the nobility in the conduct of "public affairs."[125] The feudal age was a golden age and Charlemagne was its admirable founder. "Charlemagne was a wise politician," Boulainvilliers wrote, "when he attached his preference to feudal government."[126] Indeed, "feudal government" was nothing less than "the masterpiece of the human mind," a stupendous achievement of medieval political prudence unanticipated by the ancients and unappreciated by the moderns. Classical political philosophies, such as that of Aristotle, would have to be revised to accommodate feudal government. So would modern political prejudices such as those of Louis Chantereau-Lefebvre, the royalist and antifeudal author of a highly regarded *Traité des fiefs*. Boulainvilliers wrote that

> although the Greek philosophers, and particularly Aristotle, had no notion of feudal government, and although [he] . . . did not include it among his political categories, one can regard it as the masterpiece of the human mind. . . . whether one considers it with regard to the true grandeur of kings, or whether one admires it for the liberty it secures for subjects. It is true . . . that it supposed reciprocal and inviolable rules between superiors and inferiors, rules founded on equity, faith and convention. . . . But can one regard these reciprocal duties as inconveniences, when they established common safety and a limit beyond which ambition, caprice, avidity— passions all too common among the great—could not carry them? I admit that I cannot read without indignation what Chantereau has dared to write on this subject: that is, "that feudalism injured the sovereignty of kings and

[124]Ibid., 129–30 (Letter 10).
[125]*Etat . . . Tome III*, 30–32 (Letter 4). Cf. *Etat*, 1, "Mémoires historiques": 113–14, 137–38, 142–45, 164, 179–82; see chapter 3. See also Mézeray, *Histoire de France* (1685 ed.), 1:611, 2:1–13, esp. 7, on medieval France as a "great fief."
[126]*Etat . . . Tome III*, 37 (Letter 4).

not only restricted or constrained it but also opposed and contradicted it. . . ." On the contrary is it not more judicious, more human, more reasonable to recognize that sovereignty has its laws and has had them since the existence of the monarchy?[127]

In these lines, Boulainvilliers called for nothing less than a revision of Europe's still classical political science to make room for a rehabilitated "feudal government," now medieval Europe's great gift to political wisdom.

In writing his "Lettres," however, Boulainvilliers' immediate aim was not to plead for a new and historically informed political science. Rather, his aim was to encourage noble support for the ducal cause in the *affaire du bonnet*. To that end, he spared the peers his harshest vituperation and reserved it for those other enemies of "feudal government," the legists and magistrates of the Parlement of Paris.

Boulainvilliers began their history with an angry account of the enfranchisement and ennoblement of their putative ancestors, the serfs of medieval France.[128] Here, he came as close as he ever would to imagining French history as a protracted struggle between Frankish or French nobles and enserfed Gallo-Romans.[129] And he nearly achieved a socioeconomic analysis of a feudal society in which armigerous nobles exploited a servile peasantry.[130] Appreciating feudalism's dependency upon seigneurialism, he attempted to vindicate seigneurialism and bemoan its decay, the result (he claimed) of the "inattention" of the nobility and "the Disorder, Boldness, and Insolence" of its serfs. That effort is not without interest, if only because of the later controversies occasioned by Boulainvilliers' harsh insistence that servility once had a rightful place in French society.[131] In his "Lettres," however, Boulainvilliers was

[127]Ibid., 37–38 (Letter 8). On Chantereau-Lefebvre, *Traité des fiefs et de leur origine*, see chapter 2.

[128]*Etat . . . Tome III,* 38–41 (Letter 4).

[129]For such readings of Boulainvilliers see Barzun, *The French Race,* esp. 138–47; and Devyver, *Le Sang épuré,* 353–90, 432–37. Boulainvilliers appreciated, however, that there were other causes of serfdom besides the putative Frankish Conquest and other serfs besides the presumably conquered Gauls. Cf. *Etat . . . Tome III,* 38 (Letter 4), on "serfs or . . . men of *main morte* who populated the towns and countryside of all France [and] who were either natural Gauls subjected at the time of the Conquest or unfortunates whom necessity or different accidents reduced to servitude."

[130]Cf. Marc Bloch, *Feudal Society,* tr. L. A. Manyon, 2 vols. (Chicago: University of Chicago Press, 1961).

[131]*Etat . . . Tome III,* 39–40 (Letter 4) for quotations; also 18 (Letter 2, on serfdom as "a state between Roman servitude and a sort of liberty"), 38–39 (Letter 4, on the "natural humanity of the [French or Frankish] Nation," and its self-interested concern for it serfs). For serfdom and its place in social controversies in eighteenth-century France see Barzun, *The French Race,* and Dieter Gembicki, "Le Renouveau des études sur les communes

chiefly concerned to deplore the rise of a robe nobility alongside an old or feudal nobility. It is not surprising, then, that when he turned from the enfranchisement of the serfs to their ennoblement, he pronounced it "much more monstrous."[132]

Conventional in chronology, Boulainvilliers' history of ennoblement was polemical in character. Like other writers on the subject, he dated ennoblement to the late thirteenth and early fourteenth centuries, when Philip III (1270–85) and Philip IV (1285–1314) first issued letters of nobility and when Philip VI (1328–50) began to sell them in abundance.[133] Boulainvilliers deplored these developments, although he admitted that among the enfranchised serfs were "minds [*génies*] superior to the character proper to agriculture and the arts" and rightfully destined for the churches and schools of medieval France. He lauded Raoul Gruet, the Breton commoner who negotiated the Treaty of Arras of 1435 and founded a noble line that only lately had died out.[134] But he refused to believe that ennoblement rewarded "virtue" like Raoul Gruet's. On the contrary, it rewarded only the ambition of commoners and the greed of favorites and ministers who recommended candidates for ennoblement and earned a cut of its cost. It exempted the rich from taxes and increased the fiscal burden on the poor. Worse, it encouraged *anoblis* to think that by acquiring letters of nobility they acquired "equality" with old nobles—despite the "natural" inequality of their "blood" and "origin." Here, Boulainvilliers wrote, was ennoblement's greatest "abuse."[135]

All of Boulainvilliers' works betray his suspicions about ennoblement. In his "Lettres," however, Boulainvilliers sought above all to vilify the Parlement of Paris and the great robe nobles in it. Accordingly, he paid close attention to the growing prominence of legists and magistrates in medieval France, to discover their "chicanery" behind everything that he deplored in the past. Following an old nobiliaire tradition of anti-robe complaint, he bemoaned the legists' assumption of the administration of justice, a task that should have been the nobility's alone but which the nobility in its lamentable "ignorance" abandoned.[136] "This,"

---

médiévales au XVIIIe siècle," in Centre Aixois d'Etudes et de Recherches sur le XVIIIe siècle, *La Ville au XVIIIe siècle: Colloque d'Aix-en-Provence (29 avril–1er mai 1973)* (Aix: Edisud, 1975), 205–11.

[132]*Etat . . . Tome III*, 41 (Letter 4).

[133]Ibid., 39–41 (Letter 4). Compare the similar but by no means bitter account in La Roque, *Traité de la noblesse*, 55–57, based on the registers (since destroyed by fire) of the Chambre des Comptes of Paris.

[134]*Etat . . . Tome III*, 52 (Letter 5); 149–50 (Letter 12).

[135]Ibid., 63–64 (Letter 6).

[136]Devyver, *Le Sang épuré*, 65, 70–88, 100, and (for Saint-Simon and Boulainvilliers) 287–91.

Boulainvilliers wrote, "must be regarded as their first and most essential step to their ruin, since from that moment, men accustomed themselves to regarding these legists as men of importance, the depositories of laws and usages, men whose opinions were practically never to be contradicted."[137]

No less regrettable was the legists' penetration into the baronial parlement at the beginning of the fourteenth century. Hitherto an assembly competent to treat "affairs of state," it now became "a purely judicial court" dominated by "lower clergy and legists" and disfigured by the "finesse," "chicanery," and "supposed enlightenment of jurists and churchmen."[138] Contemplating Philip IV's permanent establishment of the Parlement of Paris, Boulainvilliers commented, "It seems to me that there is no *gentilhomme* whose heart must not shudder at the thought."[139] Indeed, he lost no occasion to disparage the now sedentary Parlement of Paris and the legists who bought their offices in it.[140]

Boulainvilliers sought above all to indict legists for conspiring with kings to destroy feudalism. This great conspiracy thesis was central to his plea for the the dukes, for by detailing the legists' repeated attacks on feudalism and feudal nobility he hoped to persuade nobles to support the peers in their quarrel with the Parlement of Paris. Boulainvilliers acknowledged that the feudal nobility faced other threats besides the legists. He deplored the clergy's Peace Movement, for example: the clergy's "Associations" of the eleventh century were laudable efforts to contain feudal violence but dangerous extensions of clerical jurisdiction over nobles and laity. Because clergy were feudatories, however, Boulainvilliers refused to believe that they plotted to destroy fiefs.[141] Far more iniquitous were aggressive medieval kings such as Louis VI (1081–1137) and Philip II (1180–1223), well known for having expanded their own authority by conquering or claiming their vassals' fiefs.[142] But even

[137]*Etat . . . Tome III,* 45–46 (Letter 5).

[138]Ibid., 62 (Letter 6) for quotations, 47–50 (Letter 5), and 60–62 (Letter 6).

[139]Ibid., 65–66 (Letter 6).

[140]Cf. ibid., 69 (Letter 7, deploring the legists' admission to Estates General); 116, 123 (Letters 9 and 10, praising the Estates General of 1356 and the Ordinance of 1357 as efforts to abolish venality of office); 62, 66 (Letter 6), and 121 (Letter 10, reducing the Parlement of Paris to a mere law court); 139 (Letter 11, on the Parlement's registration the 1420 Treaty of Troyes, whereby the feebleminded Charles VI disinherited his son and made Henry V of England his heir, as "the eternal shame of the Parlement").

[141]Ibid., 43–45 (Letter 5), esp. 45 on clerical oaths as "new chains for the laity." Cf. Boulainvillier' 1700 "Dissertation" (*Essais,* 78–94) for earlier and more sympathetic views on chivalry; also discussed in Gossman, *Medievalism and Ideologies,* 276.

[142]*Etat . . . Tome III,* 51 (Letter 5). Cf. the two leading *histoires génerales* of Boulainvilliers' time: Mézeray, *Histoire* (1685 ed.), 2:74–89, 121–69, esp. 121; Daniel, *Histoire de France,* vol. 1, cols. 1129–68, 1140–41, 1269–1454.

in the reign of the "ambitious" Philip II, Boulainvilliers discovered "clerks" and "legists" behind royal efforts to destroy the feudal nobility. "Clerks" and "legists," he maintained, prepared the Ordinance of May 1, 1209, permitting the dismemberment of fiefs.[143] Those same jurists, he added, first contrived to lift a peerage above the body of the nobility. Consistently, Boulainvilliers' legists sought to make noble rank contingent on feudal tenure rather than on the "blood of the conquerors" of Gaul, in order to destroy fiefs and nobles at a stroke.[144] After describing the first appearance of a peerage in 1216, he stated,

> This will doubtless render more believable what I must propose in the following [letters], in order to show the common progress made by the ambition of kings, on the one hand, and the finesse of lettered men or jurists, on the other, in ruining little by little the prerogatives of fiefs after having destroyed the glory and the distinction of French blood by attributing all nobility to the grandeur of titles and the dignity of fiefs; and then in ruining fiefs themselves, by procuring their dismemberment and by playing with laws to make possession depend on the prince's will, notwithstanding that reciprocal fidelity of lords and vassals which ought to have established public safety.[145]

In arguing his thesis—that kings and legists conspired to destroy fiefs and feudal nobility—Boulainvilliers nearly lapsed into the antiducal and antilegist antifeudalisms that had tempted him in earlier works. But in his "Lettres sur les parlements," he managed to vindicate feudalism and the tenurial basis that it established for the "high nobility"'s preeminence. Fiefs, he argued, did not destroy the "illustriousness" that "blood" or "natural dignity" conferred on nobles. On the contrary, fiefs gave nobles their great names, those marks of distinction and grandeur that let genealogists trace noble lineages and celebrate their glory.[146] Not all families, he admitted, were so lucky. Some, even some descended from royalty, never became great feudatories. For "an infinity of oth-

---

[143]*Etat . . . Tome III*, 51–52 (Letter 5, on the ordinance of "Stabilimentum feodorum" [misdated 1204 in editions of the "Lettres"], which permitted the division of fiefs among a vassal's heirs but required that they do separate homage for their portions).

[144]Ibid., 52–54 (Letter 5, on the Parlement of Melun, 1216); and 46.

[145]Ibid., 54 (Letter 5).

[146]Ibid., 150 (Letter 12): "One can raise a powerful objection to this pretended rank of the high nobility . . . : namely, that honors and rights had passed to fiefs and consequently to their possession, with no consideration for the natural dignity of families. . . . But one must admit that the possession of great lands restored [*rendit*] to most families the illustriousness of which they had been deprived, and restored it with all the more distinction, since, having had no family names [*noms propres*] when they lost it, these families reentered into their rights with distinguished names which ought, henceforth, to have been incommunicable."

ers," however, fiefs "procured a permanent distinction by means of family names of which the first Franks [*François*] never had any idea."[147]

Boulainvilliers sustained his effort to accuse kings and legists of conspiring to destroy fiefs and feudatories to the very end of the twelve "Lettres sur les parlement" written in 1716. In his very last letter, he refused to ascribe the decay of feudal tenure and knight service to impersonal historical forces. One by one, he ruled out the reunification of great fiefs with the crown; the use of paid troops; the mortgaging, alienation, division, and female inheritance of fiefs; the death and imprisonment of feudatories during the Hundred Years' War; and even the monetary depreciation of the later Middle Ages, so devastating, he believed, for feudal landlords dependent on fixed money rents. These phenomena were not unique to France, Boulainvilliers claimed, but the decay of feudalism was. France, he concluded, owed her peculiar fate to a peculiar cause: "a formal design to ruin fiefs, conceived in the age of Louis the Fat [Louis VI, 1108–37], executed and followed under his successors, as I have shown in my preceding [letters] in recounting the principal means which the ambition and policies of monarchs aided by the finesse of men [var.: of the law] whom they employed to arrive at their ends."[148]

Having accused the peers of failing to defend French feudalism and having accused the legists of conspiring with kings to destroy it, Boulainvilliers came to his point. In the last of the twelve "Lettres" he finally made his plea for the dukes. His ostensible subject was privilege and precedence in the reign of Charles VII (1422–61). His real subject, however, was the *affaire du bonnet* and the role that untitled nobles should play in it.

His comments on privilege and precedence speak volumes about the social values that he sought to defend in 1716. Mining Jean Du Tillet's *Recueil des rangs*, Boulainvilliers hoped to demonstrate that peers and nobles still enjoyed preeminence over parlementaires in the fifteenth

---

[147]*Etat . . . Tome III*, 150, 151 (Letter 12). Here Boulainvilliers mentioned (among other houses) the "lords of Ham and S. Simon" descended, he said, from Charlemagne's own grandson, King Bernard of Italy. Thus Boulainvilliers accepted the genealogical pretensions of the duc de Saint-Simon's house (for which see A. de Boislisle, "Généalogie de la maison de Rouvroy Saint-Simon," in Saint-Simon, *Mémoires*, 1:384–427). That was no unmixed courtesy, however. Nothing proved more emphatically that the ducal dignity dear to Saint-Simon depended on royal favor and not on a glorious feudal past than the fact that Saint-Simon's house did not have one. On genealogy and the importance that genealogists (Boulainvilliers among them) attached to family names, see chapter 2.

[148]*Etat . . . Tome III*, 144–46 (Letter 12), 146 for quotation. This printing is corrupt. For the variant reading indicated here see Boulainvilliers, *Histoire de l'ancien gouvernement de la France*, 3 vols. (Amsterdam and The Hague: 1727), 3:62 (and on this edition see Bibliographical Appendix, Part 5).

century. When, for example, a "lit de justice" registered Charles VI's regency ordinance in 1407, princes and "high" nobles took precedence, followed first by ecclesiastics, and then, in carefully separated cohorts, by presidents of the Parlement on the one hand and by royal chamberlains ("the nursery of favorites") and nobles of the "second order" on the other. Councillors of the Parlement occupied the lowest rank and there were no *anoblis* at all. Doubtless Boulainvilliers appreciated that this scheme could authorize just those ducal-noble distinctions that he deplored. Hence his careful observation that the preeminence of the "high nobility" in no way impugned the dignity enjoyed by "knights and the nobility of the second order." Their inferiority of rank, in his view, did not "signify an inferiority of birth or origin but rather one of riches, possessions, or employments which have always distinguished men."[149] Boulainvilliers' admission—that nobles otherwise equal by "birth" might be unequal by virtue of their "riches, possessions, or employments"—recalls the practice of Old Regime genealogists who distinguished noble houses according to their "marks" of "honor" or "glory." But his admission clearly distinguishes him from the assembling nobles who in 1716 were asserting a rigorous and legalistic equality of all nobles old and new, sword and robe, titled and untitled. Boulainvilliers did not suddenly cease to be suspicious of the ducal dignity or its bearers in the lines just quoted. His recognition that some nobles might belong to a "second order" was not an admission that dukes and peers belonged to a "first."[150] He was not prepared, however, to assert a legalistic equality of all nobles and he clearly refused to make magistrates in the Parlement of Paris its beneficiaries. It was with satisfaction that he contemplated their inferior rank in 1407.

Boulainvilliers adduced yet further evidence of noble precedence over the robe in the fifteenth century. He was pleased to report that at the ceremonies for signing the Treaty of Arras in 1435, the "high nobility" still took took "precedence over officers, today called officers of the crown, and over every species of magistracy."[151] When Charles VII reduced his troops in 1439 and regrouped them in new "ordinance companies," Boulainvilliers wrote, he chose his captains among "the most illustrious nobility."[152] Like any ducal polemicist, finally, Boulainvilliers applauded the refusal of the Parlement of Paris to take cog-

---

[149]*Etat . . . Tome III,* 135–36 (Letter 12).
[150]Compare Boulainvilliers' similar remarks in one of his last works, the "Discours sur la noblesse"; see chapter 6.
[151]*Etat . . . Tome III,* 150 (Letter 12).
[152]Ibid., 144–45, 147, 156–59, 156 for quotation (Letter 12).

nizance of the duc d'Alençon's trial in 1458 as evidence that the court's magistrates had not yet lost all "firmness" and "modesty."[153]

Yet hints of later calamities darken Boulainvilliers' pages on rank and precedence in the fifteenth century. He admired Charles VII and his military reforms, but he saw the seeds of social "confusion" in the exemptions from the *taille* that Charles granted his soldiers.[154] And he claimed that the ceremonial signing of the Treaty of Arras "was the last occasion on which [the] high nobility was maintained in its preeminence, formerly natural and essential, without the aid of a particular privilege from the prince." As Boulainvilliers described it the fifteenth century was the Indian summer of noble preeminence, and with its passing the "true nobility" entered a new and uncongenial age in which it had to "console itself" for its "small share" of royal graces by cultivating "sentiments proper to the grandeur of its origin." Hence Boulainvilliers' lesson to his readers: "all the favor of monarchs can communicate nothing but titles and privileges but cannot make any other blood flow in a man's veins but that which is natural."[155]

Yet this was not Boulainvilliers' only lesson to his readers, for he proceeded to appeal to the age of Charles VII to rally the nobility to the peerage's side in the *affaire du bonnet*. After introducing the duc d'Alençon's trial of 1458, he interrupted his narrative to address the squabbling noble elites of regency Paris. He urged nobles to remember that peers were *gentilshommes* like themselves and that peerages were dignities reserved to nobles alone—unlike venal offices in the judiciary, available to the "meanest bourgeois." "Would it not be shameful for our government if the ease of buying offices made available to the meanest bourgeois all the dignities in the magistracy, while the illustriousness of birth, the greatness of services, and even the favor of kings could not obtain, at least for some fortunate individuals drawn from the body of the nobility, the rank and preeminence that it used to enjoy?" he asked.[156] Although he noted that the ducal dignity violated the equal dignity of all nobles of ancient birth, he defended the peers:

> I admit . . . that this distinction among persons of the same order and natural dignity [i.e. birth] might be disagreeable to those whom it does not favor; but since to combat this usage one would have to attack or rather

[153]Ibid., 161 (Letter 12); cf. [Le Laboureur], *Histoire de la pairie*, 1:152–54; and *Mémoire des pairs de France*, 6–7.

[154]*Etat . . . Tome III*, 158 (Letter 12). Boulainvilliers concluded that a family's nobility had to antedate the age of Charles's reforms to be beyond reproach.

[155]Ibid., 150–51 (Letter 12).

[156]Ibid., 161–62, or Boulainvilliers, *Histoire*, 3:127 (Letter 12). I translate from *Histoire*, because the text printed in *Etat . . . Tome III* is corrupt.

deny the plenitude of royal power which confers dignities and creates new peerages, would it not be better to console oneself with the thought that only the peers remain who can really maintain, by virtue of their privileges, the dignity of the nobility against the enterprises of men of the law, decorated today by titles of knights, counts, and marquis, while the old noble dares only at the greatest risk to take the quality of squire without the provincial intendant's permission?[157]

The dukes deserved the nobility's support, Boulainvilliers argued, because they alone enjoyed a distinction that had once been the entire nobility's. They were defending a precious remnant of the nobility's bygone glory.

His support for the dukes had its limits, however. He reminded his intended readers (the *affaire du bonnet*'s audience, dukes and peers included) that those titled dignitaries were *gentilshommes* who ought to maintain a "clearer remembrance of their first quality." And he dared to hope that less-wellborn peers might exercise a "greater modesty and good faith, so that, not presuming that the advantages of favor or fortune are equal or superior to those of birth, they will be better disposed to respect those who possess these last only by the grace of God and the order of nature and without any external helps."[158] Above all, even as he defended the dukes' preeminence he denied their constitutional "pretensions," for he reduced duchy-peerages to mere dignities created by kings and he exalted the "plenitude" of their power.

As a contributor to the *affaire du bonnet*, therefore, Boulainvilliers may be identified not with the assembling nobles but rather with that less easily discerned current of noble opinion at Paris sympathetic, with reservations, to the dukes. He was an advocate of ducal-noble solidarity, a late defender of a "tradition of union" that had all but collapsed under the weight of ducal constitutional "pretensions." His solicitude for the old nobility's "birth" and "glory" led him to take that position, for he did not share the assembling nobles' concept of nobility—a concept recalling that of Louis XIV's commissioners and intendants, whom Boulainvilliers despised—that nobility was equal membership in a legal noble order created and populated by a king.

Yet Boulainvilliers acknowledged the "plenitude" of royal power in modern France, and not just to reduce the ducal dignity to a mere product of it. Like the assembling nobles, he wanted to deflate ducal constitutional "pretensions." It has already been established that he sought also to lift the regent's authority above the reach of any noble

[157]*Etat . . . Tome III*, 162, or Boulainvilliers, *Histoire*, 3:127–28 (Letter 12).
[158]*Etat . . . Tome III*, 162, or Boulainvilliers, *Histoire*, 3:128–29 (Letter 12).

elite or body, but Boulainvilliers pursued yet another aim in writing on French constitutional history in his "Lettres sur les parlements." He hoped to exalt the absolute authority of modern kings, trace its establishment to the late Middle Ages and the destruction of "feudal government," and use that history to appeal to Orléans for the revival of the "nation"'s assemblies of Estates. Some features of that constitutional history have claimed attention already. It is now appropriate to return to it.

An Appeal to Orléans

Boulainvilliers' "Lettres sur les parlements" opens with the following lines:

> It is no longer possible, Monsieur, to resist your demands. The power of friendship has dissipated my repugnance and has caused to vanish all the reasons that I privately opposed to your request: that I inform you in writing about the nature of the assemblies that in France are called the Estates General of the Kingdom, about the causes that rendered practically all of them fruitless, [and] about what new measures might be hoped for or enacted to render them truly useful and advantageous, first for the king, by securing the tranquillity and glory of his government, and then for all subjects according to their different conditions, by securing the enjoyment of the natural goods that the fertility and happy situation of this kingdom might be able to procure to them.[159]

Boulainvilliers' subject is clear: "the assemblies that in France are called the Estates General of the Kingdom." Equally clear, now, are Boulainvilliers' intended readers, for behind the fictional friend to whom he addressed the "Lettres" stands the audience of the *affaire du bonnet*. It is arguable, however, that Boulainvilliers addressed his "Lettres" above all to the regent himself, for he orchestrated the examples of past princes as models to be shunned or emulated and exalted the legendary Charlemagne above all other princes. Like Charlemagne, Boulainvilliers sought to suggest, Orléans might use the plenitude of royal authority in his hands to revive the "nation" by restoring its "assemblies."

As a history of French representative institutions, the "Lettres" was a depressing tale of frauds and failures. Much of the story is familiar already: the atrophy of the baronial "parlement," for example, invaded by the legists and reduced to a mere law court; and the creation of the Estates General in the early fourteenth century, when the king's need

[159]*Etat . . . Tome III*, 1 (Letter 1).

for money, the legists' appetite for prominence, and the nobility's "inattention" to its own rights and preeminence all let a Third Estate dominated by men of the law acquire a political voice in the "nation's" assemblies.[160]

Boulainvilliers nevertheless desired to recount a continuous history of "parlements or estates general" in which the Estates inherit the mantle of the baronial "parlement." Like his "parlement" his Estates was an assembly of feudal vassals. These were not great feudatories, for most of France's great fiefs had now been reunited to the royal domain. But as bodies of feudal vassals the Estates still enjoyed the right to consent to taxes before paying them to their lord. Even in the fourteenth century, Boulainvilliers held, the French king taxed his subjects not as a "monarchic sovereign" but as a feudal lord—not as a king of France but as a "count of Perigord or Blois." Boulainvilliers' Estates General, therefore, was an aggregate of provincial feudal assemblies, a "general assembly" easier to work with than the many "particular assemblies" of individual fiefs but enjoying the same rights and performing the same functions.[161]

Boulainvilliers appreciated that the Estates could assist kings, but he sought to prove above all that the Estates protected the rights and properties of subjects against them. This point he made emphatically in recounting the rebellions that provincial "associations" of nobles, clergy, and commoners mounted against Philip IV's fiscal exactions after his death in 1314.[162] In response to those rebellions, Louis X (1314–16) issued charters of provincial liberties which Boulainvilliers had carefully transcribed from the originals in the *Trésor des chartes*. These he revered as "the last titles of our liberty" and as the "foundation of the authority that the Estates General assumed since that time"—the authority to consent to taxation.[163]

[160]Ibid., 69–75, esp. 69 (Letter 7): "Having to speak of the three orders which for several centuries now have composed what we call today the Estates General of the Kingdom, it is necessary to explain how they were formed and multiplied by the inattention and complacency *[facilité]* of the nobility, which alone constituted the state in the beginning and which, not content to let itself be dislodged from its rank by the clergy, has also been pleased to let men of the law—whose artifice and conduct I have had to describe—associate themselves with it."

[161]Ibid., 38 (Letter 4).

[162]Ibid., 76–86 (Letter 7). Cf. André Artonne, *Le Mouvement de 1314 et les chartes provinciales de 1315* (Paris: F. Alcan, 1912).

[163]*Etat . . . Tome III*, 76, 84 (Letter 7). See Bibliographical Appendix, Part 2, for Boulainvilliers' transcriptions of the original charters (all but two of the eight original documents have since been lost [Artonne, *Le Mouvement de 1314*, 1–2]). Among them was the celebrated *Charte normande* of 1315, still remembered and cited by Normans (like Boulainvilliers) in the seventeenth century (Bonney, *Political Change in France*, 344).

Having managed to transfer of the rights of the baronial "parlement" to the Estates, however, Boulainvilliers proceeded to tell a woeful tale about its failure to preserve them. Louis X's duplicity and his subjects' heedlessness weakened the associations of 1314, Boulainvilliers complained.[164] He applauded the Estates, it is true, when that assembly sought in 1355 and 1357 to establish consent to taxation as a "fundamental law" and to authorize resistance to illicit taxation by the king's officers and armies.[165] Yet the Estates had already established France's first "fixed" levy in 1345: the excise tax or *aides*. In 1360, he observed, King Jean II (1350–64) issued an ordinance on his own authority giving himself the right to collect the *aides* and the *gabelle:* "a great breach," Boulainvilliers wrote, in the Estates' authority. And the *taille*'s permanence after 1439, he maintained, opened the door to "despotism and arbitrary authority" by "delivering the goods of all individuals to the discretion of kings and the caprice of their ministers." An unmistakable gloom overshadows Boulainvilliers' history of the Estates General. He compared its 1355 ordinance to England's Magna Carta, it is true, but only to observe sadly that the ordinance "would have forever assured public liberty, had it been possible for France to be happy."[166]

France's was to be an unhappy fate, however, for the Estates lost not only the right of the old "parlement" to vote subsidies but also its right to make laws. By 1374, Boulainvilliers wrote, kings were legislating without the assistance of either the Estates or the barons or peers.[167] He ascribed that expansion of royal authority to two causes. One was the disorder of the 1350s—princely factionalism, conflicts between the Second Estate and the Third Estate, the violent peasant rebellion or *Jacquerie,* the popular rising in Paris led by Etienne Marcel—which discredited the Estates General and led Charles V (1364–80) to govern without it.[168] Boulainvilliers' second cause for the rise of royal authority was the Hundred Years' War, a contest for the royal succession which by the 1350s had already led Frenchmen to forget their rights and the "mixed government" that secured them:

> It is to this date, according to Mézeray, that one must assign the end of the mixed government by which France ruled herself since the beginning of

[164]*Etat . . . Tome III*, 77–84 (Letter 7).
[165]Ibid., 103–9, esp. 103, 117–18 (Letter 9), and 122–23 (Letter 10). A copy of the ordinance of 1355 is among Boulainvilliers' transcriptions of sources for his "Lettres" (see Bibliographical Appendix).
[166]*Etat . . . Tome III*, 99 (Letter 8); 123–24 (Letter 10); 158 (Letter 12); 103, 105 (Letter 9).
[167]Ibid., 129 (Letter 10).
[168]*Etat . . . Tome III*, 109–18 (Letter 9).

the monarchy, to a greater or lesser extent according to the character, capacity, and good fortune [*le bonheur particulier*] of kings. This happened not only because people were disgusted by popular violence—wrongly taken as the effect of the resolutions of the recent Estates—but also because, during a war that had lasted for more than eighty years, royal authority imperceptibly gained the upper hand thanks to the oblivion into which the rights of individuals had fallen, rights that remained unexercised amidst the confusion and disorder of a war that penetrated all parts of the kingdom.[169]

Even in its unfinished state, Boulainvilliers' history of "parlements or estates general" is clearly the history of a catastrophe that befell France in the fourteenth and fifteenth centuries. He had intended to carry his story forward to the seventeenth century and amassed documentation on later meetings of the Estates, but he sealed France's fate in the fourteenth century. He wrote ominously of the unhappy "destiny" that ·was henceforth hers:

And in essence, it is evident that states have their destinies and that these destinies are just as inevitable as those of individuals, so that the freeborn man who finds himself reduced to servitude by the enchainment of the diverse accidents of his life is the natural image of a people whom occasions, events, circumstances, even their contrary effects lead into slavery despite the certainty of its primordial rights. Such was the fortune of the Romans who, having destroyed their liberty by their own arms, could never have masters enough and in fact always anticipated their ambition with flattery and the basest submission.[170]

Inverting the Roman "parallel" dear to the celebrants of Louis XIV's "glory," Boulainvilliers used that "obligatory cliché" to deplore the Roman Empire and the French monarchy both.[171] Comparing France's monarchical destiny with Rome's imperial fate, Boulainvilliers once again introduced a dramatic discontinuity into the history of the French monarchy. Customarily, early-modern French historians wrote a continuous history of the monarchy and asserted its antiquity.[172] Boulainvilliers denied it, asserting the monarchy's modernity and representing the monarchy as the product of the fatal decline of France into an iron age of "submission," "slavery," and "despotism."

[169]Ibid., 117 (Letter 9). Cf. Mézeray, *Histoire* (1685 ed.), 1:377–78.
[170]*Etat . . . Tome III*, 118 (Letter 9).
[171]Cf. Hubert Gillot, *La Querelle des anciens et des modernes en France: De la défense et illustration de la langue française aux Parallèles des anciens et des modernes* (Paris: Edouard Champion, 1914), 319–22.
[172]See works cited in chapter 1, n. 29.

It is tempting to suppose that Boulainvilliers' darkly pessimistic history of the monarchy could only lead him to an elegiac nostalgia for a dead but adored past. In writing his "Lettres," however, he excavated that past for political lessons applicable in the present. To be sure, he did not address those lessons to a French "nation" or "nobility," whose "ignorance," "inattention," "inconsideration," "lightheadedness" (*légèreté*), and contempt for historical "study" he lamented throughout his "Lettres."[173] "Had it been the custom in France to pay attention to the past," he wrote, the French would never have forgotten the great charters of 1315 or the great Ordinance of 1357.[174] Had the French been like the English—Boulainvilliers was one of the first Anglomaniacs of eighteenth-century France—they would have defended their rights against kings and demanded "precise titles" of them.[175] And had the French emulated the ancients, Boulainvilliers maintained, they would have cultivated "virtue" while pursuing a "solid glory." Instead, Boulainvilliers complained, the Frenchman's "modern education" reduced "love of country" to a "chimera," let "arrogance" and "the king's service" replace "generous ambition" and "what we used to call greatness of soul and fidelity," and taught the Frenchman to forget his birth or "natural dignity." "We teach no one to esteem his rank and natural dignity enough to fear to dishonor them by weakness," he complained.[176] Boulainvilliers' diatribe against the failings of the French reveals once again his presumption that "birth" fosters "virtue" in the pursuit of "glory," provided that paths of "glory" remain open to the wellborn. That presumption, encouraged by his proud genealogical consciousness of what belonging to a noble lineage meant, led him in his "Lettres" to imagine a nobiliaire civic community whose members defended their "rights" jealously and cultivated their "virtue" actively in the pursuit of "glory." But Boulainvilliers asserted that nobiliaire civism only to declare it beyond the reach of a "nation" and a nobility disfigured by its "modern education" and the political vices that it entailed.

Boulainvilliers addressed his "Lettres" not to a "nation" but—remark-

[173]See, for example, *Etat . . . Tome III*, 3 (Letter 1), 64 (Letter 6), 69 (Letter 7), 146–47 (Letter 12). Such complaints had long since been commonplaces; see Miriam Yardéni, *La Conscience nationale en France pendant les guerres de religion (1559–1598)* (Louvain: Editions Nauwelaerts; Paris: Béatrice Nauwelaerts, 1971), 37–39, 40–41, and (for contemporaries of Boulainvilliers) Gossman, *Medievalism and Ideologies*, 11–2.
[174]*Etat . . . Tome III*, 77 (Letter 7), and 123 (Letter 10).
[175]Ibid., 84–85 (Letter 7): "The English are less contemptible than we think them for having perhaps forced their princes to give them exact and precise titles of incontestable notoriety when it was a matter . . . of assuring the liberty of men and the tranquil enjoyment of their goods." See 103 (Letter 9), and 122 (Letter 10), for other English comparisons.
[176]Ibid., 4–5 (Letter 1).

ably—to a prince. Vesting his hopes for the revival of the "nation" in the duc d'Orléans, he tried to convince himself and the regent that even in monarchies historians might speak the truth because even princes could face it. If French historians customarily flattered their princes, Boulainvilliers blamed that fault not on monarchy but "on the personal character of writers and on the common manner of thinking in this age."[177] Thus he invited Orléans to welcome the truth, and then deployed for the regent's edification a series of royal examples dominated by the inspiring figure of Charlemagne. Writing for the duc de Bourgogne, Boulainvilliers had already magnified Charlemagne's stature. Writing for the duc d'Orléans he did so again, representing the Carolingian emperor as a magnanimous prince who had used the fullness of royal authority in his hands to rescue France from her corruption and to revive her moribund assemblies.[178] Boulainvilliers claimed that

> at bottom Charlemagne was a better politician than his predecessors and all his successors: . . . one must return to the maxim that every prince who governs without concern [*ménagement*] for the rights of the peoples, without attention to their character or to public happiness, without foresight for those who must succeed him, and without a desire to establish his glory on the justice of his government, that prince, I say, far from meriting the title of a good king, would be regarded by posterity only as an oppressor, that is, a sovereign who abused his power, who abandoned himself to his passions, and who, concerned with his own interests alone, separated himself from the body of society to enjoy alone advantages which cannot cease to be common without politically destroying society. Consequently, Charlemagne could not make a better and more useful employment of his fortune than by admitting his subjects to sharing authority.[179]

The glorious Charlemagne dominated Boulainvilliers' "Lettres sur les parlements" as "an example for future ages," setting the standard by which Boulainvilliers judged later kings and setting the example that he hoped the duc d'Orléans would imitate. When Boulainvilliers deplored Louis X's duplicity in 1315, for example, he observed that "Louis . . . was incapable of acting upon the sentiment of generosity or upon the consideration of law and justice, which had been Charlemagne's motives when he reestablished the usage of common assemblies or parlements." And when Boulainvilliers lamented Charles V's refusal to govern with the Estates, he wrote, "there are no examples, after Charlemagne, of any

[177]Ibid., 2–3, 6 (Letter 1), 3 for quotation; cf. *Etat*, 1, "Préface": xxii (similar remarks written with the duc de Bourgogne in mind).
[178]*Etat . . . Tome III*, 13–5, 18 (Letter 2).
[179]Ibid., 15 (Letter 2).

monarch who voluntarily renounced his arbitrary power after he had acquired it by his work, skill, and *savoir-faire.*"[180] That, however, is precisely what Boulainvilliers encouraged Orléans to do, by arranging his princely examples around Charlemagne and by demonstrating, in the course of an elaborate account of France's inexorable decline into monarchical "despotism," that Orléans too held "arbitrary power" in his own hands and might use it to renounce it.

Here was Boulainvilliers' appeal to Orléans: an invitation to be a new Charlemagne and Prince-Legislator restoring to life a nobiliaire civic community that had once existed long ago. Writing in the heat of the *affaire du bonnet,* Boulainvilliers intended to lift Orléans' power above the constitutional claims to secure it which the aristocratic elites were lodging at the beginning of the regency. He appreciated the dynastic difficulties that inspired those claims and in his "Lettres" he implied that barons or nobles might take cognizance of a regency dispute in 1716, for they had done so before, in 1328.[181] But Boulainvilliers sought above all to exalt Charlemagne's "generosity" and to lead Orléans—whose authority he defended against all challengers—to emulate it.

Never were Boulainvilliers' hopes higher than when he prepared his "Lettres" as a contribution to the *affaire du bonnet* in 1716. An *orléaniste* publicist writing to defend the regent's authority, Boulainvilliers was also a nobiliaire ideologue writing to persuade Orléans that, like Charlemagne, he might revive the assemblies of the "nation", restore the nobility's preeminence, and thereby reconstitute a nobiliaire civism of "birth," "virtue," and "glory" which had once existed in Frankish and feudal times. That Boulainvilliers never finished and published his "Lettres" is only one sign that his hopes were misplaced.

[180]Ibid., 18 (Letter 2); 85 (Letter 7); 118 (Letter 9).
[181]Ibid., 94 (Letter 8).

6

The *Affaire des Princes* (1716–1717)

and Boulainvilliers' Failure

If (as one memorialist put it) the *affaire du bonnet* "distracted . . . individuals from public affairs," the *affaire des princes* "made an uncommon noise in France."[1] Gazetteers, correspondents, memorialists, and diarists commonly paid much more attention to the *affaire des princes* than they had to the *affaire du bonnet*.[2] So too, it seems, did publishers. In the course of the *affaire des princes* they printed more than forty pamphlets; some of them went through several editions before they were all gathered together in a four-volume collection published shortly after the dispute ended.[3] Among those pamphlets was one by Boulainvilliers, the *Justification de la naissance légitime de Bernard, roy d'Italie, petit-fils de Charlemagne*, a minor contribution to the *affaire des princes* but the only piece that he ever managed to publish.[4]

Modern historians, too, have attached greater importance to the *affaire des princes* than to the *affaire du bonnet*. They appreciate that the later

---

[1][Piossens], *Mémoires de la Régence*, 1:88, 2:21.

[2]For example, ibid., 1:88–92 (on the *affaire du bonnet*), and 2:21–45, 56–93, 118–26, 3:126–53 (on the *affaire des princes*); Anon., *Gazette de la Régence*, 62, 66–67, 77–78, 85, 87, 88 (on the *affaire du bonnet* and matters concerning the peerage), and 93, 95–96, 100, 101, 107, 109, 129, 134, 135–36, 140, 151–54, 167, 173, 177–80, 187, 190 (on the *affaire des princes*); Buvat, *Journal de la Régence*, 1:33 (a promise to include the polemics occasioned by the two *affaires*), 1:121–23 (on the *affaire Richelieu;* there is nothing on the *affaire du bonnet*), and 1:170, 250–51, 272–73, 284–85 (on the *affaire des princes*); Marais, *Journal et mémoires*, 1:206–15 (on the *affaire des princes;* there is nothing on the *affaire du bonnet*); Balleroy, *Les Correspondants de la marquise de Balleroy*, 1:75, 108 (on the *affaire du bonnet*), and 1:108, 157–58, 166–76, 184 (on the *affaire des princes*).

[3]*Recueil general des pieces touchant l'affaire des princes legitimes et legitimez, mises en order,* 4 vols. (Rotterdam: 1717). For the original pamphlets and the dates when some of them appeared, see Jacques Lelong, *Bibliothèque historique de la France*, ed. [Charles-Marie] Fevret de Fontette, 5 vols. (Paris: Jean-Thomas Herissant, 1768–78), and B.N., *Catalogue de l'histoire de France*, sub Lb[38] 77–121.

[4]([Paris: 1717]). As discussed later, this pamphlet was not Boulainvilliers' sole contribution to the *affaire*.

dispute was a major debate about the "fundamental law" of the royal succession and the "rights of the nation" to judge disputes about that law, a debate whose parties skillfully mobilized men of letters and learning in their causes.[5] Like the *affaire du bonnet*, however, the *affaire des princes* was also a dispute about the regent's authority and the conflicting constitutional claims lodged by the aristocratic elites of France. The issues that had divided those elites in 1715–16 continued to do so in 1716–17; once again shifts in aristocratic "public opinion" in regency Paris were to determine the outcome of the contest. By ending the *affaire* with an edict issued on his own authority, the regent finally suppressed the vague and conflicting constitutional ambitions of the aristocratic elites. Significantly, for the course of later political disputes during the regency, only the Parlement of Paris emerged from the *affaire des princes* with its political credit enhanced.[6]

Yet another step in Orléans' successful consolidation of his own authority, the *affaire des princes* was also the final step—for Boulainvilliers—in the destruction of French "liberty" and in the establishment of royal "despotism." In his contributions to the *affaire des princes*, Boulainvilliers abandoned his remarkable hopes for the regency and the regent. In his very last works, written after the *affaire* had ended, only his historical pessimism and fatalism remained. His hopes had ended in failure.

Dynastic Conflict and Aristocratic Constitutionalism

The *affaire des princes* owed its name to its leading protagonists, the princes of the blood of the House of Condé, and Louis XIV's legitimated bastards by Madame de Montespan, the duc du Maine and the comte de Toulouse. At issue was the legislation whereby the late king exalted their rank and added their lines to the order of succession to the crown. By his Declaration of May 5, 1694, Louis gave his bastards (and the descendants of Henry IV's bastards) an "intermediate rank" below the princes of the blood and above the dukes and peers. In the May 1711 Edict on the peerage, Louis made two further provisions for exalting his bas-

[5]André Lemaire, *Les Lois fondamentales de la monarchie française d'après les théoriciens de l'ancien régime* (Paris: E. Thouin et fils; Albert Fontemoing, 1907), 197–204; Henri Morel, "Les 'Droits de la nation'" 249–62; Waller, "Men of Letters and the *Affaire des Princes*"; Claire Saguez-Lovisi, *Les Lois fondamentales au XVIIIe siècle: Recherches sur la loi de dévolution de la couronne*, (Paris: Presses Universitaires de France, 1983), 47–76. Marina Valensise' doctoral dissertation on the *affaire des princes*, now in progress, will situate it firmly in the history of Old Regime convictions about an unwritten monarchical constitution.

[6]Leclercq, *Histoire de la Régence*, 2:97.

tards: that the princes and legitimated bastards first be asked to officiate at royal consecrations, before dukes and peers; and that princes be received at the Parlement of Paris at age nineteen, the legitimated bastards at age twenty, and the dukes and peers only at age twenty-five. Having exalted his bastards' rank, Louis proceeded to add his bastards and their legitimate descendants to the line of succession to the crown. By the Edict of July 1714, he provided that should the lines of the legitimate princes of the blood fail, then the right to succeed to the throne would pass to the lines of Maine and Toulouse. Finally, by his Declaration of May 23, 1715, the aging king gave Maine and Toulouse the title or "quality" of prince of the blood.[7] Measures of a doting father and an anxious dynast—it will be recalled that by 1714 Louis XIV had lost all his male descendants except Philip V of Spain and the future Louis XV—the king's legislation elicited no protests when he issued it: the Parlement registered it and the great princes and nobles acquiesced in it. After Louis XIV's death, however, such forebearance evaporated. Predictably the dukes and peers opposed the king's legislation because it demoted them in the order of court ranks.[8] So did the Condé princes of the blood, the duc de Bourbon (or the prince de Condé or "Monsieur le Duc"), his brother the comte de Charolais, and their cousin the prince de Conti. True, they continued to precede the king's bastards both in rank and in the succession to the throne, but the princes, notably the young and hotheaded duc de Bourbon, claimed nonetheless that their rank and rights were injured by Louis XIV's legislation. After his death they sought occasions to contest it.

Orléans managed to restrain Bourbon until August 1716, when the duc de Richelieu's trial for dueling was drawing to a close. The Parlement of Paris planned to assemble on August 21 to render its decision. Whereas most of the princes, legitimate and legitimated, planned not to attend because they were related to Richelieu, the comte de Toulouse let it be known that he would attend and assume the princely rank to which his father's legislation entitled him. In response, the duc de Bourbon prepared a petition to the crown which, the day after Toulouse appeared in Parlement, he presented to a reluctant Orléans. Orléans may have wished to avoid a new round of aristocratic controversy but the *affaire des princes* had now begun.[9]

The Condé princes' petition of August 22, 1716, was one of the most

[7]See printed editions of this legislation listed in B.N., *Catalogue . . . Actes royaux*, nos. 18320, 24561, 25605, 25882.
[8]Labatut, *Les Ducs et pairs*, 341–50.
[9]Anon., *Gazette de la Régence*, 67, 72, 100, 101, 107, 109; Dangeau, *Journal*, 14:424, 425, 428, 431, 432, 433, 436–37, 496, 498, 500.

important utterances of the *affaire des princes*. It defined the princes' position and the terms of the ensuing debate: a controversy about the "fundamental law" of the French royal succession and the "rights" of the "nation" to "choose" its "masters."[10] According to the petition, Louis XIV violated that "fundamental law" and injured those "rights" when, by the Edict of July 1714 and the Declaration of May 23, 1715, he added Maine's and Toulouse's lines to the French royal succession and assimilated them to the princes of the blood:

> When this Edict and this Declaration appeared, the entire nation was convinced that they directly contravened the fundamental laws of the kingdom, and that they could not subsist because the legislator lacked the power to make them. The right to succeed to the crown is attached only to the house which the nation chose to rule over it. Consequently, the nation has rejected as incapable all those who do not belong to that house. That incapacity includes taking the quality and title of prince of the blood, for that title supposes descent from the royal house, which cannot be supposed of individuals who are not legitimately born into it. And when that house dies out, the nation resumes all its rights to choose a master.
>
> However extensive and however respectable the sovereign power of kings may be, it is not above nature itself and the fundamental law of the state.[11]

A plea for *amour-propre,* the princes' petition was also a constitutional theory, for according to the princes, the French "nation" had chosen its ruling house and the "fundamental law" of the royal succession embodied the terms of a contract between that "nation" and its ruling house which kings could not violate.

The contractualist implications of that constitutional theory have impressed at least one modern historian.[12] Yet that contractualism was not a matter of controversy during the *affaire des princes*. Virtually all partici-

---

[10]It is true that some pamphlets appeared as early as May 1716 (B.N., *Catalogue de l'histoire de France,* sub Lb^{38} 80–83), well before the princes' August 22 petition. Those earlier pamphlets applied private law to the French royal succession, not public or "fundamental" law, and their authors argued about whether or not bastards might inherit their parents' estates under divine, natural, and ancient Frankish law. See *Recueil general des pieces,* 1:136–47 (*Lettre d'un espagnol à un françois*); 170–71 (*Response à la lettre d'un espagnol à un françois, au sujet de la contestation qui est entre les princes du sang & les legitimez*); and 176–204 (*Nouvelle refutation de la lettre d'un espagnol à un françois, au sujet de la contestation qui est entre les princes du sang & les legitimez, où l'on fait voir les dangereuses consequences qu'on peut tirer contre l'état, des faux principes que cet auteur établit*). The princes' August 22 petition clearly moved the debate onto the constitutionally more appropriate terrain of "fundamental law."

[11]*Recueil general des pieces,* 1:81–82 (*Requeste presentée au roi, par messieurs les princes de Condé, de Charolois, & de Conty*).

[12]Morel, "Les 'Droits de la nation.'"

pants in that debate embraced it.[13] Virtually no one denied that "funda-mental law" governed the French royal succession or even that it defined the "rights" of the French "nation."

But by appealing to French "fundamental law" in the August 22 petition, the princes invited their opponents to do so as well and to examine its history; indeed it was the bastards' pamphleteers who turned the *affaire des princes* into a historical debate. To disprove the princes' thesis that French "fundamental law" excluded bastards from the throne, Maine's and Toulouse's writers searched the Frankish past for bastard princes and kings. A short *Examen de la pretendue loi fondamen-tale, qui exclut les princes legitimez de la succession à la couronne* initiated this strategy.[14] It was the abbé Louis Legendre, one of the leading controver-sialists of the *affaire des princes,* who developed it fully in a *Lettre de M.** ** ** à un homme de qualité* published in September 1716.[15] Leg-endre agreed that the "nation" chose its royal house, bastards includ-ed.[16] But to discover the "fundamental law" by which the "nation" regulated the royal succession, he chose not to dwell on mythical juridi-cal acts performed by that "nation" in a barely discernible past. Rather, he chose to examine the historical record. There, he wrote, one might find the provisions of "fundamental law": not a written law but a "cus-tom" that became "law" with longevity.[17] Legendre proceeded to follow a clear and lucid strategy to establish that bastards did indeed succeed to the throne in Frankish antiquity and to demonstrate that no subsequent act disallowed that practice. In examining the Merovingians, he had little difficulty in adducing evidence that bastards succeeded along with legitimate sons to patrimonies customarily divided among a prince's heirs.[18] Under the Carolingians, however, he found only two examples of bastard princes. One was King Bernard of Italy, the son of Charlemagne's bastard Pepin, an admissible example, Legendre insis-ted, because Italy was a Frankish and not foreign dominion in the ninth century.[19] The other was Arnulf, Charlemagne's great-grandson who

[13]There were two exceptions. For one see *Recueil general des pieces,* 3:143–45 (*Défense des droits du roi, dans la contestation formée entre les princes legitimes, & legitimez*). The other, Boulainvilliers' "Mémoire touchant l'affaire de Mrs. les princes du sang," is discussed later.
[14]*Recueil general des pieces,* 1:275–99.
[15]Ibid., 1:300–44 ([Louis Legendre], *Lettre de M. ** ** ** à un homme de qualité, qui lui a demandé son sentiment sur la Lettre d'un espagnol à un françois, sur les réponses qu'on y a faites, & sur la Requête des princes*).
[16]Ibid., 1:315.
[17]Ibid., 1:322–23.
[18]Ibid., 1:323–26.
[19]Ibid., 1:326–27. An earlier pamphleteer for the Condé princes had rejected the admissibility of Bernard's example (1:187 [*Nouvelle réfutation de la lettre d'un espagnol à un françois, au sujet de la contestation qui est entre les princes du sang & les legitimez, où l'on fait voir les dangereuses consequences qu'on peut tirer contre l'etat, des faux principes que cet auteur établit*]).

became king of Germany in the late ninth century when the legitimate Carolingian line in that kingdom had died out, another admissible example, Legendre insisted, and an especially instructive one because it established that bastards could no longer succeed *with* legitimate princes to divided patrimonies but only *after* legitimate princes to undivided states now reserved to the eldest heir.[20] The direct Capetians, Legendre added, did not abrogate the principle of bastard succession[21] and if it was now believed that bastards were excluded from the throne, that was merely a "prejudice" encouraged by the fact that from Philip II's reign in the early thirteenth century to Henry II's in the early sixteenth century, no king sired a bastard. This "prejudice" contradicted an ancient practice that had never been abrogated and still subsisted, therefore, as part of French "fundamental law." Legendre's conclusion was simple and emphatic: when Louis XIV added Maine and Toulouse and their lines to the royal succession, he did not contravene fundamental law. Rather he declared it, and so stayed well within the bounds of his legislative authority.[22]

To the end of the *affaire des princes* the bastards' pamphleteers continued to work and rework Legendre's argument.[23] Meanwhile the legitimate princes' publicists did their best to refute it. Predictably, they raised doubts about Legendre's use of Capetian sources.[24] Predictably, too, they raised questions about Legendre's two Carolingian bastards. Arnulf of Germany inspired fairly little controversy.[25] Bernard of Italy, on the other hand, became a subject of debate as the pamphleteers working for Bourbon, Charolais, and Conti did their best to give him a legitimate pedigree.[26] It was when they examined Legendre's Mer-

[20]Ibid., 1:327–28.

[21]Ibid., 1:328–31 (an analysis of the writings of abbot Suger and the twelfth-century historian Rigord, arguing that they acknowledged the rights of royal bastards to succeed to the throne).

[22]Ibid., 1:332–35.

[23]Ibid., 4:4–82 and 296–301 (*Troisième Memoire des princes legitimez*). This massive pamphlet was still in press when the *affaire des princes* ended with a decision against Maine and Toulouse (see MS note on the B.N.'s copy of the original folio edition of the pamphlet [cote F° Lb^{38} 118]).

[24]*Recueil general des pieces*, 2:136–41 (*Réponse au dernier Memoire instructif de M. le duc du Maine*); 420–32 ([Jean de La Chapelle], *Reflexions politiques et historiques sur l'affaire des princes*); both pamphlets criticizing Legendre's use of Suger and Rigord (see n. 21).

[25]*Recueil general des pieces*, 2:131 (*Réponse au dernier Memoire instructif de M. le duc du Maine*); 318 (*Memoire des princes du sang, pour répondre au Memoire instructif des princes legitimez, du quinze novembre 1716. & à celui du neuf decembre suivant*); 416–19 ([La Chapelle], *Reflexions politiques et historiques sur l'affaire des princes*).

[26]Ibid., 2:130 (*Réponse au dernier Memoire instructif de M. le duc du Maine*); 412–13 ([La Chapelle], *Reflexions politiques et historiques sur l'affaire des princes*). In their own *Memoire des princes du sang, pour répondre au Memoire intructif des princes legitimez*, Bourbon, Charolais, and Conti (or their draftsman) conceded Bernard of Italy's illegitimacy, declared that he

ovingian examples, however, that the princes' pamphleteers gave their most interesting performances, for they effectively dissolved Legendre's clear distinctions between legitimate and illegitimate Merovingians by restoring them to their still partly pagan and polygamous world, in which concubinage coexisted with Christian marriage and both the concubine's and the wife's children might be regarded as legitimate. The princes' pamphleteers did not deny the existence of Merovingian bastardy altogether, but they insisted that the Merovingian Franks were so radically unlike the Christian Frenchmen of later times that Merovingian experience offered no valid legal analogies and precedents that might be applied to the case of Maine and Toulouse.[27] Thus the princes' pamphleteers discovered the mutability of French private law even as they sought to insist on the immutability of French "fundamental law" and its exclusion of bastards from the throne.

But the *affaire des princes* was not simply a debate, however learned and insightful, about the nature and history of "fundamental law." It was also a debate about the constitutional right to judge disputes about the royal succession. Inevitably its participants raised questions about the regent's authority to do so. The *affaire des princes*, consequently, recalls the quarrels about the right to "declare" regencies and resolve disputes about them which had divided France's aristocratic elites during the *affaire du bonnet*.

Just as both parties to the *affaire des princes* agreed that "fundamental law" governed the French royal succession, so too both parties agreed that French royal authority was absolute. In their August 22 petition, it is true, the legitimate princes declared that Louis XIV had exceeded the limits of his legislative authority. He had no right, they protested, to confer either the rights or the rank of prince of the blood upon his bastards. Only "fundamental law" and legitimate birth into the royal house—"nature," in the princes' parlance—could do that. But having insisted on the limits to the absolute authority of French kings, Bourbon,

owed his Italian throne to royal grace alone, and added that his descendants were passed by in 987 when the "nation" named Hugh Capet to succeed to the last French Carolingian king (2:296, 314–15, 321–23). But Waller clearly erred when he wrote that both parties in the *affaire des princes* agreed on Bernard of Italy's illegitimacy ("Men of Letters and the *Affaire des Princes*," 140). They did not, and the princes' pamphleteers had clear enough reasons for wishing to establish Bernard's legitimacy: to knock yet another prop out from under the bastards' case, so cogently defended by Legendre.

[27]See *Recueil general des pieces*, 2:134–35 (*Réponse au dernier Memoire instructif de M. le duc du Maine*); 305–8 (*Memoire des princes du sang, pour répondre au Memoire instructif des princes legitimez . . .*); 398–409 ([La Chapelle], *Reflexions politiques et historiques sur l'affaire des princes*—by far one of the historically most sophisticated performances of the *affaire des princes*).

Charolais, and Conti proceeded to exalt that authority, even when it was to be found in the hands of a minor king's regent, for they demanded that Orléans hold a *lit de justice* to answer their petition and quash Louis XIV's July 1714 Edict and May 23, 1715, Declaration.[28] Their pamphleteers never ceased to assert the regent's authority to judge the *affaire des princes.*[29]

Maine and Toulouse also exalted the authority of French kings. Early pamphlets for the bastards even suggested that kings might transmit their crown by testament, just as the last Carolingian king did when, presumably, he willed his crown to Hugh Capet in 987.[30] Led by Louis Legendre, the bastards' pamphleteers soon abandoned that position—the testament of 987 was a myth long since exploded by historical criticism—in order to appeal instead to a "fundamental law" whose provisions were to be discovered in ancient Frankish history.[31] Legendre insisted, however, that French kings could dispose freely of ranks and titles, including the rank and title of prince of the blood.[32] In due course, other pamphleteers writing for Maine and Toulouse would adopt Legendre's argument.

Although both parties agreed that French royal authority was absolute, critical issues divided them. Bourbon, Charolais, and Conti rejected the bastards' "dangerous" claims that kings might make "princes" at will

[28]Ibid., 1:81–82 (quoted earlier), and 82–83 (the demand that Orléans hold a *lit* to quash Louis's legislation).
[29]Ibid., 1:196–97 (*Nouvelle réfutation de la lettre d'un espagnol à un françois . . .*); 2:152 (*Réponse au dernier Memoire instructif de M. le duc du Maine*); 227–32 (*Remarques sur le second Memoire de Monsieur le duc du Maine, du 9. decembre 1716. dont le commencement n'est presque qu'un répétition du premier*); 333–49 (*Memoire des princes du sang, pour répondre au Memoire instructif des princes legitimez, du quinze november 1716. & à celui du neuf decembre suivant*); 440–41 ([La Chapelle], *Reflexions politiques et historiques sur l'affaire des princes*); 3:57–58 (*Raisons courtes et fondamentales pour les princes du sang, & pour la nation. Contre les princes legitimez*); 327–35 (*Reflexions sur la necessité de juger l'affaire des princes du sang, sur la forme du jugement, & sur l'effet des lettres de legitimation*); 347–48 (*Nouvelles reflexions sur l'affaire des princes du sang*).
[30]Ibid., 1:151–53 (*Lettre d'un espagnol à un françois*); 249–50, 256–57 (*Reflexions sur la pretention de messieurs le duc de Bourbon, comte de Charolois, & prince de Conty, contre messieurs les duc du Maine, & comte de Toulouse*); 2:30–31 (*Apologie de l'édit du mois de juillet 1714. & de la déclaration du 23. mai 1715. qui donnent aux princes legitimez, & à leurs enfans & descendans mâles, à perpetuité, nez & à naître en légitime mariage, le titre, les honneurs, & le rang de princes du sang, & le droit de succeder à la couronne après tous les princes legitimes. Ou lettre justificative d'un magistrat à un abbé, pour messieurs le duc du Maine, & comte de Toulouse*).
[31]By 1700 even narrative historians had abandoned the mythical testament of A.D. 987 (Tyvaert, "L'Image du roi," 528). And see *Recueil general des pieces* 1:308–9 ([Legendre], *Lettre de M. ** ** ** à un homme de qualité*).
[32]*Recueil general des pieces*, 1:464–66 ([Legendre], *Seconde lettre de M.*** à un homme de qualité, qui lui a proposé ses doutes sur la premiere Lettre que l'auteur lui avoit écrite touchant l'affaire des princes*).

and (so the Condé princes argued) tamper with the royal succession.[33] Maine and Toulouse, meanwhile, refused to acknowledge the regent's authority to judge the *affaire des princes*.[34]

The bastards' position in the *affaire des princes* had explosive political implications, and these quickly became apparent as Maine and Toulouse sought the support of bodies and elites in France equally prepared to challenge the regent's authority. Preeminent among them was the Parlement of Paris, with its old pretensions to legislative tutelage over minor kings and their regents. It is true that in his first *Mémoire* against the Condé princes' August 22 petition, Maine carefully rejected the Parlement's jurisdiction, because that body had already registered the royal legislation now at issue.[35] But Maine's pamphleteers also exalted the Parlement as a national representative, a body whose registration of royal legislation constituted nothing less than national consent to it.[36] Clearly, the bastards were prepared to impugn the regent's authority and seek support elsewhere—in the goodwill of a major king, in the Parlement, in the "nobility" too.[37] It is one of the ironies of the *affaire des princes* that Maine and Toulouse, despite their attachment to the values of Louis XIV's "old court," were so firmly committed to rejecting the regent's jurisdiction over the *affaire* that they appealed to the judgment of an Estates General.

Even at the beginning of the *affaire*, the bastards' most daring pamphleteer, Louis Legendre, was exploring that possibility. Legendre rea-

---

[33]Ibid., 2:286 (*Memoire des princes du sang, pour répondre au Memoire instructif des princes legitimez, du quinze novembre 1716. & à celui du neuf decembre suivant*); 3:348–49 (*Nouvelles reflexions sur l'affaire des princes du sang*), against the bastards' "maxims which are as false as they are dangerous."

[34]Ibid., 1:91–92, 94–95 (*Memoire de monsieur le duc du Maine*—Maine's first response to the princes' August 22 petition), 321–22 ([Legendre, *Lettre de M. ** ** ** à un homme de qualité*, quoted in n. 38), 3:103 (*Requeste presentée au roi par messieurs les princes legitimez*—the bastards' February 28, 1717, petition which actually altered their legal and political strategy during the *affaire*).

[35]*Recueil general des pieces*, 1:85–86, 91–101 (*Memoire de monsieur le duc du Maine*). Cf. similar arguments in 1:424–26 (*Second memoire sur la Requeste presentée au roi contre les princes legitimez*), 2:252–55 (*Suite de la Justification de monsieur le president de * * * sur la dispute des princes. Ou réfutation d'un libelle intitulé: Remarques sur les Memoires de M. le duc du Maine*).

[36]Ibid., 1:154–56 (*Lettre d'un espagnol à un françois*); 215–16 (*Réponse d'un solitaire à une lettre qu'un de ses parens de province lui avoit écrite sur l'affaire des princes du sang, dont il lui demandoit son sentiment*); 268–69 (*Reflexions sur la pretention de messieurs les duc de Bourbon, comte de Charolois, & prince de Conty, contre messieurs les duc du Maine, & comte de Toulouse*); 399–400 (*Memoire instructif sur la Requeste presentée au roi contre les princes legitimez*); 2:74–75 (*Apologie de l'édit du mois de juillet 1714. & de la déclaration du 23. mai 1715 . . .*).

[37]One of their pamphleteers professed to find in Bourbon, Charolois, and Conti's defense of the "rights" of the "nation" a threat to open the floodgates of "democracy," and invited the "nobility" to raise an "invincible rampart" against "rebellion and sedition"; see ibid., 1:215–16, 234–35 (*Réponse d'un solitaire . . .*).

soned that neither a minor king nor an interested regent (Orléans was, after all, first in the line of succession) had the right to decide whether or not Louis XIV's legislation of 1714 and 1715 conformed to the will of the "nation" embodied in its "fundamental law." Only the "nation" itself, assembled in "estates," could be a competent tribunal, and Legendre claimed that he wrote about French "fundamental law" to edify the delegates to such a body should it ever assemble.[38]

Legendre was proposing nothing less than turning the *affaire des princes* over to a revived Estates General, but no pamphleteer on either side of the dispute responded to that suggestion, either to rebut it or to embrace it, until February 28, 1717, when the bastards finally submitted a petition of their own to the crown. In it they demanded, once again, that any judgment of the *affaire* be remitted to Louis XV's majority. But if an earlier judgment could not be avoided, they demanded that the three estates of the realm, "juridically assembled," deliberate on the "interest" that the "nation" might take in the provisions of Louis XIV's Edict of July 1714.[39]

Thus, midway through the *affaire des princes,* the bastards appropriated the legitimate princes' appeal to the "nation" and turned it into a literal call for convoking the Estates General. That was a startling move for men attached to the values of the "old court," but it was explicable and not just because of the rivalry between Maine and Orléans. Like the *affaire du bonnet,* the *affaire des princes* was a public conflict whose protagonists appealed not only to the throne but also to an aristocratic public with conflicting convictions and aspirations of its own.

During the *affaire des princes,* printed pamphlets played a far greater role than they had during the *affaire du bonnet,* but the *affaire des princes*'s audience may not have been appreciably larger. Once again rumor,

[38]Ibid., 1:321–22 (*Lettre de M. ** ** ** à un homme de qualité*):
Such grave complaints [as those advanced in the princes' August 22 petition] merit all our attention. But before examining them each individually, let us see who shall be the judge.
The king not being old enough to take cognizance of any dispute, and M. the Regent being just as interested in it as the princes, it seems that at present one cannot and should not end it.
The Petition calls upon a tribunal that would be able to judge these complaints [and] it is the tribunal of the nation; for just as it is certain that only the nation has the right to choose a king for itself, should the august house of Bourbon altogether fail, it seems that only the nation might decide the fate of the two legitimated princes by confirming or rejecting what Louis XIV did for them.
Let us suppose then that the Estates are assembled, and let us discuss by what principle, if they were the judges of these complaints, they might reach a decision.
[39]Ibid., 3:101–3, esp. 103 (*Requeste presentée au roi, par messieurs les princes legitimez*).

personal contact, the carefully controlled distribution of printed pamphlets, and the continued use of manuscript polemics suggest a narrow, aristocratic, and Parisian audience. So too does the decisive role played in the *affaire des princes* by the aristocratic conflicts that had dominated the *affaire du bonnet* a year earlier.

In mobilizing "public opinion," the princely parties used tactics that implied a narrow public indeed. Throughout the *affaire* the princes cultivated opinion by making rounds of visits in Paris and by attending the Parlement.[40] In addition the princes—or their wives, for the indefatigable duchesse du Maine was a leading protagonist in the *affaire*—supervised not only the composition of pamphlets but also their distribution. The Parisian *hôtels* of Maine and Toulouse were notorious centers for the dissemination of pamphlets: on those grounds a hostile writer declared that the bastards "avowed" pamphlets even when they did not sign them.[41] Maine and Toulouse also used peddlers (*colporteurs*) to distribute their pamphlets. These peddlers were not necessarily commercial booksellers; they could also be princely servants, like the peddler Maine engaged to toss pamphlets into elegant carriages in the capital's streets and who had the misfortune to throw one into the carriage of the old princesse de Condé. Her son, the duc de Bourbon, took the incident as a personal insult and had the peddler jailed until Maine, "fort en colère," got him released into the duc de La Force's custody.[42] The incident is amusing, but instructive too, for it indicates the bastards' concern to select the recipients of their printed pamphlets. The legitimate princes were equally concerned to do so; they used letter carriers to convey their elegant prints to the "public" whose "opinion" they wished to cultivate. A contemporary gazetteer exclaimed, "You would not believe the innumerable number of pamphlets [*mémoires*] . . . the princes have sent to Paris by letter carriers; I mean those which are on large paper [*en grand*], folded in two, and sealed with a subscription at the bottom of which is written, 'the duc de Bourbon.' There are some that have been sent into the great towns. But the result of all that will be that this *affaire* will be pushed vigorously for the holding of a *lit de justice* and that, at bottom, it will be public opinion that judges the contest."[43]

The pamphlet referred to here was the *Memoire des princes du sang, pour répondre au Memoire instructif des princes legitimez, du quinze november*

[40]Anon., *Gazette de la Régence*, 109; A.N., K.566 (1): "Détail sommaire de l'affaire des princes légitimés pour la succession à la couronne."
[41]*Recueil general des pieces*, 2:98–99 (*Réponse au dernier Memoire instructif de M. le duc du Maine*). And see Waller, "Men of Letters and the *Affaire des Princes*."
[42]Anon., *Gazette de la Régence*, 167, 172, 177.
[43]Ibid., 151–52 (February 22, 1717).

1716. & à celui du neuf decembre suivant, which the princes had begun to distribute on February 8.[44] With its appearance, rumors that Orléans was about to decide the *affaire des princes* began to fly. Naturally, the dispute became "noisier than ever."[45]

It was at this point that aristocratic controversies recalling the *affaire du bonnet* revived, for the dukes and peers now entered the dispute. Since August they had been planning to petition to the regent to ask that he quash the May 5, 1694, Declaration and the relevant sections of the May 1711 Edict by which Louis XIV had created an "intermediate rank" for Maine and Toulouse. On February 22 they finally submitted their petition to the regent and sent it to their printer as well.[46] To a contemporary who sympathized with the bastards, it now appeared that they faced a formidable opposition.[47]

The peerage's entry into the *affaire des princes,* however, soon provoked other parties to enter the conflict as well. About a month after the peers' petition, there appeared a *Lettre écrite par un chanoine de Luçon, à un de ses amis, contenant ses réflexions sur la Requête presentée au roi par les pairs de France le 22. février 1717.*[48] The author was in fact Claude Blanchard, who had probably written the Parlement's "libelle généalogique" during the *affaire du bonnet.*[49] During the *affaire des princes* he was still writing to deflate ducal aspirations. Like the dukes and peers he supported the princes. Louis XIV had contravened French "fundamental law" when he added his bastards' lines to the order of royal succession, Blanchard wrote, and he accordingly supported the princes' demand that the king's July 1714 Edict and May 23, 1715, Declaration be nullified.[50] But Blanchard refused to support the dukes' demand that

[44]*Recueil general des pieces,* 2:257–382; Anon., *Gazette de la Régence,* 140; Dangeau, *Journal,* 17:19.

[45]Dangeau, *Journal,* 17:25–26.

[46]A.N., K.648 (53–55) (minutes of ducal assemblies for August 1716 and February 1717); A.N., K.648 (58–61) (drafts of the ducal petition); A.N., K.648 (80, 82) (printed copies of the ducal petition: *Requeste des pairs de France, présentée au roy le 22. février 1717* [Paris: Antoine-Urbain Coustelier, 1717]; for copies at the B.N., see B.N., *Catalogue des factums,* 4:103).

[47]Dangeau, *Journal,* 17:28–29, 30 (February 20 and 22, 1717).

[48] In *Recueil general des pieces,* 3:302–26. At the end the pamphlet is dated "At Luçon, March 30, 1717."

[49]Waller, "Men of Letters and the *Affaire des Princes,*" 133, 134, 147; see chapter 5.

[50]*Recueil general des pieces,* 3:303–4. Blanchard, it will be recalled, served first president de Mesmes (see chapter 5, n. 52), who led an in fact divided Parlement that both parties were courting in spring 1717 (Leclercq, *Histoire de la Régence* 2:92, 95, 96). Indeed, just as Maine and Toulouse sought to flatter the court so did the princes, who in the *Mémoire* of February 1717 significantly refined their demand of August 22 petition for a *lit de justice* to quash Louis XIV's legislation of 1714 and 1715. During minorities, the princes now argued, *lits* were not vehicles for imposing the king's will on Parlement but occasions for free votes by its members (*Recueil general des pieces,* 2:335 [*Memoire des princes du sang, pour répondre au Memoire instructif des princes legitimez . . .*]).

the regent suppress the legislation of the late king exalting his bastards' rank. Louis XIV was entirely within his rights when he gave his bastards whatever "precedences," "prerogatives," and "honors" he chose; of such things, Blanchard wrote, the king was "master."[51] Blanchard devoted the rest of his pamphlet to reducing the peerage to yet another "honor" subject to the arbitrary will of French kings. Peerage, he wrote, was a dignity dating only to 1179 (when Du Tillet first found peers officiating at royal consecrations) and so not the ancient and essential institution— the "law of the state"—the dukes said it was.[52] Blanchard steered a delicate course between the two princely parties, but he roundly rejected the constitutional claims that dukes and peers had been making since the beginning of the regency.

Still more emphatically antiducal were the assembling nobles, who also entered the *affaire des princes* in spring 1717 to resist ducal ambitions.[53] In petitions to Louis XV and the regent, the assembling nobles demanded a royal declaration designed "to repress . . . the enterprises of the peers of France," including their aspirations to constitute a body apart from the nobility that might alone deliberate on "important affairs of state" and resolve disputes about regencies and the royal succession.[54] Nothing in their petitions of 1717 suggests that the *affaire des princes* concerned the assembling nobles; they were still fighting the battles of the *affaire du bonnet*. They continued to fight those battles in the elaborate *Mémoire pour la noblesse de France, contre les ducs et pairs* which they submitted to the regent on April 18.[55] A lengthy refutation of the peerage's *Recueil des écrits qui ont esté faits sur le différend entre les pairs de France & les présidens à mortier du Parlement de Paris* published the year before, the *Mémoire pour la noblesse* denounced once again the social and constitutional "pretensions" of the dukes.[56] Many of its arguments will be familiar. The dukes were seeking to revive "aristocratic government" and with it the power of "sovereign" feudal peers whose "usurpations"

[51]*Recueil general des pieces*, 3:304.

[52]Ibid., 3:305–25. Blanchard even suggested that kings sought to suppress the peerage when, in their ordinances of 1579 and 1582, they provided that peerages escheat to the crown upon the failure of male lines.

[53]Dangeau, *Journal*, 17:66–68; Lassaigne, *Les Assemblées de la noblesse*, 136–37.

[54]Texts in Lassaigne, *Les Assemblées de la noblesse*, 244–46.

[55]Anon., *Mémoire pour la noblesse de France, contre les ducs et pairs* ([Paris: 1717]). The B.N. has several copies of this rare pamphlet: Réserve des imprimés, F.320; 4° Fm 23113; and a copy bound into MS. Clairambault 721 at p. 735. For a MS copy see Bibliothèque du Sénat (Paris), MS. 9198, fols. 363–443. See sources cited in n. 53. On the *Mémoire*'s authorship and limited distribution see notes 64 and 67.

[56]Anon., *Mémoire pour la noblesse*, 14, 64–108. Cf. *Recueil des écrits* (1716 ed.), copies in A.N., K.619 [43], K.622 [10], U.907; Bibliothèque de l'Assemblée Nationale (Paris), MS. 336; and at the B.N., *Catalogue des factums* 4:103; see chapters 2 and 5.

had injured royal authority.[57] Despite their ambitions they were merely officers in the Parlement who had taken an oath to it, not members of a "court of peers" which the peers sought to discover in *lit de justice* assemblies. Indeed, the dukes' Parlement-*lit* distinction was "chimerical."[58] Members of Parlement, the dukes were merely members of the nobility, too, an order whose members were all legally equal whatever their titles, their professions, or their ancestries.[59]

Unlike their petitions, however, the nobles' *Mémoire* did not ignore the *affaire des princes*. For during that dispute about the royal succession, the ducal claim to be the "only" or "necessary" judges of such a conflict inevitably aroused the untitled nobility's jealousy. Not surprisingly, the *Mémoire pour la noblesse* roundly denied that ducal claim and lodged a competing claim for the "nobility" and the "nation": "The peers are not the judges of the succession to the crown. At least, they are not unless they constitute a body with the nobility and with the nation."[60] The "nobility" and the "nation" had regulated the royal succession before: in 752 when it called the Carolingians to the throne, in 987 when it gave the crown to Hugh Capet, and in 1328 when it awarded the kingdom to Philippe de Valois and his descendants. In 1717, the assembling nobles' memorandum implied, the "nobility" and the "nation" might regulate the royal succession once again, by adjudicating the *affaire des princes*. The nobles were indeed jealous of that putative constitutional right, they refused to let the dukes and peers preempt it, and they spared no effort to rebut the peers' ideas, "ideas so contrary to the authority of kings and to the fundamental laws of the state and the monarchy" and injurious not only to the "nobility" but also the "clergy" and, indeed, the "entire nation."[61]

The positions taken by the assembling nobles and the royal bastards thus converged, both parties appealing over the head of the regent to the "nation" assembled in Estates. Indeed, as rumors of an impending Estates General started to fly in Paris contemporaries began to suspect

---

[57]Anon., *Mémoire pour la noblesse*, 9–10, 16–35, esp. 28–30.

[58]Ibid., 41–48, 50–51.

[59]Ibid., 48–63. The assembling nobles acknowledged the claims of "birth" and "illustriousness": "Illustrious names are above titles [like the dukes'], birth above recompenses" (Anon., *Mémoire pour la noblesse*, 52). But they subordinated those claims to the legal equality of all nobles: "The nobility is a republic subject to its king. In the nobility all its members shed all titles, honoring themselves only with the title of *gentilhomme;* in the nobility, amid all the advantages deriving from high birth, dignities, alliances, and fortune, equality has always reigned; in the nobility, equality is the fundamental law and the indissoluble bond" (60). Their concept of nobility remained what it had been in 1716: not protoracist but legalistic (cf. Devyver, *Le Sang épuré*, 243–78, esp. 258–60).

[60]Anon., *Mémoire pour la noblesse*, 73.

[61]Ibid., 73–77.

that the duc and duchesse du Maine were directing "this extravagant nobility."[62] The assembling nobles were indeed "extravagant," if they were responsible for the manuscript pamphlet that circulated in Paris in June, which proposed that a sworn "confederation" assemble to demand an Estates General and disband only when that body should convene.[63] They probably were acting in collusion with Maine and Toulouse and may even have owed their *Mémoire pour la noblesse* to abbé Louis Legendre, the bastards' premier pamphleteer and the first to raise the possibility that an assembly of Estates might take cognizance of the *affaire des princes*.[64]

Because they appealed over the regent's head to the "nation" assembled in Estates, bastards and nobles challenged his authority and pushed him to use it. His first step was to disarm the assembling nobles, a party that he had encouraged in 1716 but that now escaped his control.[65] He refused to let the nobles submit their petitions and memoranda to the king.[66] He also forced them to withdraw the *Mémoire pour la noblesse* from circulation.[67] Finally, on May 14, 1717, he issued a council decree suppressing their assemblies. Authoritatively, that decree denied the no-

---

[62]Balleroy, *Les Correspondants de la marquise de Balleroy*, 1:166–69, esp. 166 (Caumartin de Boissy to the marquise, June 21, 1717), naming the cardinal de Polignac (a close friend of the duchesse du Maine) as instigator of "cette noblesse extravagante." In one of his "Additions" to Dangeau's *Journal*, Saint-Simon wrote, "These rumors of [an] Estates General had no other foundation than the declaration of M. du Maine and the desires of this noble mob [*cette noblesse rassemblée*]" (Dangeau, *Journal*, 17:97 [May 27, 1717]).

[63]"Mémoire pour les trois estats du royaume" (B.N., MS. Clairambault 721, pp. 921–26, esp. 924–25 on the "confederation"). This was probably the pamphlet that Dangeau knew as "Des trois états" and which, though he sympathized with the bastards' party, he pronounced "most seditious" (Dangeau, *Journal*, 17:115).

[64]The *Mémoire* is ascribed to Legendre in B.N., *Catalogue général des livres imprimeés de la Bibliothèque Nationale, Auteurs*, 231 vols. (Paris: B.N., 1897–1981), 93, col. 44. The same catalog ascribes the work to Boulainvilliers too (albeit tentatively: ibid., 17, col. 392). So does B.N., *Catalogue des factums*, 4:103, "according to Barbier." But that nineteenth-century bibliographer clearly confused the nobles' *Mémoire* with Boulainvilliers' "Dissertation" or "Traité" or "Mémoire sur la noblesse" written in 1700 and published in 1732 as *Essais*, as Barbier's entry indicates: "Mémoire pour la noblesse de France, contre les ducs et pairs. (Par le comte Henri de Boulainvilliers.) s.l. (avril 1717), in-12.—Amsterdam (Trévoux), 1732, in-8" (A. Barbier, *Dictionnaire des ouvrages anonymes*, 4 vols. [Paris: 1872–89], vol. 3, col. 143). Legendre is the likelier author of the *Mémoire*, given its style and substance, although his *Mémoires*, which detail his services to the duc and duchesse du Maine, make no mention of any work for the assembling nobles (abbé [Louis] Legendre, *Mémoires*, ed. Roux [Paris: Charpentier, 1865], 324–25, 329–38).

[65]Lassaigne, *Les Assemblées de la noblesse*, 148–49.

[66]Dangeau, *Journal*, 17:66–68; Lassaigne, *Les Assemblées de la noblesse*, 137.

[67]Three copies of the *Mémoire*—one MS (Bibliothèque du Sénat [Paris], MS. 9198, fols. 363–443) and two printed (B.N., 4° Fm 23113, and Réserve des imprimés, F.320)—bear identical MS notes: "This memorandum appeared in April 1717. Only a few copies were distributed and quickly withdrawn." The regent apparently forced the pamphlet's withdrawal from circulation.

bility's right to assemble and petition—to "constitute a body" or *faire corps*—without the king's authorization: "The nobility, though one of the first orders of the realm and that which His Majesty regards as the principal force of his state, cannot constitute a body or sign petitions in common without the express permission of the king."[68]

On May 14, the regent issued a second council decree directing the Condé princes and the royal bastards to submit their petitions and memoranda to a commission composed of the first president, the king's advocate, and the procurator general of the Parlement of Paris, and thirty-two other nominees. The princes haggled about the commission's composition. The bastards refused to recognize its competence. Its parlementary members hesitated to proceed, embarrassed by their sudden obligation to pass judgment on princes who might one day hold authority and influence over them. But the regent persisted in his resolve to end the *affaire des princes* by his own authority. On June 6 he issued yet another council decree commissioning six councillors of state to receive the princes' and the bastards' petitions and render a judgment in their dispute.[69]

As the regent's commission set about its task, the assembling nobles and the royal bastards took their last desperate steps in the *affaire des princes*. They prepared formal protestations against the commission's impending judgment and appealed to Louis XV's majority. Proclaiming the nullity of the "judgment without the nation" that the regent's commission was about to render, the nobles claimed cognizance of the *affaire des princes* for themselves and the "nation" assembled in Estates, "since the nobility has a capital interest in a question which concerns the succession to the crown, since the finest of the nobility's privileges would be nullified if it were not summoned to this decision according to the laws of the kingdom, [and] since it would not be just that the nobility had

[68]Text in Lassaigne, *Les Assemblées de la noblesse,* 247. The council decree alluded to "a great number of *gentilshommes,* not only in Paris but also in the provinces," who were participating in the assembling nobles' activities. And the chancellor, Henri-François d'Aguesseau, soon instructed all provincial Parlements to suppress noble assemblies and report the efforts of recalcitrant nobles to him (Francis Monnier, *Le Chancelier d'Aguesseau: Sa conduite et ses idées politiques* [Paris: 1863, repr. Geneva: Slatkine/Megariotis, 1975], 176). But there is no other evidence that Parisian and provincial nobles were in league during the *affaires* of 1715–17 (see also chapter 5, n. 62).

[69]Marais, *Journal et mémoires,* 1:210, 211; Dangeau, *Journal,* 17:68, 82, 84, 85–86, 102, esp. 85–86 (May 13, 1717): "Monsieur the duke of Orléans—pressed by the princes of the blood, goaded by the declared resolution of the legitimated [princes] to recognize no judge but the major king or the estates general, and recognizing what a threat it posed to his regency's authority and what an example it might set—resolved to wait no longer and hastened, by a decree preparatory to a quick and certain judgment, to show that he felt his power and was resolved not to let it be compromised."

no voice to state its claims on so important an occasion where the conservation of its greatest right is at stake."[70]

The nobles' protestation was bold, but stillborn. On June 17, they persuaded an usher of the Châtelet court to "signify" their protestation to the Parlement of Paris, but on June 18 the embarrassed company rebuked him, suppressed the signatures of its own officers who had received the nobles' protestation, and issued a decree of its own reiterating the regent's prohibition of noble assemblies. Finally, on June 19, the regent arrested and imprisoned six leaders of the assembling nobles.[71] There were to be no more noble assemblies.

On that same day, however, Maine and Toulouse went to the Parlement with a protestation of their own. Like the nobles' it promised to appeal to Louis XV's majority against any judgment that the regent's commission might render.[72] The embarrassed (and divided) court hesitated to dismiss this protestation, but on June 21, the party of the legitimate princes prevailed. By a vote of 204 to 134, the Parlement resolved not to accept the bastards' protestation, but to depute to the regent instead to report on its recent proceedings. The regent received that deputation graciously on June 30.[73]

On July 5, the *affaire des princes* ended with a decision—for the legitimate princes—issued by the regent's commission and on the regent's royal authority alone. Framed as an edict, it was registered by the Parlement of Paris on July 6 and published two days later.[74] The regent's decision was at once indulgent and firm.[75] It was indulgent, for though it stripped Maine and Toulouse of their rights to succeed to the throne, it let them keep their princely ranks and titles. Predictably, that indulgence angered the dukes and peers and it was now their turn to resort to futile protestations against the regent's conduct—no easy task since he had suppressed unauthorized assemblies, the dukes' included.[76] The

---

[70]Text in Lassaigne, *Les Assemblées de la noblesse*, 248–49.

[71]Ibid., 138, 149.

[72]Text in *Recueil general des pieces*, 3:4, 10–15.

[73]Marais, *Journal et mémoires*, 1:207–8.

[74]Not that the Parlement abandoned its own constitutional pretensions. True, 113 magistrates voted for registering the regent's edict on July 6 and only 74 voted for remitting it to commissioners for scrutiny—that is, delay. But the first president, speaking in favor of quick registration, did not fail to claim that the Parlement of Paris was the only French court competent to discuss great affairs of state, and Mathieu Marais did not fail to record the first president's claim (ibid., 1:210–11).

[75]See printed editions listed in B.N., *Catalogue . . . Actes royaux*, no. 27019.

[76]See A.N., K.624 (1–5) for the July 9, 1717, protestations, and A.N., K.648 (55) for an invitation to a "little assembly" at Saint-Simon's in July, indicating that some guests were to pass through "hidden doors" (*portes derobées*) undetected even by domestics. In fact contemporaries quickly learned of the dukes' illicit assemblies (Balleroy, *Les Correspondants de*

edict was also firm, for it carefully delimited the "rights" of the "nation" that had become so controversial during the *affaire des princes*. True, it acknowledged that the "nation" had chosen the dynasty that governed it. This official statement in a public royal act was to be cited repeatedly in prerevolutionary political debate. Nonetheless, the edict's draftsmen carefully avoided any language suggesting that "fundamental laws" were the terms of a contract between the "nation" and its chosen dynasty. Nowhere did the July 1717 Edict acknowledge the right of the "nation" to intervene in politics to uphold the terms of that contract.[77] The July 1717 Edict was a vigorous assertion of the regent's royal authority, not the authority of the "nation" and certainly not of the nobility, the peerage, or the Parlement.

In the summer of 1717 two years of public aristocratic controversy came to an end. Certainly the dukes and peers continued to defend their dignity against the royal bastards and the Parlement of Paris—with uneven results. At the great *lit de justice* of August 16, 1718, called chiefly to overcome the Parlement's resistance to Orléans' financial experiments, the regent had the court register legislation stripping Maine and Toulouse of their "intermediate rank." Saint-Simon had helped plan that double victory over magistrates and royal bastards and wrote a richly satisfied account of it in his *Mémoires*.[78] In 1721, however, dukes and peers were appealing from Orléans' regency to Louis XV's majority in a new set of protestations, these against the Parlement's trial of the duc de La Force for engaging in retail trade.[79] Plainly, aristocratic conflicts about rank and precedence did not cease in 1717, but aristocratic conflicts about an unwritten French constitution and the roles that noble elites and bodies might play in it did. In 1717 the regent suppressed not only ducal and noble assemblies but also ducal and noble aspirations to judge disputes about regencies and the royal succession. Only the Parlement's political credit remained unimpaired.

Of course, during Louis XV's minority the most serious dispute about regencies and the royal succession concerned the dubious validity of

---

la marquise de Balleroy, 1:108 [Caumartin de Saint-Ange to the marquise, July 13, 1717]), and jealous nobles denounced them in one last MS "Mémoire pour la noblesse" in August (Lassaigne, *Les Assemblées de la noblesse,* 138–39).

[77] As noted by Lemaire, *Les Lois fondamentales,* 197–204, and Brancourt, *Le Duc de Saint-Simon et la monarchie,* 44. On the July 1717 edict's later uses see Morel, "Les 'Droits de la nation.'"

[78] Leclercq, *Histoire de la Régence,* 2:51–58, 97, 129–87 (for Saint-Simon's role in and description of the 1718 *lit*), and 189–207; see also Labatut, *Les Ducs et pairs,* 349–50.

[79] Leclercq, *Histoire de la Régence,* 3:310–14; A.N., K.624 (12) (copies of peers' notarized protestations of March 31, 1721).

Philip V's renunciation of his rights to the French throne. As heir to Louis XV, Philip inspired (and even directed) plots against the regent by the duc and duchesse du Maine and by noble rebels in Brittany, plots which Orléans took seriously indeed. It is not surprising, then, that the problem of Philip V's renunciation inspired the regent's foreign policy, and a corpus of tracts and pamphlets on French dynastic custom and the possibility that international laws and treaties might change it.[80]

Yet it may be argued that even before Philip's renunciation became a topic for polemicists in 1718, it had become a subject of public debate. The parties to the *affaire du bonnet* and the *affaire des princes* made only oblique or private references to the renunciation, but in lodging their competing constitutional claims to "declare" regencies, judge disputes about them, and take cognizance of contests for the royal succession, they doubtless had the Spanish king's renunciation in mind.[81] Dynastic conflicts intensified aristocratic controversy in 1715–17 and inspired the elaboration of conflicting aristocratic constitutionalisms and the public debates about them examined in the preceding pages.

Boulainvilliers and the *Affaire des Princes*

The *affaire des princes* elicited nothing from Boulainvilliers but a minor pamphlet and an unpublished memorandum to the regent. These are slight performances, compared with the "Lettres sur les parlements ou états généraux" that Boulainvilliers had written during the *affaire du bonnet*. They are also strangely contradictory and (at times) surprisingly friendly to the "arbitrary" authority of French kings. Yet in taking these contradictory and unexpected positions, Boulainvilliers realized possibilities implicit in his understanding of the French monarchy's history. He also pursued an aim he had long served, defending the regent's authority. A "zealous servant" and client of the duc d'Orléans,[82] Boulainvilliers wrote with the regent's interest uppermost in mind even as he commented on the exalted rank of Louis XIV's bastards or on the legitimate birth of an all but forgotten Carolingian prince. His interventions in the *affaire des princes* were those of a devoted *orléaniste* ideologue.

It was during the *affaire des princes* that Boulainvilliers published his *Justification de la naissance légitime de Bernard, roy d'Italie, petit-fils de Charle-*

---

[80]See discussion in chapter 4 and sources cited there in notes 82 and 83.

[81]As did the dukes and peers, in their unsubmitted petition of January 1715 on the *bonnet* (see chapter 5, n. 20).

[82]See chapter 4, and notes 26 and 27 there.

magne.[83] His only publication, that pamphlet was not one of the *affaire*'s major polemics, and its first edition may have amounted to only twenty copies![84] Some historians have denied that it was a polemic at all. Taking Boulainvilliers at his word, they have described the *Justification* as a savant's attempt to correct pamphleteers on both sides of the dispute (the "learned historians and jurisconsults employed by Messieurs the legitimate and legitimated princes") who all claimed that Bernard of Italy was a bastard.[85] A learned little performance, the *Justification* was a polemic nonetheless, written by an author acutely sensitive to the political and constitutional debates of the early regency.

Boulainvilliers' personal sympathies lay with the legitimate princes. In a later work, he made no secret of his antipathy to the exalted rank of the royal bastards and (like Saint-Simon) condemned Père Gabriel Daniel's *Histoire de France* (1713) as an apology for it.[86] In the *Justification* he attacked only one pamphlet directly and by name, a brochure for the bastards.[87] And in asserting Bernard of Italy's legitimacy, he took a position already embraced by some of the pamphleteers writing for the Condé princes. Boulainvilliers probably sympathized also with the ducal supporters of the legitimate princes, for when he finished his *Justification* he seems to have put it at the disposal of dukes and peers.[88]

In the *Justification,* however, Boulainvilliers ignored the great issues of the *affaire des princes.* Did Louis XIV transgress "fundamental law" when he added his bastards' lines to the royal succession? Boulainvilliers left that question unanswered. What body in France might judge contests about the royal succession? Even that problem failed to absorb Boulain-

[83][Boulainvilliers], *Justification de la naissance légitime de Bernard, roy d'Italie, petit-fils de Charlemagne* ([Paris: 1717]), reprinted in *Recueil general des pieces,* 3:201–14. By 1719, contemporaries knew that Boulainvilliers was the pamphlet's author, for Jacques Lelong ascribed it to him in his 1719 *Bibliothèque historique de la France,* 604. On MSS see Bibliographical Appendix, Part 2.

[84]B.M., Angoulême, MS. 23, p. 24.

[85][Boulainvilliers], *Justification,* 1; Simon, *Henry de Boulainviller,* 109; Waller, "Men of Letters and the *Affaire des Princes,*" 140.

[86]Boulainvilliers, *Un Révolté,* 93 ("Préface critique au Journal de Saint Louis"), on Père Daniel as "an author who wrote only to write, who used his fellows' pen when his own needed to rest, who interested himself in nothing, who overturned the common order making bastards legitimate and the legitimate bastards." For Saint-Simon's similar critique of Daniel see Brancourt, *Le Duc de Saint-Simon,* 196.

[87][Boulainvilliers], *Justification,* 12–14, contra the *Justification de monsieur le president de * * * sur la dispute des princes* (n.p.: 1717), reprinted in *Recueil general de pieces,* 2:157–219.

[88]See Simon, *Henry de Boulainviller,* between pp. 112 and 113, for a photographic reproduction of a May 8 letter that Boulainvilliers wrote to accompany a MS copy of his *Justification.* Boulainvilliers addressed the unidentified recipient as "Monseigneur," indicating his superior rank: it was very likely the ducal rank, as Boulainvilliers also asked him to convey the pamphlet ("if you think it suitable") to the duc d'Humières and the duc de La Force.

villiers. Nowhere did he exalt the power of Carolingian "parlements," as he had in his "Lettres" when he reflected on the fate of Bernard of Italy. There, Boulainvilliers wrote that in 813 a "parlement" had assigned Charlemagne's crown to his younger son, Louis the Pious, despite Bernard's presumably greater right as the son of Charlemagne's elder son Pepin. In the "Lettres," Boulainvilliers reported that in 818 yet another "parlement" condemned Bernard to death for having rebelled against Louis the Pious, to conclude that in the early ninth century the "parlement" was nothing less than "arbiter of the crown."[89] But even in his "Lettres," Boulainvilliers appreciated that the "nation" had since lost its mastery over its kings, who now owed their throne to an autonomous dynastic custom. In his *Justification,* Boulainvilliers made no effort to reclaim for the "nation" its putative "rights" to arbitrate disputes about the royal succession. The great hopes that the *affaire des princes* inspired in the assembling nobles seem not to have burned in Boulainvilliers' breast.

Boulainvilliers drew other lessons from Bernard of Italy's unhappy career and he spelled them out plainly for anyone familiar with the dynastic and constitutional problems raised by the dubious validity of Philip V's renunciation.

> They [writers for both princely parties] seem to have chosen deliberately to regard him [Bernard] as a bastard, rather than recognize that he was justly delivered up to the severity of a general assembly of the French nation because he had made himself guilty of wanting to incite civil war, by rebelling against his uncle, Louis the Pious, in order to defend his own right of primogeniture—a right Bernard had renounced in submitting to Louis by swearing to obey him.
>
> In our unhappy age, men are so convinced that treaties and the most religious oaths do not bind princes as they do other men and that politics has rights superior to the rights of sincerity and good faith, that it is difficult to imagine that Charlemagne's legitimate grandson could have been condemned to death for having retracted the submission and fidelity he had promised to his father's younger brother [*son oncle puîné*] and for having retracted the renunciation he had made of his elder's right to succeed [*son droit d'aînesse*], a renunciation he had made at least by taking oaths, if not expressly.

In short, the *Justification* was one more effort by Boulainvilliers to defend the validity of Philip V's renunciation and, therefore, the political fortunes of the duc d'Orléans. He continued, "This example, however, is not so far removed from present circumstances that one cannot usefully

[89]*Etat . . . Tome III,* 24 (Letter 3) on the 818 "parlement."

apply it to them in the interests of the government and in the interest of our princes."[90]

Boulainvilliers continued to defend the duc d'Orléans in his "Mémoire touchant l'affaire de Mrs. les princes du sang."[91] Now, however, he addressed the great questions of the *affaire des princes* too, taking an unexpectedly positive attitude to the royal bastards while directing his harshest criticism at the legitimate princes' August 22 petition. In earlier works he had declared that the Carolingian and Capetian dynasties had usurped the throne. In his "Mémoire" he did so again to destroy the supposition, critical to the legitimate princes' argument, that a "nation" had chosen those dynasties and that "fundamental law" embodied the "nation"'s will.[92] He admitted (as he had earlier) that French kings now enjoyed an incontestable right to their throne, but he grounded that right in 700 years of "possession," not in "fundamental law."[93]

In his "Mémoire" on the *affaire des princes,* Boulainvilliers took what was, even for him, an extremely royalist and absolutist position. Like Maine's and Toulouse's pamphleteers, he claimed that bastards had succeeded to the throne in Merovingian antiquity, but unlike the bastards' pamphleteers, he denied that a fundamental law regulated the royal succession to call the eldest legitimate prince to the throne. Had such a law existed in the ninth century, he reasoned, not Louis the Pious but Bernard of Italy would have succeeded to Charlemagne's throne, and Charles the Bald—yet another younger brother—would have never become the Franks' emperor.[94] Thus, even Boulainvilliers' argument for Bernard's legitimate birth served the cause of Maine and Toulouse.

Yet Boulainvilliers wrote not to sustain a princely party but to uphold the regent's authority. He defended Louis XIV's exaltation of his bastards in order to defend the larger thesis that the authority of modern French monarchs was "absolute" and even "arbitrary." Ever since the fifteenth century, Boulainvilliers wrote, when Charles VII pacified France by virtually reconquering her from the English, French kings had the right to impose "practically arbitrary laws": "France is therefore accustomed to the usage of this absolute power." That "arbitrary" or "absolute" power certainly made kings masters of all ranks. "Rank is a grace, a favor of kings, a new distinction," he stated, and like the bas-

---

[90][Boulainvilliers], *Justification*, 1–2. Boulainvilliers' earlier defense of the renunciation's validity was discussed in chapter 4.

[91]In Boulainvilliers, *Mémoires présentés*, 1:115–61. See Bibliographical Appendix, Part 4.

[92]Boulainvilliers, *Mémoires présentés*, 1:132–33, 136–37.

[93]Ibid., 1:137–38.

[94]Ibid., 1:142–43.

tards' pamphleteers he refused to make any exception for the princely rank.[95] Boulainvilliers even extended the "absolute" or "arbitrary" power of kings over the royal succession itself.[96] With only one exception, as noted earlier, the bastards' pamphleteers had never gone so far. Boulainvilliers did, to defend royal authority and the prince who held it against *all* parties to the *affaire des princes:* legitimate princes and bastards too, not to mention assembling nobles. Abandoning his Anglomania, Boulainvilliers deplored the temerity with which princes sought "to discuss the rights of royalty in an odious manner, after the sole fashion of English Puritans," and warned the regent against such dangerous "novelties" as letting an Estates General resolve the *affaire des princes.*[97]

Boulainvilliers' harsh insistence on the "arbitrary" power of modern French monarchs has not escaped the notice of historians, nor have his remarkable inconsistencies during the *affaire des princes.*[98] Explaining them is not so easy, however. Boulainvilliers' antipathy to the dukes cannot explain his solicitude for the bastards (such as it was), as he could easily plead the ducal case when he wanted to.[99] Two forces drove Boulainvilliers to defend the extraordinary positions that he took during the *affaire des princes.* One was his devotion to Orléans. The *Justification* was plainly an *orléaniste* tract. The "Mémoire" too was an effort to serve the regent: with its uncharacteristic approval of the bastards and its equally uncharacteristic denunciation of Estates as "novelties," the "Mémoire" offered Orléans a strategy for coopting Maine and Toulouse while dissolving any alliance between them and the assembling nobles clamoring for a meeting of Estates. Like the rest of Boulainvilliers' advice to Orléans, this suggestion fell on deaf ears. Its interest lies chiefly in what it reveals about the possibilities of politics as Boulainvilliers and his contemporaries imagined them. The monarchy's dynastic problems, matters of public debate in the controversies about Louis XIV's bastards and Philip V's renunciation, raised the possibility that French "fundamental law" might become an object of willful political action, be it by aristocratic bodies "judging" disputes about the provisions of "fundamental law," or by princes and monarchs seeking to adjust or alter its operation. In this light, Boulainvilliers' determination to vindicate both Philip V's renunciation and Louis XIV's addition of his bastards to the line of succession become part of a still larger tendency to assert the "arbitrary" character of the modern French monarchy and to subject

[95]Ibid., 1:147–55, 149 and 155 for quotations.
[96]Ibid., 1:145–47.
[97]Ibid., 1:147, 156–61.
[98]Cf. Morel, "Les 'Droits de la nation,'" 254–55; Simon, *Henry de Boulainviller,* 100–109.
[99]Cf. Ford, *Robe and Sword,* 185 n. 40.

even the royal succession to its authority. This tendency lies deep in Boulainvilliers' understanding of the monarchy's history and is the second force that drove him to take the positions that he took during the *affaire des princes*. His "Mémoire" advising the regent on how to manage that conflict now appears not only as a client's service to his patron, though it was surely that, but also as the realization of Boulainvilliers' deepest convictions about the modern monarchy's character, convictions now unrelieved by any of the hopes for the future of the "nation" and the nobility that Boulainvilliers had once placed in the duc d'Orléans.

After the *Affaire des Princes:* Valedictory Works

The pamphlet and memorandum just considered were Boulainvilliers' last efforts to write on French history as a princely client, counselor, and controversialist. He wrote them for Orléans and never ceased to serve him, but after the *affaire des princes* any sign that he wrote to or even for the prince vanishes from his writings in French history. His last works—two additional "Lettres sur les parlements"; an essay on the reign of Louis IX (1226–70), and a "Discours sur la noblesse"—exude an unrelieved historical fatalism and pessimism. In effect, he now admitted that he had misplaced his hopes and in his last, valedictory works he reflected bitterly on the bleak and "despotic" future that awaited France and on his own failure to persuade a prince to reverse her fate.

After the *affaire des princes,* Boulainvilliers returned to his "Lettres sur les parlements ou états généraux" to revise his text, add two more letters to it, and abandon it unfinished once again.[100] Whatever his aims, they did not include edifying or persuading a prince, for Boulainvilliers now pronounced all princes hopelessly devoted to "rendering their authority despotic":

> In my previous letters, Monsieur, I have surveyed the reigns of a great number of princes of diverse character. They have all sat upon the same throne, but they have conducted themselves upon it in such different fashions that with the exception of one sole point—which was the idea of subjugating their peoples, annihilating the great lords, and rendering their authority despotic—one might say that their maxims of government had no greater connection with each other than with those of the Chinese or

[100]*Etat . . . Tome III,* 164–89 (Letters 13 and 14). For dating see 181 (Letter 14), a bitter allusion to the May 14, 1717, council decree forbidding unauthorized noble assemblies and petitions. On MSS and editions see Bibliographical Appendix, Parts 2 and 5.

Tartar monarchy. However, one may observe that they did not fail to lead their posterity to the goal that they already proposed many centuries ago: but that to attain that goal effectively, the administration of the Cardinal Richelieu and the reign of Louis XIV have done more in 90 years than all the enterprises of earlier kings had accomplished in 1,200.[101]

Indeed, Boulainvilliers wrote his "Lettres sur les parlements" to vilify French princes, not to educate them. He still admired "Charlemagne, the institutor of fiefs, restorer of parlements or common assemblies, faithful conservator of equality among the French." But he had only contempt for Charlemagne's successors. Not one sustained the "equality" that Charlemagne had revived. Not one could match Charlemagne's "knowledge" and goodwill. "Ignorance" vitiated the goodwill of Louis the Pious (814–40), and the saintly Louis IX also "lacked the knowledge to govern his kingdom according to a solid plan suitable to his intentions."[102] An "ignorant" prince, Boulainvilliers maintained, could not achieve "the great and supreme views of a wise legislator," and ignorance, he was convinced, was an abiding fault of French kings.[103]

Equally deplorable was their ill will, which could destroy a good "education" if a prince happened to receive one.[104] Despite his examples of Louis the Pious and Saint Louis, Boulainvilliers insisted that ill will was a fault of all French princes, not a merely personal failing of particular monarchs but a flaw inherent in the French monarchy itself and arising out of the fatal tendencies of feudal kingship to particularism. Writing about Hugh Capet's son, Robert the Pious (996–1031), Boulainvilliers said:

> France was not governed during his reign except as a great lordship in which vassals granted or refused obedience while the king lacked the force and authority to constrain them to obey. Thus, one need not be astonished that, reduced to a particular condition although decorated with the magnificent title of kings of France, neither Robert nor his successors had any general views beyond those of acquiring and of expanding when they had the opportunity and the power to do so and—when necessity required—of employing the most extreme violence, to the point of plundering travelers on highways and in forests.[105]

That is a surprising remark for a man who had proclaimed "feudal government" to be "the masterpiece of the human mind." Now Boulain-

[101]*Etat . . . Tome III*, 164 (Letter 13).
[102]Ibid., 165, 168 (Letter 13).
[103]Ibid., 165 (Letter 13).
[104]Ibid., 167 (Letter 13), on Philip II (1180–1223).
[105]Ibid., 166 (Letter 13).

villiers (who dropped that encomium to feudalism from his revised "Lettres") was moving toward a subtler, if less admiring understanding of "feudal government" as an inherently unstable and conflict-ridden system carrying the seeds of its own destruction in the antagonism between feudatories and their equally egoistic kings.[106]

By looking for despotism's roots in feudalism, Boulainvilliers came very close to damning his beloved feudal past. But he refused to assimilate it to a despotic modernity which he traced clearly and emphatically to the reign of Louis XI (1461–83). French historians traditionally described that king as an evil genius. So did Boulainvilliers, who called him "the ablest and at the same time the most ill-intentioned of our kings up to the fifteenth century." Louis XI gave French kings "the maxims and practices by which they established the despotic power they exercise today." His reign was "the origin of despotism exercised without restraint and without good faith, to the total ruin of subjects great and small."[107]

Thus, after discovering the roots of modern despotism in medieval feudalism, Boulainvilliers restored the distinction between them. With heavy irony, he remarked that Louis XI had served France well, "if one supposes that one must regard the union of the body of the monarchy and the destruction of all particular powers as the basis of the repose and welfare of subjects."[108] The "particular powers" to which Boulainvilliers alluded were the national assemblies and autonomous provinces of the barbarian and feudal pasts, bulwarks of liberty that survived—Boulainvilliers' Anglomania now reemerges—only in England: "One must conclude that there can be no security for the peoples except in states governed on the models given by the ancient destroyers of the Roman Empire—models of which no vestiges remain any longer except in England—or at least in states where there remain enough great lords and established princes to offer refuge to some miserable [subjects], whose misery unlimited power cannot fail to produce, at least unwittingly if not by bad intention."[109] Clearly and emphatically, Boulainvilliers distinguished modern monarchical "despotism," first established by Louis XI, from the "feudal" or "mixed" or Germanic government that France had enjoyed in earlier centuries.

[106]Compare ibid., 37 (Letter 4, 1716 version), with Boulainvilliers, *Histoire de l'ancien gouvernement*, 3:291–320 (the revised Letter 4).

[107]*Etat . . . Tome III*, 164 (Letter 13); 187–88 (Letter 14, against Père Daniel's departure from historiographical convention to censor Charles VII and laud Louis XI); 171 (Letter 13); 176 (Letter 14).

[108] Ibid., 176 (Letter 14).

[109]Ibid., 176–77 (Letter 14). Cf. ibid., 20 (Letter 3), also on the Germanic provenance of the "diets," "parliaments," "estates," and "*cortes*" of European monarchies.

"Despotism" was not the only evil that plagued modern France. Equally deplorable to Boulainvilliers' mind was the "confusion" of social orders, "the great handiwork of despotism" and yet another innovation of Louix XI.[110] Scrutinizing rank and precedence at the Estates General of 1468 and at the Assembly of Notables two years later, Boulainvilliers claimed to discover a royal design to confuse ranks, destroy the nobility's preeminence, and confound "nobility of birth" with "the privilege of nobility and the knighthood of the law" that any *anobli* or Parlementaire might enjoy.[111]

These remarks recall the aristocratic controversies of 1715–17 when peers, parlementaires, and untitled nobles fought for preeminence. Boulainvilliers abandoned his narrative to cast one last glance at those disputes. He admitted that the old nobility could not consign magistrates and the Third Estate to "the rank of serfs from which they emerged."[112] He even accepted the magistracy's and the Third Estate's importance in modern society. In his view, "It would be . . . unsuitable perpetually to reproach the Third Estate and the magistracy for their original condition. The advantages which the entire state derives from commerce and the habit of honoring the judges who daily render decisions concerning our property and our fortunes are powerful reasons to restore equality and to persuade the nobility, which has the greatest interest in the loss of its original rank, to acept that equality."[113] Boulainvilliers insisted, however, that the nobility had paid a high price for these benefits of modern society, because the nobility had lost its social and political autonomy. It was now a socially "confused" elite doomed to political silence. Boulainvilliers did not cite the regency council's May 14, 1717, decree forbidding unauthorized noble assemblies and petitions, but he clearly had it in mind when he described the "decadence" of the modern French nobility:

> Unfortunately for this nobility, it is no longer even a question of equality. The nobility has fallen into the last rank, so that one would be incapable of believing that it existed at all, if we did not see in the commons a measureless passion to take the nobility's place, by means of letters [of nobility] of the prince, or by means of purchasing privileged offices. It has been declared in our own days that the nobility did not constitute a body [*ne faisoit point de Corps*], and that no noble individual could even represent its common rights before the prince, by means of petitions permitted to all other

[110]Ibid., 180 (Letter 14).
[111]Ibid., 177–84, 188 for quotation (Letter 14). Boulainvilliers relied on documents in Jean Du Tillet's *Recueil des roys de France* (several editions between 1580 and 1618).
[112]Ibid., 180 (Letter 14).
[113]Ibid., 181 (Letter 14).

subjects. Events have not disproved that statement. Thus the augury of a still greater decadence in the future has become all too certain for the honor of French blood.[114]

Modernity had its charms, Boulainvilliers admitted. "Each age has its advantages and its afflictions which compensate for each other," he wrote, adding that "the total society of the nation and of all conditions is more advantageous to the nobility itself than that superior and incommunicable rank which it so long enjoyed in the age of ignorance and grossness."[115] That was a passing admission, however, and a painful one, for in acquiring its present advantages the French nobility had lost its past glory and condemned itself to a future of "despotism" and "confusion" from which no escape was possible.

The vices of despotism and the virtues of feudalism preoccupied Boulainvilliers in another late work, the "Préface critique au journal de Saint Louis."[116] The "journal" that Boulainvilliers prefaced was a history in journal form of Louis IX. Its author was Antoine Aubery, a barrister at the Royal Council whom Colbert had directed to write journal-histories on the reigns of all French kings. Aubery completed journals for Louis IX and his successors through Louix XI. Intended as monuments to the glory of France's kings and to the plenitude of their power, Aubrey's journals never got into print even after Colbert had another author (one sieur Péan) revise them. Copies circulated in manuscript, however, reaching collectors and connoisseurs such as Boulainvilliers who set himself the task of annotating and prefacing each of the journals. In fact, he annotated only the journals of Louis IX and Philip III and wrote a preface only for the first.[117]

Like the last two "Lettres sur les parlements," the "Préface critique au journal de Saint Louis" manifests the bitterness of its author, now convinced that he had misplaced his hopes when he lodged them in Orléans' regency. Royal "minorities," Boulainvilliers was now convinced, "have served only to augment the power of kings, despite all the efforts appar-

---

[114]Ibid.

[115]Ibid.

[116]Boulainvilliers, "Préface critique au journal de Saint Louis. Anecdotes curieuses du règne de Saint Louis, roy de France, depuis 1226 jusqu'en l'année 1270," in Un Révolté, 85–131. On MSS and editions see Bibliographical Appendix, Part 2.

[117]On the Aubery-Péan journals see Boulainvilliers' contemptuous comments in his "Préface critique" (Un Révolté, 94–97); and see Lelong, Bibliographie historique de la France (ed. Fevret de Fontette), 2:57, 158, 160, 207 (a description barely less contemptuous than Boulainvilliers'); 4:388–89, 392. For MSS of the Aubery-Péan journals with Boulainvilliers' annotations see Bibliographical Appendix, Part 2.

ently intended to submerge [*engloutir*] or restrict it." Indeed, the invariably vain efforts that the French made to reclaim their "rights" during minorities served only to reinforce the power of kings. As an example, Boulainvilliers cited the Fronde's failure during Louis XIV's minority: "Louis XIV could never forget the barricades of Paris and never examined if it was right to arrest Broussel and his colleagues." Boulainvilliers must have been reflecting on Louis XV's minority, too, and on his own failed hopes for the regency.[118]

Boulainvilliers' disappointment is visible not only in his bitter comments on royal minorities, but also in his harsh reflections on the failure of French history to enlighten the French. The "Préface critique," it is true, reiterates much that Boulainvilliers had written earlier, notably in the first of his "Lettres sur les parlements." He still claimed that history might teach the prince and that the historian, like a faithful counselor, might tell him the truth. He still believed that "the plan of history" was the education of princes. History, he still insisted, teaches right conduct to living princes by adducing for their edification the "examples," good and bad, set by dead princes.[119] His countrymen, he still complained, could not read or write a history that truthfully depicted the "ancient liberty" once enjoyed by a "French nation," for they were accustomed to "masters," prone to "flattery," and blinded by "corruption," "agitation" and "covetousness" to the "happiness" of a better but simpler time that "bores us today by its very description."[120] In the "Préface critique," however, Boulainvilliers went on to make a proposal he had not made earlier. He now invited the lover of the past to abandon didactic eloquence for a retiring and contemplative erudition. He proclaimed his admiration for seventeenth-century *érudits*. He applauded André Duchesne, who found French history "dry and arid" and left it enriched by the sources he collected and published. He commended the Benedictine and Bollandist fathers, who had continued Duchesne's work and had assembled at last the "necessary materials" for a reliable French history.[121] He did not propose the writing of such a history, however. "Corruption" and "adulation" had made that impossible. Instead he proposed that the "truth" that modern historians and their readers feared be left half-buried in the compilations of *érudits* where true lovers

[118]Boulainvilliers, *Un Révolté*, 113. The crown's arrest in 1648 of Pierre Broussel, the aged councilor of the Parlement of Paris and a popular opponent of royal taxation, occasioned the rebellion of Paris during the civil wars of the French.
[119]Ibid., 97.
[120]Ibid., 90–93. Boulainvilliers' condemnation included the most recent "general histories" of France, Mézeray's and Daniel's.
[121]Ibid., 85–86.

of liberty might contemplate its past undisturbed by their timorous contemporaries. "We owe . . . eternal gratitude to the memory of André Duchesne for having projected and partially executed a work in which truth will always be found, not shining and open—that is, capable of arousing hate in those who fear it—but rather like gold buried in mines, causing neither jealousy nor debates among men who do not know how to extract it from the envelopes in which nature sought to hide it."[122] History, Boulainvilliers suggested, had now become a form of esoteric connoisseurship restricted to pious initiates alone.

In that spirit Boulainvilliers turned once again to the feudal past, and the Aubery-Péan journals on the reigns of feudal kings. He did not rewrite those journals (though he thought them "in a certain sense premature") because their authors had worked before the great advances of late-seventeenth-century erudition. In annotating and prefacing the journals, however, Boulainvilliers vigorously defended medieval feudalism against modern "despotism." He detected some symptoms of "despotism" in Louis IX's France, but he denied that anyone in the thirteenth century had "the slightest notion of a despotic monarchy" or of the dynastic principle on which (Boulainvilliers held) it rested.[123] He deplored the efforts of Aubery and Péan to discover "sovereignty" in thirteenth-century France and to denounce fiefs, feudatories, and the rights of vassals to make war on their suzerains as attacks on it. "Sovereignty," in Boulainvilliers' view, did not even exist in the age of Louis IX. To suppose that it did was to fall prey to "the disproportion of our ideas" and "judge all past ages by present usage."[124]

Always, Boulainvilliers insisted on the difference between past and present. He did not seek to assert a historical relativism, however, for he condemned the present while he admired the past, and he sought to contemplate the past undisturbed by the misapprehensions of modern historians who feared it unless they could remold it in their own image in writing its history. "Oh, extreme misery of our age!" he wrote. "Far from being contented with the subjection in which we live, we seek to carry slavery back into times when men had not even formed an idea of it."[125]

---

[122]Ibid., 94.

[123]Ibid., 85; 120–29; 114; 98–105. On regencies, notably Blanche of Castile's during Louis IX's minority, see 106–13 (arguments that in the thirteenth century feudal law still regulated the royal succession—Louis IX's rights to the throne rested on primogeniture and the oaths sworn by the barons to his dying father to secure his consecration as quickly as possible).

[124]Boulainvilliers, *Un Révolté*, 92 (for quotation), and 91, 114–20, 130–31.

[125]Ibid., 131.

In the "Préface critique," historical study became an act of pious contemplation of a buried but better past.

Admiration for a dead past informed not only Boulainvilliers' "Préface critique" but also his "Discours sur la noblesse," a work he wrote (or left unfinished) in 1719.[126] Like his very first work on French history, the "Dissertation" on the "old nobility" written in 1700, the "Discours sur la noblesse" was the preface to a genealogical work, an unfinished province-by-province catalog of French nobility. Unlike the "Dissertation," however, the "Discours" attenuates the activist functions of genealogy. It is not a pedagogical or hortatory work using ancestral "examples" to teach the wellborn young to love "virtue" and pursue "glory." It is a contemplative work using the history of the "true nobility" to teach its members, now unable to realize their "virtue" and "glory" in the present, to recognize themselves in the past grandeur of their families.

In the "Discours," it is true, Boulainvilliers made the same assumptions that he had made in the "Dissertation." He still held that "birth" and "virtue" constituted nobility and obliged it to pursue "glory." Indeed, he stated those assumptions more forcefully than he had in 1700. Although he began his "Dissertation" by claiming that "conquest" and "violence" constitute nobility, he opened his "Discours" by arguing that "virtue" first established nobility among the Greeks and Romans, who honored "those who had been useful to the fatherland" with statues, festivals, games, and sacrifices. Only when kings subverted the virtuous aristocracies of antiquity—only when Philip of Macedon vanquished the Greeks and only when Romulus and the Tarquins subdued the Romans—did "favor," "industry," "adulations," and "personal attachment" replace "virtue" and "illustriousness" as the qualities that constitute "true nobles."[127] "Conquest," Boulainvilliers admitted, constituted the nobilities of postclassical Europe. "Conquest" was the "principle of another sort of nobility which established itself [*se reproduit*] among us," an "odious" nobility perhaps, but sanctioned by the "law of the victor." He added that this nobility—clearly he had the French in mind—sustained itself "until the reign of Philip the Fair and the year 1300" when (Boulainvilliers complained once again) kings began to ennoble commoners and dilute the nobility of "blood" with a new nobility distinguished only by its "privileges."[128] "Conquest" and "blood"

---

[126]According to dates on MSS, for which see Bibliographical Appendix, Part 2. The MS cited here will be Bibliothèque de l'Institut (Paris), MS. 321, fols. 547v–589.

[127]Bibliothèque de l'Institut (Paris), MS. 321, fols. 547v–549.

[128]Ibid., fols. 551–52.

notwithstanding, however, Boulainvilliers still claimed that "virtue" was essential to the nobilities of postclassical Europe. He even conceded that "personal virtue" should admit new lineages into the nobility: "Virtues being personal," he declared, "they make those who practice them equal or approach very closely true nobility."[129] He hesitated to base "true" or "high nobility" on "personal virtue" alone, it is true, but for reasons consonant with his genealogical concept of nobility as a body of glorious lineages constituted by "virtue" and "birth" both: "But the great and high nobility has something more; it has for itself a tradition of virtues, of honor, of sentiments, of dignities and of possessions, a tradition which has perpetuated itself through a long succession of generations [*Races*], and which bears no comparison with the personal merit of a mere individual denuded of all these great advantages."[130] This is the familiar language of genealogical consciousness, to which Boulainvilliers remained as firmly committed at the end of his career as at the beginning. In 1719 as in 1700 he believed that familial tradition formed the virtuous nobleman and compelled him to pursue his glory.

Boulainvilliers was equally sensitive to the implications of genealogical erudition. This too remained with him in 1719. Again he identified the old nobility with the feudal nobility, since (he admitted) it was "absolutely impossible" to trace noble lineages further back in time than the age of fiefs when feudal patrimonies and patronyms appeared to help the genealogist do his work.[131] Identifying nobility with feudalism, however, could invite one to identify the nobility's "decadence" with feudalism's decay: Boulainvilliers did so in the "Dissertation" on the "old nobility" that he wrote in 1700. Because one of his reasons for writing that work, however, was to prepare his sons to pursue "glory" and restore their house's name, he allowed himself to hope the nobility's "decadence" might be reversible, a transitory aberration that "princes as informed and equitable as ours" would suppress.[132] In 1719, however, no such aspirations deflected the powerfully pessimistic drift of his thinking on the old nobility's history. In the "Discours," that history became yet another history of a dead but admirable past, the social and genealogical past of the old nobility.

Boulainvilliers' "Discours" was not a history of the feudal nobility's bygone glory; it was a plea that the feudal nobility's modern descendants might remember, against all odds, that their ancestry ought to have

---

[129]Ibid., fol. 575.
[130]Ibid., fols. 575–575v.
[131]Ibid., fols. 552v–553. See chapter 2.
[132]*Essais*, 300. See chapter 2.

given them precedence over nobility descended from royal officers, magistrates, or mere *anoblis*.[133] Boulainvilliers refined that plea for pre-eminence in the last pages of his "Discours," where he divided his old nobility into two "orders."[134] He had done so already in his "Lettres sur les parlements," where he carefully refused to impugn the "birth" of second-order nobles; their inferiority, he had written, arose only from an inferiority of "riches, possessions, and employments which have always distinguished men."[135] Boulainvilliers manipulated his categories of social analysis no less carefully in the "Discours"—as well he might, since ducal "pretensions" during the *affaire du bonnet* and the *affaire des princes* had lately sharpened aristocratic sensitivities to all efforts at social categorization—where he denied that his first order of nobility was "a separate and dominant body."[136] The first order's members, he explained, were distinguished "not by the titles and qualities of princes and dukes and peers, titles by which many are adorned today, but by the grandeur of their origin, along with their long-continued enjoyment of an honorable prosperity, with regard to property, dignities, and the merit of the different members [*sujets*] who succeeded each other in these houses."[137] Ready as ever to acknowledge legitimate distinctions within the nobility, he still refused to include the ducal title among them. Indeed, his first order of old nobility was most unlike the ducal corps, for it contained only ten families, of which four were either extinct or "fallen into the second order" because (as he explained while commenting on one of his unfortunate houses) they had had "the misfortune to have subsisted for more than three centuries without producing a member [*sujet*] capable of elevating it."[138]

At this point Boulainvilliers' plea for the old nobility's preeminence is complicated by an appreciation that social and historical contingencies never ceased to surround the enjoyment of great fiefs, high offices, and brilliant marriages that sustain membership in the first order:

[133]Bibliothèque de l'Institut (Paris), MS. 321, fols. 571–80, on Boulainvilliers' seven "ranks" of nobility. He assigned the highest to families descended from ancient Franks (by his own admission a category "absolutely impossible" to trace genealogically), and reserved the next three to families descended from feudatories. Families founded by royal officers, magistrates, and *anoblis* occupied the last three ranks.

[134]Ibid., fols. 579–85.

[135]*Etat . . . Tome III*, 136 (Letter 12).

[136]Bibliothèque de l'Institut, MS. 321, fol. 579v.

[137]Ibid., fol. 580.

[138]Ibid., fol. 585v (on the House of Poitiers, subsisting still in the collateral lines of Saint-Vallier and Poitiers). The other three unfortunate houses were those of Coucy, Châlons, and Lusignan. See fols. 580 r–v on Boulainvilliers' ten first-order houses: "Couci, Châtillon, Melun, Montmorency, Rohan, Harcourt, Châlons and Vienne whom I do not separate, La Tour, Poitiers and Lusignan."

It is impossible that any house subsist for several centuries in the state that we have described, in order to accord it first rank. Consequently, they redescend necessarily into the second order, which we compose of the pure French nobility which possesses neither great fiefs, nor great dignities, nor high alliances; or of houses which, having possessed all these advantages, failed to keep them because of adverse fortune; or of houses which issuing directly from royal houses or other sovereign houses were forced, either by the necessity of events or by the loss of property, to follow the common route and to forget what used to distinguish them.[139]

Boulainvilliers' remark about "loss of property" notwithstanding, he was not concerned about the nobility's so-called decline, nor was he protesting the plight of an impoverished *plèbe nobiliaire*.[140] He made that remark about "property" while writing of houses of royal extraction, and he had nothing at all to say about poor nobles. Decayed gentry find no place in his seven "ranks" of nobility old and new. They include only propertied houses, and even the lowest of the three reserved to nobles of feudal extraction required property enough "to conserve the rank and quality of lord" and to perform "all the duties of their state."[141] Indeed, in the lines just quoted he wrote about the contingencies of familial glory with something like equanimity.

Yet the contingencies surrounding the nobility's pursuit of glory did preoccupy Boulainvilliers. At times he expanded that preoccupation into a concern for "service" to the "state," as in his proposal to abolish hereditary office in the military and the magistracy; that measure, he claimed, would encourage "emulation" and make room for the "merit" of the nobleman ever ready to exert himself "for fear of falling from the rank of his fathers."[142] That proposal for a noble meritocracy belongs to

[139]Ibid., fols. 583v–584.

[140]Cf. Devyver, *Le Sang épuré*, 353–90, 432–37; Bluche, *La Vie quotidienne de la noblesse*, 230–31.

[141]See n. 133, and Bibliothèque de l'Institut (Paris), MS. 321, fols. 571v–573, fol. 573 for quotation.

[142]Ibid., fols. 588–89:
It would be more advantageous for the . . . state if dignities in it were only granted for life rather than that they be hereditary, for then everyone would endeavor to merit them and make himself worthy of them, for fear of falling from the rank of his fathers, whereas the certainty of acquiring one's rank makes one content with fulfilling common duties which produces only common actions. From that certainty springs also the lack of emulation which one sees today among officers of war and in the Robe. The first, assured of ascending through the ranks of the military according to their seniority in service, avoid perilous occasions which might elevate them a little sooner, but at the risk of their lives. The second, certain to possess one day their fathers' charges, do not deign to acquire the knowledge necessary to exercise these charges worthily, for that would cost them some effort. I conclude that to produce great men in a state, it is necessary that everything be accorded to merit and service, and that

a tradition of noble complaint and noble calls for military reform that led eventually to the Ségur regulation of 1781.[143] In Boulainvilliers' hands, however, it was only a paper project. In the "Discours," his chief aim was not to open up paths to glory, but to teach his readers to distinguish between worthy and worthless glory: between "grandeur" enjoyed in a better feudal past and distinctions since acquired by the personal "favor" of "despotic masters." This is the reason for his vituperation of dukes and peers, whom he vilified with unprecedented enthusiasm and hatred as the nobility's "truest enemies."[144] The peerage, he claimed, destroyed the "political body" that was once the French nobility:

> The nobility, I mean that of extraction, which participates in one of the attributes of grandeur mentioned earlier [i.e. fiefs, dignities, alliances, etc.] is in reality a political body. In it one can introduce no division, any more than one can do so in a natural body, without damaging the body and the members one detaches from it. For that very reason our fathers refrained from seeking titles and ranks which some use today, not only to lift themselves above their fellows but also above themselves, without thinking that these added dignities, which they respect so highly, are the gifts of arbitrary favor granted always to address, to intrigues, and rarely to merit. These dignities always incriminate those who obtain them; those who are wise enough to distinguish fiction from truth always and sincerely hold these dignities in contempt. And we see that there were no dukes and peers in the order of the nobility before the reigns of Henry II and his children.[145]

Familial glory had become so difficult to acquire and sustain, Boulainvilliers sought to suggest, because a "despotic" and "arbitrary" French monarchy dispensed it and discredited it.

Boulainvilliers' response to this problem was not to level the French monarchy but to oppose its "fictions"—among them "dignities" such as

---

nothing passes to heirs who often dishonor the memory of their ancestors by the indignity of their own lives.

[143]See Bien, "La Réaction aristocratique," 23–48, 505–34; Bien, "The Army in the French Enlightenment," 68–98; Brancourt, *Le Duc de Saint-Simon*, 113; Brancourt, "Un Théoricien de la sociéte." Guy Chaussinand-Nogaret has also called attention to the meritocratic opinions circulating in the eighteenth-century nobility, but he takes "merit" to be a "bourgeois" notion, "virtue" an antiquated and aristocratic one closely aligned with "valor." See Chaussinand-Nogaret, "Aux origines de la Révolution: Noblesse et bourgeoisie," *Annales. E.S.C.*, 30 (1975):267–70; Chaussinand-Nogaret, "Un Aspect de la pensée nobiliaire au XVIIIe siècle: L'"antinobilisme,'" *Revue d'histoire moderne et contemporaine*, 29 (1982): 442, 447; and Chaussinand-Nogaret, *La Noblesse au XVIIIe siècle*, 23–38. But Boulainvilliers' plea for "merit" in both the military and the magistracy is at variance with Chaussinand-Nogaret's interpretative model.

[144]Bibliothèque de l'Institut (Paris), MS. 321, fols. 584v–585; 586v.

[145]Ibid., fols. 585r–v. Henry II was indeed the first king to grant the ducal dignity to French nobles and not just to lords of the blood royal (Labatut, *Les Ducs et pairs*, 57–65).

duchy-peerages which "incriminate those who obtain them"—by elaborating a "sound idea" of nobility. He cast a critical eye on the standards his contemporaries used to distinguish noble houses and hold them up for esteem. And he reserved his most acerbic comments for the leading genealogical compilation of late-seventeenth- and early-eighteenth-century France: the *Histoire de la maison royale de France et des grands officiers de la couronne* by Père Anselme and his collaborators and continuators. When Boulainvilliers wrote his "Discours," that work had already gone through two editions designed to associate aristocratic "glory" with the grandeur of French kings, and plans were afoot for a third edition that would insert genealogies of ducal houses in the place of highest honor, right after the royal genealogy and before everyone else's.[146] It is tempting to suppose that Boulainvilliers knew of that project since the dukes and peers, Saint-Simon preeminent among them, were behind it.[147] In any case, Boulainvilliers' contempt for offices of the crown and for Père Anselme's compendium is unmistakable. Offices of the crown, he claimed, were merely domestic charges, and "well into the third race" the great vassals of France held them in contempt.[148] He questioned even the glory conferred by military charges, such as those of constable and marshal, for "wealth" and "favor" usually filled those offices and thereby discredited them.[149] His contemporaries' high esteem for offices of the crown dismayed him, and for that reason so did Père Anselme's genealogical compendium on families "illustrated" by those offices. "In our time," wrote Boulainvilliers, "opinion has reached such a point that the most illustrious houses of the present day would lose the

[146][Pierre de Guibours, called] Père Anselme, *Histoire de la maison royale de France et des grands officiers de la couronne*, 2 vols. (Paris: Estienne Loyson, 1674), a work that included the royal genealogy and genealogies of families that had produced officers of the crown or knights of the royal Order of the Holy Spirit. An enlarged edition appeared in 1712: Père Anselme [and Honoré Caille Du Fourny et al.], *Histoire généalogique et chronologique de la maison royale de France, des grands officiers de la couronne et de la maison du roy*, 2 vols. (Paris: Michel Guignard and Claude Robustel; or G. Cavelier, 1712).

[147]The project goes back to the beginning of the regency. At a December 27, 1715, meeting of ducal syndics Louis-Auguste d'Albert, duc de Chaulnes suggested a new edition of Père Anselme's *Histoire* revised to include ducal genealogies. Louis-Hector, duc de Villars was instructed to speak about the project to the chancellor (A.N., K.648 [9]). Later, probably in 1719 when Boulainvilliers was preparing his "Discours," there circulated a "Projet Pour l'histoire des Ducs et Pairs de France" that explicitly described the plan to be followed by Père Ange and his associates when they revised Père Anselme's compendium (B.N., MS. Clairambault 720, fols. 443–51, esp. fols. 443–44; undated but bound with documents dated 1719). The "Projet" bears marginalia by the duc de Saint-Simon, the duc de La Force, and the duc d'Humières, all of whom Boulainvilliers knew. And see the nine-volume third edition of 1726–33: Anselme, Du Fourny, Ange, and Simplicien, *Histoire généalogique et chronologique*.

[148]Bibliothèque de l'Institut (Paris), MS. 321, fols. 568–569v.

[149]Ibid., fols. 574v–578, esp. 576v–577.

greater part of their high relief if one did not find them inscribed in the catalog of Père Anselme, who took the liberty to erect into charges of the crown as many employments as possible, so he could make everyone happy. I would not care to assert that this was the best means for conserving the sound idea that one should have of nobility."[150]

To "conserve" a "sound idea" of nobility, Boulainvilliers planned his own genealogical compendium: a catalog of forty old, well-married, well-endowed provincial families illustrated by their "courage" and their "hereditary virtue" and distinguished by glorious feudal pasts attested faithfully by mentions in charters and chronicles.[151] Thus the "Discours sur la noblesse" and the genealogical survey that it introduced furnished an alternative social manual for proud (but not poor) nobles of old extraction. It did not use family history to exhort the wellborn to pursue glory. The "arbitrary" and "despotic" French monarchy had made that impossible—the nobleman's path to glory was now a treacherous route that corrupted him as he traveled it. Boulainvilliers now muted the activist implications of genealogy, to propose instead a contemplative genealogical connoisseurship that might let "true" nobles recognize and admire each other in contemplating their ancestral "glory" acquired in the feudal past.

Why did Boulainvilliers write his last works on French history? Why did he refuse to put down his pen after the *affaire des princes*, when he proclaimed the futility of historical writing and the vanity of the hopes he had lodged in the duc d'Orléans' regency? Even at his most pessimistic and contemplative Boulainvilliers was an author performing for an audience still aroused by the social and political conflicts of 1715–17. Both the last "Lettres sur les parlements" and the "Discours sur la noblesse" may be read as bitter comments on those controversies and

---

[150]Ibid., fol. 570.

[151]Ibid., fols. 586v–587: "One can count in the provinces more than forty families so distinguished by the accounts that can easily be made of their origins or their alliances or their wealth or the high esteem that courage or hereditary virtue procured for them, that one can hardly discover in them any inferiority [to first-order houses], excepting with regard to their subordinate vassalage." On Boulainvilliers' procedure cf. Bibliothèque du Sénat (Paris), MS. 986, p. 51 (his introduction to his account of Burgundian nobility):
> The method I propose [to follow] . . . is to determine which are the illustrious houses mentioned in charters or on the great occasions in history; to judge sincerely the remaining posterity of those houses; to judge those who usurped the names of those illustrious houses to separate from them their glory; and finally to enumerate the most considerable of those whose riches, sustained by ennoblements, lifted up to the possession of those same fiefs and who pretend consequently to replace those ancient families. By this means, the reader will find himself in a position to judge the true distance or the equality that might be encountered between these same families and the ten which I had imagined preferable to all the others.

their outcomes. During those quarrels, however, Boulainvilliers aspired to reach his public in print. It is not likely that he entertained any such hopes after 1717. He was not writing for the desk drawer, however. When he died, his friend Nicolas Fréret did not know that he had added two more "Lettres sur les parlements" to the twelve written in 1716.[152] But Fréret did report that Spinozist works by Boulainvilliers circulated commercially in manuscript.[153] Boulainvilliers' historical works did too. Just as he read Le Laboureur, or Longuerue, or the Aubery-Péan journals in manuscript, others read Boulainvilliers in manuscript and with his own connivance. In 1716, for example, he let manuscripts of his "Lettres sur les parlements" and other pieces be copied and circulated.[154] It may be surmised, therefore, that Boulainvilliers was still writing for a public at the end of his life, a contemporary public still aroused by the *affaire du bonnet* and the *affaire des princes*, but also a future public which he could consciously have addressed in manuscript. And indeed not long after his death, contemporaries began to report that they were acquiring his works, commenting on their boldness with nervous pleasure. In his "Mémoires" for September 1722, Mathieu Marais reported having obtained and read Boulainvilliers' "Préface critique." "Nothing is stronger and bolder than all this talk," he wrote; "it seems that the authorities shall have to stop the circulation of these manuscripts which teach things so curious and so contrary to sovereignty that one is nearly a criminal in reading them!" If Marais can be believed, Boulainvilliers became a dangerous author whose works circulated in manuscript "samizdat editions" until the pressure of later controversies led English and Dutch publishers to print and sell them.[155]

To carry this story forward requires embarking on a new history, a history of Boulainvilliers' posthumous career. The career he actively pursued, as a princely client, counselor, and controversialist writing French history for French princes, ended with the *affaire des princes*. It can only be called a failure. For the regent's refusal to play the role Boulainvilliers prepared for him—Orléans never became a new Charlemagne magnanimously reviving the Estates and restoring French nobility to preeminence—left Boulainvilliers an inner émigré, marooned in a monarchical modernity he hated and nostalgic for an irretrievably lost past.

[152]Fréret, "Lettre de M. Fréret," 202.
[153]Fréret, "Lettre de M. Fréret," 203.
[154]See Bibliographical Appendix, n. 51; Moréri et al., *Le Grand Dictionnaire historique,* 2:133.
[155]Marais, *Journal et mémoires,* 2:349. See Bibliographical Appendix, pp. 248–49.

7

Conclusion

In 1707, Boulainvilliers consigned some thoughts on how to read and write French history to a "Lettre à Mademoiselle Cousinot sur l'histoire et sa méthode."[1] There he condemned the crown-centered histories of France that his contemporaries customarily wrote: "ces histoires toutes monarchiques," he called them. He demanded instead a larger history of government, *moeurs,* and the "passions" that make men act.

> Do you believe, Mademoiselle, that one has gotten very far when one knows the dates of a few events, the names of princes and their ministers and generals or mistresses, while one ignores the reasons for their actions and their government, while one fails to learn about the genius of each age, [its] predominant opinions, *moeurs,* and ideas, or, to be brief, the passions that make men act? I have hardly been interested in princes and I would give them no thought at all if the unhappiness of the human condition had not caused the felicity of peoples to depend upon their will, or rather their caprice. . . . What connection is there between our fortune and theirs? What lessons can I draw from their conduct to govern mine? I see in their character only haughtiness, ill will, and hatred for other men. Consequently, one cannot examine the lives of princes (excepting a few more happily born than the rest and formed in their youth by adversity) without one way or another casting shame upon their successors. On the other hand, I find it pleasing and useful to learn about men of a lower level: the similarity of condition and fortune necessarily interests me in what happens to them.[2]

---

[1]Boulainvilliers, "Lettre à Mademoiselle Cousinot sur l'histoire et sa méthode (1707)," in *Un Révolté,* 71–81. For MSS see Bibliographical Appendix, Part 2. "Mademoiselle Cousinot" remains unidentified but she probably belonged to the prominent Parisian medical family.

[2]Boulainvilliers, *Un Révolté,* 72. On the crown-centered history of the Old Regime see studies cited in chapter 1, n. 29.

Convinced that history had to be morally edifying, yet equally convinced that the distance between haughty princes and their humble subjects rendered princely history all but useless to "men of a lower level," Boulainvilliers proposed an alternative history, a history of ordinary men for ordinary men, a new history with uses of its own.[3]

It is tempting to read this rejection of kings-and-battles history as an antimonarchical plea for a history of a French "nation," a history that Boulainvilliers eventually sought to write himself, as Mona Ozouf and François Furet have demonstrated.[4] Yet it is one of the ironies of Boulainvilliers' career that despite a powerful suspicion of monarchy, he worked in the shadow of princes and wrote most of his pieces on French history for them or to them.

The preceding chapters have charted the itinerary that Boulainvilliers followed in writing French history as nobiliaire ideologue, polemicist, and princely client and adviser. His journey began in the privacy of his Norman château where he wrote his first works for his sons; eventually he entered the entourages of princes for whom he wrote virtually all his other pieces on French history until, bitter and disappointed, he penned his last works. Throughout his career a powerful "genealogical consciousness" of the burdens and glories of noble birth impelled him. Whether he was exhorting his sons to pursue "glory" or persuading princes to prefer men of "birth" and "virtue" to men recommended by "wealth" and "favor" alone, Boulainvilliers was always reflecting on the conditions in which old nobles had to pursue their "glory" in modern France. He was convinced that they had to because he believed that noble "birth" obliged the wellborn to "illustrate" the houses whose names they bore by cultivating a "personal virtue" and acquiring a personal "glory." Boulainvilliers wished to make the French monarchy safe for noble "glory." He counted on the magnanimity of the princes he served and for whom he wrote: Louis XIV's grandson and (for ten heady

[3]The humanist concept of didactic history survived vigorously into Boulainvilliers' time. See Nadel, "Philosophy of History before Historicism," and Joseph M. Levine, "Ancients, Moderns, and History: The Continuity of English Historical Writing in the Later Seventeenth Century," in *Studies in Change and Revolution: Aspects of English Intellectual History 1640–1800*, ed. Paul J. Korshin (Menston, Yorkshire: Scolar Press, 1972), 43–75. On Boulainvilliers' concept of history in the "Lettre à Mademoiselle Cousinot," see Corada, "La Concezione della storia nel pensiero di Henry de Boulainvillier," 319–23; Simon, *Henry de Boulainviller*, 48–49, 52–54, 56.

[4]Ozouf and Furet, "Two Historical Legitimations of Eighteenth-Century French Society," 140–49. In her studies on the late-seventeenth-century *histoire raisonnée*, Phyllis K. Leffler has clearly identified the antimonarchical implications of demands such as Boulainvilliers' (his was not the only one) for a new history: "The '*Histoire raisonnée*,' 1660–1720"; "French Historians and the Challenge to Louis XIV's Absolutism," *French Historical Studies*, 14 (1985–86): 1–22.

months in 1711–12) heir, the duc de Bourgogne; and the young Louis XV's heir and regent, the duc d'Orléans. Bourgogne and (then) Orléans were to be the architects of the new order that Boulainvilliers ardently desired.

Restoring Boulainvilliers and his historical writings to the contexts in which he wrote them has several consequences. The most obvious is the discovery that this aristocratic reactionary—he is not the ideological monster that lives in the pages of some historians but he remains an aristocratic reactionary nonetheless—did not operate on the periphery of French society and politics. Ideologies of aristocratic reaction were certainly languages of complaint against personal failure and, at a higher level of generalization, against ministerial absolutism and the elites of bureaucrats and dignitaries that arose in its service. Boulain-villiers' vituperation against intendants and against dukes and peers may be understood in this sense. Yet these languages of noble complaint could be encountered at court and even in the highest reaches of the king's service, in the Burgundy Circle, for example, which Boulain-villiers sought to serve. Aristocratic reaction, it bears repeating, was no monopoly of the marginalized, for it could also be a symptom of the antagonisms that continued to divide French elites despite the Old Regime's vigorous social mobility and fusion, and despite the monarchy's equally vigorous mobilization of those elites in its service.[5]

Restoring Boulainvilliers and his works to the circumstances in which he wrote also discloses the political and constitutional meanings of aristocratic reaction: meanings at once monarchical and constitutionalist, and constitutionalist in a variety of competing senses. It is true that none of the nobiliaire ideologues considered in the preceding chapters, not even the antimonarchical Boulainvilliers, managed to escape the monarchical orthodoxies of the Old Regime. They appreciated that France was a formally absolute monarchy and they deferred to their kings and princes. Yet their ideologies of aristocratic reaction were not bereft of constitutionalist implications. And thanks to the French monarchy's dynastic difficulties at the end of Louis XIV's reign and at the beginning of Louis XV's minority, nobiliaire ideologues could transform those constitutionalist implications into explicit claims to play authoritative roles prescribed by an unwritten French constitution.

These dynastic difficulties and the aristocratic controversies that they occasioned are rich in implications for the history of constitutional

---

[5]See Willaim Beik, *Absolutism and Society in Seventeenth-Century France: State Power and Provincial Aristocracy in Languedoc* (Cambridge, Engl.: Cambridge University Press, 1985), on the mobilization and pacification of elites in one province.

theory and political argument in the Old Regime. From 1712 to 1717 what can only be called a French succession problem bedeviled the monarchy and subjected the dynastic transmission of sovereign authority to debate. At issue were the Spanish king Philip V's exclusion from the French succession, the duc d'Orléans' standing as Louis XV's heir (which depended on Philip V's exclusion), and, finally, Louis XIV's efforts to add his bastards and their lines to the order of succession. Matter for discussion among ministers, royal counselors, and princely entourages while Louis XIV lived, those dynastic difficulties became subjects for public debate after his death, when the French peerage, the Parlement of Paris, and diverse sectors of the untitled nobility at Paris all lodged conflicting constitutional claims to settle disputes about regencies and the royal succession, and defended those claims before the bar of "public opinion." Herein lies the political significance of the *affaire du bonnet* (1715–17) and the *affaire des princes* (1716–17). In the course of their quarrels, the aristocratic parties to those disputes began to rethink the French monarchy's unwritten constitution and to reinvent political argument about it.

It has been argued that Louis XIV subverted the unwritten constitution of the French monarchy by tampering with the indefeasible dynastic custom that sustained it.[6] Whether or not the king took it seriously (and there is reason to suspect that he did not), his legislation excluding the Spanish Bourbons from the succession and adding his bastards to it shook the mystique of the old monarchy and encouraged eighteenth-century Frenchmen to imagine the French constitution—that is, the body of "fundamental law"—not as an untouchable deposit of custom but as an act of legislative will. For whereas Louis XIV seemed to be subordinating fundamental law to the expanded authority of kings, the noble elites soon made similar claims of their own. As early as 1712 there were efforts to assign the right to regulate the royal succession to the dukes and peers. After 1715 nobles and parlementaires made competing claims to "judge" the royal succession and disputes about it. All these claims were on behalf of a "nation," and during the *affaire des princes*, it was even possible to imagine that fundamental law constituted the terms of a contract between a "nation" and its kings of which the "nation" was sovereign arbiter.[7] In early-eighteenth-century France, therefore, and

---

[6]See Sixte de Bourbon, *Le Traité d'Utrecht;* Saguez-Lovisi, *Les Lois fondamentales au XVIIIe siècle;* and Marina Valensise' forthcoming work on the *affaire des princes.*

[7]See Morel, "Les 'Droits de la nation,' " 249–62; also chapter 6. This understanding of "fundamental law" as contractual enactment rather than as indefeasible custom recalls the original sixteenth-century usages of the term (see Martyn P. Thompson, "The History of Fundamental Law in Political Thought from the French Wars of Religion to the American Revolution," *American Historical Review,* 91 [1986]: 1103–7).

Conclusion

in response to the monarchy's dynastic difficulties, the aristocratic elites developed a myth of the "nation"—it was to be one of the grand authorizing myths of political discourse in eighteenth-century France—and asserted their conflicting claims to act on its behalf in altering the provisions of fundamental law or in adjudicating disputes about it.

These were exalted claims indeed, but they were public claims too. During the *affaire du bonnet* and the *affaire des princes* the aristocratic elites self-consciously appealed to the "opinion" of a "public" which, they claimed, was to be reached by "print." That public was a small one, basically Parisian and aristocratic, and it is tempting to neglect it. Uninvolved contemporaries seem to have dismissed the *affaire du bonnet*, despite the big constitutional questions raised by the parties to it, as a risible spat about rank and genealogy. And even the *affaire des princes* failed to generate the flood of print that quarrels about Jansenism and *Unigenitus* could inspire during the regency. The "Constitution" mattered more to most Frenchmen than did France's unwritten constitution, as peers and nobles imagined it, and it may be arguable that the diverse publics mobilized by constitutional and religious controversy did not really coalesce until the 1750s.[8] It is certainly arguable that the aristocratic constitutional conflicts of 1715–17 turned out to be sterile. The regent managed them effectively, aided no doubt by the mutual antagonisms of the noble elites which reduced their politics to a politics of jealousy. Yet it cannot be denied that in 1715–17 those elites created in France a "public sphere" or "space" for political and constitutional conflict.[9] Nor can it be denied that they explored the possibilities for political publicity and rhetoric in it. They resorted to print, as well as to manuscript and rumor, in order to address publics as well as princes. Expanding the circuits of political speech, they attempted to persuade public opinion as well as to counsel or petition a royal lord.[10]

By restoring Boulainvilliers and his works to the contexts in which he wrote and by following him into the thickets of aristocratic controversy in early-eighteenth-century France, it has been possible to read his

[8]Baker, "On the Problem of the Ideological Origins of the French Revolution," 212–19; Daniel Carroll Joynes, "Parlementaires, Peers, and the *Parti Janséniste:* The Refusal of Sacraments and the Revival of the Ancient Constitution in Eighteenth Century France," in *Proceedings of the Annual Meeting of the Western Society for French History* [1980], 8 (1981): 229–38; Van Kley, *The Damiens Affair.* For printed production during the *affaire des princes* see Pierre M. Conlon, *Le Siècle des Lumières: Bibliographie chronologique: Tome I 1716–1722* (Geneva: Droz, 1983).
[9]Cf. Habermas, *Strukturwandel der Öffentlichkeit,* and his "The Public Sphere."
[10]The history of early-eighteenth-century attempts to imagine, constitute, and address a political "public" remains to be written, but see Thomas E. Kaiser's valuable contribution, "The Abbé de Saint-Pierre, Public Opinion, and the Reconstitution of the French Monarchy," *Journal of Modern History,* 55 (1983): 618–43.

historical writings as acts performed at identifiable moments and for identifiable purposes, be they familial, nobiliaire, or *orléaniste*. This procedure—which recalls the procedure Christian Jouhaud used with telling effect in his study of pamphlet literature during the Fronde—enhances the historian's sensitivity to the circumstances in which an author writes and expects to be read, and teaches the historian to appreciate how texts may be marked and scarred by the circumstances in which they were written.[11] Boulainvilliers' *oeuvre* clearly bears such marks and scars. When he contemplated the "arbitrary" or "absolute" authority that he claimed to find in the hands of modern French monarchs, he oscillated between vituperation and acquiescence. Reflecting on French feudalism, he could proclaim it the "masterpiece of the human mind" and, elsewhere, deplore it as the seedbed of the monarchical "despotism" and the ducal preeminence that he lamented in modern France. Indeed, the varieties of antifeudalism to which this champion of "feudal government" was susceptible are astonishing. He even came close to denouncing feudalism as a plot by legists to undo the French nobility. These equivocations, like Boulainvilliers' remarkable reversals in the *affaire des princes,* are intelligible only when restored to their ideological contexts and understood as ideological acts performed by an author pursuing contradictory aims: denouncing the ducal dignity while defending it against nobles and magistrates; bemoaning the reduction of rank and nobility to acts of royal will while asserting it to sustain the regent's authority; deploring the "absolute" and "arbitrary" authority of kings while inviting a prince to use it to revive the assemblies of the "nation" and restore its nobility to preeminence.

But in taking leave of Boulainvilliers and in bringing this history of his career to a close, it is suitable to remember that he did indeed seek to write an *oeuvre* and that other histories of it may be written. He imagined that his works represented to their readers the consistent views of a single author. Seeking to assert royal authority in one work, he remembered that he had denounced "despotic authority" in another (see chapter 4). Writing on Capetian France in his "Lettres sur les parlements," he claimed to be continuing "what I already wrote on the history of the first two families of our kings" (in the "Mémoires historiques," see chapter 5). Dominant features of his historical thought have emerged repeatedly in the preceding pages, devoted though they were to a closely contextualist reading of his writings in French history. Despite the antifeudalisms to which he was susceptible, he sustained his admiration for the feudal order from the beginning of his career to the end. Despite the hopes for

---

[11]Christian Jouhaud, *Mazarinades: La Fronde des mots* (Paris: Aubier, 1985).

the French "nation" and nobility that he vested in princes, he never ceased to believe that the French monarchy was a pernicious novelty. Consistently, he sought to locate in the fourteenth and fifteenth centuries a momentous historical watershed dividing a modern and monarchical France from an older France in which "feudal" or "mixed government" still survived. In short, throughout his career he propounded a thesis: that the French monarchy was a "despotism," that this "despotism" was modern, and that it was built on the ruins of a nobiliaire civic order which decayed with the demise of "feudal government." This was the thesis of a pessimistic and nostalgic reactionary. His efforts to believe in the magnanimity of French princes in order to pin his hopes on them and write history for them must have been costly efforts indeed.

Boulainvilliers' nostalgia for a nobiliaire civism that he associated with "feudal government" situates him in other, longer histories apart from his own efforts to write for princes. The most celebrated, of course, is the controversy about the legendary Frankish Conquest and what Boulainvilliers took to be its consequences: the Franks' enserfment of the inhabitants of Roman Gaul, and the exclusive liberty that they claimed for themselves by the sword and transmitted to their putative descendants, the old nobility. An early critic of Boulainvilliers—who may have written while Boulainvilliers still lived—deplored his "design . . . to exalt to excess the state and glory of three or four thousand persons in this nation, and to lower all the rest into servitude and the deepest baseness," and this complaint may be taken as the first contribution to a long and celebrated quarrel.[12] But Boulainvilliers presented yet other faces to his eighteenth-century readers. Just after his death, Nicolas Fréret applauded "the rectitude of his sentiments" and his "love of the common good."[13] A later critic of his ideas on the Frankish Conquest conceded that he was a firm if misguided lover of "liberty."[14] Mid-eighteenth-century ideologues for the Parlement of Paris (an institution Boulainvilliers roundly detested) cited his historical works with sympathy and enthusiasm.[15] Finally, his thesis that the French monarchy was a mod-

---

[12][Abbé de Trianon], "Lettre d'un conseiller du parlement de Rouën au sujet d'un écrit du comte de Boulainvilliers," in Père Desmolets, ed. *Continuation de Mémoires de littérature et d'histoire de M. de Sallengre*, 9 (1730): 107–244, 247–311, esp. 108 (for quotation) and 115 (for an allusion to the regent, who outlived Boulainvilliers only by a year, as a currently reigning prince). On the Frankish Conquest debate, see works cited in chapter 1, notes 13 and 18.

[13]Fréret, "Lettre de M. Fréret," 201–2.

[14]Président [Charles-Jean-François] Hénault, *Histoire critique de l'établissement des français dans les Gaules*, 2 vols. (Paris: F. Buisson, 1801), 2:170 (a posthumous edition of Hénault's reading notes on Boulainvilliers and on his trenchant critic, the abbé Dubos).

[15]See Carcassonne, *Montesquieu et le problème de la constitution au XVIIIe siècle*, 275–78, on [Louis-Adrien Le Paige], *Lettres historiques sur les fonctions essentielles du Parlement*, 2 vols. (Amsterdam: 1753–54).

ern and "despotic" regime built on the ruins of a nobiliaire civic order initiated a debate about ancient republics, "feudal government," and modern monarchies and their despotic proclivities, a debate that engaged the attention of the abbé de Saint-Pierre, the marquis d'Argenson, the abbé de Mably, and, of course, Montesquieu. That debate, it may be argued, embedded French history in larger and larger frameworks of moral and political philosophy until, during the Revolution, Frenchmen seeking to discover pasts that realized humanity's civic possibilities abandoned the French past altogether—a recalcitrant past linked with the nobility and burdened by the ideological claims of "aristocratic" elites that proponents of a nobiliaire civism like Boulainvilliers readily deplored—to celebrate and emulate the republican achievements of antiquity instead.[16] It is not necessary to pursue these suggestions further to conclude that nobiliaire ideologues like Boulainvilliers cannot be confined to the ranks of aristocratic reactionaries, though they certainly belong there. For they were aristocratic constitutionalists too and may even be located in traditions of liberal or civic discourse.[17] These sometimes rebarbative ideologues have yet to be located firmly and fully in the manifold history of French political culture on the eve of the monarchy's crisis of authority at the end of the eighteenth century, but doubtless they belong there.

[16]Hunt, *Politics, Culture, and Class in the French Revolution*, 27.

[17]These discourses—one concerns private rights and their defense and the other concerns public virtue and its realization—should be distinguished although they are not mutually exclusive. See, to begin, the essays collected in Istvan Hont and Michael Ignatieff, eds., *Wealth and Virtue: The Shaping of Political Economy in the Scottish Enlightenment* (Cambridge, Engl.: Cambridge University Press, 1983) and Pocock, *Virtue, Commerce, and History*.

Bibliographical Appendix:

Boulainvilliers' Works on French History

Although Renée Simon published an exhaustive bibliographical essay on Boulainvilliers in 1941, new bibliographical foundations had to be laid for this study.[1] Poor typographical design makes Simon's work difficult to use. Worse, it can be misleading. It lists manuscripts of Boulainvilliers' texts by their titles, although different titles may designate a single work and single works may survive in different versions.[2] And, it will soon be evident, Simon relies on sources lacking the authority she imputed to them. To prepare the present study, consequently, it was necessary to compile a fresh list of extant editions and manuscript copies—there are no autographs—of works by or ascribed to Boulainvilliers and to examine those editions and manuscripts anew. The first task was easy enough, given the abundant and well-indexed library catalogs and bibliographies at the modern scholar's disposal. Rather more laborious was the second task of inspecting manuscripts and editions. Only about half of the extant manuscripts were examined and no systematic collection of variants was attempted. A few weeks' work on that project yielded only copiests' errors, divergent spellings, and diverse word orders in lists of adjectives. I found, however, that several of Boulainvilliers' works survive in more than one version, and that some manuscripts contain useful information for dating texts or for identifying the circumstances in which they were written. This information, along with that contained in other bibliographical sources of the eighteenth century, constitutes the basic "hard" evidence for dating and for ascribing or denying texts to Boulainvilliers. Equally important for mak-

[1] Renée Simon, *A la recherche d'un homme et d'un auteur: Essai de bibliographie des ouvrages du comte de Boulainviller* (Paris: Boivin, 1941).

[2] Simon herself noticed that two basic versions exist of Boulainvilliers' "Dissertation" on the old nobility (Simon, *Henry de Boulainviller*, 76–80).

ing those decisions, however, was the effort to place his works plausibly within a coherent account of his career as client, counselor, and would-be controversialist. At this point the bibliographer's task fused with the historian's.

This five-part appendix collects and reviews the bibliographical information used to select the texts and editions employed in the preceding chapters. Part 1 examines the problems surrounding any effort to define the Boulainvilliers corpus. Here, in the course of an attempt to determine what happened to Boulainvilliers' manuscripts after he died, it will be possible to identify and assess the eighteenth-century bibliographical sources at the modern bibliographer's and historian's disposal. Part 2 lists manuscripts and (with certain exceptions to be treated in part 5) editions of the texts examined in the body of this book. In addition, manuscripts of ancillary texts (notably, reading notes and extracts made by Boulainvilliers preparatory to composing his historical writings) will be listed and described. Part 3 concerns texts whose traditional ascription to Boulainvilliers is rejected. Part 4 treats a collection of memoranda for the duc d'Orléans which may not all be by Boulainvilliers. Part 5 reports on editions of Boulainvilliers' major historical writings and explains the selection of editions used in this book.

1. Bibliographical Problems: Defining a Boulainvilliers Corpus

In her effort to identify and list Boulainvilliers' writings, Renée Simon relied on a number of sources. Among them were the comments of Nicolas Fréret and Mathieu Marais—reasonable choices, as Boulainvilliers knew these men and let them see his manuscripts.[3] But Simon attached still greater value to three other sources. One was a library sale catalog compiled in 1747 for the liquidation of the estate of Boulainvilliers' son-in-law Gabriel Bernard de Rieux.[4] The two other sources were identical manuscripts at the Bibliothèque de l'Arsenal in Paris listing works said to be Boulainvilliers'. One manuscript is entitled "Catalogue des ouvrages de M. le comte de Boulainvilliers fait par luy même."[5] The other is untitled but according to the Bibliothèque de

---

[3]See Fréret, "Lettre de M. Fréret", 201, 203. (Fréret wrote this letter just after Boulainvilliers' death; see chapter 1, n. 3); Marais, *Journal et mémoires*, 2:212–14.

[4]*Catalogue des livres de la bibliothèque de feu Monsieur le président Bernard de Rieux* (Paris: Barrois, 1747) (B.N., *cotes* Δ 3386, Δ 9897, Δ 10948, Δ 48699 [copy used here]).

[5]Bibliothèque de l'Arsenal (Paris), MS. 7464, fols. 65–66 (no. 26). Hereafter Bibliothèque is abbreviated Bibl.

l'Arsenal's catalog was written by one Isaac Milsonneau.[6] Simon relied on the Bernard de Rieux sale catalog because she supposed, on no clear evidence, that Bernard de Rieux and his wife purchased Boulainvilliers' library after Boulainvilliers died.[7] Simon relied on the Arsenal lists because she held, again on no clear evidence, that Boulainvilliers compiled them sometime between 1705 and 1710.[8] In fact these documents are not what Simon thought they were.

The Arsenal lists are manifestly not Boulainvilliers', not even the one said to be his.[9] Boulainvilliers could not have listed manuscript copies of a single work, or of its parts, as if they were entirely distinct compositions.[10] Nor could he have listed Leibniz's "Principes de la nature et de la grâce" as his own. Indeed, that work's inclusion in the Arsenal lists puzzled Simon.[11] She might have found some other titles on the Arsenal lists equally puzzling, among them the "Astronomie phisique [sic]." In her book on Boulainvilliers, Simon devoted considerable space to that theoretical and experimental effort to introduce weight into a Cartesian vortex theory of the solar system, but in 1722, Nicolas Fréret wrote that the "system on weight" (the "système de la pesanteur") was not Boulainvilliers'. Unaccountably, Simon ignored that remark.[12] Far more understandable is Simon's willingness to believe that Boulainvilliers wrote the two Paracelsan tracts listed in the Arsenal manuscripts (an "Extrait des Archidoxes de Paracelse" and the "Avant propos pour entendre la doctrine de Paracelse"), for in a letter to his elder son written in 1700 he confessed his youthful passion for "chemistry."[13] Had Simon located manuscripts of those Paracelsan tracts—they survive, though she thought them lost—she would have recognized them as works written not by Boulainvilliers but by his friend, the Italian astrologer and alchemist Francesco Maria Pompeo Colonna.[14] Clearly, Simon erred when

[6]Ibid., MS. 7463, fol. 251 (Recueil de Valentin Conrart et de Milsonneau); *Catalogue général des manuscrits des bibliothèques publiques de France: Paris: Bibliothèque de l'Arsenal*, 10 vols. (Paris: Plon, 1885–92), 6:420.

[7]Simon, *Henry de Boulainviller*, 41.

[8]Simon, *A la Recherche*, 7–8.

[9]The lists are reproduced in ibid., 20–24.

[10]For example, an "Hist. universelle. F°. 2 vols.," an "abregé de l'hist. Universelle, 4°.," an "hist. de l'ancienne Grece," and an "hist. des Iers hommes et des Patriarches" are all references to a single work or to parts of it: Boulainvilliers' ancient history (for which see Simon, *Henry de Boulainviller*, 256–320).

[11]Simon, *A la Recherche*, 22.

[12]Simon, *Henry de Boulainviller*, 590–630. Cf. Fréret, "Lettre de M. Fréret," 204: "The *système de la pesanteur* is not his [Boulainvilliers'] but the late M. Gardien's, whose paper had been placed in the hands of the younger M. Cassini. M. de Boulainvilliers simply expanded and clarified the writing of this latter."

[13]Boulainvilliers, *Oeuvres philosophiques*, 2:147 (a 1700 letter to his elder son, prefixed to his 1683 Helmontian treatise, "Idée d'un système général de la nature").

[14]Compare "Extrait des Archidoxes de Paracelse avec un préface sur les principes de

she supposed that the Arsenal lists were Boulainvilliers' authoritative catalogs of his own writings.

Simon erred again when she assumed that the 1747 Rieux library sale catalog listed manuscripts of Boulainvilliers' works which Rieux and his wife had purchased from Boulainvilliers' estate after his death. No records concerning the settlement of Boulainvilliers' estate support that supposition. On January 25, 1722 (two days after Boulainvilliers' death), the duc d'Orléans, regent of France, ordered the dead man's heirs to send his autograph manuscripts on "history and other sciences" to Paris for inspection. Obeying that order, Boulainvilliers' sons-in-law went to his Norman château at Saint-Saire where, aided by his domestics, they tried to identify manuscripts in his own hand and pack them up for the prince. On January 29, two large boxes were ready for shipment to Paris.[15] What then happened to Boulainvilliers' manuscripts can only be a matter of conjecture.[16] On May 22, 1722, his heirs had his "titles and papers together with all the books composing the library" at Saint-Saire sent to Paris to be inventoried.[17] But manuscripts of Boulainvilliers' works were not among them. His postmortem inventory enumerates the contents of his library and describes his family and estate papers, but makes no mention of his manuscript writings.[18] Indeed, in the records, there is only one further mention of only one of Boulainvilliers' works: in August 1722, according to the *procès verbal de mise sous scellés*, Boulainvilliers' heirs chose not to sell his family history (the "memoirs on the houses of Crouÿ and Boulainviller bound together in one large volume") but rather to assign it to his elder daughter after having a copy made for the younger.[19] No record evidence, therefore, authorizes the suppositions that Boulainvilliers' younger daughter and her husband bought the dead man's manuscripts and, consequently, that the Bernard de Rieux library sale catalog lists those manuscripts fully and accurately.

---

l'art chimique" (Bibl. de l'Arsenal [Paris], MS. 2899) with [Francesco Maria Pompeo Colonna], *Abrégé de la doctrine de Paracelse, et de ses Archidoxes. Avec une explication de la nature des principes de chymie* (Paris: d'Houry fils, 1724). On Colonna see Costa, "Un Collaboratore italiano del conte di Boulainviller," esp. 219–23, on Colonna's and Boulainvilliers' association.

[15]A.N., Y.10976, [fols. 3–5v]; Simon, *Henry de Boulainviller*, 40–41, who mistook this *procès verbal de mise sous scellés* for a postmortem inventory. For that document (unknown to Simon, who wrote before the opening of the A.N.'s Minutier Central des Notaires Parisiens) see n. 18.

[16]No records confirm the picturesque story, which circulated later in the eighteenth century, that a friend of Boulainvilliers' went to Saint-Saire to hold off at pistol point the men the regent had sent to fetch Boulainvilliers' manuscripts to Paris. See Simon, *Henry de Boulainviller*, 39–40, citing a now destroyed MS "Moréri des normands" from B.M., Caen.

[17]A.N., Y.10976, [fol. 17v].

[18]A.N., M.C., XIV, 255 (February 13, 1722), under the dates July 18, 20, and 21 (library), and July 31 to September 12 (family and estate papers).

[19]A.N., Y.10976, under the dates August 1 and 3; Simon, *Henry de Boulainviller*, 41–42.

To the degree that Simon's account of the Boulainvilliers corpus depends on the sources just considered, it cannot inspire confidence. But these sources, like others now to be considered, are indeed documentary traces left by Boulainvilliers' manuscripts—manuscripts of his own works and of works by other authors in his possession and later ascribed to him—as they passed from library to library across the eighteenth century. All these sources can assist the bibliographer or historian, provided that one appreciates their character and the fact that they owe their existence not to an author or to a conscientious bibliographer but rather to lawyers and booksellers engaged in liquidating the estates of wealthy collectors of books and manuscripts.

The historian seems to lose track of Boulainvilliers' manuscripts very soon after his death. Indirect evidence suggests that eventually they found their way into the hands of Samuel Bernard, the fabulously wealthy and influential banker who helped finance Louis XIV's War of the Spanish Succession.[20] Boulainvilliers may not have been one of Bernard's many aristocratic debtors, but the two men did know each other.[21] In 1719 Boulainvilliers' younger daughter married Bernard's younger son, the Gabriel Bernard de Rieux whose library sale catalog Simon used in her bibliographical essay.[22] Although Bernard's testament makes no mention of his library and his postmortem inventory is now lost, numerous manuscripts of works by Boulainvilliers or attributed to him bear Bernard's arms handsomely embossed on their leather bindings.[23] It is inviting to suppose, therefore, that Boulainvilliers' manuscripts eventually found their way into Bernard's library.

[20]On Bernard, his career, and his family see Victor de Swarte, *Un Banquier du Trésor Royal au XVIIIe siècle: Samuel Bernard, sa vie, sa correspondance (1651–1739)* (Paris: Berger-Levrault, 1893); the vicomte de Bonald, *Samuel Bernard, banquier du Trésor Royal et sa descendance* (Rodez: 1912); E. de Clermont-Tonnerre, *Histoire de Samuel Bernard et de ses enfans* (Paris: Honoré Champion, 1914); and Jacques Saint-Germain, *Samuel Bernard, le banquier des rois* (Paris: Hachette, 1960).

[21]For a list of Bernard's debtors (it may not be complete) see Saint-Germain, *Samuel Bernard,* 271–72.

[22]Clermont-Tonnerre, *Histoire de Samuel Bernard,* 155–61.

[23]On the testament see ibid., 119–32; Saint-Germain, *Samuel Bernard,* 83. The postmortem inventory should be but is not in A.N., M.C., LXXXXVIII, 564 (January 27, 1739). Examples of manuscripts with Bernard's arms embossed on the bindings: "Opuscules politiques, par M. le comte de Boulainvilliers" (Bibliothèque de la Faculté de Droit [Bibliothèque Cujas, Paris], MSS. 13–15); "Extraits de lectures de M. le comte de Boulainviller, avec des réflexions" (B.N., MSS. n.a.f. 11071–76); "Extrait de l'Introduction à l'histoire de France de Mr. l'abbé de Longuerue" (B.N., MS. n.a.f. 11077); Antoine Aubery's "Journals" of the reigns of French kings from Louis IX to Louis XI, with Boulainvilliers' "Préface critique au Journal du règne de Louis IX" and annotations (B.N., MSS. n.a.f. 11078–89); "Extrait de l'Histoire de France de Mézeray par M.r le comte de Boulainviller" (B.N., MSS. n.a.f. 11090–94); "Extrait des Archidoxes de Paracelse, avec une préface sur les principes de l'art chimique" (Bibliothèque de l'Arsenal [Paris], MS. 2899); transcribed documents concerning meetings of the Estates General and the Assem-

Admittedly, that supposition is open to criticism, for no extant manuscripts of Boulainvilliers' works, not even those bearing Samuel Bernard's arms, are autographs that may be identified with the manuscripts packed up at Boulainvilliers' château in 1722 and sent to the regent. Even those manuscripts may not have been autographs, however, because to assemble them Boulainvilliers' sons-in-law relied not on his secretary (one Estienne de Mortemer, whom they left behind in Paris) but rather on "officers and domestics" at the château.[24] Those manuscripts, therefore, may have been nothing more than fair copies prepared by a secretary whose hand resembled Boulainvilliers' and therefore easily mistaken for autographs.[25]

There is, moreover, further evidence supporting the hypothesis that Samuel Bernard acquired Boulainvilliers' manuscripts. In 1739 one of the executors of Bernard's estate was the Parisian lawyer Isaac Milsonneau—the same Milsonneau who drafted one of the Arsenal lists of Boulainvilliers (and pseudo-Boulainvilliers) manuscripts considered earlier.[26] Very likely the harried lawyer prepared it because those manuscripts constituted a valuable collection in the dead banker's library, one that could have had appreciable monetary value.

It does not appear that Bernard's library was sold, however. No catalog listing its contents for sale survives. Such catalogs do exist for the libraries of his two sons, however; both lists are rich in Boulainvilliers manuscripts very likely acquired from their father's library after his death. The Bernard de Rieux catalog lists ten manuscripts of works by or attributed to Boulainvilliers.[27] Richer still are the sale catalogs for the books and manuscripts of Bernard de Rieux's elder brother, Samuel-Jacques Bernard, comte de Coubert, who died in 1753. The final pages of these catalogs list no less than twenty-eight manuscripts of works by or attributed to Boulainvilliers.[28]

---

bly of Notables from 1355 to 1627 (B.M., Rouen, MSS. 1875–87); "L'Astronomie phisique" (University of Minnesota Wilson Library [Minneapolis]. MS. Z 520 qB 663). For Samuel Bernard's arms see Saint-Germain, *Samuel Bernard*, 21; and Eugène Olivier, Georges Hermal, and R. de Roton, *Manuel de l'amateur de reliures armoriées françaises*, 30 vols. (Paris: C. Bosse 1924–38), vol. 10, plates 1042, 1043, 1044 (reproducing, respectively, Samuel Bernard's arms, those of his older son Samuel-Jacques Bernard de Coubert, and those of Boulainvilliers' younger daughter, Suzanne-Henriette-Marie de Boulainvilliers de Bernard de Rieux). Library catalogs often mistake Bernard's arms for Boulainvilliers'.
[24]A.N., Y.10976, [fols. 1r, 4r–v].
[25]Compare the MSS cited in n. 23 with Boulainvilliers' hand in the letter reproduced in Simon, *Henry de Boulainviller*, between pp. 112 and 113.
[26]Clermont-Tonnerre, *Histoire de Samuel Bernard*, 121.
[27]*Catalogue des livres de . . . Bernard de Rieux*, 264, 299, and 321, for items 1272, 2216, 2363, 2530, 2859, 2860, 2862, 2865, 2866, 3062.
[28]See *Catalogue des livres de feu M. Bernard, conseiller d'état, dont la vente commencera lundy*

Bernard de Coubert's manuscripts found a wealthy purchaser in the Parisian parlementaire Barthélemy-Antoine Nouveau de Chennevières, who outbid even Louis-Philippe, duc d'Orléans (the regent's grandson) to acquire them.[29] And when Nouveau's library went on the market twenty years later, its sale catalog inevitably featured Boulainvilliers manuscripts.[30] Indeed, the bookseller in charge of selling Nouveau's library called public attention to the Boulainvilliers manuscripts in the catalog's *avertissement*. He misconstrued the exact connections between the Boulainvilliers and Bernard families. And he misrepresented the provenance of the Boulainvilliers manuscripts in the Bernard de Coubert library that Nouveau had purchased. But the bookseller deftly used the Boulainvilliers manuscripts to excite interest.[31]

He was successful. Henri-Léonard-Jean-Baptiste Bertin, the reform-

---

18 mars, 1754, & continuera les jours suivans, depuis deux heures de relevée jusqu'au soir, en son hôtel, rue du Bacq (Paris: Barrois, 1754) (B.N., *cotes* Q 7781, Δ 284, Δ 10909, Δ 48738); and above all the separate sales catalog for Bernard de Coubert's MSS sold in 1756, *Catalogue des manuscrits de la bibliothèque de feu M. Bernard, conseiller d'état, ordinaire, &c.* (Paris: Barrois, 1756) (B.N., *cotes* Δ 283, Δ 287, Δ 4161(8), Δ 11103), 28–30.

[29]See *Catalogue des manuscrits . . . de feu M. Bernard* (B.N., *cote* Δ 287), 2, for a MS note that Orléans offered Bernard de Coubert's creditors 20,000 *livres* for his manuscripts, but Nouveau offered them 26,000.

[30]*Catalogue des livres imprimés et manuscrits de la bibliothèque de feu M. Nouveau, chevalier, seigneur de Chennevieres & autres lieux, ancien conseiller au Parlement. Dont la vente, qui se fera rue neuve Saint-Paul, commencera le lundi 21 février, & jours suivans de relevée sans interruption* (Paris: Debure, 1774) (B.N., *cote* Δ 3030), 23, 42–44, 62, 64–67, 75, 77–78, 84, 88–89, 91, 93, 95, for 28 MSS of works by or attributed to Boulainvilliers. There are yet other entries for works by Boulainvilliers but not ascribed to him here.

[31]Ibid., iii:
The library whose catalog we present here will doubtless arouse the curiosity of book lovers [*Amateurs*], thanks principally to the great number of interesting and priceless manuscripts which compose it. Monsieur Nouveau de Chennevières, a former councillor in the Parlement, a magistrate as honest as he was enlightened, had acquired the entire collection of manuscripts in the library of Monsieur Bernard de Boulainvilliers [sic]. The importance and the merit of that fine collection are already known to the public, thanks to the catalog that the late Monsieur Barrois, our colleague [and] celebrated bibliographer, published in 1756. . . . One can only consider it the complete collection, or the most complete collection known of the works of Monsieur le comte de Boulainvilliers. We presume that Monsieur Bernard, son-in-law of that famous man, had collected with the greatest possible care all his works and had them carefully copied.
The author, nephew of the esteemed eighteenth-century book expert Guillaume François De Bure, claimed to be a scientific and methodical bibliographer in his own right (ibid., iii–iv; cf. Guillaume-François De Bure, *Bibliographie instructive: ou Traité de la connoissance des livres rares et singuliers,* 7 vols. (Paris: Guillaume-François Debure le Jeune, 1763–68), but his casual attention to biographical information and to the details of a library's provenance inspire doubts. It is obvious that the author confused Bernard de Coubert with his younger brother Bernard de Rieux, for Rieux, not Coubert, was Boulainvilliers' son-in-law. It should also be observed that the author confused Bernard de Coubert with Rieux's son—Bernard de Rieux, marquis de Boulainvilliers—who lived into the 1790s (see works cited, n. 20).

ing comptroller-general of France, bought the entire Nouveau de Chennevières collection for just under 34,000 *livres* (the manuscripts alone
cost him 28,000).[32] And when Bertin sought to dispose of his own
collection in May 1797, the sale catalog listed Boulainvilliers manuscripts once again.[33] With the sale of Bertin's collection, unfortunately,
one loses track of the Boulainvilliers manuscripts.[34]

Since Boulainvilliers' manuscripts seem to have fallen into Comptroller-General Bertin's possession, it may be tempting to speculate
about the uses to which he put them. In the later eighteenth century,
competing authorities in the Old Regime amassed "ideological arsenals"
of historical documents for political battle. Presiding over ministerial
efforts to establish the Dépôt des Chartes under Jacob-Nicolas Moreau
was none other than Comptroller-General Bertin himself.[35]

Here, however, it is enough to observe that the hypothesis just argued—that Boulainvilliers' manuscripts entered the libraries of Samuel
Bernard and his sons to pass later into the hands of Nouveau de Chennevières and Comptroller-General Bertin—can be tested by the careful
use of the Arsenal lists and the sale catalogs for the Bernard de Rieux,
Bernard de Coubert, Nouveau de Chennevières, and Bertin collections
in defining the corpus of Boulainvilliers' historical writings. These docu-

[32]Lelong, *Bibliothèque historique de la France* (ed. Fevret de Fontette), 4:389. For the price
paid see *Catalogue des livres imprimés et manuscrits de la bibliothèque de feu M. Nouveau*, 95 (MS
note in the B.N.'s copy, *cote* Δ 3030).

[33]See *Catalogue d'une précieuse collection de manuscrits sur l'histoire de France, au nombre
d'environ 2,000 volumes, et de quelques livres imprimés* (Paris: Lamy, "An Cinquième" [1797])
(B.N., *cote* Δ 4865), 11–14 for items 156, 173, 187, 197, 199, 201, which are identified as
Boulainvilliers'; other items listed (it will soon be evident) may also be associated with him.

[34]A nineteenth-century writer suggested that the Jariel de Forges library, sold in 1810,
included books and manuscripts originally Boulainvilliers'. See M. Michaud, *Biographie
universelle ancienne et moderne*, 45 vols. (Paris: Desplace, 1843–65), 5:224 n.; and *Notice de
livres rares et précieux, formant environ 2500 volumes, provenant de la bibliothèque de feu M. Jariel
de Forges, quai de Béthune, n° 26, île Saint-Louis, à Paris: Dont la vente se fera le 15 octobre et
jours suivans, à cinq heures précises de relevée* ([Paris: 1810]). The cover of the B.N.'s copy
of this catalog bears a manuscript note that also asserts that the Jariel collection included
Boulainvilliers' collection. In fact Jariel's library, rich in literature on the occult, dwarfed
Boulainvilliers' little collection of a few hundred titles of which only a handful were on the
occult (for Boulainvilliers' library see his postmortem inventory, cited in n. 18). But cf. [A.-
A. Barbier], *Examen critique et complément des dictionaires historiques les plus répandus, depuis le
Dictionnaire de Moréri, jusqu'à la Biographie universelle inclusivement*, I (A–J) (Paris: Rey et
Gravier, 1820), 145. Barbier denied that the Jariel catalog was of any use for bibliogra-
phers interested in Boulainvilliers, and (ignoring the utility of the Bertin sale catalog) he
pronounced the Nouveau de Chennevières catalog the last reliable source for defining the
Boulainvilliers corpus.

[35]On "ideological arsenals" see Keith Michael Baker, "Memory and Practice: Politics and
the Representation of the Past in Eighteenth-Century France," *Representations*, 11 (1985):
135–43. Bertin's efforts as Moreau's superior and patron may be followed in Dieter
Gembicki, *Histoire et politique à la fin de l'Ancien Régime: Jacob-Nicolas Moreau (1717–1803)*
(Paris: Nizet, 1979).

ments have their limits, because their authors were executors of estates and sellers of libraries chiefly concerned to dispose of books and manuscripts, not to identify them as accurately as possible. Nevertheless, it will soon be apparent that these documents can be used profitably by the bibliographer interested in Boulainvilliers. It is ironic, perhaps, that his manuscripts probably found their way into the hands of men belonging to the financial, parlementaire, and ministerial elites of eighteenth-century Paris, elites whose preeminence Boulainvilliers deplored. But the historian and bibliographer seeking to define the Boulainvilliers corpus can only be grateful for the avidity with which these wealthy men amassed their prestigious collections of books, and for the efforts of Parisian booksellers to catalog and sell them.

2. Boulainvilliers' Historical Writings

What follows is an annotated bibliography of Boulainvilliers' historical writings arranged chronologically. For each text all manuscripts in Parisian, provincial, and finally foreign repositories are cited, and an asterisk (*) identifies each manuscript actually consulted. With certain exceptions that will be indicated, all editions of each text are cited. Information on dating is given here, unless already given in the preceding chapters (to which the reader is referred when necessary).

Among Boulainvilliers' earliest works on French history (works examined in chapter 2) is his family history, which has a prefatory "Dissertation" on France's old nobility prefixed to it. Two or perhaps three copies of the family history circulated in the eighteenth century.[36] Today, unfortunately, there survive only manuscript notes and extracts prepared in the eighteenth and early nineteenth centuries.

[36]Even before Boulainvilliers' death the existence of the family history was public knowledge, announced in 1719 in the first edition of Père Lelong's historical bibliography (Lelong, *Bibliothèque historique de la France* [1719 ed.], 845). When Boulainvilliers died three years later, the family history, bound in "one large volume," passed to his elder daughter after his younger daughter (married to Bernard de Rieux) had a copy prepared for herself (see n. 19). That second copy may have remained in the Bernard de Rieux family to the end of the eighteenth century. It does not appear among the manuscripts listed in the sale catalog of Bernard de Rieux's library. Moreover, a mid- or late-eighteenth-century genealogist working on the history of the Croy family thought Boulainvilliers' family history an essential work to consult and declared it to be in the possession of Bernard de Rieux's son, who called himself the marquis de Boulainvilliers (B.N., MS. f.f. 29770 [Dossiers bleus, 225, Croy]). There may have been yet a third copy of Boulainvilliers' genealogical history, however: a three-volume copy that may be traced in the library sale catalogs of Bernard de Coubert, Nouveau de Chennevières, and Comptroller-General Bertin. It is possible, however, that this three-volume copy was the copy originally made for Boulainvilliers' younger daughter.

Boulainvilliers' Family History: Manuscript Notes and Extracts

*A.N., M.353(2²⁴) (short résumé).
*B.N., MS. f.f. 29664 (Dossiers bleus, 119), fols. 124–132v.
*B.N., MS. f.f. 32948 (Cabinet des titres).
*B.M., Amiens, MSS. 811–12 (early-nineteenth-century reading notes).
*B.M., Toulouse, MS. 598(II 31) (detailed notes and verbatim extracts dating the work to 1700).
Boulainvilliers' "Dissertation," however, may be consulted in several editions and in numerous manuscripts.

Boulainvilliers' "Dissertation" on the Old Nobility: Editions

Essais.
"Traité sur l'origine et les droits de la noblesse," in Père Desmolets, ed., *Continuation des mémoires de littérature et d'histoire de M. de Sallengre,* 9 (1730): 3–106.
"Dissertation sur la noblesse françoise servant de préface aux mémoires de la maison de Croï et Boulainviller," in André Devyver, *Le Sang épuré: Les préjugés de race chez les gentilshommes français de l'Ancien Régime (1560–1720)* (Brussels: Editions de l'Université de Bruxelles, 1973), 501–48.

Boulainvilliers' "Dissertation" on the Old Nobility: Manuscripts

 B.N., MS. Clairambault 929.
 B.N., MS. f.f. 1228.
*B.N., MS. f.f. 7508.
 B.N., MS. f.f. 7535.
 B.N., MS. f.f. 7536.
 B.N., MS. f.f. 8195.
 B.N., MS. f.f. 11467.
*B.N., MS. f.f. 32948 (Cabinet des titres, incomplete copy).
 B.N., MS. n.a.f. 1513.
*B.N., MS. n.a.f. 9813.
*Bibl. de l'Ecole Supérieure de Guerre (Paris), MS. 26.
*Bibl. de l'Institut (Paris), MS. 741.
*Bibl. du Sénat (Paris), MS. 984.
*Bibl. Mazarine (Paris), MS. 3060.
*B.M., Bordeaux, MS. 828.
*B.M., Nantes, MS. 1822.
 B.M., Vire, MS. 50.
 B.M., Vire, MS. 51.

Least satisfactory of the editions is that of Père Desmolets, which omits important opening paragraphs in which Boulainvilliers addressed his sons. The entirety of the text printed by Père Desmolets may be consulted in *Essais*. That edition, however, differs considerably from Devyver's. Most obvious are the subtitles, footnotes, and appendixes in *Essais*, all added to the text by the editor. More important, however, are textual differences which Devyver imputed to the carelessness of Boulainvilliers' eighteenth-century editors. Devyver based his own edition solidly on manuscripts.[37] But his claim that Boulainvilliers' Old Regime editors did not is false. Most of the manuscripts consulted contain the text that Devyver printed, but three (the Ecole Supériere de Guerre, Nantes, and Bordeaux manuscripts) contain texts that partly conform to the Old Regime editions. Two manuscripts (the Cabinet des titres and Mazarine manuscripts) reproduce it perfectly. And one of these (the Cabinet des titres manuscript) dates its version of the text to 1700. As Boulainvilliers is known to have revised his works and let them circulate in their various states, it is reasonable to suppose that his eighteenth-century editors printed the "Dissertation" as written in 1700 for his sons, whereas Devyver published a different version prepared at some other time.[38] The Devyver version, moreover, is probably the later version, because the substantial differences between it and the eighteenth-century editions all turn on the history of allods, benefices, and fiefs in pre-Capetian France: a history (it is argued in the body of this work) that Boulainvilliers sought to rethink under the impact of reading Jean Le Laboureur's "Traité" or "Histoire de la pairie de France."[39]

Boulainvilliers' notes on Le Laboureur—the "Extrait d'un manuscrit de M. l'abbé de Le Laboureur intitulé: De l'Origine de la Pairie de France"—survive in two manuscripts.

Boulainvilliers' Notes on Le Laboureur: Manuscripts

*B.N., MS. f.f. 7504.
*B.N., MS. f.f. 7508, fols. 1–55v.

Boulainvilliers wrote his history of Merovingian and Carolingian France (the "Mémoires historiques") for the duc de Bourgogne and the men around him. That text was part of a bulky preface to a still bulkier

---

[37]Devyver, *Le Sang épuré*, 498–99. The MSS Devyver used are B.M., Angoulême, MS. 23, and B.N., n.a.f., MSS. 1513 and 9813.

[38]Moréri et al., *Le Grand Dictionnaire historique*, 2:133.

[39]See various editions in and after 1740, some erroneously ascribed to Boulainvilliers; that used here is [Le Laboureur], *Histoire de la Pairie de France et du Parlement de Paris* (1745).

compilation, that is, Boulainvilliers' abridgments of the celebrated intendants' reports of 1697–1700. The entire project got into print in 1727 as the *Etat de la France*. This was the first of several editions published in the eighteenth century, although numerous manuscripts also survive which reproduce all or part of the collection, and which must be consulted along with the (in fact faulty) editions. Since questions of textual authenticity and dating are central to a historical account of Boulainvilliers' work for the duc de Bourgogne's circle, they are examined in chapter 3. Here it suffices to list editions and manuscripts.

Boulainvilliers' Etat de la France: *Editions*

Etat, I and II.

Histoire de l'ancien gouvernement de la France, avec XIV. Lettres historiques sur les parlements ou états généraux de la France, 3 vols. (Amsterdam and The Hague: 1727), 1:1–168 (an abridged edition of the "Mémoires historiques").

See Part 5.

Boulainvilliers' Prefatory "Discours sur les intendants": Manuscripts

*B.M., Dijon, MS. 682 (409[1]).
*B.M., Angoulême, MS. 23, pp. 241–306.

Boulainvilliers' "Mémoires Historiques": Manuscripts

*A.N., MM.959.
*B.N., MS. f.f. 6489.
*B.N., MS. f.f. 6490.
*B.N., MS. f.f. 13613.
*B.N., MSS. f.f. 13614–17.
*B.N., MS. f.f. 14330,
*B.N., MSS. f.f. 22194–95.
  Bibl. de l'Arsenal (Paris), MSS. 3420–21.
  Bibl. de l'Université de Paris (Sorbonne), MS. 340.
*Bibl. du Sénat (Paris), MSS. 256–57.
*Bibl. du Sénat (Paris), MS. 258.
*Bibl. Mazarine (Paris), MSS. 1977–78.
*Bibl. Mazarine (Paris), MSS. 3179–80.
  Bibl. du Musée Condé, Chantilly, MS. 1102.
  B.M., Angoulême, MS. 26.
  B.M., Beauvais, MSS. 4–5.

B.M., Lisieux, MS. 15.
B.M., Nancy, MS. 620(191), vol. 2.
B.M., Rouen, MSS. 1167–68 (U.89).
B.M., Saint-Brieuc, MS. 77.
B.M., Sémur, MS. 59.
B.M., Sens, MSS. 231–32.
B.M., Sens, MSS. 266–67.
B.M., Troyes, MS. 1288.
B.M., Vitry-le-François, MS. 89.

Boulainvilliers' Abridgments of the Intendants' Reports: Manuscripts

*A.N., MM.960–75.
*A.N., MM.976–86.
*B.N., MSS. f.f. 8137–40.
*B.N., MSS. f.f. 13588–13612.
*B.N., MSS. f.f. 14331–34.
*B.N., MSS. n.a.f. 2031–36.
 Bibl. de l'Arsenal (Paris), MSS. 7162–65.
 B.M., Angers, MS. 969 (incomplete copy).
 B.M., Angoulême, MSS. 16–21.

Boulainvilliers' Extracts on Nobility from the Intendants' Reports: Manuscript

Bibl. de l'Ecole de Médecine de Montpellier, MS. H.193.

The editions and manuscripts just enumerated all reproduce texts examined in the body of this study. Others now to be listed contain Boulainvilliers' reading notes on François Eudes de Mézeray's *Histoire de France* and on the chronological dissertations of the learned abbé de Longuerue. These notes constitute nothing less than the sources for the bulk of Boulainvilliers' narrative in the "Mémoires historiques." Although they were not examined in the body of this study, these reading notes merit attention here.

Boulainvilliers' Reading Notes on Mézeray: Editions

Etat . . . Tome III, 190–501 (for new emissions of this edition later in the eighteenth century see Part 5).
Abrégé chronologique de l'histoire de France, par M. le c^{te} de Boulainvilliers, 3 vols. (The Hague: Gesse & Neaulme, 1733).
An Historical Account of the Antient Parliaments of France, or States-General of the Kingdom. In Fourteen Letters . . . to which is added a Chronological

Abridgment of the History of France under the Reigns of the Kings of the First Race, tr. Charles Forman, esq., 2 vols. (London: J. Brindley, 1739), 2:291–364.

An Accurate tho' Compendious History of the Ancient Parliaments of France. Compriz'd in Fourteen Letters . . . , together with a Chronological Abstract of the History of France from its First Foundation, tr. Charles Forman, esq., 2 vols. (London: J. Brindley, 1754), 2:291–364 (new emission of the preceding).

Boulainvilliers' Reading Notes on Mézeray: Manuscripts

*B.N., MSS. n.a.f. 11090–94.
*Bibl. du Ministère de la Guerre (Paris), MSS. 612–17.
Bibl. Albert I (Brussels), MS. 6964.

Boulainvilliers' Reading Notes on Longuerue: Manuscripts

*B.N., MS. n.a.f. 11077 (an unfortunately misbound copy).
B.M., Aix, MS. 397.
Bibl. Royale (Brussels), MS. 1743.

Despite official dissatisfaction with the work and its author, François Eudes de Mézeray's *Histoire de France*—notably its second edition (1685)—was the authoritative general history of France during most of Boulainvilliers' lifetime. Boulainvilliers read it carefully, preparing on it lengthy and polished notes in prose.[40] It is not surprising, therefore, that the notes could be mistaken for or misrepresented as an original work, as indeed they were in the editions just listed. But one must not be taken in.[41] As some eighteenth-century Frenchmen knew, Boulainvilliers' notes on Mézeray were simply a running abridgment and paraphrase of the original, in which Boulainvilliers only occasionally intervened to criticize the earlier historian.[42] Here, consequently, it is less

[40]At least (in the case of the MSS consulted) up to the reign of Charles VIII, where the notes dissolve into mixtures of grammatical sentences and ungrammatical fragments: see B.N., MS. 11094, at fol. 947, and Bibl. du Ministère de la Guerre, MS. 617, at fol. 119v. And see Mézeray, *Histoire de France,* 2d ed.; and Ranum, *Artisans of Glory,* 223–32.

[41]As was Simon, *Henry de Boulainviller,* 184–94.

[42]For two examples see B.N., MS. n.a.f. 11090, fol. 2v (against Mézeray's decision to begin French history with the legendary Pharamond); B.N., MS. n.a.f. 11091, fols. 161v–163 (against Mézeray's interpretation of Hugh Capet's accession to the throne in 987 as an "election" by a "parlement"—a point of considerable importance to Boulainvilliers). For eighteenth-century Frenchmen who knew that the work published as Boulainvilliers' "Abrégé" of French history was really a set of notes on Mézeray, see B.N., MS. f.f. 21990, fol. 18v (Registre des livres d'impression étrangère présentés pour la permission de débiter 1718–42): in 1731 or 1732 one Morin requested permission to sell in France an "Extrait de Lhist. de France de Mezeray par M. Le Comte de Boulainvilliers"; the censor (none other than Boulainvilliers' posthumous critic, the abbé Jean-Baptiste Du Bos) granted Morin the

important to assess the merits of the several editions just listed than to establish the use Boulainvilliers made of his Mézeray notes in writing his "Mémoires historiques."[43] In effect they furnished the basic narrative text and most of the detail of his "Mémoires historiques." For example, it was from his Mézeray notes that Boulainvilliers derived his account of Charlemagne's discovery of Lombard feudalism in Italy in 774.[44] From those same notes, Boulainvilliers lifted the report that Charlemagne imported Gregorian chant into France in 786, and the assertion that in 790 Charlemagne established the traditional Scottish-French Alliance and invited Alcuin and Clement to Paris to found its university.[45] Such examples need not be multiplied; they simply reveal that in Boulainvilliers' hands the art of historical writing remained what it had been for Mézeray and his predecessors, the compilation of narratives cribbed from the work of earlier writers. Of course, in neither Mézeray's nor Boulainvilliers' cases did this procedure preclude original research and writing.[46] Boulainvilliers' debt to his Mézeray notes was massive, nevertheless, for those notes furnished the narrative armature of his "Mémoires historiques."

When he turned to the details of Frankish antiquity, however, Boulainvilliers had a better scholar to rely upon. The works of the abbé Louis du Four de Longuerue (1652–1733), learned author of careful chronological essays on the Merovingian dynasty, were printed after Boulainvilliers and Longuerue had both died, but the abbé's essays had long since been circulating in learned circles. In 1719 the Oratorian historical bibliographer Jacques Lelong relied on Longuerue to fix the canon, order, and dates of early French kings.[47] Boulainvilliers, too, used Lon-

---

permission he sought, but it was later withdrawn. It follows, then, that the 1733 *Abrégé chronologique* may well have been an illicit Parisian printing of a prohibited book (thus Lelong, *Bibliothèque historique de la France* [ed. Fevret de Fontette], 2:41).

[43]With respect to the editions, it should be noted that their texts differ in length if not in substance. The London editions in French end with Charles VIII's reign, like the MSS consulted. The London editions in English translation, however, end with the fall of the Merovingian dynasty and probably served only to fill out the space of a volume. Finally, the Dutch (or Parisian?) edition of 1733 continues through the reign of Henry IV, which suggests that Boulainvilliers or a later editor recast his fragmentary notes on sixteenth-century history into prose.

[44]Compare Mézeray, *Histoire* (1685 ed.), 1:398; B.N., MS. n.a.f. 11090, fols. 73v–74; *Etat*, 1, "Mémoires historiques": 110.

[45]Compare Mézeray, *Histoire* (1685 ed.), 1:409; B.N., MS. n.a.f. 11090, fol. 77; *Etat*, 1, "Mémoires historiques": 112. And compare Mézeray, *Histoire* (1685 ed.), 1:412–13; B.N., MS. n.a.f. 11090, fols. 78–79v; *Etat*, 1, "Mémoires historiques": 113.

[46]Evans, *L'Historien Mézeray et la conception de l'histoire en France au XVIIe siècle*, 99–108.

[47]Lelong, *Bibliothèque historique de la France* (ed. Fevret de Fontette), 2:69. And see [Louis du Four de] Longuerue, "Introduction à l'histoire de France" (for the years 270–627), in *Recueil de pièces intéressantes pour servir à l'histoire de France, et autres morceaux de littératures rrouvés [sic] dan [sic] les papiers de M. l'abbé de Longuerue* (Geneva: 1769), 97–236; Longuerue, "Annales ab anno sexto Dagoberti I. Christi DCXXVIII. ad annum DCCLIV et

guerue's works, having read and annotated them. His notes may be consulted in the three manuscript copies just listed.[48] And like the Mézeray notes, the Longuerue notes aided Boulainvilliers as he prepared his "Mémoires historiques." Countless details, learned references, and even turns of speech in that work derive from Longuerue, or from Boulainvilliers' notes on Longuerue.[49] Boulainvilliers was no less indebted to Longuerue than to Mézeray.

Indeed, so massive were Boulainvilliers' debts to Mézeray and Longuerue that when one compares his notes on their work with his own "Mémoires historiques" one discovers that not even half of that work's bulk contains original writing by Boulainvilliers.[50]

Boulainvilliers' first work for the duc d'Orléans was a short manuscript memorandum criticizing an earlier (and longer) memorandum by the duc de Saint-Simon: the "Réflexions et considérations sur le mémoire des formalités nécessaires pour valider la renonciation du roi d'Espagne." The text survives in print and in several manuscripts.

Boulainvilliers' "Réflexions et considérations": Edition and Manuscripts

[Chevalier de Piossens], *Mémoires de la Régence: Nouvelle édition, considérablement augmentée*, [ed. Nicolas Lenglet-Dufresnoy], 5 vols. (Amsterdam: 1749), 2:231–88.
  B.N., MS. n.a.f. 7808, fols. 186–201.
*Bibl. de l'Ecole Supérieure de Guerre (Paris), MS. 25, fols. 222–73.
*Bibl. du Sénat (Paris), MS. 987.
*B.M., Angoulême, MS. 23, pp. 307–64.

Pippini regnantis tertium," in *Recueil des historiens des Gaules et de la France*, ed. Dom Martin Bouquet (Paris: Imprimerie Royale, 1741): 3:685–707. See also ibid., 681–84, for Longuerue's "Disquisitio de annis Childerici I. francorum regis" (for the years 445–82).

[48]For some details in the MS consulted it has not been possible to find sources in Longuerue's work; see for example B.N., MS. n.a.f. 11077, fols. 13v–15v. This may indicate that there were several different versions of Longuerue's work in circulation.

[49]For turns of speech one example must suffice: "Theodebert avoit épousé Belichilde que Brunehaut haïssoit à mort . . ." (Longuerue, "Introduction," 223); "Brunehaut haïssoit à mort Bilichilde femme de Theodebert . . ." (B.N., MS. n.a.f. 11070, fol. 112v); "Brunehaut haïssoit avec fureur Belichelde femme de Theodebert . . ." (Boulainvilliers, *Etat*, 1, "Mémoires historiques": 64). For references to chronicles compare Longuerue, "Annales," 702–3, B.N., MS. n.a.f. 11070, fols. 71v–77v; and *Etat*, 1, "Mémoires historiques": 96–99 (under the rubric "Interregne"). Boulainvilliers lifted countless narrative and interpretative details from Longuerue too, for example, the report of the first Frankish attack on the Romans, which was led by Marcomir (compare Longuerue, "Introduction," 100–101; and *Etat*, 1, "Mémoires historiques": 1), or the rejection of the authenticity of the chronicle of Tiro Prosper, the only chronicle to have mentioned Pharamond (compare Longuerue, "Introduction," 101–3; and *Etat*, 1, "Préface": xxvii).

[50]*Etat*, 1, "Mémoires historiques": 11–49, 74–76, 88–89, 93–94, 102–3, 133–35, 117–19, 127–28, 141–46, 150–64, 174–82. The text is 182 pages long.

B.M., Mâcon, MS. 10, fols. 50–67.
B.M., Rouen, MS. 1186 (U.87), fols. 20–85 (second foliation).
B.M., Sens, MS. 228, pp. 106–208.
Bibl. Albert I (Brussels), MS. 6851, pp. 1–57.

All manuscripts consulted conform (with only minor variants) to Leng-let-Dufresnoy's edition. Lenglet misdates the text to 1717, however. As argued in chapter 4, Boulainvilliers wrote his "Réflexions et considé-rations" on the eve of the regency.

Boulainvilliers continued to write memoranda for Orléans after he became regent. Chapter 4 examines two such pieces dating to the beginning of the regency. One urges Orléans to assemble the Estates General. The other asks that he establish a "General Chamber of the Nobility" charged with compiling a "nobiliaire général." The memorandum on calling the Estates survives in manuscript and printed collections which, because they include pieces of doubtful ascription to Boulainvilliers, are examined in Part 4. The "Mémoire présenté à Son Altesse Royale Mgr. le duc d'Orléans dans le commencement de sa régence pour la con-struction d'un nobiliaire général" may be consulted in several manu-script copies, all (but for minor variants) identical to each other.

Boulainvilliers' "Mémoire Pour Un Nobiliaire Général": Manuscripts

*Bibl. du Sénat (Paris), MS. 990.
*Bibl. de l'Ecole Supérieure de Guerre (Paris), MS. 26, fols. 384–98.
*B.M., Angoulême, MS. 23, pp. 609–34.

As a polemic and as a piece of historical writing, Boulainvilliers' unfinished "Lettres sur les parlements ou états généraux" is by far his most ambitious work: a complex contribution to the *affaire du bonnet* of 1715–16 (see chapter 5) and part of what would have been a massive history of the Estates General had Boulainvilliers completed it.

The work consists of twelve letters which Boulainvilliers composed and circulated in 1716 and to which he later returned, to revise the text, add two more letters to it, and abandon unfinished once again. This work survives in several states in editions and manuscripts.

Boulainvilliers' "Lettres sur les parlements": Editions

Etat . . . Tome III, 1–189.
Histoire de l'ancien gouvernement de la France, avec XIV. Lettres historiques sur les parlements ou états généraux de la France, 3 vols. (Amsterdam and The Hague: 1727).
See Part 5.

Boulainvilliers' "Lettres sur les parlements": Manuscripts

*Archives du Ministère des Affaires étrangères (Paris), Mémoires et documents, France, MS. 22.

*Archives du Ministère des Affaires étrangères (Paris), Mémoires de documents, France, MS. 23.

*Archives du Ministère des Affaires étrangères (Paris), Mémoires et documents, France, MS. 144.

*Archives du Ministère des Affaires étrangères (Paris), Mémoires et documents, France, MS. 744.

*B.N., MS. f.f. 4784.

*B.N., MS. f.f. 10177.

*B.N., MS. f.f. 10882.

*B.N., MS. f.f. 13634 (14 letters).

*B.N., MSS. f.f. 14024–26 (14 letters).

*B.N., MSS. f.f. 21401–2 (14 letters).

*B.N., MSS. n.a.f. 93–94 (14 letters).

*B.N., MS. n.a.f. 95.

*B.N., MS. n.a.f. 2079 (14 letters).

Bibl. de l'Arsenal (Paris), MSS. 3418–19.

*Bibl. de l'Assemblée Nationale (Paris), MSS. 400–401.

*Bibl. de l'Assemblée Nationale (Paris), MS. 402.

*Bibl. de l'Institut (Paris), MS. 321 (14 letters).

*Bibl. de l'Institut (Paris), MS. 582.

*Bibl. de l'Institut (Paris), MSS. 684–85 (14 letters).

*Bibl. de la Faculté de Droit (Paris), MSS. 11–12.

*Bibl. du Sénat (Paris), MSS. 400–401 (14 letters).

Bibl. du Musée Condé, Chantilly, MS. 1103 (incomplete; breaks off in Letter 11).

B.M., Aix, MSS. 398–99.

B.M., Aix, MSS. 400–406.

*B.M., Angoulême, MS. 23, pp. 144–240 (Letters 13 and 14).

B.M., Angoulême, MS. 27.

B.M., Besançon, MS. 894.

*B.M., Bordeaux, MS. 828.

B.M., Bourges, MS. 364.

B.M., Cahors, MSS. 9–10.

B.M., Chartres, MS. 734.

B.M., Châteaudun, MSS. 25–27.

B.M., Grenoble, MS. 1009.

B.M., Lille, MSS. 24–25.

*B.M., Nancy, MS. 622 (14 letters).

B.M., Nantes, MSS. 1149–50.

B.M., Nantes, MSS. 1151–53.
B.M., Poitiers, MS. 266.
*B.M., Rouen, MS. 1170 (U.88).
*B.M., Rouen, MS. 1171 (U.101) (10 letters).
*B.M., Rouen, MS. 1807 (Montbret 451).
*B.M., Rouen, MS. 1808 (Montbret 364).
*B.M., Rouen, MS. 2562 (Martainville 105).
B.M., Saint-Brieuc, MS. 78.
B.M., Saint-Pol, MS. 12.
B.M., Sens, MS. 230.
University of Michigan Library (Ann Arbor), MS. JN 2413 b 76.
Of the forty-seven manuscripts listed, twenty-eight have been consulted, and of these more than half—that is, sixteen—reproduce texts containing only twelve letters. Boulainvilliers wrote this version at the beginning of the regency, for two manuscript copies of it (B.M., Angoulême, MS. 27, and B.M., Saint-Brieuc, MS. 78) bear the indication "copied from the author's original in 1716."[51] It is not clear when and why Boulainvilliers added two more letters to the set, but (as argued in chapter 6) they clearly postdate the aristocratic controversies of 1715–17. Indeed they may date to shortly before his death (if a notation on a separate manuscript of the last two letters can be believed) and that may explain why Nicolas Fréret, writing only weeks after Boulainvilliers died, ignored their existence.[52] All but one of the nine manuscripts containing fourteen letters that I consulted contain the twelve letters as written in 1715–16, but MS. 321 at the Bibliothèque de l'Institut contains a revised version of the first twelve. One may conclude that after adding two letters to the original set, Boulainvilliers embarked on revising the entire text before abandoning it altogether. Both editions just listed print all fourteen letters, but *Etat . . . Tome III* reproduces the 1715–16 version of the first twelve, and *Histoire* contains a version yet more extensively revised than that found in MS. 321 at the Institut.

To prepare his "Lettres sur les parlements," Boulainvilliers assembled a body of documentary evidence hitherto unknown, but preserved largely intact and largely at the Bibliothèque Municipale de Rouen. There one may consult thirteen manuscript volumes dating to the eighteenth century and containing transcribed documents on the history of French representative institutions. With those volumes may be associated another at the Bibliothèque Nationale (Paris). Boulainvilliers (it will

[51] According to *Catalogue général des manuscrits des bibliothèques publiques de France: Départements*, 56 vols. [Paris: Plon/B.N., 1886–1962), 13:370, and 20:300.
[52] See Simon, *A la Recherche*, 13, n. 9 (quoting B.M., Angoulême, MS. 23, p. 144); and Fréret, "Lettre de M. Fréret," 202.

be argued) may be held responsible for them all. Although these volumes of documents claimed little attention in the preceding chapters, they merit attention here. Like his notes on Mézeray and Longuerue, these collections of documents were materials that he used in writing French history.

Boulainvilliers' Transcriptions of Documents on the History of Representative Institutions: Manuscripts

*B.N., MS. f.f. 7508 (Boulainvilliers' reading notes on Le Laboureur's *Histoire de la pairie;* a transcription of Jehan Masselin's diary recording the debates at the Estates General of Tours, 1484; transcriptions of the provincial charters of 1314–15 preserved at the Trésor des Chartes; Boulainvilliers' 1700 "Dissertation" on the "old nobility"; a "Copie du carton biffé en l'article: Connestables de France, au sujet de *Charles* d'Albert, connétable de *Luynes*"; "Observations" on the condition of Franche-Comté and Burgundy).

*B.M., Rouen, MSS. 1875–76 (Montbret 318) (copies of the ordinance of 1355 and of Jehan Masselin's diary).[53]

*B.M., Rouen, MSS. 1877–79 (Montbret 319), three of originally four volumes (the first is lost) (documents on the Estates General of Fontainebleau and Orleans, 1559 and 1560).

*B.M., Rouen, MS. 1880 (Montbret 320) (Etienne Bernard's journal of the Estates General of Blois, 1588–89).

*B.M., Rouen, MSS. 1881–82 (Montbret 321) ("Recueil journalier de ce qui s'est negotié et arresté en la chambre et compagnies du tiers-état de France en l'assemblée générale des trois états . . ." [1614–15]; the July 1618 ordinance based on *cahiers* submitted by the Assembly of Notables, Rouen; "De l'origine de la convocation des trois estats de France qui estoit jadis soubs la première et seconde lignée de nos roys. Tenir le parlement. 1651").

*B.M., Rouen, MSS. 1883–85 (Montbret 322) ("Recueil de ce qui s'est observé et passé durant la tenue des états généraux convoquez à Paris par ordre du roy, depuis le 27 octobre 1614 jusques au 23 février 1615"; extracts from *cahiers* of the nobility submitted at the 1614–15 Estates).

*B.M., Rouen, MSS. 1886–87 (Montbret 323) (*procès verbal* of the Assembly of Notables, Paris, 1626–27; associated documents).

All these manuscripts may be associated with Boulainvilliers. The Pari-

---

[53]For another MS volume of these transcriptions, see B.N., MS. latin 11797.

sian manuscript contains texts clearly by Boulainvilliers.[54] The Rouen manuscripts bear Samuel Bernard's arms, and are almost fully described in the library sale catalogs of Bernard de Rieux, Bernard de Coubert, Nouveau de Chennevières (here many are ascribed to Boulainvilliers), and Comptroller-General Bertin.[55] The most telling evidence that these manuscripts belonged to Boulainvilliers, however, is the use that he made of the earliest documents transcribed in them. In his "Lettres sur les parlements," he based his account of the provincial rebellions following the death of Philip IV on the charters issued in 1314 and 1315. He included lengthy extracts of and commentaries on those documents and

[54]Including the item on Luynes, which corrects a genealogical error in Père Anselme et al., *Histore généalogique et chronologique de la maison royale de France, des grands officiers de la couronne et de la maison du roy* (1712 ed.), 1:337–41. This little piece of genealogical connoisseurship was probably Boulainvilliers' for he was associated with the Luynes family: the constable's descendant, Charles d'Albert, duc de Luynes, witnessed Boulainvilliers' marriage contract in 1689 (A.N., M.C., CII, 148, August 20, 1689).

[55]*Catalogue des livres de . . . Bernard de Rieux*, 298, 299: "Etats généraux du Royaume de France tenus à Paris en 1355. & à Tours en 1483. Mss. 2 *vols. in-4. v. f.*"; "Journal des Etats de Blois des années 1588. & 1589. Ms. *in-4. v. f.*" *Catalogue des manuscrits de la bibliothèque de feu M. Bernard* [de Coubert], 29: "Etats généraux du Roîaume de France, depuis 1355, jusq. 1483, par le même [Boulainvilliers]. 2 *vol. in-4*"; "Autres en 1560. 4 *vol. in-4*"; "Journal des Etats tenus à Blois, en 1588, & 1589. *in-4*"; "Autre assemblée des Etats de 1614 & 1615. 3 *vol. in-4.*" *Catalogue des livres imprimés et manuscrits de la bibliothèque de feu M. Nouveau*, 84–85: "Assemblée des Etats généraux du royaume de France, contenant ce qui s'est passé à ceux tenus à Paris, en 1355, & ceux tenus à Tours, en 1483. 2 *vol. in-4*. Mss. Veau marbré filets d'or"; "Recueil de ce qui s'est passé aux Etats Généraux tenus à Fontainebleau sous le regne de François II, & à ceux d'Orleans, sous le régne de Charles IX, en 1560. Par M. le comte de Boulainvilliers. 4 *vol. in-4*. Mss. Veau marbré filets d'or"; "Journal des Etats de Blois, des années 1588 & 1589. 1 *vol. in-4*. Ms. Veau marbré filets d'or"; "Propositions & délibérations arretées en la chambre du Clergé, en l'assemblée tenue à Paris pendant la Ligue, sous le nom des Etats Généraux du Royaume, en l'année 1593. 2 *vol. in-4*. Mss. Veau marbré filets d'or"; "Assemblée des Notables, tenue à Rouen en 1597. 1 *vol. in-4*. Ms. Veau marbré filets d'or"; "Recueil de ce qui s'est observé & passé durant la tenue des Etats Généraux tenus à Paris, depuis le 27 Octobre 1614 jusqu'au 23 Février 1615; par M. le Comte de Boulainvilliers. 2 *vol. in-4*. Mss. veau marbré filets d'or"; "Recueil de ce que s'est négotié dans la chambre du Tiers-Etat, durant l'assemblée des Etats en 1614 & 1615. 2 *vol. in* Mss. Veau marbré filets d'or"; "Procès verbal de l'Assemblée des Notables, tenue à Paris en 1626 & 1627. 2 *vol. in-4*. Mss. Veau marbré filets d'or"; "Cahier présenté par la Noblesse aux Etats Généraux assemblés à Paris en 1614 & 1615. 1 *vol. in-4*. Ms. Veau marbré filets d'or." The documents for the 1593 and 1597 assemblies do not figure in the Rouen collection as it now exists. *Catalogue d'une précieuse collection* [Bertin], 2–3: "Etats-généraux du royaume de France, tenus à Paris en 1355, et à Tours en 1483. *in-4. v.m.*"; "Les Etats tenus à Fontainebleau sous le règne de François II, et ceux d'Orléans sous le règne de Charles IX en 1560. 4 vol. in-4. v.m. (Manque le premier vol.)"; "Journal des Etats de Blois des années 1588 et 1589. in-4. v.m."; "Cahier présenté par la noblesse aux états-généraux en 1614 et 1615. in-4. v.m."; "Recueil de ce qui s'est observé et passé durant la tenue des états-généraux, convoqués à Paris par ordre du roi, dupuis le 27 octobre 1614 judqu'au 23 février 1615. 2 vols. in-4. v.m."; "Recueil de ce qui s'est négocié en la chambre du tiers-état, durant l'assemblée des trois états en 1614. et 1615. 2 vol. in-4. v.m."; "Procès-verbal de l'assemblée des notables, tenue à Paris depuis le mois de décembre 1626 jusqu'en février 1627. 2 vol. in-4. v.m."

pronounced them "the last titles of our liberty."[56] In the same work he observed that the 1355 Estates was the first assembly whose deliberations the historian could follow, thanks to the earliest of the documents transcribed in the Rouen collection: the 1355 ordinance preserved at the Bibliothèque du Roi.[57] The importance Boulainvilliers attached to that ordinance cannot be underestimated, for he wrote that it "would have forever assured public liberty, had it been possible for France to be happy."[58] Boulainvilliers abandoned his "Letters" unfinished; he never brought his narrative past the reign of Louis XI and so he never made use of the remaining sources collected in the transcriptions at Rouen. Yet one may conclude that those transcriptions were indeed his and that they constitute part of the documentary basis on which he intended to build his account of French representative institutions.

The debates occasioned by the *affaire des princes* elicited from Boulainvilliers a minor pamphlet (his only published work) and a memorandum to the regent. These works are examined in chapter 6, along with three texts postdating the regency's aristocratic controversies and containing Boulainvilliers' last and bitterest reflections on French history, and on the (now evident) futility of the hopes he had lodged in the duc d'Orléans.

Boulainvilliers' pamphlet, *Justification de la naissance légitime de Bernard, roy d'Italie,* may be consulted in two editions of 1717 and in two manuscript copies.

Boulainvilliers' "Justification de la naissance légitime de Bernard, roy d'Italie": Editions and Manuscripts

[Boulainvilliers], *Justification de la naissance légitime de Bernard, roy d'Italie, petit-fils de Charlemagne* ([Paris: 1717]).
Recueil general des pieces touchant l'affaire des princes legitimes et legitimez, mises en ordre, 4 vols. (Rotterdam: 1717), 3:201–14.
*Bibl. du Sénat (Paris), MS. 988.
*B.M., Angoulême, MS. 23, pp. 23–50.
The editions reproduce the text contained in the manuscripts, but omit the extracts from ancient chronicles that Boulainvilliers had appended to his text and used in it. By 1719 if not earlier, contemporaries knew that Boulainvilliers was the pamphlet's author, for Père Lelong ascribed

---

[56]*Etat . . . Tome III,* 76–86, esp. 76 for the quotation.
[57]Ibid., 102.
[58]Ibid., 105. Cf. ibid., 112, on another ordinance preserved at the Bibliothèque du Roi (but not among the transcribed documents at Rouen): the 1357 ordinance.

it to him in his *Bibliothèque historique de la France*.[59] Although it was reprinted in the Rotterdam *Recueil*, Boulainvilliers' *Justification* was not one of the major polemics of the *affaire des princes*, as its first edition may have amounted to only twenty copies.[60]

Boulainvilliers' other contribution to the *affaire des princes* was a memorandum to the regent, "Mémoire touchant l'affaire de Mrs. les princes du sang." Because this memorandum develops arguments contrary to those elaborated in *Justification*, and because it is found in printed and manuscript collections containing other works doubtfully ascribed to Boulainvilliers, the reader is referred to discussions of this text in chapter 6 and in Part 4 of this appendix.

Boulainvilliers' last works on French history all postdate the end of the *affaire des princes* and include not only the last two "Lettres sur les parlements" examined already, but also annotations on Antoine Aubery's histories in journal form of the reigns of Louis IX (1226–70) and Philip III (1270–85) along with a preface to the first entitled "Préface critique au journal de Saint Louis: Anecdotes curieuse du règne de Saint Louis, roy de France, depuis 1226 jusqu'en l'année 1270." The evidence for dating this work is adduced in chapter 6. Here it suffices to list and describe editions and manuscripts.

Boulainvilliers' "Préface critique": Editions

[abbé Saint-Martin de Chassonville], *Les Délassemens d'un galant homme, ou fruits agréables de la lecture et de la conversation, recueil des bons mots, aventures, pièces fugitives, etc., où l'on a ajouté un journal anecdote très curieux sur l'histoire de Saint Louis, roi de France par l'abbé S. M. D. C.* (Amsterdam: 1742), 85–179, 191–201, 204–14, 224–38, 258–73.

Boulainvilliers, *Un Révolté du grand siècle. Henry de Boulainviller*, ed. Renée Simon, pref. Henri Gouhier (Garches: Editions du Nouvel Humanisme, 1948), 85–131.

Boulainvilliers' "Préface critique": Manuscripts

B.N., MS. n.a.f. 4964.
Bibl. de l'Arsenal (Paris), MS. 6335.
*Bibl. de l'Ecole Supérieure de Guerre (Paris), MS. 18.
*Bibl. de l'Institut (Paris), MS. 322.
Bibl. Sainte-Geneviève (Paris), MS. 1997.

---

[59]Lelong, *Bibliothèque historique de la France* (1719 ed.), 604.
[60]B.M., Angoulême, MS. 23, p. 24 ("Avertissement").

*B.M., Angoulême, MS. 23, pp. 51–142.
 B.M., Dijon, ancien fond, MS. 798 (fond Baudot 1218), fols. 249–72.
*B.M., Rouen, MS. 1169 (U.90).

Aubery's Journals with Boulainvilliers' Annotations: Manuscripts

 B.N. MSS. f.f. 6956–57.
*B.N. MSS. n.a.f. 11078–81 (on Louis IX), 11082–83 (on Philip III),
 11084–89 (on later kings, unannotated).
*Bibl. de l'Arsenal (Paris), MSS. 3432–33 (on Louis IX, incomplete).
*Bibl. de l'Ecole Supérieure de Guerre (Paris), MSS. 18–19 (on Louis
 IX—incomplete).
 Bibl. Mazarine (Paris), MS. 2014.
 Bibl. Sainte-Geneviève (Paris), MS. 1917.
Incomplete and difficult to obtain and use, Saint-Martin de Chasson-
ville's edition of the "Préface critique" may safely be avoided. Simon's
edition, based on the manuscripts listed here, is far more is reliable,
though at page 104 it omits a paragraph found in manuscripts.[61]

The third of Boulainvilliers' three historical works postdating the
regency's aristocratic controversies is the "Mémoire" or "Discours sur la
noblesse," dated in manuscripts to 1719, and intended as an introduction to an unfinished province-by-province catalog of French nobility.

Boulainvilliers' "Discours sur la noblesse": Manuscripts

*Bibl. de l'Arsenal (Paris), MS. 4152.
*Bibl. de l'Institut (Paris), MS. 321., fols. 547v–589.
*Bibl. du Sénat (Paris), MS. 986.
*B.M., Angoulême, MS. 23, pp. 506–608.
 B.M., Mâcon, MS. 10, fols. 2–49.
The Sénat, Angoulême, and Mâcon manuscripts date the "Discours" to
1719. But for minor variants all manuscripts consulted are identical and
all (except the Institut manuscript) include the catalog, or at least the
parts on Burgundy; on the Franche-Comté; on Lorraine, Bar, and the
Three Bishoprics of Metz, Toul, and Verdun; and on Champagne
which are the only parts that Boulainvilliers seems to have finished.

Boulainvilliers wrote not only on French history but also on the art of
writing it, in the first of his "Lettres sur les parlements" and above all in
his "Lettre à Mademoiselle Cousinot sur l'histoire et sa méthode" (1707),

---

[61]Cf. Bibl. de l'Institut (Paris), MS. 322, pp. 39–40.

examined in chapter 7. This work—it is Boulainvilliers' credo as a historian—survives in manuscripts and in a modern edition.

Boulainvilliers' "Lettre à Mademoiselle Cousinot": Edition and Manuscripts

Boulainvilliers, *Un Révolté du grand siècle: Henry de Boulainviller*, ed. Renée Simon, pref. Henri Gouhier (Garches: Editions du Nouvel Humanisme, 1948), 71–81.

B.M., Aix, MS. 398.

*B.M., Angoulême, MS. 23, pp. 1–21.

B.M., Poitiers, MS. 266.

Simon based her edition on the Angoulême manuscript and on a manuscript in her own possession. The date 1707 appears on manuscripts.

3. Works Excluded from the Boulainvilliers Corpus

A number of historical or political works ascribed to Boulainvilliers by library catalogs of books and manuscripts are not his. Le Laboureur's "Histoire de la pairie de France" is but one well-known example.[62] Others may be added, preeminent among them the *Mémoire pour la noblesse, contre les ducs et pairs* ([Paris: 1717]), an important work examined in chapter 6.

Barely less important for efforts to assess Boulainvilliers' character as a historical writer are the "Opuscules politiques" and the five learned little treatises on French nobility, heraldry, and dynastic custom, treatises that survive in two identical manuscript collections where they are bound with works definitely by Boulainvilliers.[63] Simon ascribes these works to Boulainvilliers largely, it appears, because she believes they enhance his stature. In the "Opuscules politiques" she discovers "material for some *Spirit of the Laws* that Boulainviller was thinking of writing."[64] And in the short treatises on French nobility, heraldry, and

---

[62]Simon, *A la Recherche*, 34.

[63]For the "Opuscules politiques" see Bibl. de la Faculté de Droit (Bibl. Cujas) (Paris), MSS. 13–15. For the five treatises see B.M., Bordeaux, MS. 828, pp. 311–426; B.M., Nantes, MS. 1822, pp. 91–253: (1) "De la qualité de baron, de celle de prince, de l'invention des armes et du surnom"; (2) "Remarque troisième sur les armes et sur ce que l'épée signifie en symbole"; (3) "Traité sur l'origine de l'épée"; (4) "Introduction à l'abrégé chronologique de l'histoire des reines de France depuis le commencement de la monarchie françoise jusqu'à François I."; (5) "Traité des apanages et des partages des enfants de France." In both MSS these treatises are bound in the same order, and even with the same copiests' or binders' errors (indicated by abrupt interruptions and discontinuities in the texts): compare, for example, the Bordeaux MS at pp. 314, 339, and 371, with the Nantes MS at pp. 94, 129, and 169. Clearly one MS is a copy of the other, or both are copies of a third.

[64]Simon, *Henry de Boulainviller*, 246.

dynastic custom she sees erudite papers that Boulainvilliers read to a little "academy" of the learned where he may have met Nicolas Fréret.[65]

In fact these works are not Boulainvilliers'. The title page of the "Opuscules politiques" manuscript attributes that work to him, it is true, but in a hand unlike the original copiest's. Moreover, the work's language is archaic by comparison with Boulainvilliers'.[66] Its citations include no authors more recent than late-sixteenth and early-seventeenth-century figures like Jean de Serres and Justus Lipsius. Finally, the "Opuscules politiques" belongs to a set of similarly titled works to which it alludes—the "Opusc. Eccles." and the "opusc. du droit françois" or "Nos opuscules du Droit françois"—and these works are not ascribed to Boulainvilliers even when listed in the sale catalogs for Bernard de Coubert's books and manuscripts.[67] It is possible that Boulainvilliers owned these works, but it is not likely that he wrote them.

It is no more likely that he wrote the learned little essays on French nobility, heraldry, and dynastic custom. Two are definitely not his: the fifth, on appanages, is by the abbé de Longuerue, and the fourth, on French queens, is by the abbé de Camps.[68] Very likely the first three (on French noble titles and arms) are also by the abbé de Camps, well known in the early eighteenth century as an authority on such matters.[69]

There are three further works of lesser importance wrongly or doubtfully ascribed to Boulainvilliers. The "Corrections et additions des 2. prem.ers tomes de l'histoire de Lorraine" concerns Dom Calmet's history of Lorraine—a work published in 1728, six years after Boulainvilliers' death in 1722.[70] The "Minorité d'Edouard VI, règne de Marie, révolu-

[65]Ibid., 86–88, 682.

[66]Cf. Bibl. de la Faculté de Droit, MS. 13, fol. 78: "Les femmes de leur naturel ne sont pas nées pour commander ains pour obeir et servir."

[67]Ibid., fol. 224v, MS. 14, fol. 128v, MS. 15, fol. 106v. See *Catalogue des livres de feu M. Bernard* [de Coubert], 140, 141: "Opuscules ecclesiastiques, sur la Religion, le Droit canon, Ec. *in-fol*"; "Opuscules de Droit Romain. *in-fol*"; "Opuscules de Droit françois. *in fol.*" The Bertin sale catalog lists, just before the "Opuscules politiques, par M. le comte de Boulainvilliers. 3 vol. in-4. v.m.," an "Opuscules de Pierre de Marca. 3 vol. in-fol. v.f." (*Catalogue d'une précieuse collection*, 13), but the possible ascription of the "Opuscules" to the learned seventeenth-century archbishop of Toulouse remains to be verified. On the *Opuscula Petri de Marca . . . nunc primum in lucem edita cura Stephani Baluzii* (Paris: F. Muguet, 1681), see Jean-Pierre Nicéron, *Mémoires pour servir à l'histoire des hommes illustres dans la République des Lettres: Avec un catalogue raisonné de leurs ouvrages*, 41 vols. (Paris: Briasson, 1727–40), 12:342–47.

[68][Abbé Jacques de Guijon], *Longuerueana, ou recueil de pensées, de discours et de conversations, de feu M. Louis du Four de Longuerue, abbé de Sept-Fontaines, & de Saint-Jean-du-Jard*, 2 parts in 1 vol. (Berlin: 1754), 1:xxii–xxiii. Lelong, *Bibliothèque historique de la France* (ed. Fevret de Fontette), 3:644.

[69]Cf. *Journal des sçavans* (Amsterdam edition, March 1721): 305–47.

[70]B.N., MS. f.f. 8678; cf. Dom Augustin Calmet, *Histoire ecclésiastique et civile de Lorraine* (Nancy: Jean-Baptiste Cusson, 1728).

tion d'Angleterre" is on a subject to which Boulainvilliers paid no attention elsewhere and the only surviving manuscript of the work bears no ascription to him.[71] Finally, the "Extrait d'un discours de l'abbé de St. Réal en 1692" is also on a subject to which Boulainvilliers paid no attention elsewhere in his work: French relations with Savoy during the War of the League of Augsburg.[72] He may have written or owned it, however. It was his habit to take notes or make "extracts" on his reading. And the "Extrait de St. Réal" is listed as the "Réflexions sur la grande alliance" in the Arsenal lists of Boulainvilliers (and pseudo-Boulainvilliers) works drawn up by Isaac Milsonneau.[73]

4. Bibliographical Problems: Boulainvilliers' Regency Memoranda

In chapters 4 and 6, two minor memoranda to the regent claimed attention: a plea for assembling the Estates General (1716), and a defense of the princely rank and title conferred by Louis XIV on his bastards, the duc du Maine and the comte de Toulouse (1717). These texts belong to a set of six memoranda usually ascribed to Boulainvilliers and usually said to have been submitted by him to Orléans.

1. "Mémoire sur la convocation d'une assemblée d'états généraux."
2. "Mémoire pour rendre l'état puissant & invincible, & tous les sujets de ce même état heureux & riches."
3. "Mémoire touchant la taille réelle et proportionnelle."
4. "Mémoire touchant l'affaire de Mrs. les princes du sang."
5. "Mémoire concernant les moyens d'établir le droit d'amortissement des gabelles, & la conversion du revenu des aides en droit de bouchon, avec les avantages que le roi & les sujets en peuvent tirer."
6. "Mémoire au sujet des domaines du roi," a memorandum accompanied in some editions and manuscripts by "Extrait d'un mémoire de Mr. de Fougerolle en 1711. . . . Projet qui peut aider à un règlement général pour assurer les revenus du roi, et répartir l'imposition avec plus d'égalité qu'il n'a été pratiqué jusqu'à présent, & fortifier les arts, le commerce & l'emploi utile des sujets."

Because especially delicate bibliographical questions surround these

[71]B.N., MS. f.f. 9034. It may be observed that this MS and the MS cited in the preceding note both bear the arms of the duc de Belle-Isle, as does "Recherches curieuses de philosophie" (B.N., MS. f.f. 9107), another MS wrongly ascribed to Boulainvilliers (as Simon argues in *A la Recherche*, 28–29, and in *Henry de Boulainviller*, 362–63 and n. 14). One suspects that these faulty ascriptions, like so many others, may be blamed on eighteenth-century booksellers.

[72]Bibl. de l'Ecole Supérieure de Guerre (Paris), MS. 25, fols. 319–26.

[73]Simon, *A la Recherche*, 22.

memoranda, discussion of their editions, manuscripts, and ascription to Boulainvilliers is included here. These six memoranda may be consulted in the following editions (full bibliographical descriptions are given of the first three to enable readers to distinguish between them):

Editions

(Only the first is cited in this study. On the multiple "Dutch" editions of Boulainvilliers' works—some of these editions are actually French—see Part 5).

MEMOIRES / PRESENTÉS / A MONSEIGNEUR / LE DUC / D'ORLEANS, / *Contenant les moyens de rendre ce / Royaume très-puissant, & d'augmen- / ter considerablement les revenus du / Roy & du Peuple.* / Par le Comte DE BOULAIN-VILLIERS. / Tome I. [II.] / [vignette]

A LA HAYE ⎱ Aux dépens
& ⎰ de la
A AMSTERDAM. ⎰ Compagnie.

[rule] / M. DCC. XXVII.

Collations. 12°: Vol. 1: A^8 B^4 C^8 D^4 E^8 F^4 G^8 H^4 I^8 K^4 L^8 M^4 N^8 O^4; Vol. 2: TP A^8 B^4 C^8 D^4 E^8 F^4 G^8 H^4 I^8 K^4 L^8 M^4 N^8 O^4 P^8 Q^4 R^8 S^4 T^4 V^2
Paginations. Vol. 1: [6] 161; Vol. 2: [2] 226 [2]
French Printing and Paper.
Copies consulted: B.N. *cote* R.29729–29730; Washington University, St. Louis.

[The first, fourth, sixth, tenth, and last lines are printed in red.]
MEMOIRES / PRESENTÉS / A Monseigneur le Duc [small capitals] / D'OR-LEANS, / RÉGENT DE FRANCE. / Contenant / Les moyens de rendre ce Royaume très puis- / sant, & augmenter considerablement les / revenus du Roi & du Peuple. / Par le c. de Boulainvilliers. [small capitals] / TOME I. [II.] / [vignette]

A LA HAYE ⎱ Aux dépends
& ⎰ de la
A AMSTERDAM ⎰ Compagnie.

[rule] / M. DCC. XXVII.

Collations. 12°: Vol. 1: TP *^{8} A–K^8; Vol. 2: TP A^8(-A1) B^8–O^8 P^4
Paginations: Vol. 1: [6] 158; Vol. 2: [2] 230 [2]
Dutch Printing and Paper (Lion de Flandre watermark)
Copy consulted: B.N. *cote* R.29725–29726.

[The first, fourth, sixth, tenth, and last lines are printed in red.]
MEMOIRES / PRESENTEZ / A Monseigneur le Duc [small capitals] / D'OR-LEANS, / REGENT DE FRANCE. / CONTENTANT / Les moyens de rendre ce Roïaume très-puis- / sant, & d'augmenter considérablement / les Re-

venus du Roi & du Peuple. / PAR LE C. DE BOULAINVILLIERS / Tome I.
[or II.] / [vignette]

A LA HAYE ⎫ Aux dépens
& ⎬ de la
A AMSTERDAM ⎭ Compagnie

[rule] / M. DCC. XXVII.

Collations. 12°: Vol. 1: a⁴ *⁸ **⁴ A⁸ B⁴ C⁸ D⁴ E⁸ F⁴ G⁸ H⁴ I⁸ K⁴ L⁸ M⁴ N⁴
O²; Vol. 2: TP A⁸ B⁴ C⁸ D⁴ E⁸ F⁴ G⁸ H⁴ I⁸ K⁴ L⁸ M⁴ N⁸ O⁴ P⁸ Q⁴ R⁸ S⁴
T⁴ V²

Paginations. vol. 1: [32] 156; vol. 2: [2] 228

French Printing and Paper (papermaker named in watermark, C. B.
Chantemerle)

Copy consulted: B.N. *cote* R.29727–29728.

MEMOIRES / PRESENTEZ / A MONSEIGNEUR LE DUC / D'ORLEANS, REGENT DE
FRANCE. / CONTENANT / Les moyens de rendre ce Royaume tres-puis-
sant, / & d'augmenter considerablement les / revenus du Roi & du
Peuple. / PAR LE C. DE BOULAINVILLIERS. / TOME PREMIER. [or SECOND] /
[vignette]

A LA HAYE ⎫ Aux dépens
& ⎬ de la
A AMSTERDAM ⎭ Compagnie

[rule] / MDCCXXVII.

Collations. 12°: Vol. 1: ā^{iiij} (-āiiij) A⁸ B⁴ C⁸ D⁴ E⁸ F⁴ G⁸ H⁴ I⁸ K⁴ L⁸ M⁴ N⁴
O²; Vol. 2: TP A⁸ B⁴ C⁸ D⁴ E⁸ F⁴ G⁸ H⁴ I⁸ K⁴ L⁸ M⁴ N⁸ O⁴ P⁸ Q⁴ R⁸ S⁴
T⁸

Paginations. Vol. 1: [6] 156; Vol. 2: [2] 230 [2]

French Printing and Paper

Copy consulted: B.N. *cote* R.29731–29732

Etat de la France . . . Tome III, 502–90 (for later emissions of this 1728
edition see Part 5).

[Chevalier de Piossens], *Mémoires de la Régence: Nouvelle édition, considérablement augmentée,* [ed. Nicolas Lenglet-Dufresnoy], 5 vols. (Amsterdam: 1749), 2:217–30 (the first memorandum just listed, here
entitled "Mémoire sur le gouvernement, présenté à monsieur le duc
d'Orléans. Par M. le comte de Boulainvilliers. 1716").

Manuscripts

*Archives du Ministère des Affaires étrangères (Paris), Mémoires et
documents, France, MS. 1212 (complete).

B.N., MS. f.f. 7732 (memorandum 5 only).[74]

*B.N., MS. n.a.f. 6875 (lacks memorandum 4 and Fougerolles extract).

*Bibl. de l'Ecole Supérieur de Guerre (Paris), MS. 25, fols. 1–303 (complete).

*Bibl. du Sénat (Paris), MS. 989 (memorandum 1 only).

*Bibl. du Palais de Fontainebleau, MS. 19 (C.852) (lacks memorandum 4 and Fougerolles extract).

*B.M., Angoulême, MS. 23, pp. 365–80 (memorandum 1 only).

*B.M., Rouen, MS. 1166 (U.87), fols. 2–212ᵛ (first foliation) and fols. 2–16 and 91–158ᵛ (second foliation) (complete).

*B.M., Sens, MSS. 228–29 (complete).

There are no significant discrepancies between the texts as reproduced in the manuscripts and editions. Of the editions, the "Dutch" are to be preferred. Though their slightly different paginations can be confusing they contain all the texts just listed.

Some scholars happily ascribe all six memoranda under consideration to Boulainvilliers in order (it appears) to enhance his reputation—for once an attractive reputation—as an "aristocratic liberal" or progressive reformer of the eighteenth century.[75] In fact, a nineteenth-century historian dated memorandum 5 to the 1680s, to conclude that Boulainvilliers was well in advance of such better-known writers on French economic and fiscal affairs as Vauban and Boisguilbert.[76]

Doubts surround Boulainvilliers' authorship of these texts, however. Voltaire, who admired neither these memoranda nor their putative author, denied that Boulainvilliers wrote them.[77] More recently, Bernard Faÿ claimed that Boulainvilliers wrote only a third of them.[78] Neither Voltaire nor Faÿ gave reasons for this opinion, but Paul Harsin and Lionel Rothkrug have argued cogently for rejecting Boulainvilliers'

[74]See n. 79.

[75]Jacqueline Hecht, "Trois précurseurs de la sécurité sociale au XVIIIe siècle: Henry de Boulainvilliers, Faiguet de Villeneuve, Du Beissier de Pizany d'Eden," *Population*, 14 (1959): 74–79; Jacques-Mariel Nzouankeu, "Boulainvilliers: Questions de légitimité monarchique et théorie du pouvoir politique" (Mémoire D.E.S. d'histoire de droit et des faits sociaux, Faculté de Droit, Paris, 1968 [Bibl. Cujas]), 94–116; Simon, *Henry de Boulainviller*, 228–45, esp. 230–37; J. B. Maurice Vignes, *Histoire des doctrines sur l'impôt en France: Les causes de la Révolution française considérées par rapport aux principes de l'imposition*, rev. ed. Emanuele Morselli (Padua: CEDAM, 1961), on Boulainvilliers as indexed.

[76]Th. Ducrocq, "Le Mémoire de Boulainvilliers sur le droit d'amortissement des gabelles et la conversion du revenu des aides antérieur au Détail de Boisguillebert et à la Dîme royale de Vauban,"*Mémoires de la Société des Antiquités de l'Ouest (Poitiers)*, ser. 2, 6 (1882): 425–57.

[77]Voltaire, *Oeuvres complètes*, ed. [Louis] Moland, 52 vols. (Paris: Garnier, 1877–85), 14:45 (*Siècle de Louis XIV*).

[78]Bernard Faÿ, *La Franc-maçonnerie et la révolution intellectuelle du XVIIIe siècle*, 2d ed. (Paris: Librairie française, 1961), 50.

authorship of memorandum 5 which dates to the 1680s. According to Harsin and Rothkrug, Boulainvilliers would have been too young and inexperienced in the 1680s to have written it. Moreover the original manuscript of the memorandum—it survives—bears no ascription to Boulainvilliers. Finally, Vauban appears to have had a copy of the piece and so remains a likely candidate for its authorship.[79]

It appears that Simon's confidence in Boulainvilliers' authorship of the six memoranda under consideration may be misplaced.[80] But which (if any) of these texts did Boulainvilliers write? To answer that question, one cannot look to the collected memoranda on taxation, banking, and finance submitted to Orléans's regency council or (more specifically) its subsidiary Council of Finances.[81] None of the pieces ascribed to Boulainvilliers may be found there. Consequently, one must make bibliographical decisions on the basis of what one knows about his ideological and intellectual character. He was, it is clear, interested in economic and fiscal matters. He did not ignore them in his historical writing and at the end of his life he continued to take an interest in them. Mathieu Marais, who visited him the day before he died and spoke with him about French trade, described him as a "man well instructed" in such questions.[82] But informed interest is not expertise and Boulainvilliers disclaimed any expertise in economic and fiscal affairs.[83] In keeping with his habits, therefore, he may well have kept copies or made "extracts" of memoranda on financial affairs. He need not have been their author.

In fact, one may exclude from the Boulainvilliers corpus two or even three of the six memoranda under consideration. To the 1680s memorandum already taken from Boulainvilliers by Harsin and Rothkrug may be added memorandum 6 on the royal domain; it is merely a copy of someone else's work with annotations.[84] Appended to memorandum 6 is a another text with no claim to consideration as an original work by Boulainvilliers; that is, the "extract" on a piece by one Fougerolles. Also

[79]See Paul Harsin, "Boulainvilliers ou Vauban?" *Bulletin de la Société d'Histoire Moderne* (October 1936): 183–84; Rothkrug, *Opposition to Louis XIV*, 157–58 and n. 41. Harsin and Rothkrug identify B.N., MS. f.f. 7732, as the original version of the 1680s memorandum.
[80]Simon, *Henry de Boulainviller*, 227 and n. 2.
[81]B.N., MSS. f.f. 7765–69. There are frequent references to these memoranda in the official correspondence of the Council of Finances president the duc de Noailles; see B.N., MS. f.f. 6931, pp. 55–56, 58, 63; MS. f.f. 6932, p. 94; MS. f.f. 6933, pp. 59, 81–82, MS. f.f. 6934, fols. 25, 31r–v, 85.
[82]Marais, *Journal*, 2:227.
[83]*Etat*, I, "Préface": xviii ("Avertissement"): "I do not esteem myself a competent judge of matters concerning finances, jurisdictions, and others like them."
[84]Cf. the remark at the end of the text in *Memoires presentés*, 2:110: "The author of this memorandum, who is abreast of matters concerning the domain, has taken on the duty of having it executed."

unlikely is Boulainvilliers' authorship of the remarkable memorandum 2 calling for government "companies of commerce" in all localities to collect taxes, extend credit, provide public education for workers and peasants, and offer a kind of social security to the old and unemployed. These extraordinary proposals find no echo in Boulainvilliers' known works and the memorandum itself makes no mention of one of his clearest concerns, the right to vote and collect taxes which, he believed, once belonged to the Estates General and which, he hoped, might be restored to it. Until doubts about the authorship of this memorandum are resolved it too may be excluded from the Boulainvilliers corpus.

Three of the six memoranda under consideration may be left in Boulainvilliers' possession. One is memorandum 3, comparing the productivity of Boulainvilliers' own Norman *seigneuries* with the taxes they yielded in 1719 in order to recommend adoption of the proportional *taille*.[85] The others are memorandum 1, in which the author urged the regent to assemble the Estates General and let that body retire Louis XIV's debts, and memorandum 4, defending the princely rank and title that Louis XIV had conferred on his bastard sons the duc du Maine and the comte de Toulouse. In keeping with Boulainvilliers' character, the author of memorandum 1 claims no expertise in fiscal matters, recommends instead that "some faithful, enlightened, and wise persons" screen any financial advice or projects submitted to the regent, and urges him above all to assemble the Estates.[86] Equally consonant with Boulainvilliers' character is memorandum 4. This may seem surprising, for Boulainvilliers deplored Louis XIV's decision to add his bastards to the order of royal succession.[87] As was argued in chapter 6, however, memorandum 4 is chiefly a defense of the duc d'Orleans' absolute authority as regent, and defending it was one of Boulainvilliers' central tasks during the regency.

5. Editions of Boulainvilliers' Major Historical Works

The most frequently cited edition of Boulainvilliers' major historical writings is the first Dutch edition: the *Histoire de l'ancien gouvernement de*

---

[85]This memorandum may be used to estimate the size of Boulainvilliers' fortune. See Ellis, "Genealogy, History, and Aristocratic Reaction in Early Eighteenth-Century France," 449–51.

[86]Boulainvilliers, *Memoires presentés*, 1:6–7, 12–5.

[87]Boulainvilliers, *Un Révolté*, 91 ("Préface critique"), deploring "our easy acceptance of as many masters as present themselves, our easy recognition of princes from within or without the royal family." Cf. ibid., 93, denouncing Père Gabriel Daniel's *Histoire de France* (1713) as (among other things) a defense of Louis XIV's addition of his bastards to the order of royal succession.

la France (1727). Like Boulainvilliers' *Mémoires* for the regent, the *Histoire* was the work of one of the many consortia of bookprinters and sellers that flourished in eighteenth-century Holland. The *Histoire* too was counterfeited by French printers, but full bibliographical descriptions will let the reader distinguish between these editions.[88]

The First Dutch (and French) Editions

(Only the first listed here is cited in this study.)
[The first, third, fifth, ninth, and last lines are printed in red.]
HISTOIRE / DE L'ANCIEN / GOUVERNEMENT / DE LA / FRANCE, / Avec XIV.
Lettres Historiques sur les / Parlemens ou Etats-Généraux. / Par feu /
M. LE C. DE BOULAINVILLIERS. / TOME I. [II., III.] / [vignette]

A LA HAYE ⎫ Aux dépens
& ⎬ de la
A AMSTERDAM ⎭ Compagnie.
[rule] / M. DCC. XXVII.

Collations. 12°: Vol. 1: TP *8 **4 A8 B4 C8 D4 E8 F4 G8 H4 I8 K4 L8 M4 N8
O4 P8 Q4 R8 S4 T8 V4 X8 Y4 Z8 Aa4 Bb8 Cc4 Dd8 Ee4 Ff8; Vol. 2: TP A8
B4 C8 D4 E8 F4 G8 H4 I8 K4 L8 M4 N8 O4 P8 Q4 R8 S4 T8 V4 X8 Y4 Z8
Aa4 Bb8 Cc4 Dd4 Ee2 Q4(-Q4); Vol. 3: TP Λ8 B4 C8 D4 E8 F4 G8 H4 E8
(sic) F4 G8 H4 I8 K4 L8 M4 N8 O4 P8 Q4.

Paginations. vol. 1: [26] 352; vol. 2: [2] 324 [6]; vol. 3: [2] 240 [table]
French Printing and Paper (papermaker named in watermark, C. B.
Chantemerle)
Copy Consulted: B.N. *cote* Le¹ 4 A

HISTOIRE / DE L'ANCIEN / GOUVERNEMENT / DE LA / FRANCE. / Avec XIV
Lettres Historiques sur les / Parlemens ou Etats-Generaux. / Par Feu /
M. le C. de BOULAINVILLIERS. / *Tome I.* [*II., III.*] / [vignette]

A LA HAYE ⎫ Aux dépens
& ⎬ de la
A AMSTERDAM, ⎭ Compagnie.
[rule] / M. DCC. XXVII.

Collations. 12°: Vol. 1: a8 b4 c6(-c6) A4(-A4) B4 C8 D4 E8 F4 G8 H4 I8 K4
L8 M4 N8 O4 P8 Q4 R8 S4 T8 V4 X8 Y4 Z8 Aa4 Bb8 Cc4 Dd8 Ee4 Ff8, Gg2;
Vol. 2: TP A8 B4 C8 D4 E8 F4 G8 H4 I8 K4 L8 M4 N8 O4 P8 Q4 R8 S4 T8

---

[88]I thank Jean-Dominique Mellot of the B.N. for his kind assistance in distinguishing French from Dutch editions. Errors in the descriptive bibliographies below are of course mine. On companies of Dutch printers see I. H. van Eeghen, *De Amsterdamse Boekhandel 1680–1725*, 5 vols. in 6 (Amsterdam: Scheltema & Holkema NV/N. Israel, 1965–78), 5¹:327–31.

V⁴ X⁸ Y⁴ Z⁸ Aa⁴ Bb⁸ Cc⁴ Dd⁴ Ee²(-Ee2); Vol. 3: TP A⁸ B⁴ C⁸ D⁴ E⁸ F⁴
G⁸ H⁴ I⁸ K⁴ L⁸ M⁴ N⁸ O⁴ P⁸ Q⁴ R⁸ S⁴ T⁸ V⁴ X⁴
Paginations. vol. 1: [34] 346; vol. 2: [2] 322; vol. 3: [2] 240 [6]
Probably French Printing and Paper (shield and fleur de lis watermark)
Copy consulted: B.N. *cote* Le¹ 4

[The first, third, fifth, ninth, and last lines are printed in red.]
HISTOIRE / DE L'ANCIEN / GOUVERNEMENT / DE LA / FRANCE. / Avec XIV.
  Lettres Historiques sur les / Parlemens ou Etat-Generaux. / Par feu /
  M. le C. de BOULAINVILLIERS. / *TOME. I. [II., III.]* / [vignette] /
  A LA HAYE   ⎫ Aux dépends
      &   ⎬   de la
  A AMSTERDAM   ⎭ Compagnie.
  [rule] / M. DCC. XXVII.
Collations. 12°: Vol. 1: TP *⁸ **⁸ A–Y⁸; Vol. 2: TP A–V⁸ X²; Vol. 3: TP
  A–P⁸ Q⁴(-Q4)
Paginations. vol. 1: [34] 368; vol. 2: [2] 324; vol. 3: [2] 240 [6]
Dutch Printing and Paper.
Copy consulted: B.N. *cote* Le¹ 4 B

While Dutch bookseller-printers were bringing out their little duodecimo editions of Boulainvilliers' works, a far more ambitious and luxurious folio edition was being prepared in England.

The First English Editions

Etat de la France, dans lequel on voit tout ce qui regarde le gouvernement
  ecclesiastique, le militaire, la justice, les finances, le commerce, les manufac-
  tures, le nombre des habitans, & en general tout ce qui peut faire connoître à
  fond cette monarchie: extrait des memoires dressez par les intendans du
  royaume, par order du roi, Louis XIV. à la sollicitation de monseigneur le duc
  de Bourgogne, pere de Louis XV. à présent règnant. Avec des memoires
  historiques sur l'ancien gouvernement de cette monarchie jusqu'à Hugues
  Capet. Par monsieur le comte de Boulainvilliers. On y a joint une nouvelle
  carte de la France divisée en ses generalitez, reveuë & approuvée par Mess. de
  l'Académie Royale des Sciences, ed. Philippe Mercier, 2 vols. (London: T.
  Wood & S. Palmer, 1727), cited earlier as *Etat.*
Etat de la France, contenant XIV lettres sur les anciens parlements de France,
  avec l'histoire de ce royaume depuis le commencement de la monarchie jusqu'à
  Charles VIII. On y a joint des mémoires présentés à M. le duc d'Orléans. Par le
  Cte de Boulainvilliers. Tome III. (London: W. Roberts, 1728), cited
  earlier as *Etat . . . Tome III.*
Why did Boulainvilliers' writings on French history burst into print in
1727? The answer lies partly in their reputation as grist for the mill of

malcontents: these were works that "surely . . . will not be printed, except in time of war and in another country."[89] In 1727, France was not at war, but quarrels about Jansenism were again dividing Frenchmen.[90] And thanks to the delicate health of the still childless Louis XV, it was again possible to imagine that Philip V of Spain might assert his rights to succeed to the French throne (see chapter 4). In such a context, so reminiscent of that in which the *orléaniste* Boulainvilliers first prepared his works on French history, English and Dutch efforts to print them may be understandable. So may attempts by French authorities to prevent their circulation in print. The publishers of the luxurious English edition failed to secure permission to sell it in France, even though its subscribers included such French luminaries as Chancellor d'Aguesseau.[91] Officials of the Communauté des Libraires de Paris seized it when and where they could, at the city gates or in bookshops in town; they pursued the Dutch (or French) duodecimo editions with even greater alacrity.[92]

The politics of publishing and the uses of (Boulainvilliers') history in the 1720s are beyond the scope of this appendix. Here it suffices to remind the reader that the English folio editions, while hardly flawless, are to be preferred because they present Boulainvilliers' "Mémoires historiques" and "Lettres sur les parlements" in their entirety and in the states in which he first wrote them. The Dutch editions, however, abridge the first work and print the second with Boulainvilliers' later revisions. For that reason these editions have uses of their own (see Part 2). The texts they reproduce should not be confused with Boulainvilliers' original and unrevised contributions to the Burgundy Circle or to the debates occasioned by the *affaire du bonnet*.

Later eighteenth-century editions of Boulainvilliers' major works may be reviewed quickly, as they all derive from the first English editions.

[89]Thus one of Montesquieu's correspondents explained his purchase of some manuscript works on French history and genealogy, including two by Boulainvilliers: "Though many people have these works, I bought them because surely they will not be printed, except in time of war and in another country" (Montesquieu, *Correspondance*, ed. François Gebelin and André Morize, 2 vols. [Paris: Honoré Champion, 1914], 1:39 [Dodart to Montesquieu, Paris, November 23, 1723]).

[90]J. Carreyre, "Le Concile d'Embrun (1727–1728)," *Revue des questions historiques*, 110 (1929): 47–106, 318–67; and Robert Kreiser, *Miracles, Convulsions, and Ecclesiastical Politics in Early-Eighteenth-Century Paris* (Princeton, N.J.: Princeton University Press, 1978), 39–54.

[91]B.N., MS. f.f. 21990, fol. 11 (Registre des livres d'impression étrangère présentés pour la permission de débiter, 1718–42); and see subscription lists bound in the B.N.'s copy of *Etat*, 1 (*cote* f° L¹3, vol. 1).

[92]B.N., MS. f.f. 21931, pp. 226 (for the English edition), 227, 234, 237, 238, 243, 246, 250, 282, 283 (for the Dutch or French editions) (Registre des livres arrêtés dans les visites faites par les syndics et adjoints de la Communauté des Libraires de Paris, 1703–42).

The 1727 *Etat de la France* was twice reprinted during the eighteenth century—but in smaller, cheaper formats and with no improvement in typographical and editorial care.[93] The 1728 *Etat de la France* also spawned a series of later publications, bu these are no more than later emissions of the 1728 edition marketed with new title pages and publication dates.[94] There are also two separate editions of Boulainvilliers' "Lettres sur les parlements." One, printed in 1753, reproduces the entire text as printed in the London 1728 edition.[95] The other, printed in 1788, abridges it severely.[96] This publication was part of a collection of documents and studies on the Estates General published on the eve of elections to the revived Estates of 1789. The editor felt obliged to apologize for "the opinions peculiar to the well-known system of this writer."[97] In fact, he excised Boulainvilliers' harsh remarks against French kings, legists, and *anoblis*.[98] Thus the 1788 edition is a poor edition of Boulainvilliers' work—though it may well be a valuable indicator of French opinion in the early months of the Revolution. Finally, an English translation of Boulainvilliers' "Lettres" may be noted. Based on the text printed in the 1728 *Etat de la France*, it appeared in 1739.[99] Indeed, the same publisher was responsible for both publications and marketed them similarly. Just as the 1728 *Etat de la France* reappeared three times under new title pages, the 1739 translation reappeared in two 1754 publications.[100]

The market for Boulainvilliers' historical works ended with the Old Regime: only two editions have appeared since the Revolution. In 1838, a collection devoted to Old Regime historical scholarship reprinted the

[93]Esmonin, *Etudes sur la France des XVIIe et XVIIIe siècles*, 114–15. And see Boulainvilliers, *Etat de la France*, ed. Philippe Mercier, 6 vols. (London: T. Wood & S. Palmer, 1737); Boulainvilliers, *Etat de la France*, ed. Philippe Mercier, 8 vols. (London: T. Wood & S. Palmer, 1752).

[94]Boulainvilliers, *Histoire des anciens parlements de France, ou etats generaux du royaume. Avec l'histoire de France depuis le commencement de la monarchie jusqu'à Charles VIII. A quoi l'on a joint des mémoires presentez au duc d'Orleans* (London: J. Brindley, 1737, 1739, 1787).

[95]Boulainvilliers, *Lettres sur les anciens parlements de France que l'on nomme états généraux*, 3 vols. ([Rouen] London: T. Wood & S. Palmer, 1753).

[96]Boulainvilliers, *Lettres sur les anciens parlemens de France, que l'on nomme états généraux*, in [Charles-Joseph Mayer, ed.], *Des Etats généraux et autres assemblées nationales*, 18 vols. (The Hague: 1788), vol. 4.

[97]Ibid., 4:iv.

[98]For example, ibid., 4:94, 95, 102; cf. *Etat . . . Tome III*, 60, 64.

[99]*An Historical Account of the Antient Parliaments of France, or Estates-General of the Kingdom. In Fourteen Letters . . . to which is added a Chronological Abridgment of the History of France under the Reigns of the Kings of the First Race*, tr. Charles Forman, esq., 2 vols. (London: J. Brindley, 1739), vol. 1, and 2:1–290.

[100]*An Accurate tho' Compendious History of the Antient Parliaments of France. Compriz'd in Fourteen Letters*, 2 vols. (London: J. Brindley, 1754), vol. 1 and 2:1–290; *History of the Antient Parliaments of France* (London: J. Brindley, 1754), vol. 1 (1 vol. only).

"Mémoires historiques" (as abridged in the Dutch and French editions of 1727).[101] In 1867, a local antiquarian printed Boulainvilliers' digest of the 1697 intendant's memorandum on the *généralité* of Orleans.[102] Boulainvilliers was now on his way to becoming an author read only by historians contemplating their craft's history or deploring the aristocratic and reactionary vision of the French past that they discovered in his work.[103]

[101]"Histoire de l'ancien gouvernment de la France, par le comte de Boulainvilliers," in C. Leber, ed., *Collection des meilleures dissertations, notices et traités particuliers relatifs à l'histoire de France*, 20 vols. (Paris: 1838), vol. 5.

[102]*La Généralité d'Orléans: Mémoire dressé pour S. A. R. Monseigneur le duc de Bourgogne, par le comte de Boulainvilliers* (Orleans: Herluison, 1867).

[103]For example, Thierry, *Récits des temps mérovingiens précédés de Considérations sur l'histoire de France*, 1:60, 66; Monod, "Du progrès des études historiques en France depuis le XVIe siècle," 25.

Bibliography

Eighteenth-Century Bibliographical and Reference Works

Almanach Royal. 93 vols. Paris d'Houry, 1700–92.

Catalogue des livres de feu M. Bernard, conseiller d'état, dont la vente commencera lundy 18 mars, 1754, & continuera les jours suivans, depuis deux heures de relevée jusqu'au soir, en son hôtel, rue du Bacq. Paris: Barrois, 1756. B.N., *cotes* Q 7781, Δ 284, Δ 10909, Δ 48738.

Catalogue des livres de la bibliothèque de feu Monsieur le président Bernard de Rieux. Paris: Barrois, 1747. B.N., *cotes* Δ 3386, Δ 9897, Δ 10948, Δ 48699 (copy used here).

Catalogue des livres imprimés et manuscrits de la bibliothèque de feu M. Nouveau, chevalier, seigneur de Chennevieres & autres lieux, ancien conseiller au Parlement. Dont la vente, qui se fera rue neuve Saint-Paul, commencera le lundi 21 février, & jours suivans de relevée sans interruption. Paris: Debure, 1774. B.N., *cote* Δ 3030.

Catalogue des manuscrits de la bibliothèque de feu M. Bernard, conseiller d'état, ordinaire, &c. Paris: Barrois, 1756. B.N., *cotes* Δ 283, Δ 287, Δ 4161(8), Δ 11103.

Catalogue d'une précieuse collection de manuscrits sur l'histoire de France, au nombre d'environ 2,000 volumes, et des quelques livres imprimés. Paris: Lamy, "An Cinquième" [1797]. B.N., *cote* Δ 4865.

De Bure, Guillaume-François. *Bibliographie instructive: Ou traité de la connoissance des livres rares et singuliers.* 7 vols. Paris: Guillaume-François Debure le Jeune, 1763–68.

Lelong, Jacques. *Bibliothèque historique de la France.* Paris: Gabriel Martin, 1719.

———. *Bibliothèque historique de la France.* Ed. [Charles-Marie] Fevret de Fontette. 5 vols. Paris: Jean-Thomas Hérissant, 1768–78.

Moréri, Louis, et al. *Le Grand dictionnaire historique.* Ed. M. Drouet. 10 vols. Paris: 1759.

Nicéron, Jean-Pierre. *Mémoires pour servir à l'histoire des hommes illustres dans la République des Lettres: Avec un catalogue raisonné de leurs ouvrages.* 41 vols. Paris: Briasson, 1727–40.

Bibliography

Notice de livres rares et précieux, formant environ 2500 volumes, provenant de la bibliothèque de feu M. Jariel de forges, quai de Béthune, n° 26, île Saint-Louis, à Paris: Dont la vente se fera le 15 octobre et jours suivans, à cinq heures précises de relevée [Paris: 1810].

Modern Bibliographical and Reference Works

Barbier, A. *Dictionnaire des ouvrages anonymes.* 4 vols. Paris: 1873–89.

[Barbier, A.-A.]. *Examen critique et complément des dictionnaires historiques les plus répandus, depuis le Dictionnaire de Moréri, jusqu'à la Biographie universelle inclusivement,* vol. 1 (A–J). Paris: Rey et Gravier, 1820.

B.N. *Catalogue des factums et d'autres documents judiciaires antérieures à 1790.* 10 vols. Paris: Imprimerie Nationale, 1890–1936.

———. *Catalogue général des livres imprimés de la Bibliothèque Nationale. Actes royaux.* 7 vols. Paris: B.N., 1910–60.

———. *Catalogue général des livres imprimés de la Bibliothèque Nationale. Auteurs.* 231 vols. Paris: B.N., 1897–1981.

———. *Catalogue de l'histoire de France.* 16 vols. Paris: B.N., 1968.

Catalogue général des manuscrits des bibliothèques publiques de France: Départements. 56 vols. Paris: Plon / B.N., 1886–1962.

Catalogue général des manuscrits des bibliothèques publiques de France: Paris: Bibliothèque de l'Arsenal. 10 vols. Paris: Plon, 1885–92.

Conlon, Pierre M. *Le Siècle des Lumières: Bibliographie chronologique: Tome I 1716–1722.* Geneva: Droz, 1983.

Dictionary of National Biography. 22 vols. London: Oxford University Press, 1949–50.

Dictionnaire de biographie française. 13 vols. to date. Paris: Letouzet et Ané, 1933–.

Inventaire sommaire des Archives du Département des Affaires Etrangères: Mémoires et documents. 3 vols. Paris: Imprimerie Nationale, 1883–96.

Michaud, M., dir. *Biographie universelle ancienne et moderne.* 45 vols. Paris: Desplace, 1843–65.

Olivier, Eugène; Hermal, Georges; Roton, R. de. *Manuel de l'amateur de reliures armoriées françaises.* 30 vols. Paris: C. Bosse, 1924–38.

Simon, Renée. *A la Recherche d'un homme et d'un auteur: Essai de bibliographie des ouvrages du comte de Boulainviller.* Paris: Boivin, 1941.

Primary Sources (Manuscript)

For manuscripts of Boulainvilliers' French historical writings see Bibliographical Appendix.

Archives du Ministère des Affaires étrangères (Paris): Mémoires et Documents (France), MSS. 204, 205.

Archives Nationales (Paris): K.566; K.619; K.622; K.624; K.648; M.353; U.907; Y.10976; MM.923.

Bibliography

Archives Nationales (Paris), Minutier Central des Notaires Parisiens: XIV, 255 (February 13, 1722); CII, 148 (August 20, 1689).

Bibliothèque de l'Arsenal (Paris): MSS. 2899, 7463, 7464.

Bibliothèque de l'Assemblée Nationale (Paris): MS. 336.

Bibliothèque Mazarine (Paris): MS. 1577.

Bibliothèque Municipale (Troyes): MS. 1288.

Bibliothèque Nationale (Paris): Collection Clairambault, MSS. 719, 720 721; fonds français, MSS. 4282, 4319, 6929, 6931, 6932, 6933, 6934, 6938, 6942, 7502, 9724, 9726, 15467, 21931, 21990, 32309 (Cabinet des Titres, 483); nouvelles acquisitions françaises, MSS. 2083, 7417, 9730.

Primary Sources (Printed)

For a full list of editions of Boulainvilliers' writings on French history see Bibliographical Appendix. This bibliography lists only those editions of his works (whether historical or not) referred to in the body of this book.

Angerville, Moufle d'. *Vie privée de Louis XV.* 4 vols. London: John Peter Lyton, 1781.

Anon. *Conférence d'un anglois & d'un allemand sur les Lettres de Filtz-Moritz.* Cambrai: P. Secret, 1722.

———. *Gazette de la Régence, janvier 1715–juin 1719.* Ed. E. de Barthélemy. Paris: Charpentier, 1887.

———. *Mémoire pour la noblesse de France, contre les ducs et pairs.* [Paris: 1717].

———. Notice of Boulainvilliers' death. *Mercure de France* (January 1722): 193–94.

———. "Paris." *Nouvelles littéraires, contenant ce qui se passe de plus considérable dans la republique des lettres*, 4 (The Hague: Henri de Sauzet, 1716): 156–68.

———. *Réponse au libelle injurieux, qui attaque les maisons des ducs et pairs.* N.p.: [1716] (B.N., cote 8° Ll³9).

———. Review of *Lettres de Monsieur Filtz-Moritz* by the abbé de Margon. In *L'Europe savante*, 11, no. 1 (May 1719): 3–47.

Anselme, [Pierre de Guibours, called] Père. *Histoire de la maison royale de France et des grands officiers de la couronne.* 2 vols. Paris: Estienne Loyson, 1674.

Anselme, Père; [and Honoré Caille Du Fourny et al.] *Histoire généalogique et chronologique de la maison royale de France, des grands officiers de la couronne et de la maison du roy.* 2 vols. Paris: Michel Guignard and Claude Robustel; or G. Cavelier, 1712.

Anselme, Père; Du Fourny [Honoré Caille]; [Raffard, François]; Ange [de Sainte Rosalie], Père; Simplicien, [Paul Lucas,] Père. *Histoire généalogique et chronologique de la maison royale de France, des pairs, grands officiers de la couronne & de la maison du roy.* . . . 9 vols. Paris: 1726–33.

Balleroy, marquise de, et al. *Les Correspondants de la marquise de Balleroy d'après les originaux inédits de la Bibliothèque Mazarine.* Ed. Edouard de Barthélemy. 2 vols. Paris: Hachette, 1883.

Barbier, [Edmond-J.-F.] *Chronique de la Régence et du règne de Louis XV (1718–*

1763 ou Journal de Barbier, avocat au Parlement de Paris, nouvelle édition complète.
8 vols. Paris: G. Charpentier, 1885.

[Belleguise, Alexandre.] *Traité de la noblesse et de son origine.* 2d ed. Paris: Jacques
Morel, 1700.

[Bignon, Jerome] H. B. P. *De l'excellence des roys, et du royaume de France.* Paris:
Hiérosme Drouart, 1610.

Bodin, Jean. *Les Six Livres de la République.* 1576. 3d ed. Paris: 1586; repr. in facs.
Aalen: Scientia, 1961.

Bolingbroke, Henry St. John, Viscount. *The Works of Lord Bolingbroke.* 4 vols.
London: 1844; repr. New York: Augustus M. Kelley, 1967.

Boulainvilliers, Henri de. *Astrologie mondiale: Histoire du mouvement de l'apogée du
soleil; ou, Pratique des règles d'astrologie pour juger des événements généraux, 1711.*
Ed. Renée Simon et al. Garches: Editions du Nouvel Humanisme, 1949.

———. *Essais sur la noblesse de France.* [Ed. J.-F. de Tabary.] Amsterdam [Rouen]:
1732.

———. *Etat de la France . . . extrait des mémoires dressez par les intendans du royaume,
par ordre du roi, Louis XIV. à la sollicitation de monseigneur le duc de Bourgogne, père
de Louis XV. à présent régnant. Avec des mémoires historiques sur l'ancien gouvernement de cette monarchie jusqu'à Hugues Capet.* Ed. Philippe Mercier. 2 vols.
London: T. Wood and S. Palmer, 1727.

———. *Etat de la France, contenant XIV. lettres sur les anciens parlements de France,
avec l'histoire de ce royaume depuis le commencement de la monarchie jusqu'à Charles
VIII. On y a joint des mémoires présentés à M. le duc d'Orléans . . . Tome III.* London:
W. Roberts, 1728.

———. *Histoire de l'ancien gouvernement de la France.* 3 vols. Amsterdam and The
Hague: 1727 (see Bibliographical Appendix).

[———.] *Justification de la naissance légitime de Bernard, roy d'Italie, petit-fils de
Charlemagne.* [Paris: 1717].

———. *Mémoires présentés à monseigneur le duc d'Orléans, contenant les moyens de
rendre ce royaume très-puissant, & d'augmenter considérablement les revenus du roy &
du peuple.* 2 vols. The Hague and Amsterdam: 1727 (see Bibliographical
Appendix).

———. *Oeuvres philosophiques.* Ed. Renée Simon. 2 vols. The Hague: Martinus
Nijhoff, 1973.

———. *Un Révolté du grand siècle: Henry de Boulainviller.* Ed. Renée Simon et al.
Garches: Editions du Nouvel Humanisme, 1948.

———. *Traité d'astrologie par le comte Henry de Boulainviller (1717).* Ed. Renée
Simon et al. Garches: Editions du Nouvel Humanisme, 1947.

[Brizard, abbé Gabriel.] *Histoire généalogique de la maison de Beaumont, en Dauphiné: Tome premier, contenant l'histoire.* Paris: L'Imprimerie du Cabinet du Roi,
1779.

Brussel, Nicolas. *Nouvel Examen de l'usage général des fiefs.* 2 vols. Paris: C.
Prud'homme, 1727.

Buvat, Jean. *Journal de la Régence (1715–1723).* Ed. E. Campardon. 2 vols. Paris:
Plon, 1865.

Calmet, Dom Augustin. *Histoire ecclésiastique et civile de Lorraine.* Nancy: Jean-Baptiste Cusson, 1728.

[Caseneuve, Pierre.]. *Le Franc-alleu de la province de Languedoc.* Toulouse: Jean Bonde, 1645.

Chansonnier historique du XVIIIe siècle. Ed. E. Raunié. 6 vols. Paris: 1879–84.

Chantereau-Lefebvre, Louis. *Traité des fiefs et de leur origine.* 2 vols. Paris: Louis Billaine, 1662.

Chasot de Nantigny, [Louis]. *Les Généalogies historiques des rois, empereurs, etc., et de toutes les maisons souveraines qui ont subsisté jusqu'à présent.* 4 vols. Paris: P.-F. Giffart, 1736–38.

Chorier, Nicolas. *Histoire généalogique de la maison de Sassenage.* Grenoble: Jean Nicolas, 1669.

[Colonna, Francesco Maria Pompeo.] *Abrége de la doctrine de Paracelse, et de ses Archidoxes. Avec une explication de la nature des principes de chymie.* Paris: d'Houry fils, 1724.

Dangeau, Philippe de Courcillon, marquis de. *Journal . . . avec les additions du duc de Saint-Simon.* Ed. Eud. Soulié et al. 19 vols. Paris: Firmin Didot, 1854–60.

Daniel, Père Gabriel. *Histoire de France.* 3 vols. Paris: Jean-Baptiste Delespine, 1713.

———. *Histoire de la milice françoise.* 2 vols. Amsterdam: 1724.

Dubos, abbé [Jean-Baptiste]. *Histoire critique de l'établissement de la monarchie françoise dans les Gaules.* 2 vols. 2d ed. Paris: Nyon, 1742.

Du Cange, Charles Du Fresne, sieur. *Glossarium mediae et infimae latinitatis.* Eds. G. A. L. Henschel, L. Favre. 10 vols. in 5. 1833–87. Graz: Akademische Druck- und Verlagsanstalt, 1954.

Duchesne, André. *Généalogie de l'ancienne et illustre maison de La Rochefoucauld.* Paris: Edme Martin, 1622.

———. *Histoire de la maison de Chastillon sur Marne.* Paris: Sebastien Cramoisy, 1621.

Du Fourny, [Honoré Caille]. *Histoire généalogique de la maison de Faudoas.* Montauban: F. Descausset, 1724.

Du Haillan, Bernard de Girard. *De l'Estat et succez des affaires de France.* 1570. 2d ed. Paris: 1571.

———. *L'Histoire de France.* Paris: 1576.

Dupléix, Scipion. *Histoire générale de France.* 3 vols. Paris: Laurent Sonnius, 1621–28.

Dupuy, Pierre. *Traité de la majorité de nos rois, et des régences du royaume.* 1655. 2 vols. 2d ed. Amsterdam: Jansons à Waesberge, 1722.

Du Tillet, Jean, and Du Tillet, Jean. *Recueil des roys de France, leur couronne et maison. Ensemble, le rang des grands de France, par Iean du Tillet, sieur de La Bussière, protonotaire & secrétaire du roy, greffier en son Parlement. Plus une chronique abbrégée . . . par M. I. du Tillet, evesque de Meaux, frères.* Paris: Barthélemy Macy, 1607.

Encyclopédie méthodique: Jurisprudence. 10 vols. Paris: Pancoucke; Liège: Plomteux, 1782–91.

[Estaing, Joachim, d'.] *Dissertations sur la noblesse d'extraction et sur l'origine des fiefs.* Paris: Gabriel Martin, 1690.

Fénelon, [François de La Mothe Salignac-]. *Ecrits et lettres politiques.* Ed. Ch. Urbain. Paris: Bossard, 1920.

Fleury, abbé [Claude]. *Droit public de France.* Ed. J.-B. Daragon. 2 vols. Paris: Veuve Pierres, Saillant, Veuve Duchesne, Cellot, La Combe, 1769.

Foncemagne, Etienne Laureault de. "Examen critique d'une opinion de M. le comte de Boulainvilliers sur l'ancien gouvernement de la France." In *Mémoires de littérature, tirez des registres de l'Académie Royale des Inscriptions et Belles Lettres,* vol. 10. Paris: Imprimerie Royale, 1736.

Fréret, Nicolas. "De l'origine des français et de leur établissement dans la Gaule." In *Mémoires de l'Institut Impérial de France: Académie des Inscriptions et Belles-Lettres,* vol. 23, pt. 1. Paris: Imprimerie Impériale, 1868.

———. "Lettre de M. Fréret de l'Académie des Belles-Lettres, écrite à M.***, au sujet de la personne et des ouvrages de M. le comte de Boulainviller." In M.-H. Guervin, "Deux amis. Nicolas Fréret (1688–1749). Henry de Boulainviller (1658–1722)." *Dix-septième siècle,* nos. 7–8 (1950): 201–4.

[Guijon, abbé Jacques de.] *Longuerueana, ou recueil de pensées, de discours et de conversations, de feu M. Louis du Four de Longuerue, abbé de Sept-Fontaines, & de Saint-Jean-du-Jard.* 2 parts in 1 vol. Berlin: 1754.

Guillaume de Nangis. *Chronique latine de Guillaume de Nangis de 1113 à 1300 avec les continuations de cette chronique de 1330 à 1368.* Ed. H. Géraud. 2 vols. Paris: Jules Renouard for Société de l'Histoire de France, 1843; repr. New York: Johnson Reprint Corporation, 1965.

Hénault, Président [Charles-Jean-François]. *Histoire critique de l'établissement des français dans les Gaules.* 2 vols. Paris: F. Buisson, 1801.

Hincmar of Rheims, *De ordine palatii.* Ed. and tr. Maurice Prou. Paris: F. Vieweg, 1884.

[Hozier, Louis-Pierre d', and Antoine-Marie d'Hozier de Sérigny.] *Armorial général de la France.* 6 registers in 10 vols. Paris: Jacques Colombat, 1738–68.

Hubert, [Robert]. *Traitté de la noblesse, où sont ajoutez deux discours, l'un de l'origine des fiefs, & l'autre de la foy et homage.* Orleans: Jean Boyer, 1681.

L'Aloüete, François de. *Traité des nobles et des vertus dont ils sont formés . . . : Avec une histoire & description généalogique de la très-illustre & très-ancienne maison de Couci, & de ses alliances.* Paris: Robert Le Manier, 1577.

La Roque, Gilles-André de. *Histoire généalogique de la maison d'Harcourt.* 4 vols. Paris: Sebastien Cramoisy, 1662.

———. *Traité de la noblesse.* 1678. 3d ed. Rouen: Pierre Le Boucher, 1735.

Legendre, abbé [Louis]. *Mémoires.* Ed. Roux. Paris: Charpentier, 1865.

Legrand, Joachim. *Traité de la succession à la couronne.* Paris: Gabriel Martin, 1728.

[Le Laboureur, Jean], Boulainvilliers, Henri de [sic]. *Histoire de la pairie de France et du Parlement de Paris.* 2 vols. bound together. London: Samuel Harding, 1745.

Longuerue, [Louis du Four, abbé de]. "Annales ab anno sexto Dagoberti I. Christi DCXXVIII. ad annum DCCLIV et Pippini regnantis tertium." In

Recueil des historiens des Gaules et de la France, ed. Dom Martin Bouquet, 3:685–707. Paris: Imprimerie Royale, 1741.

———. "Disquisitio de annis Childerici I. francorum regis." In *Recueil des historiens des Gaules et de la France,* ed. Dom Martin Bouquet, 3:681–84.. Paris: Imprimerie Royale, 1741.

———. "Introduction à l'histoire de France." In Longuerue, *Recueil de pièces intéressantes pour servir à l'histoire de France, et autres morceaux de littératures rrouvés* [sic] *dan* [sic] *les papiers de M. l'abbé de Longuerue,* 97–236. Geneva: 1769.

Louvet, P[ierre]. *Anciennes remarques de la noblesse beauvaisine, et de plusieurs familles de France.* 1 vol. and 80 pp. of vol. 2. Beauvais: Veuve G. Valet, 1640.

Loyseau, Charles. *Traité des seigneuries.* 3d ed. N.p: Balthazard l'Abbe, 1613.

Mably, Gabriel Bonnot de. *Oeuvres complètes.* 12 vols. London: 1789.

Marais, Mathieu. *Journal et mémoires.* Ed. M. Lescure. 4 vols. Paris: Firmin Didot, 1863–68.

Marcel, Guillaume. *Histoire de l'origine et des progrez de la monarchie françoise.* 4 vols. Paris: Denys Thierry, 1686.

[Margon, Plantavit de la Pause, abbé de.] *Lettres de Monsieur Filtz-Moritz, sur les affaires du temps & principalement sur celles d'Espagne sous Philippe V. & les intrigues de la princesse des Ursins. Traduites de l'anglois par Monsieur de Garnesai. Seconde Edition augmentée d'une reponse à ces Lettres.* Amsterdam: Du Villard & Changuion, 1718.

[Maynier, B. de.] *Histoire de la principale noblesse de Provence.* Aix: Joseph David, 1719.

Mémoire des pairs de France, servant de preuve à leur requeste du 28 mars 1716, sur l'affaire de M. le duc de Richelieu. Paris: Antoine-Urbain Coustelier, 1716.

Mémoires concernant les pairs de France avec les preuves. Paris: Antoine-Urbain Coustelier, 1720 (B.N., Réserve des imprimés, F 323).

Menestrier, Père [Claude-François]. *Les Diverses Espèces de noblesse, et les manières d'en dresser les preuves.* 1684. 2d ed. Paris: R.-J.-B. de La Caille, 1685.

Mézeray, François Eudes de. *A General Chronological History of France.* Tr. John Bulteel. London: 1683.

———. *Histoire de France.* 3 vols. Paris: Mathieu Guillemot, 1643–51.

———. *Histoire de France.* 3 vols. 2d ed. Paris: Denys Thierry, Jean Guignard, Claude Barbin, 1685.

Montesquieu. *Correspondance.* Ed. François Gebelin and André Morize. 2 vols. Paris: Honoré Champion, 1914.

Pasquier, Etienne. *Les Oeuvres.* 2 vols. Amsterdam: 1723.

[Piossens, chevalier de.] *Mémoires de la Régence: Nouvelle édition, considérablement augmentée.* [Ed. Nicolas Lenglet-Dufresnoy.] 5 vols. Amsterdam: 1749.

Poquet de Livonière, Claude. *Traité des fiefs.* Paris: Jean-Baptiste Coignard; Angers: Pierre Foureau, 1729.

Proyart, abbé [Liéven-Bonaventure]. *Oeuvres complètes.* 17 vols. Paris: Mequignon fils, 1819.

Recueil de pièces concernant les différends des pairs de France avec les présidens à mortier du Parlement de Paris. Paris: Antoine-Urbain Coustelier, 1716.

Recueil des écrits qui ont esté faits sur le différend d'entre messieurs les pairs de France, &

messieurs les présidens au mortier du Parlement de Paris, pour la manière d'opiner aux lits de justice. Avec l'arrest donné par le roy en son conseil en faveur de messieurs les pairs. Paris: 1664.

Recueil des écrits qui ont esté faits sur le différend entre les pairs de France & les présidens à mortier du Parlement de Paris, pour la manière d'opiner aux lits de justice, avec l'arrêt donné par le roy en son conseil en faveur des pairs en 1664. 2d ed. Paris: Antoine-Urbain Coustelier, 1716.

Recueil des ecrits qui ont été faits sur le différend d'entre messieurs les pairs de France, & messieurs les présidens au mortier du Parlement de Paris, pour la maniere d'opiner aux lits de justice. Avec l'arrêt donné par le roi en son conseil en faveur de messieurs les pairs. Paris: 1771.

Recueil general des pieces touchant l'affaire des princes legitimes et legitimez, mises en order. 4 vols. Rotterdam: 1717.

Requeste du duc de Richelieu . . . présentée à sa majesté le 26 mars 1716 and *Requeste des pairs de France . . . présentée à sa majesté le 28 mars 1716* (a single publication). Paris: Antoine-Urbain Coustelier, 1716.

Rival, Pierre. *Examen d'une partie de la dissertation de M. l'abbé de Vertot, qui a pour titre "Sur l'origine des loix saliques," etc.* London: frères Vaillant, 1722; 2d ed. Amsterdam: Pierre Humbert, 1726.

[Sacy, Louis-Silvestre de.] *Mémoire des pairs de France, contre les présidens à mortier du Parlement de Paris.* Paris: Antoine-Urbain Coustelier, 1716.

[Sainte-Hyacinthe, Thémiseul de.] *Entretiens dans lesquels on traite des enterprises de l'Espagne, des prétentions de M. le Chevalier de S. George. Et de la renonciation de Sa Majesté Catholique. O.D.A.* The Hague: A. de Rogissart, 1719.

Sainte-Marthe, Louis, and Sainte-Marthe, Scévole de. *Histoire généalogique de la maison de France.* 2 vols. Paris: Abraham Picard, 1619.

Saint-Simon, [Louis de Rouvroy, duc de]. *Ecrits inédits.* Ed. P. Faugère. 8 vols. Paris: Hachette, 1880–92.

———. *Mémoires.* Ed. A. de Boislisle et al. 43 vols. Paris: Hachette, 1879–1930.

———. *Projets de gouvernement du duc de Bourgogne.* Ed. P. Mesnard. Paris: Hachette, 1860.

Salvaing de Boissieu, Denis de. *De l'usage des fiefs et autres droits seigneuriales.* 2d ed. Grenoble: Robert Philippes, 1668.

[Sautour.] *A Messeigneurs les états généraux de Bourgogne.* N.p.: n.d.

Savaron, Jean. *Chronologie des estats généraux, où le tiers estat est compris, depuis l'an MDCXV. iusques à CCCCXXII.* Paris: Pierre Chevalier, 1615.

Serres, Jean de. *Inventaire général de l'histoire de France.* Paris: Guillaume Pelé, 1636.

Sourches, Louis-F. Du Bouchet, marquis de. *Mémoires.* Ed. Gabriel-Jules de Cosnac et al. 13 vols. Paris: Hachette, 1882–93.

Tiraqueau, André. *Commentarii de nobilitate et iure primigeniorum.* 3d ed. Lyon: "apud Guliel. Rouillium," 1559.

[Trianon, abbé de.] "Lettre d'un conseiller du parlement de Rouën au sujet d'un écrit du comte de Boulainvilliers." In Père Desmolets, ed., *Continuation de Mémoires de littérature et d'histoire de M. de Sallengre,* 9 (1730): 107–244, 247–311.

Bibliography

Vertot, abbé [René] de. "Dissertation sur l'origine des loix saliques, et si c'est précisément en vertu de l'article LXII. paragraphe 6. que les filles de nos rois sont excluës de la succession à la couronne." In *Mémoires de littérature tirez des registres de l'Académie Royale des Inscriptions et Belles Lettres, depuis le renouvellement de cette Académie jusqu'en M.DCCX.: Tome second.* Paris: Imprimerie Royale, 1717.

Vignier, Nicolas. *La Bibliothèque historiale.* 3 vols. Paris: Abel Langelier, 1587.

———. *Sommaire de l'histoire des françois.* Paris: Sebastien Nivelle, 1579.

Vipart, François-Augustin de. *Généalogie de la maison de Vipart, en Normandie.* N.p.: 1751.

Voltaire. *Oeuvres complètes.* Ed. [Louis] Moland. 52 vols. Paris: Garnier, 1877–85.

Secondary Literature

Adam, Antoine. *Le Mouvement philosophique dans la première moitié du XVIIIe siècle.* Paris: Société d'Edition et d'Enseignement Supérieur, 1967.

Andt, E. "Sur la théorie de la directe universelle présenté par l'édit de 1692." *Revue historique de droit français et étranger,* ser. 4, 1 (1922): 604–36.

Antoine, Michel. *Le Conseil du roi sous le règne de Louis XV.* Geneva: Droz, 1970.

Arendt, Hannah. *The Origins of Totalitarianism.* 2d ed. Cleveland: Meridien, 1958.

Ariès, Philippe. *Le Temps de l'histoire.* Monaco: Editions du Rocher, 1954.

Armogathe, Jean-Robert, and Joutard, Philippe. "Bâville et la guerre des Camisards." *Revue d'histoire moderne et contemporaine,* 19 (1972): 44–72.

Artonne, André. *Le Mouvement de 1314 et les chartes provinciales de 1315.* Paris: F. Alcan, 1912.

Baker, Keith Michael. "Memory and Practice: Politics and the Representation of the Past in Eighteenth-Century France." *Representations,* 11 (1985): 134–64.

———. "On the Problem of the Ideological Origins of the French Revolution." In *Modern European Intellectual History: Reappraisals and New Perspectives,* ed. Dominick LaCapra and Steven L. Kaplan. Ithaca, N.Y.: Cornell University Press, 1982.

Barzun, Jacques. *The French Race: Theories of Its Origin and Their Social and Political Implications prior to the Revolution.* New York: Columbia University Press, 1932.

Baudrillart, Alfred. *Philippe V et la cour de France.* 5 vols. Paris: Firmin Didot, 1890–1901.

Beik, William. *Absolutism and Society in Seventeenth-Century France: State Power and Provincial Aristocracy in Languedoc.* Cambridge, Engl.: Cambridge University Press, 1985.

Bérenger, Jean, and Meyer, Jean. "Introduction." In *La Bretagne de la fin du XVIIe siècle d'aprés le rapport de Béchameil de Nointel,* ed. Jean Bérenger, Jean Meyer et al. Paris: C. Klincksieck, 1976.

Betts, C. J. *Early Deism in France: From the So-Called 'Deistes' of Lyon (1564) to Voltaire's 'Lettres philosophiques' (1734).* The Hague: Martinus Nijhoff, 1984.

Bien, David D. "The Army in the French Enlightenment: Reform, Reaction and Revolution." *Past and Present,* 85 (November 1979): 68–98.

————. "La Réaction aristocratique avant 1789: L'exemple de l'armée." *Annales, E.S.C.,* 29 (1974): 23–48, 505–34.

Bloch, Marc. *Feudal Society.* Tr. L. A. Manyon. 2 vols. Chicago: University of Chicago Press, 1961.

Bluche, François. *La Vie quotidienne de la noblesse française au dix-huitième siècle.* Paris: Hachette, 1973.

————. *La Vie quotidienne au temps de Louis XIV.* Paris: Hachette, 1984.

Bluche, François, and Durye, Pierre. *Les Honneurs de la cour.* 2 vols. Paris: Les Cahiers Nobles, 1957.

Boislisle, A. de. "Les Etudes du duc de Bourgogne." *Annuaire-Bulletin de la Société de l'Histoire de France,* 11 (1874): 54–60.

————. "Généalogie de la maison de Rouvroy Saint-Simon." In [Louis de Rouvroy, duc de] Saint-Simon, *Mémoires,* ed. A. de Boislisle, 1:384–427. Paris: Hachette, 1879.

————. "Introduction." In *Mémoires des intendants sur l'état des généralités, dressés pour l'instruction du duc de Bourgogne,* vol. 1, *Mémoire de la généralité de Paris,* ed. A. de Boislisle. Paris: 1881.

————. "Note sur les mémoires dressés par les intendants en 1697 pour l'instruction du duc de Bourgogne." *Annuaire-Bulletin de la Société de l'Histoire de France,* 10 (1873): 149–60, 167–75.

Bonald, vicomte de. *Samuel Bernard, banquier du Trésor Royal et sa descendance.* Rodez: 1912.

Bonney, Richard. *The King's Debts: Finance and Politics in France, 1589–1661.* Oxford: Clarendon Press, 1981.

————. *Political Change in France under Richelieu and Mazarin 1664–1661.* Oxford: Oxford University Press, 1978.

Bosher, J. F. "*Chambres de Justice* in the French Monarchy." In *French Government and Society 1500–1850: Essays in Memory of Alfred Cobban,* ed. J. F. Bosher. London: University of London Press / Athlone, 1973.

Bouchard, Constance. "The Origins of the French Nobility: A Reassessment." *American Historical Review,* 86 (1981): 501–32.

Bourbon, [prince de Parme] Sixte de. *Le Traité d'Utrecht et les lois fondamentales du royaume.* Paris: Honoré Champion, Edouard Champion, 1914.

Bourde de La Rogerie, [H.] "Etude sur la réformation de la noblesse en Bretagne (1668–1721)." *Mémoires de la Société d'Histoire et d'Archéologie de Bretagne,* 3 (1922): 237–312.

Bourgeois, Emile. *Le Capitulaire de Kiersy-sur-Oise (877): Etude sur l'état et le régime politique de la société carolingienne à la fin du IXe siècle d'après la législation de Charles le Chauve.* Paris: Hachette, 1885.

Boutruche, Robert. *Une Société provinciale en lutte contre le régime féodal: L'alleu en Bordelais et en Bazadais du XIe au XVIIIe siècle.* Rodez: P. Carrère, 1947.

Brancourt, Jean-Pierre. *Le Duc de Saint-Simon et la monarchie.* Paris: Cujas, 1971.

————. "Un Théoricien de la société au XVIIIe siècle: Le chevalier d'Arcq." *Revue historique,* 250 (1973): 337–62.

Bibliography

Brejon, André. *André Tiraqueau, 1488–1558*. Paris: Recueil Sirey, 1937.

Brocher, Henri. *A la cour de Louis XIV: Le rang et l'etiquette sous l'Ancien Régime.* Paris: Félix Alcan, 1934.

Buranelli, Vincent. "The Historical and Political Thought of Boulainvilliers." *Journal of the History of Ideas*, 18 (1957): 475–94.

Carcassonne, Elie. *Montesquieu et le problème de la constitution française au XVIIIe siècle.* Paris: Presses Universitaires de France, 1927.

Carré, Henri. *La Noblesse de France et l'opinion publique au XVIIIe siècle.* Paris: Honoré Champion, 1920.

Carreyre, J. "Le Concile d'Embrun (1727–1728)." *Revue des questions historiques*, 110 (1929): 47–106, 318–67.

Chartier, Roger; Compère, Marie-Madeleine; and Julia, Dominique. *L'Education en France du XVIe au XVIIIe siècle.* Paris: Société d'Edition et d'Enseignement supérieur, 1976.

Chaussinand-Nogaret, Guy. "Un Aspect de la pensée nobiliaire au XVIIIe siècle: L''antinobilisme.'" *Revue d'histoire moderne et contemporaine*, 29 (1982): 442–52.

———. "Aux origines de la Révolution: Noblesse et bourgeoisie." *Annales. E.S.C.*, 30 (1975): 265–78.

———. *Gens de finance au XVIIIe siècle.* Paris: Bordas, 1972.

———. *Une Histoire des élites 1700–1848: Recueil de textes présentés et commentés.* Paris: Mouton, 1975.

———. *La Noblesse au XVIIIe siècle: De la féodalité aux lumières.* Introd. Emmanuel Le Roy Ladurie. 2d ed. Brussels: Editions Complexe, 1984.

Chénon, Emile. *Etude sur l'histoire des alleux en France.* Paris: L. Larose et Forcel, 1888.

Chevallier, Jean-Jacques. "Montesquieu ou le libéralisme aristocratique." *Revue internationale de philosophie*, 9, nos. 33–34 (1955): 330–45.

Church, William Farr. *Constitutional Thought in Sixteenth-Century France.* Cambridge: Harvard University Press, 1941.

———. "The Decline of the French Jurists as Political Theorists, 1660–1789." *French Historical Studies*, 5 (1967–68): 1–40.

———. *Richelieu and Reason of State.* Princeton, N.J.: Princeton University Press, 1972.

Clair, Pierre. *Libertinage et incrédules (1665–1715?).* In *Recherches sur le XVIIe siècle*, vol. 6. Paris: Editions du Centre National de la Recherche Scientifique, 1983.

Clermont-Tonnerre, E. de. *Histoire de Samuel Bernard et de ses enfans.* Paris: Honoré Champion, 1914.

Cole, Charles Woolsey. *French Mercantilism, 1683–1700.* New York: Columbia University Press, 1943.

Coleman, D. C. "Editor's Introduction." In *Revisions in Mercantilism*, ed. Coleman. London: Methuen, 1969.

Colonna d'Istria, F. "Introduction." In Baruch Spinoza, *Ethique*, tr. Boulainvilliers [?], ed. F. Colonna d'Istria. Paris: Armand Colin, 1907.

Bibliography

Constant, Jean-Marie. "L'Enquête de noblesse de 1667 et les seigneurs de Beauce." *Revue d'histoire moderne et contemporaine*, 21 (1974): 548–66.

———. *La Vie quotidienne de la noblesse française au XVIe–XVIIe siècles*. Paris: Hachette, 1985.

Corada, Gian Carlo. "La Concezione della storia nel pensiero di Henry de Boulainviller." *A.C.M.E.: Annali della Facoltà di Lettere e Filosofia dell'Università degli Studi di Milano*, 28, fasc. 3 (1975): 311–33.

Costa, Gustavo. "Un Collaboratore italiano del conte di Boulainviller: Francesco Maria Pompeo Colonna (1644–1726)." *Atti e memorie dell'Accademia Toscana di Scienze e Lettere: La Colombaria*, 29, n.s., no. 15 (1965): 205–95.

Courcy, [Marie-René-Roussel,] marquis de. *Renonciation des Bourbons au trône de France*. Paris: E. Plon, Nourrit, 1889.

Daumard, Adeline, and Furet, François. *Structures et relations sociales à Paris au milieu du XVIIIe siècle*. Paris: Armand Colin, 1961.

Davis, Natalie Zemon. "Ghosts, Kin, and Progeny: Some Features of Family Life in Early Modern France." *Daedalus*, 106, no. 2 (Spring 1977): 87–114.

Denault, Gerard Francis. "The Legitimation of the Parlement of Paris and the Estates General of France 1560–1614." Ph.D. diss., Washington University, St. Louis, 1975.

Denis, Jacques. "Politiques: Fleuri, Saint-Simon, Boulainvilliers et Duguet." *Mémoires de l'Académie des Sciences, Arts et Belles-Lettres de Caen* (1871): 227–98.

Deschamps-Juif, Martine. "L'Historiographe André Du Chesne (1584–1640)." *Ecole nationale des chartes: Positions des thèses soutenues par les élèves, de la promotion de 1963* . . . (Paris: Ecole des Chartes, 1963), 45–9.

Devyver, André. *Le Sang épuré: Les préjugés de race chez les gentilshommes français de l'Ancien Régime (1560–1720)*. Brussels: Editions de l'Université de Bruxelles, 1973.

Dickson, P. G. M. *The Financial Revolution in England: A Study in the Development of Public Credit, 1688–1756*. London: Macmillan; New York: St. Martin's Press, 1967.

Dodge, Guy Howard. *The Political Theory of the Huguenots of the Dispersion: With Special Reference to the Thought and Influence of Pierre Jurieu*. New York: Octagon, 1972.

Doolin, Paul Rice. *The Fronde*. Cambridge: Harvard University Press; London: Humphrey Milford/Oxford University Press, 1935.

Doyle, William. *Origins of the French Revolution*. Oxford: Oxford University Press, 1980).

———. "Was There an Aristocratic Reaction in Pre-Revolutionary France?" *Past and Present*, 57 (November 1972): 97–122.

Drews, Dorit. *Das fränkisch-germanische Bewusstsein des französischen Adels im 18. Jahrhundert*. Historische Studien 368. Berlin: Emil Ebering, 1940.

Duby, Georges. *Hommes et structures au Moyen âge: Recueil d'articles*. Paris: Mouton, 1973.

Ducrocq, Th. "Le Mémoire de Boulainvilliers sur le droit d'amortissement des gabelles et la conversion du revenu des aides antérieur au Détail de Boisguillebert et à la Dîme royale de Vauban." *Mémoires de la Société des Antiquités de l'Ouest (Poitiers)*, ser. 2, 6 (1882): 425–57.

Duméril, Henri. "La Légende politique de Charlemagne au XVIIIe siécle et son influence à l'époque de la Révolution française." *Mémoires de l'Académie des Sciences, Inscriptions et Belles-Lettres de Toulouse*, ser. 7, vol. 10 (1878): 145–77.

Dumont, François. "French Kingship and Absolute Monarchy in the Seventeenth Century." In *Louis XIV and Absolutism*, ed. Ragnhild Hatton. London: Macmillan, 1976.

Duranton, Henri. "L'Épisode du vase de Soissons vu par les historiens du XVIIIe siècle: Quelques aspects de la pensée historique sous l'Ancien Régime." *Revue de synthèse*, 96 (1975): 283–316.

————. "Le Mythe de la continuité monarchique chez les historiens français du XVIIIème siècle." In *Modèles et moyens de la réflexion politique au XVIIIe siècle: Tome troisième: Débats et combats idéologiques*. Lille: Université de Lille III, 1979.

Edelman, Nathan. *Attitudes of Seventeenth-Century France toward the Middle Ages*. New York: King's Crown Press, 1946.

Eeghen, I. H. van. *De Amsterdamse Boekhandel 1680–1725*. 5 vols. in 6. Amsterdam: Scheltema & Holkema NV/N. Israel, 1965–78.

Egret, Jean. *Louis XV et l'opposition parlementaire 1715–1774*. Paris: Armand Colin, 1970.

Ellis, Harold A. "Boulainvilliers Ideologue and Publicist: Ideologies of Aristocratic Reaction and the Uses of History in Early-Eighteenth-Century France." Ph.D. Diss., Washington University, St. Louis, 1981.

————. "Genealogy, History, and Aristocratic Reaction in Early Eighteenth-Century France: The Case of Henri de Boulainvilliers." *Journal of Modern History*, 58 (1986): 414–51.

Emmanuelli, François-Xavier. "Introduction." In *L'Intendance de Provence à la fin du XVIIe siècle: Edition critique des mémoires "pour l'instruction du duc de Bourgogne"*, ed. François-Xavier Emmanuelli. Paris: B.N., 1980.

Esmonin, Edmond. *Etudes sur la France des XVIIe et XVIIIe siècles*. Paris: Presses Universitaires de France, 1964.

————. *La Taille en Normandie au temps de Colbert (1661–1683)*. Paris: Hachette, 1913.

Evans, Wilfred Hugo. *L'Historien Mézeray et la conception de l'histoire en France au XVIIe siècle*. Paris: Librairie Universitaire J. Gamber, 1930.

Faure, Edgar. *La Banqueroute de Law: 17 juillet 1720*. Paris: Gallimard, 1977.

Faÿ, Bernard. *La Franc-maçonnerie et la révolution intellectuelle du XVIIIe siècle*. 2d ed. Paris: Librairie française, 1961.

Ford, Franklin L. *Robe and Sword: The Regrouping of the French Aristocracy after Louis XIV*. Cambridge: Harvard University Press, 1953.

Forster, Robert. "The French Revolution and the 'New' Elite, 1800–50." In *The American and European Revolutions, 1776–1848: Socio-political and Ideological Aspects*, ed. Jaroslav Pelenski. Iowa City: University of Iowa Press, 1980.

Fox, Paul W. "Louis XIV and the Theories of Absolutism and Divine Right." *Canadian Journal of Economics and Political Science*, 26 (1960): 128–42.

Furet, François. *Interpreting the French Revolution.* Tr. Elborg Forster. Cambridge, Engl.: Cambridge University Press; Paris: Editions de la Maison des Sciences de l'Homme, 1981.

Furet, François, and Richet, Denis. *The French Revolution.* Tr. Stephen Hardman. New York: Macmillan, 1970.

Fyot, E. "L'Affaire du bonnet avec deux documents inédits." *Annales de l'Académie de Mâcon, Société des Arts, Sciences, Belles-Lettres et Agriculture de Saône-et-Loire,* ser. 3, vol. 6 (1901): 222–25.

Gallouédec-Genuys, Françoise. *Le Prince selon Fénelon.* Paris: Presses Universitaires de France, 1963.

Gaquère, François. *La Vie et les oeuvres de Claude Fleury (1640–1723).* Paris: J. de Gigord, 1925.

Gargallo di Castel Lentini, Gioacchino. *Boulainvilliers e la storiografia dell'Illuminismo francese.* Naples: Giannini, 1954.

Gembicki, Dieter. *Histoire et politique à la fin de l'Ancien Régime: Jacob-Nicolas Moreau (1717–1803).* Paris: Nizet, 1979.

———. "Le Renouveau des études sur les communes médiévales au XVIIIe siècle." In Centre Aixois d'Etudes et de Recherches sur le XVIIIe siècle, *La Ville au XVIIIe siècle: Colloque d'Aix-en-Provence (29 avril–1er mai 1973).* Aix: Edisud, 1975.

Gembruch, Werner. "Reformforderungen in Frankreich um die Wende vom 17. zum 18. Jahrhundert: Ein Beitrag zur Geschichte der Opposition gegen System und Politik Ludwigs XIV." *Historische Zeitschrift,* 209 (1969): 265–317.

Gerhardi, G. "L'Idéologie du sang chez Boulainvilliers et sa réception au 18e siècle." In *Etudes sur le XVIIIe siècle,* vol. 11, *Idéologies de la noblesse,* ed. Roland Mortier, Hervé Hasquin. Brussels: Editions de l'Université de Bruxelles, 1984.

Giesey, Ralph E. "The Juristic Basis of Dynastic Right to the French Throne." *Transactions of the American Philosophical Society,* n.s., 51, no. 5 (1961): 3–42.

———. *The Royal Funeral Ceremony in Renaissance France.* Geneva: Droz, 1960.

———. "Rules of Inheritance and Strategies of Mobility in Prerevolutionary France." *American Historical Review,* 82 (1977): 271–89.

Gillot, Hubert. *La Querelle des anciens et des modernes en France: De la Défense et illustration de la langue française aux Parallèles des anciens et des modernes.* Paris: Edouard Champion, 1914.

———. *Le Règne de Louis XIV et l'opinion publique en Allemagne.* Paris: Honoré Champion, 1914.

Ginzburg, Carlo. *The Cheese and the Worms: The Cosmos of a Sixteenth-Century Miller.* Tr. John Tedeschi and Anne Tedeschi. Harmondsworth: Penguin, 1982.

Göhring, Martin. *Weg und Sieg der modernen Staatsidee in Frankreich (vom Mittelalter zu 1789).* Tübingen: J. C. B. Mohr, 1947.

Gossman, Lionel. *Medievalism and Ideologies of the Enlightenment: The World and Work of La Curne de Sainte-Palaye.* Baltimore: Johns Hopkins Press, 1968.

Goubert, Pierre. *The Ancien Régime: French Society, 1600–1750.* Tr. Steve Cox. New York: Harper and Row, 1974.

———. *Beauvais et le Beauvaisis: Contribution à l'histoire sociale du XVIIe siècle.* 2 vols. Paris: S.E.V.P.E.N., 1960.

———. *Louis XIV and Twenty Million Frenchmen.* Tr. Anne Carter. New York: Pantheon, 1968.

Grellet-Dumazeau, André. *L'Affaire du bonnet et les Mémoires de Saint-Simon.* Paris: Plon, 1913.

Guervin, M.-H. "Deux amis. Nicolas Fréret (1688–1749). Henry de Boulainviller (1658–1722)." *Dix-septième siècle,* nos. 7–8 (1950): 197–204.

Habermas, Jürgen. "The Public Sphere: An Encyclopedia Article (1964)." *New German Critique,* 3 (1974): 49–55.

———. *Strukturwandel der Öffentlichkeit: Untersuchungen zu einer Kategorie der bürgerlichen Gesellschaft.* Neuweid: Hermann Luchterhand Verlag, 1962.

Hamscher, Albert N. *The Parlement of Paris after the Fronde, 1653–1673.* Pittsburgh: University of Pittsburgh Press, 1976.

Hanley, Sarah. *The* Lit de Justice *of the Kings of France: Constitutional Ideology in Legend, Ritual, and Discourse.* Princeton, N.J.: Princeton University Press, 1983.

Hardy, James D., Jr. *Judicial Politics in the Old Regime: The Parlement of Paris during the Regency.* Baton Rouge: Louisiana State University Press, 1967.

Harsin, Paul. "Boulainvilliers ou Vauban?" *Bulletin de la Société d'Histoire Moderne* (October 1936): 183–84.

Hasquin, Hervé. "Introduction." In *L'Intendance de Hainaut en 1697: Edition critique du mémoire pour l'instruction du duc de Bourgogne,* ed. Hervé Hasquin. Paris: B.N., 1975.

Hecht, Jacqueline. "Trois précurseurs de la sécurité sociale au XVIIIe siècle: Henry de Boulainvilliers, Faiguet de Villeneuve, Du Beissier de Pizany d'Eden." *Population,* 14 (1959): 73–88.

Herval, René. "Un Historien normand oublié: Henri de Boulainvilliers (1658–1722)." *Etudes normandes,* 34 (1960): 51–53;

Hölzle, Erwin. *Die Idee einer altgermanischen Freiheit vor Montesquieu: Fragmente aus der Geschichte politischer Freiheitsbestrebungen in Deutschland, England und Frankreich von 16.–18. Jahrhundert.* Beihefte 5 der Historischen Zeitschrift. Munich: R. Oldenbourg, 1925.

Hont, Istvan, and Ignatieff, Michael, eds. *Wealth and Virtue: The Shaping of Political Economy in the Scottish Enlightenment.* Cambridge: Cambridge University Press, 1983.

Hunt, Lynn. *Politics, Culture, and Class in the French Revolution.* Berkeley and Los Angeles: University of California Press, 1984.

Hurpin, Gérard. "Introduction." In *L'Intendance de Rouen en 1698: Mémoire rédigé par l'intendant pour l'instruction du duc de Bourgogne,* ed. Gérard Hurpin. Paris: Comité des Travaux Historiques et Scientifiques, 1985.

Jackson, Richard A. "Peers of France and Princes of the Blood." *French Historical Studies,* 7 (1971–72): 27–46.

———. *Vive le Roi! A History of the French Coronation from Charles V to Charles X.* Chapel Hill: University of North Carolina Press, 1984.

Jacob, Margaret C. *The Radical Enlightenment: Pantheists, Freemasons and Republicans.* London: Allen & Unwin, 1981.

Jardin, André. *Histoire du libéralisme politique de la crise de l'absolutisme à la constitution de 1875.* Paris: Hachette, 1985.

Jouanna, Arlette. *L'Idée de race en France au XVIe et au début du XVIIe siècle (1498–1614).* 3 vols. Lille: Atelier de Reproduction de Thèses; Paris: Honoré Champion, 1976.

Jouhaud, Christian. *Mazarinades: La Fronde des mots.* Paris: Aubier, 1985.

Joynes, Daniel Carroll. "Parlementaires, Peers, and the *Parti Janséniste:* The Refusal of Sacraments and the Revival of the Ancient Constitution in Eighteenth Century France." *Proceedings of the Annual Meeting of the Western Society for French History* [1980], 8 (1981): 229–38.

Kaiser, Thomas E. "The Abbé de Saint-Pierre, Public Opinion, and the Reconstitution of the French Monarchy." *Journal of Modern History,* 55 (1983): 618–43.

Kanter, Sanford B. "Archbishop Fénelon's Political Activity: The Focal Point of Power in Dynasticism." *French Historical Studies,* 4 (1965–66): 320–34.

Kantorowicz, Ernst H. *The King's Two Bodies: A Study in Mediaeval Political Theology.* Princeton, N.J.: Princeton University Press, 1957.

Kelley, Donald R. *Foundations of Modern Historical Scholarship: Language, Law, and History in the French Renaissance.* New York: Columbia University Press, 1970.

Keohane, Nannerl O. *Philosophy and the State in France: The Renaissance to the Enlightenment.* Princeton, N.J.: Princeton University Press, 1980.

King, James E. *Science and Rationalism in the Government of Louis XIV 1661–1683.* Baltimore: Johns Hopkins Press, 1949.

Klaits, Joseph. *Printed Propaganda under Louis XIV: Absolute Monarchy and Public Opinion.* Princeton, N.J.: Princeton University Press, 1976.

Koebner, Richard. "Despot and Despotism: Vicissitudes of a Political Term." *Journal of the Warburg and Courtauld Institutes,* 14 (1951): 275–302.

Kreiser, Robert. *Miracles, Convulsions, and Ecclesiastical Politics in Early-Eighteenth-Century Paris.* Princeton, N.J.: Princeton University Press, 1978.

Labatut, Jean-Pierre. *Les Ducs et pairs de France au XVIIe siècle: Etude sociale.* Paris: Presses Universitaires de France, 1972.

Lanson, Gustave. "Questions diverses sur l'histoire de l'esprit philosophique en France avant 1750." *Revue d'histoire littéraire de la France,* 10 (1912): 1–29, 293–317.

Lassaigne, Jean-Dominique. *Les Assemblées de la noblesse en France aux dix-septième et dix-huitième siècles.* Paris: Cujas, 1965.

Leclercq, Henri. *Histoire de la Régence pendant la minorité de Louis XV.* 3 vols. Paris: Honoré Champion, 1923.

Leffler, Phyllis K. "French Historians and the Challenge to Louis XIV's Absolutism." *French Historical Studies,* 14 (1985–86): 1–22.

———. "The '*Histoire Raisonnée*' 1660–1720: A Pre-Enlightenment Genre." *Journal of the History of Ideas,* 37 (1976): 219–40.

Lemaire, André. *Les Lois fondamentales de la monarchie française d'après les théoriciens de l'ancien régime.* Paris: E. Thouin et fils; Albert Fontemoing, 1907.

Le Maire, Octave. *L'Imprescriptibilité de l'ancienne noblesse et la dérogeance d'après la jurisprudence ancienne.* Brussels: 1953.

Le Roy Ladurie, Emmanuel. "Auprès du roi, la cour." *Annales. E.S.C.,* 38 (1983): 21–41.

Levine, Joseph M. "Ancients, Moderns, and History: The Continuity of English Historical Writing in the Later Seventeenth Century." In *Studies in Change and Revolution: Aspects of English Intellectual History 1640–1800,* ed. Paul J. Korshin. Menston, Yorkshire: Scolar Press, 1972.

Lévy, Claude-Frédéric. *Capitalistes et pouvoir au siècle des Lumières,* vol. 2, *La Révolution libérale.* Paris: Mouton, 1979.

———. *Capitalistes et pouvoir au siècle des Lumières,* vol. 3, *La Monarchie buissonnière 1718–1723.* Paris: Mouton, 1980.

Lewis, Andrew W. "Anticipatory Association of the Heir in Early Capetian France." *American Historical Review,* 83 (1978): 916–27.

Lewis, P. S. *Later Medieval France: The Polity.* London: Macmillan; New York: St. Martin's Press, 1968.

Lightman, Harriet. "Queens and Minor Kings in French Constitutional Law." *Proceedings of the Annual Meeting of the Western Society for French History, 1981,* 9 (1982): 26–36.

Lizerand, Georges. *Le Duc de Beauvillier 1648–1714.* Paris: Les Belles Lettres, 1933.

Loirette, François. "The Defense of the Allodium in Seventeenth-Century Agenais: An Episode in Local Resistance to Encroaching Royal Power." In *State and Society in Seventeenth-Century France,* ed. and tr. Raymond F. Kierstead. New York: New Viewpoints, 1975.

Lombard, A. *L'Abbé Du Bos: Un initiateur de la pensée moderne (1670–1742)* Paris: Hachette, 1913.

Lucas, Colin. "Nobles, Bourgeois and the Origins of the French Revolution." *Past and Present,* 60 (August 1973): 84–126.

McKay, Derek, and Scott, H. M. *The Rise of the Great Powers 1648–1815.* London: Longman, 1983.

Mackrell, J. Q. C. *The Attack on 'Feudalism' in Eighteenth-Century France.* London: Routledge and Kegan Paul, 1973.

Major, J. Russell. *Representative Government in Early Modern France.* New Haven, Conn.: Yale University Press, 1980.

Malettke, Klaus. *Opposition und Konspiration unter Ludwig XIV.: Studien zu Kritik und Widerstand gegen System und Politik des französischen Königs während der ersten Hälfte seiner persönlichen Regierung.* Göttingen: Vandenhoeck und Ruprecht, 1976.

Malssen, P. J. W. van. *Louis XIV d'après les pamphlets répandus en Hollande.* Amsterdam: H. J. Paris; Paris: A. Nizet and M. Bastard, 1937.

Martin, Henri-Jean. *Livre, pouvoirs et société à Paris au XVIIe siècle (1598–1701).* 2 vols. continuously paginated. Geneva: Droz, 1969.

Martindale, Joan. "The French Aristocracy in the Early Middle Ages: A Reappraisal," *Past and Present,* 75 (May 1977): 5–45.

Mathiez, Albert. "La Place de Montesquieu dans l'histoire des doctrines politiques au XVIIIe siècle." *Annales historiques de la Révolution française*, 7 (1930): 97–112.

Meinecke, Friedrich. *Historism: The Rise of New Historical Outlook*. 1936. Tr. J. E. Anderson. New York: Herder and Herder, 1972.

Menant-Artigas, Geneviève. "Boulainvilliers et Madame de Lambert." In *Studies on Voltaire and the Eighteenth Century*, vol. 219. Oxford: Voltaire Foundation at the Taylor Institution; Paris: Jean Touzot, 1983.

Mesnard, Pierre. "Introduction." In [Louis de Rouvroy], duc de Saint-Simon, *Projets de gouvernement du duc de Bourgogne*, ed. P. Mesnard. Paris: Hachette, 1860.

Mettam, Roger. "The Role of the Higher Aristocracy in France under Louis XIV with Special Reference to the 'Faction of the Duke of Burgundy' and the Provincial Governors." Ph.D. Diss., Cambridge University, 1967.

Meuvret, Jean. "Fiscalism and Public Opinion under Louis XIV." In *Louis XIV and Absolutism*, ed. Ragnhild Hatton. London: Macmillan, 1976.

Meyer, Jean. *Colbert*. Paris: Hachette, 1981.

———. *La Noblesse de Bretagne au XVIIIe siècle*. 2 vols. Paris: S.E.V.P.E.N., 1966.

———. "Un Problème mal posé: La noblesse pauvre, l'exemple breton au XVIIe siècle." *Revue d'histoire moderne et contemporaine*, 18 (1971): 175–88.

———. *Le Régent*. Paris: Ramsay, 1985.

———. *La Vie quotidienne en France au temps de la Régence*. Paris: Hachette, 1979.

Monnier, Francis. *Le Chancelier d'Aguesseau: Sa conduite et ses idées politiques*. Paris: 1863; repr. Geneva: Slatkine/Megariotis, 1975.

Monod, Gabriel. "Du progrès des études historiques en France depuis le XVIe siècle." *Revue historique*, 1 (1876): 5–38.

Moreil, François. "Introduction." In *L'Intendance de Languedoc à la fin du XVIIe siècle: Mémoire pour l'instruction de duc de Bourgogne*, ed. François Moreil. Paris: Comité des Travaux Historiques et Scientifiques, 1985.

Morel, Henri. "Les 'Droits de la nation' sous la Régence." In Centre Aixois d'Etudes et de Recherches sur le Dix-huitième Siècle, *La Régence*. Paris: Armand Colin, 1970.

Mousnier, Roland. *La Dîme de Vauban*. Les Cours de Sorbonne. Paris: Centre de Documentation Universitaire, 1969.

———. *Les Institutions de la France sous la monarchie absolue: 1598–1789: Tome I: Société et état*. Paris: Presses Universitaires de France, 1974.

Nadel, George H. "Philosophy of History before Historicism." *History and Theory*, 3 (1963): 291–315.

Neumann, Franz. "Introduction. In Montesquieu, *The Spirit of the Laws*, tr. Thomas Nugent. New York: Hafner, 1966.

Neveu, Bruno. "La Vie érudite à Paris à la fin du XVIIe siècle d'aprés les papiers du P. Léonard de Sainte-Catherine (1695–1706)." *Bibliothèque de l'Ecole des Chartes*, 124 (1966): 432–511.

Nzouankeu, Jacques-Mariel. "Boulainvilliers: Questions de légitimité monarchique et théorie du pouvoir politique." Mémoire D.E.S. d'histoire de droit et des faits sociaux, Faculté de Droit, Paris, 1968 (Bibliothèque Cujas).

O'Higgins, James. *Yves de Vallone: The Making of an Esprit-Fort.* The Hague: Martinus Nijhoff, 1982.

Ozouf, Mona. "War and Terror in French Revolutionary Discourse." *Journal of Modern History,* 56 (1984): 579–97.

Ozouf, Mona, and Furet, François. "Two Historical Legitimations of Eighteenth-Century French Society: Mably and Boulainvilliers." In François Furet, *In the Workshop of History,* tr. Jonathan Mandelbaum. Chicago: University of Chicago Press, 1984.

Petrocchi, Massimo. "Il Mito di Maometto in Boulainvilliers." *Rivista storica italiana,* 9 (1948): 367–77.

Picciola, André. "Sur l'établissement de la Régence: Mémoire inédit du chancelier de Pontchartrain." *Dix-huitième Siècle,* 8 (1976): 305–18.

Pocock, J. G. A. *The Ancient Constitution and the Feudal Law: English Historical Thought in the Seventeenth Century.* Cambridge: Cambridge University Press, 1957.

———. *Politics, Language, and Time: Essays on Political Thought and History.* New York: Atheneum, 1971.

———. *Virtue, Commerce, and History: Essays on Political Thought and History, Chiefly in the Eighteenth Century.* Cambridge: Cambridge University Press, 1985.

Poitrineau, Abel. "Introduction." In *Mémoire sur l'état de la généralité de Riom en 1697 dressé pour l'instruction du duc de Bourgogne par l'intendant Lefèvre d'Ormesson,* ed. Abel Poitrineau. Publications de l'Institut d'Etudes du Massif Central. Clermont-Ferrand: 1971.

Poliakov, Leon. *The Aryan Myth: A History of Racist and Nationalist Ideas in Europe.* Tr. Edmund Howard. London: Chatto-Heinemann/Sussex University Press, 1974.

Potter, John Milton. "The Development and Significance of the Salic Law of the French." *English Historical Review,* 52 (1937): 235–53.

Price, Robin. "Boulainviller and the Myth of the Frankish Conquest of Gaul." In *Studies on Voltaire and the Eighteenth Century,* vol. 199. Oxford: Voltaire Foundation at the Taylor Institution; Paris: Jean Touzot, 1981.

Prou, Maurice. "Introduction." In Hincmar of Rheims, *De Ordine palatii,* introd., ed., and tr. Maurice Prou. Paris: F. Vieweg, 1884.

Ranum, Orest. *Artisans of Glory: Writers and Historical Thought in Seventeenth-Century France.* Chapel Hill: University of North Carolina Press, 1980.

———. "Fathers and Sons: Social Values in Seventeenth-Century Robe Society." *Proceedings of the Annual Meeting of the Western Society for French History, 1982,* 10 (1984): 215–26.

Richet, Denis. "Autour des origines idéologiques lointaines de la Révolution française: Elites et despotisme." *Annales. E.S.C.,* 24 (1969): 1–24.

———. *La France moderne: L'esprit des institutions.* Paris: Flammarion, 1973.

Richter, Melvin. "The History of the Concept of Despotism." In *Dictionary of the History of Ideas,* 4 vols. New York: Charles Scribner's Sons, 1973.

Robinet, A. "Boulainviller auteur du 'Militaire philosophe'?" *Revue d'histoire littéraire de la France,* 73 (1973): 22–31.

Rothkrug, Lionel. *Opposition to Louis XIV: The Political and Social Origins of the French Enlightenment*. Princeton, N.J.: Princeton University Press, 1965.

Rowen, Herbert H. *The King's State: Proprietary Dynasticism in Early Modern France*. New Brunswick, N.J.: Rutgers University Press, 1980.

Saguez-Lovisi, Claire. *Les Lois fondamentales au XVIIIe siècle: Recherches sur la loi de dévolution de la couronne*. Paris: Presses Universitaires de France, 1983.

Saint-Germain, Jacques. *Samuel Bernard, le banquier des rois*. Paris: Hachette, 1960.

Salmon, J. H. M. "Storm over the *Noblesse*." *Journal of Modern History*, 53 (1981): 242–57.

Schaeper, Thomas J. *The Economy of France in the Second Half of the Reign of Louis XIV*. Interuniversity Centre for European Studies Research Report 2. Montreal: Interuniversity Centre for European Studies, 1980.

———. *The French Council of Commerce, 1700–1715: A Study of Mercantilism after Colbert*. Columbus: Ohio State University Press, 1983.

Scoville, Warren G. "The French Economy in 1700–1701: An Appraisal by the Deputies of Trade." *Journal of Economic History*, 22 (1962): 231–52.

Sée, Henri. *L'Evolution de la pensée politique en France au XVIIIe siècle*. Paris: Marcel Giard, 1925.

Seillière, Ernest. *Le Comte de Gobineau et l'aryanisme historique*. Paris: Plon, 1903.

———. *L'Impérialisme démocratique*. Paris: Plon, 1907.

Sewell, William H., Jr. "Ideologies and Social Revolutions: Reflections on the French Case." *Journal of Modern History*, 57 (1985): 57–85.

Shennan, J. H. *The Parlement of Paris*. Ithaca, N.Y.: Cornell University Press, 1968.

———. *Philippe, Duke of Orléans, Regent of France, 1715–1723*. London: Thames and Hudson, 1979.

———. "The Political Role of the Parlement of Paris, 1715–1723." *Historical Journal*, 8 (1965): 179–200.

Simon, Renée. *Henry de Boulainviller: Historien, Politique, Philosophe, Astrologue: 1658–1722*. Paris: Boivin, 1941.

———. *Nicolas Fréret, académicien*. In *Studies on Voltaire and the Eighteenth Century*, ed. Theodore Besterman, vol. 17. Geneva: Institut et Musée Voltaire, 1961.

Skinner, Quentin. "Meaning and Understanding in the History of Ideas." *History and Theory*, 8 (1969): 3–53.

Skocpol, Theda. "Cultural Idioms and Political Ideologies in the Revolutionary Reconstruction of State Power: A Rejoinder to Sewell." *Journal of Modern History*, 57 (1985): 86–96.

Smith, Pauline M. *The Anti-Courtier Trend in Sixteenth Century French Literature*. Geneva: Droz, 1963.

Spiegel, Gabrielle. "The *Reditus Regni ad Stirpem Karoli Magni*. A New Look." *French Historical Studies*, 7 (1971–72): 145–74.

Spink, John Stephenson. *French Free-Thought from Gassendi to Voltaire*. London: University of London Press/Athlone, 1960.

Stadler, Peter. *Geschichtschreibung und historisches Denken in Frankreich, 1789–1871*. Zurich: Berichthaus, 1958.

Stone, Bailey. *The Parlement of Paris, 1774–1789.* Chapel Hill: University of North Carolina Press, 1981.

Sturdy, D. J. "Tax Evasion, the *Faux Nobles,* and State Fiscalism: The Example of the *Généralité* of Caen, 1634–35." *French Historical Studies,* 9 (1975–76): 549–72.

Swarte, Victor de. *Un Banquier du Trésor Royal au XVIIIe siècle: Samuel Bernard, sa vie, sa correspondance (1651–1739).* Paris: Berger-Levrault, 1893.

Theis, Laurent. *L'Avènement d'Hugues Capet: 3 juillet 987.* Paris: Gallimard—N.R.F., 1984.

Thierry, Augustin. *Récits des temps mérovingiens, précédes de Considérations sur l'histoire de France.* 2 vols. Paris: Garnier, [1867].

Thireau, Jean-Louis. *Les Idées politiques de Louis XIV.* Paris: Presses Universitaires de France, 1973.

Thompson, Martyn P. "The History of Fundamental Law in Political Thought from the French Wars of Religion to the American Revolution." *American Historical Review,* 91 (1986): 1103–28.

Thomson, Ann. Review of *Oeuvres philosophiques,* by Henri de Boulainvilliers, ed. Renée Simon. *Dix-huitième siècle,* 7 (1975): 364–65.

Torrey, Norman. "Boulainvilliers: The Man and the Mask." In *Travaux sur Voltaire et le dix-huitième siècle,* ed. Theodore Besterman, vol. 1. Geneva: Institut et Musée Voltaire, 1955.

———. Review of *The Clandestine Organization and Diffusion of Philosophic Ideas in France from 1700 to 1750,* by Ira O. Wade. *Revue d'histoire littéraire de la France,* 45 (1938): 529–31.

———. Review of *The Clandestine Organization and Diffusion of Philosophic Ideas in France from 1700 to 1750,* by Ira O. Wade. *Romanic Review,* 30 (1939): 205–9.

Tréca, G. *Les Doctrines et les réformes de droit public en réaction contre l'absolutisme de Louis XIV dans l'entourage du duc de Bourgogne.* Paris: Librairie de la Société Générale des Loix & des Arrêts & du Journal du Palais, 1909.

Trénard, Louis. "Introduction." In *L'Intendance de Flandre Wallonne en 1698: Edition critique du mémoire rédigé "pour l'instruction du duc de Bourgogne,"* ed. Louis Trénard. Paris: B.N., 1977.

———. *Les Mémoires des intendants pour l'instruction du duc de Bourgogne (1698): Introduction générale.* Paris: B.N., 1975.

Tyvaert, Michel. "L'Image du roi: Légitimité et moralité royales dans les histoires de France au XVIIe siècle." *Revue d'histoire moderne et contemporaine,* 21 (1974): 521–47.

Van Kley, Dale. "Church, State, and the Ideological Origins of the French Revolution: The Debate over the General Assembly of the Gallican Clergy in 1765." *Journal of Modern History,* 51 (1979): 629–66.

———. *The Damiens Affair and the Unraveling of the Ancien Régime.* Princeton, N.J.: Princeton University Press, 1984.

———. "The Jansenist Constitutional Legacy in the French Prerevolution 1750–1789." *Historical Reflections/Réflexions historiques,* 13 (1986): 393–453.

Venturi, Franco. *Europe des lumières: Recherches sur le 18e siècle.* Paris: Mouton, 1971.

Bibliography

———. "Oriental Despotism." *Journal of the History of Ideas*, 24 (1963): 133–42.

Venturino, Diego. "Metodologia della ricerca e determinismo astrologico nella concezione storica di Henry de Boulainvilliers." *Rivista storica italiana*, 95 (1983): 389–418.

Vernière, Paul. *Spinoza et la pensée française avant la Révolution*. 2 vols. Paris: Presses Universitaires de France, 1954.

Vignes, J. B. Maurice. *Histoire des doctrines sur l'impôt en France: Les causes de la Révolution française considérées par rapport aux principes de l'imposition*. Rev. ed. Emanuele Morselli. Padua: CEDAM, 1961.

Voss, Jürgen. *Das Mittelalter im historischen Denken Frankreichs: Untersuchungen zur Geschichte des Mittelalterbegriffs und der Mittelalterbewertung von der zweiten Hälfte des 16. bis zur Mitte des 19. Jahrhunderts*. Munich: Wilhelm Fink, 1972.

Vovelle, Michel. "L'Elite ou le mensonge des mots." *Annales. E.S.C.*, 29 (1974): 49–72.

Wade, Ira, O. *The Clandestine Organization and Diffusion of Philosophic Ideas in France from 1700 to 1750*. Princeton, N.J.: Princeton University Press; London: Oxford University Press, 1938.

Waller, R. E. A. "Men of Letters and the *Affaire des Princes* under the Regency of the Duc d'Orléans." *European Studies Review*, 8 (1978): 129–50.

Weil, Françoise. *Jean Bouhier et sa correspondance*. 3 vols. Paris: Université Paris-Sorbonne, 1972–76.

Wolf, John B. *Louis XIV*. New York: W. W. Norton, 1968.

Wolfe, Martin. *The Fiscal System of Renaissance France*. New Haven, Conn.: Yale University Press, 1972.

———. "Jean Bodin on Taxes: The Sovereignty-Taxes Paradox." *Political Science Quarterly*, 83 (1968): 268–84.

Wood, James B. *The Nobility of the Election of Bayeux, 1463–1666: Continuity through Change*. Princeton, N.J.: Princeton University Press, 1980.

Yardéni, Miriam. *La Conscience nationale en France pendant les guerres de religion (1559–1598)*. Louvain: Editions Nauwelaerts; Paris: Béatrice Nauwelaerts, 1971.

Zaccone Sina, Maria G. "L'Interpretazione della *Genesi* in Henry de Boulainvilliers. Fonti: Jean Le Clerc e Thomas Burnet." *Rivista di filosofia neo-scolastica*, 72 (1980): 494–532, 705–33, and 73 (1981): 157–78.

Index

References in italics direct the reader to discussions of Boulainvilliers' writings on or his connections with the topics, institutions, groups, or persons indexed.

Index

Maine, Louis-Auguste de Bourbon, duc du, 92, 115–16, 117 n. 82, 119–20, 122, 135 n. 62, 141, 170–79, 180 n. 50, 183, 185–86, *190–91, 241, 246. See also* Legitimated princes

Maintenon, Françoise d'Aubigné, marquise de, 61, 61 n. 12, 116

Manuscript circulation of aristocratic polemics, 2, 15, 20, 42, 129, 130 n. 47, 131, 136, 179, 183, *206. See also* Print circulation of aristocratic polemics

Marais, Mathieu, 1, 142 n. 88, 185 n. 74, 206, 216, *245*

Marca, Pierre de, 240 n. 67

Margon, Guillaume Plantavit de la Pause, abbé de, 117 n. 82

Mary Tudor (queen of England, 1553–58), 240

Masselin, Jehan, 234

Masters of Requests (*Maîtres des requêtes*), 66–67, *69*

Mazarin, Jules (Cardinal, First Minister), 38, 40, 61

Melun, house of, *201 n. 138*

Mercantilism, 58–59, 62 n. 15

Mercier, Philippe, 64–65 n. 25, 66–68

Merit (*mérite*), 22 n. 26, 27–28, 69, *202–3*

Merovingian dynasty, *78–83, 85,* 97, 173–75, *190,* 225, 229 *n. 43*

Mesmes, Jean-Antoine de (First President of the Parlement of Paris), 132 n. 52, 185 n. 74

Metz, *238*

Mézeray, François Eudes de, *73–74,* 77 n. 70, 83 n. 90, *84–85,* 90 n. *119,* 197 n. *120,* 227–30

Milsonneau, Isaac, 217, 220, 241

Mixed government, *154, 213*

Moeurs, 207

Montespan, Francoise-Athénaïs de Rochechouart de Mortemart, marquise de, 115, 170

Montesquieu, Charles-Louis de Secondat, baron de, 249 n. 89

Montmorency, house of, 50, *201 n. 138*

Montpellier, 90 n. 119

Moreau, Jacob-Nicolas, 222

Mortemer, Estienne de (secretary to Boulainvilliers), *220*

Moufle d'Angerville. *See* Angerville, Moufle d'

Nation, *9,* 52–53, 63, *76, 78–80, 82–83, 87, 91, 94,* 102, *104, 110–11,* 137–38, 140, *143–44,* 154 n. 131, *162, 166,*

172–73, 175 n. 26, 177–78, 182–84, 186, *189, 196–97, 208,* 211, *212–13*

Natural dignity (*dignité naturelle*), *157, 160, 166. See also* Birth (*naissance*); Blood (*sang*)

Noailles, Adrien-Maurice, duc de, *19,* 96, *103,* 133, 245 n. 81

Noailles, house of, 133 n. 54

Noailles, Louis-Antoine de (Cardinal), 112

Nobility: 5–8, 10, 18–20; average fortunes of, 19 n. 8; familial education of, 21–22; honors of the court for, 22 n. 25; inquests (*recherches*) into usurpation of, 107–8, 135

Nobility (early modern writing on): confusion (*confusion, dérangement*) of noble ranks and conditions, 5, 29 n. 57, 135 n. 63, *160, 195;* decadence of the nobility, 24, *26–30,* 107, 139–40, *196–200;* education of nobility (familial), *17–20,* 21–22, *23, 30;* education of nobility (modern), *166;* feudal nobility, *24–26, 53–54,* 83 n. 90, *155,* 200–202, 205, *239–40;* high nobility, 125, 133 n. 58, 133 n. 59, 139, *147, 149,* 157 n. 146, *159, 200;* inquests (*recherches*) into usurpation of nobility, *107–8,* 135; marks of honor or glory of noble families, 22, *159,* 182 n. 59, 200–202; new nobility (*anoblis*), 7, *109–10,* 135, *155, 159, 195, 199, 201, 250;* nobiliaire civism, *120, 168, 213–14;* nobility as described by ducal ideologues, 46, 49–50, 97–98, 103, 133–34, 140–41; nobility as described as parlementaire ideologues, 45, 133; noble barons, 125, *147–48, 164, 198* n. *123,* 239 n. 63; old nobility (= nobility in Boulainvilliers), 7, *17, 18 n. 2, 24–26, 53–55,* 61, *91, 109–10, 145, 147–53, 155–57, 160–61, 163, 166, 168, 192, 195–96, 199–203, 205–6, 212–13, 223–25, 238;* provincial nobility, *89 n. 117,* 134 n. 62, 183 n. 68, *205;* theoretical hierarchies of nobility, *24–25,* 108–9, *109–10,* 135–36, *195–96, 200–202;* true nobility, *17, 18 n. 2*

Nobility (untitled court nobility) and assemblies of (1716–17), 14–15, 120, 134–38, *143,* 144, *148–50,* 154, *159, 161,* 177, 181–85, *183 n. 64, 189, 191, 195–96,* 210–11, *239. See also* Dukes and peers

Nouveau de Chennevières, Barthélemy-Antoine, 221–22, 235

Novion, André III Potier de (*Président à*

Index

Novion, André III (*cont.*)
mortier of the Parlement of Paris), 132 n. 52

Omnibus regni fidelibus formula, 48, 79 n. 76
Order of the Holy Spirit, 103, 204 n. 146
Orléans, généralité of, *251*
Orléans, house of, 115
Orléans, Louis-Philippe, duc d', 221
Orléans, Philippe, duc d' (Regent, 1715–23), 2, 3, *11*, 92–93, *93*, 95, *102*, *106–12*, 112–18, 119, *120*, 122–33, 136, 141–43, *143–50*, *162–68*, 170–71, 176–79, 181–82, 183 n. 67, 184–87, *187*, *189–92*, 205–6, 209, 210, *218*, *230–31*, *236*, *241*, 245, *246*
Ozouf, Mona, 9, 208

Paracelsan chemistry, *217*
Parlement (*Parlamentum*, assembly of magnates, baronial assembly), *53*, 76, *83–84*, 97–99, *104–5*, 151, 156, *162–64*, *189*. See also Assembly, Frankish (*Champs de mars*)
Parlement of Paris, 15, 32, 40–42, 44–46, 50–51, 93, 98–100, 102, 112–13, 115–16, 119–43, *149–51*, *154–56*, *159–60*, 170–71, 177, 179–80, 182, 184–86, 195, 197 n. 118, 210–11, 213; *lits de justice* and royal sessions in, 41–42, 44, 98–99, 121–23, 150 n. 113, 176, 180 n. 50, 182, 186
Pasquier, Etienne, 31–32, 44, *51 n. 134*
Peace of God Movement, *156*
Péan, sieur, 196, *198*, 206
Peerage, ceremonial (royal consecration ceremony), 43–44, *151*, 181
Peerage, feudal, 43–44, 49–50, *105–6*, *145–46*, *149*, *151–53*, *164*. See also Court of peers; Dukes and peers; Nobility (early modern writing on)
Pepin (king of Italy, 781–810, son of Charlemagne), 173, *189*
Pepin the Short, *83–84*
Pharamond (legendary French king), 228 n. 42
Philip II (1180–1223), 32 n. 64, *156*, 174, *193 n. 104*
Philip III (1270–85), 155, *196*, 237
Philip IV (1285–1314), 155–56, *163*, *199*
Philip V (1317–22), 138 n. 72, *145–46*
Philip VI (1328–50), 99, *145–48*, 155
Philip V (king of Spain, 1700–1746), 92–97, 114, 171, 210, 249; his renun-

ciation of his right to succeed to the French throne, 93, 95–97, 99–101, *100–103*, 106, 112, 114, 116–17, 141, 144, 187, *189*, *191*
Philip of Macedon, *199*
Poisson, père (Franciscan), 117 n. 82
Poitiers, house of, *201 n. 138*
Polignac, Melchior de (Cardinal), 183 n. 62
Polysynody, 14, 112–13, 117 n. 81
Ponchartrain, Louis Phélypeaux, comte de (Chancellor), 116 n. 78
Presidents á mortier. See Parlement of Paris
Princes of the blood royal (*Princes du sang royal*), 41, *104*, 123, 125, *159*, *201*, 203 n. 145; princes of the house of Condé (the legitimate princes), 115, 123, 170–80, 184–85, *188*, *190–91*, *237*; their rank and title, 115, 171–72, 176. *See also* Bourbon, Louis-Henri, duc de (prince de Condé); Charolais, Charles, comte de; Conti, Louis-Armand II, prince de
Print circulation of aristocratic polemics, 15, 42, 129–31, 136, 178–80, 183, *206*, 211. See also Manuscript circulation of aristocratic polemics
Property, 32–39, 47–49, *51–52*, *54*, *75*, 77, *79–80*, 86, 88
Proyart, abbé Liéven-Bonaventure, 57 n. 2
Public, 15, 69 n. 37, 120, 129–31, 136, 141, 178–79, 187, 211
Public Opinion, 15–16, 59–60, 129, 130 n. 45, 136, 141–42, 170, 179, 211

Quadruple Alliance (1718), 116
Quiercy-sur-Oise, edict of (877), *86*

Race consciousness, *18–20*, *30*. See also Genealogical consciousness
Regencies (aristocratic controversialists on), 93, 99–100, 114, 120, 122–23, 125, 132–33, 136–38, 140–42, *146–50*, 175, 181, 186, *198 n. 123*. See also Orléans, Philippe, duc d' (Regent, 1715–1723); Royal minorities
Regency (1715–23). See Orléans, Philippe, duc d' (Regent, 1715–23)
Regency Council (*Conseil de Régence*), 116, 119, 127–28, 134 n. 62, 183–84, 245. *See also* Council of conscience (Polysynody); Council of Finances (Polysynody); Polysynody
Renunciation of Philip V. *See* Philip V (king of Spain, 1700–1746)

281

Index

Valois succession. *See* Philip VI (1328–50)
Vassalage, *55, 80,* 97
Vauban, Sébastien Prestre, seigneur de, 60, 244–45
Venturi, Franco, 9
Verdun, 238
Vertot, René de, 117 n. 82, 138 n. 74
Vienne, house of, *201 n. 138*
Villars, Louis-Hector, duc de, 204 n. 147

Virtue (*vertu*), 18, *19–20,* 21–22, *23,* 25, 27, *69,* 107, *166, 199–200,* 203 n. 143, *205 n. 151, 208*

War of the League of Augsburg (1689–97), 62, 241
War of the Spanish Succession (1702–13), 62, 63 n. 21, 92–95, 108 n. 46, 117 n. 82, 219
Wealth, *28, 204, 205 n. 51, 208*

Library of Congress Cataloging-in-Publication Data

Ellis, Harold A.
   Boulainvilliers and the French monarchy.

   Bibliography: p.
   Includes index.
   1. Boulainvilliers, Henri, comte de, 1658–1722. 2. Historians—France—Biography. 3.
France—History—Louis XIV, 1643–1715—Historiography. 4. Monarchy—France—
History—18th century—Historiography. I. Title
DC36.98.B58E44   1988   944'.033'0924   87–47971
ISBN 0–8014–2130–6 (alk. paper)